Travels Through Central Africa To Timbuctoo; And Across The Great Desert, To Morocco
Vol. 1

by

Réné Caillié

Double9
BOOKS

Travels Through Central Africa To Timbuctoo; And Across The Great Desert, To Morocco Vol. 1
by Réné Caillié

Copyright © 2023

All Rights reserved.

ISBN: 978-93-59396-41-5

Published by

DOUBLE 9 BOOKS

2/13-B, Ansari Road
Daryaganj, New Delhi – 110002
info@double9books.com
www.double9books.com
Tel. 011-40042856

ABOUT THE AUTHOR

The book "Travels Through Central Africa to Timbuctoo and Across the Great Desert to Morocco," written by the French adventurer René Caillié, describes his amazing expedition through West Africa. Caillié embarked on a risky voyage across the deserts and jungles of West Africa in 1824 from Senegal. The famous city of riches known as Timbuktu was his ultimate destination. Along the voyage, Caillié had to overcome several difficulties, including sickness, starvation, and the threat of robbers and dangerous animals. He persisted nevertheless, and his accomplishment of becoming the first European to reach Timbuktu earned him worldwide recognition. Caillié gives a thorough description of his travels in his book, including the geography, history, and traditions of the people he met along the route. He also offers a thorough examination of Timbuktu, covering its marketplaces, architecture, and distinct way of life.

CONTENTS

INTRODUCTION

Having cherished from my earliest infancy a strong desire to become a traveller, I have always seized with avidity any occasion that could facilitate the means of acquiring knowledge; but, notwithstanding all my efforts to supply the want of a good education, I have not been able to procure more than a scanty store of information. My thorough conviction of the inadequacy of my means frequently grieved me, when thinking of all that I needed for the performance of the task which I had imposed on myself; but still, while reflecting on the dangers and difficulties of such an enterprise, I hoped that the notes and observations which I should bring back from my travels would be received with interest by the public. I did not, therefore, relinquish for a moment the hope of exploring some unknown portion of Africa; and in the sequel the city of Timbuctoo became the continual object of all my thoughts, the aim of all my efforts, and I formed a resolution to reach it or perish. Now that I have had the happiness to accomplish this design, the public will perhaps grant some indulgence to the narrative of an unpresuming traveller, who relates simply what he has seen, the events which have befallen him, and the facts which he has witnessed.

I was born in 1800, at Mauzé, in the department of the Deux-Sèvres; my parents who were poor, I had the misfortune to lose in my childhood. I received no other education than what the charity-school of my village afforded; and as soon as I could read and write, I was put to learn a trade, to which I soon took a dislike, owing to the reading of voyages and travels, which occupied all my leisure moments. The History of Robinson Crusoe, in particular, inflamed my young imagination: I was impatient to encounter adventures like him; nay, I already felt an ambition to signalize myself by some important discovery springing up in my heart.

Geographical books and maps were lent to me: the map of Africa, in which I saw scarcely any but countries marked as desert or unknown, excited my attention more than any other. In short, this predilection grew into a passion for which I renounced every thing: I ceased to join in the sports and amusements of my comrades; I shut myself up on Sundays to read all the books of travels that I was able to procure. I talked to my uncle, who was my guardian, of my desire to travel: he disapproved it, forcibly representing the dangers which I should incur at sea, and the regret which I should feel far away from my country and my family—in short, he neglected nothing to divert me from my project. My resolution, however, was irrevocable; I still insisted on setting out, and he made no further opposition.

All that I possessed was sixty francs, and with this trifle I proceeded to Rochefort in 1816, and embarked in the brig La Loire, bound to Senegal.

This vessel, as it is well known, sailed in company with La Méduse, on board which was M. Mollien, with whom I was not then acquainted, and who has since made such interesting discoveries in the interior of Africa. Our brig, having luckily parted company with La Méduse, arrived without accident in the road of St. Louis. From that place I proceed to Dakar, a village in the peninsula of Cape Verd, whither the unfortunate persons saved from the wreck of La Méduse were conveyed by La Loire. After a stay of some months at this dreary spot, when the English had restored the colony to the French, I set out for St. Louis.

At the moment of my arrival, the English government was preparing an expedition, under the direction of Major Peddie, for exploring the interior of Africa: when ready, it proceeded to Kakondy, a village situated on the Rio Nuñez. The major died on his arrival there. Captain Campbell, who assumed the command of the expedition, set out with his numerous caravan to cross the high mountains of Fouta-Diallon: in few days he lost part of his beasts of burden and several men; he nevertheless determined to pursue his journey, but no sooner had he entered the territories of the *almamy* [1] of Fouta-Diallon than the expedition was detained by order of that sovereign. It was obliged to pay a heavy contribution to the almamy for permission to return by the way it had come, to recross rivers which it had passed with great difficulty, and to endure such persecutions that, to put an end to them and to render his march less embarrassing, the commander caused the dry goods to be burned, the muskets to be broken, and the gunpowder to be thrown into the river. On this disastrous return Captain Campbell and several of his officers ended their lives at the same place where Major Peddie died: they were interred at the same spot with him, at the foot of an orange tree, at the factory of Mr. Bethmann, an English merchant.

The rest of the troops of Captain Campbell's expedition sailed for Sierra Leone.

Some time afterwards, a new expedition was formed, and the command of it given to Major Gray. The English spared neither trouble nor expense to render it still more imposing and more numerous than the first. To avoid the terrible almamy of Timbo, the travellers proceeded by water to the Gambia and sailed up the river. As soon, as the expedition had landed, it traversed Oulli and Gabou, and at length arrived in Bondou; but the inhabitants of Bondou are like those of Fouta-Diallon, equally fanatic, and equally malevolent, and their king showed not less ill will towards the English. Upon pretext of some old debt or other contracted by the English government, he demanded such a quantity of goods that Major Gray was soon entirely stripped, and obliged, as will be seen, hereafter, to send an officer to the Senegal to procure more, in the hope of obtaining a passage by means of them.

I was ignorant of these unpleasant circumstances when I heard of the English expedition; and not doubting that Major Gray, standing in need of hands, would eagerly accept the offer of my services, though I was a stranger to him, I determined to proceed by land to the Gambia. I set out from St. Louis, accompanied by two negroes who returned to Dakar, and took the road leading from Gandiolle to the peninsula of Cape Verd. We travelled on foot: I was then very young, and my companions were two vigorous walkers, so that I was obliged to run in order to keep up with them. I cannot express the fatigue I felt, under the oppressive heat, journeying over a burning and almost moving sand. If I could but have obtained a little fresh water to allay the thirst which consumed me!—none was to be found but at some distance from the sea; and we were obliged to keep near the beach, that we might have a more solid footing. My legs were covered with blisters, and I thought that I should have been knocked up before we reached Dakar: at length, however, we arrived at that village, where I made no stay, but immediately took a passage in a boat which conveyed me to Goree.

The torments which I had already endured led me to reflect on the still greater hardships to which I was about to expose myself: the persons who felt a friendship for me, and M. Gavol in particular, had not therefore much trouble to divert me from, my design; and, to gratify in some measure my fondness for travel, that worthy officer procured me a gratuitous passage on board a merchantman which was sailing for Guadeloupe.

I arrived in that colony with some letters of recommendation, and obtained a petty appointment, which I held but for six months. My passion for travelling began to revive; the perusal of Mungo Park gave new strength to my projects; and lastly, my constitution, having withstood a residence of some length at the Senegal and in Guadeloupe, gave me hopes of this time executing them with success.

I sailed from Pointe-à-Pitre for Bordeaux, and thence returned to the Senegal. Arriving at St. Louis, at the conclusion of 1818, with scanty resources, for I had exceedingly diminished them by useless voyages, I was not to be deterred by any consideration: every thing seemed possible to my adventurous spirit, and chance seemed to second my designs.

M. Adrien Partarrieu, who had been sent by Major Gray to purchase at St. Louis the goods required by the King of Bondou, was preparing to rejoin the expedition. I called upon M. Partarrieu, and proposed to accompany him without salary or engagement of any kind for the moment. He replied that he could not promise me any thing for the future, but that I was at liberty to join him if I pleased. I had soon decided—happy to seize so favourable an opportunity of visiting unknown countries and participating in an expedition of discovery.

M. Partarrieu's caravan was composed of sixty or seventy men both white and black, and thirty-two camels richly laden.

We set out, on the sixth of February, 1819, from Gandiolle, a village in the kingdom of Cayor, situated at a short distance from the Senegal. The damel, or king, whom our presents had rendered favourable to us, issued orders that we should be well treated; we met every where with an hospitable reception, and in several places the people carried their generosity so far as to subsist our whole company without accepting any remuneration. On reaching the frontiers of Cayor, we came to a desert which separates it from the country of the Yolofs. It is well known that formerly these two countries belonged to the same sovereign, who governed them with the title of *boor*, or emperor, and that the damel is only an independent vassal: we experienced the same kind reception from the subjects of the boor of Yolof.

It was not long before we had to regret the generous, hospitality of the Yolofs. On quitting their country we entered a desert, where, for five days' journey, we were exposed to a thousand hardships. I hope to be forgiven for entering into these details, the only ones which could have fixed themselves in the memory of a mere youth, travelling rather in quest of adventures than for the purpose of making observations.

Our camels were so laden with goods, that we had been able to take with us but a very small quantity of water: it was soon found necessary to deal out but a very small portion to each person: mine was not more abundant. How could I complain—I, a useless consumer, attached to the expedition through the mere condescension of the leader! I had no right to find fault, but I suffered extremely from thirst. I was sometimes reduced to extremity; for, having no beast to ride upon, I was obliged to follow on foot. I have been since told that my eyes were hollow, that I panted for breath, and that my tongue hung out of my mouth: for my own part, I recollect that at every halt, I fell to the ground from weakness, and had not even the courage to eat. At length my sufferings excited the pity of all; and M.

Partarrieu had the kindness to divide with me his portion of water as well as a fruit which he had found. This fruit resembles the potatoe; its pulp is white and of an agreeable flavour: we subsequently found many such, which were of great service to us.

A sailor, having in vain tried all means to allay his thirst, and set about seeking fruits, was deceived by the resemblance borne by one to that which M. Partarrieu had given to me. He ate it, and it set his mouth on fire as if it had been pimento: from the retching and the violent pains with which he was seized we concluded that he was poisoned; every one cheerfully gave up to him some of his allowance of drink; but he appeared to be relieved so suddenly that I have since thought his illness was only a feint to excite pity and get a little more water. I was not, however the worst off, for I saw several drink their urine.

We arrived at length at Boulibaba, a village inhabited by pastoral Foulahs, who live during part of the year in the woods and subsist entirely upon milk seasoned with the fruit of the baobab. To us Boulibaba was a paradise; we there found limpid and abundant springs: the water which we eagerly drank seemed to us excellent, but we had to pay a high price for it, the Foulahs to whom it belonged being poor and very selfish. We encamped near the village, the straw houses of which are in the form of a sugar-loaf truncated at top: the door is so low that, in order to enter, the inhabitants are obliged to crawl on all fours.

No sooner was our arrival known than the whole village sallied forth to look at us: a Foulah came to the foot of the tree where I was resting and asked me in the Wolof, which I understood, for a *grigri* [2] to confer riches. I wrote one for him, and out of gratitude he gave me a bowl of milk. I was nevertheless his dupe, for scarcely was he gone when I perceived that he had stolen my black silk cravat.

On quitting Boulibaba we had another desert without water to traverse: before we entered it, we thought it advisable to recruit ourselves from the fatigues which we had undergone and to sojourn some days with the Foulah herdsmen. A stock of water was procured: guides were hired, and we set out.

After we had made half a day's journey we arrived at Paillar, where we laid in a fresh store of water. It would not have been prudent to traverse Fouta-Toro, the inhabitants of which are thieves and fanatics: we avoided it by turning a little to the south. The precautions which we had taken to obviate the want of water cheered our minds. The country in general appeared to us to be fine: we beheld with admiration trees of great height, with umbrageous foliage, covered with birds of various kinds, which by their song enlivened these solitudes. It was no doubt the agreeable sensations produced by this scenery that caused us partly to forget our fatigues, though we travelled from sun-rise till near ten o'clock at night, taking but a few moments' rest during the day. On the fifth day, however, we were all exhausted: we suffered from thirst, and our water was nearly spent. European ingenuity came to our succour: peppermint-drops were distributed among us, and we experienced immediate relief. Our camels suffered severely for want of water and forage, having no other food than young branches of trees, cut off here and there.

At length we reached a hamlet where the negroes readily brought us some calebashes of water, but they were not prodigal of it, and this was prudent, considering the number of men and animals to be supplied: for my part, I received no more than about a large glassful. But no sooner did we begin to drink than swarms of bees settled upon the vessels containing the water, and even upon our lips, disputing it with us; and to this horrid punishment, these grievous pangs, we had been several times exposed during the journey. I have frequently seen the water-skins covered with bees, which we had no means of driving away but by burning green wood, the smoke of which forced them to quit.

At length we entered Bondou. M. Partarrieu, who was extremely afraid of falling in with the almamy, wished to avoid Boulibaneh, his usual residence, and to reach Bakel speedily and by the direct route; but the inhabitants of Potako, the second village we came to, manifested a disposition to oppose this design. It was therefore necessary to encamp for the purpose of holding a *palaver*. [3] This palaver still continued; we were near wells, but were not supplied either with water or provisions; no millet was brought, and a war of famine was commenced. This system of attack upon us was the worst and the most dangerous of all: it behoved us to meet it with firmness and resolution. M. Partarrieu, who was not deficient in these qualities, was preparing to pursue his route directly towards Bakel, and we were on the point of starting, when Major Gray, the commander of the expedition, who came to meet us, appeared on horseback, and directed us to go to Boulibaneh, under the idea that the almamy would keep his word, and that, after he had received our goods he would suffer us to pass. Major Gray was rather credulous. For the rest, the inhabitants, as soon as they saw us change our route, readily permitted us to draw water and brought us abundance of provisions of all kinds. Peace being concluded and both parties on good terms, traffic commenced.

The day after the arrival of Major Gray we received orders to set out and to take the road to Boulibaneh: we could do no other than obey; but, that the inhabitants of that capital might not remark the great quantity of goods which we brought with us, we entered the place at night. I was in the rear-guard, with some English soldiers mounted on asses: these poor fellows were exhausted with fatigue: never had they made so arduous a campaign; they proposed to stay behind: I prevented them from so doing and we at length rejoined, though rather late, the head of the caravan, which we found asleep in the camp that it had formed outside the town. This camp was nothing more than a cluster of straw huts, surrounded by a palisade four feet high, formed of trunks of trees interlaced with branches.

Our people had neglected to inclose the wells within the palisade of the camp—an unpardonable oversight, which in the sequel exposed us to the most severe privation. The chiefs of the expedition proceeded on their arrival to pay their respects to the old almamy, carrying with them valuable presents to dispose him in our favour.

This was not all: they were obliged to make him fresh presents every day, for the greedy almamy was incessantly craving. Curious to see this sovereign, I repaired to his residence: I penetrated thither without impediment, and found the king of Bondou seated on a mat spread upon the ground, watching a negro mason belonging to our expedition, for whom he had applied, that he might build him a stone powder-room destined to contain the ammunition with which we had presented him.

The almamy of Bondou, a man of about severity, had quite white hair, a long beard, and a face deeply wrinkled. He was dressed in two pagnes[4] of the country and covered with amulets down to the ancles. He eyed me with a look of indifference and seemed to pay much more attention to the work of the mason than to my presence, which afforded me leisure to examine without giving him offence.

Having staid some days at Boulibaneh, during which we were on the best terms with the inhabitants, Major Gray made arrangements for quitting this royal residence. But before his departure he deemed it right to make the almamy a farewell present: it consisted of a piece of Guinea cloth,[5] and a few trifling articles. Whether the prince was dissatisfied with it, or apprehensive that the English were going to join the French for the purpose of attacking his dominions, or had vowed not to allow us to pass, he declared with feigned regret that he could not permit us to proceed to Bakel; that he would suffer us to go to Clego, but we must traverse his territories and those of Kaarta: otherwise there was no alternative for us but to take the road of Fouta-Toro, to reach the Senegal. These two routes were equally arduous and dangerous for us, since we were sure to find in both those countries people as fanatic and as barbarous as the inhabitants of Bondou. It was evidently the almamy's design to cause us to be plundered and perhaps murdered. Our situation became alarming. A council was held, and the indignation excited by the almamy's conduct caused the adoption of the violent measure of opening by force a passage to Bakel. The animals were immediately laden, and preparations made for breaking up: but no sooner was our intention known than the king's soldiers, fifty in number, armed with lances and muskets, came and possessed themselves of the wells and surrounded our camp. We had but little water, through the imprudence which I have mentioned above; and notwithstanding the economical manner in which we employed it, we were on the point of being totally cut off from it. In Africa it is easier to reduce a place by thirst than by famine.

This was not the only danger that threatened us; the war-drums were already heard on all sides. At the sound of this tocsin of alarm, crowds of armed men hastened to obey the summons of their chiefs; and a tremendous uproar every where prevailed. In less than two hours a numerous army was on foot, ready to rush upon us: resistance became impossible, since we were no more than one hundred and thirty persons. Notwithstanding the ardour and the despair which animated all of us, we could not hope to withstand so many foes united. It was useless therefore, to think of fighting, and all that could now be done was to endeavour by new negociations to avert the calamities which threatened us: such were the sentiments of the chief officers of the expedition; they conceived that a battle could not fail to have a most disastrous issue; and that, independently of the loss of men and the pillage of goods, it would thenceforward render the whites objects of horror and execration in the interior of Africa. These prudent reflexions induced our chief to demand a palaver, which was granted by our enemies, but with the superiority and haughtiness of men sure of victory.

The almamy rejected all the propositions that were made to him, and arrogantly, dictated the conditions of peace: all that could be wrung from him by dint of solicitations and presents was permission to keep as near the Senegal as possible, that we might not be in want of water: but he was inflexible in regard to the route which we were to pursue; *Fouta-Toro, or no water*, was his definitive answer. We submitted thankfully to every thing, and, when once assured of our obedience, he made a sign to the soldiers who guarded the wells to retire, and we could then drink with security. The anxiety in which we were during this parley, added to the heat, caused us to consider this permission of the almamy's as a kindness, especially for our animals, which had been on their legs with their loads ever since day-break, without eating or drinking.

Our departure for Fouta-Toro was deferred till the following day. Our caravan resembled a long file of prisoners: a multitude of horsemen hovered upon our wings, to prevent our straggling. The almamy was more vigilant on this point than any other; the traitor, to make the more sure that this valuable booty would not escape his allies of Fouta-Toro, followed us to our first halting-place, and did not leave us till he had received a fresh present; but, on retiring, he committed the duty of superintending our march to several princes of his family, who accompanied us with a numerous escort of soldiers, horse and foot. Night having come on, a large fire was lighted, and, that we might no longer be embarrassed by the baggage which retarded our progress, orders were issued that every one should throw into it all he possessed, excepting such articles of clothing as were absolutely necessary. This useful sacrifice was made before the faces of the Foulahs, who in vain entreated us to desist. In our just indignation against them we would rather have suffered death than have allowed them to save so much as a handkerchief from the flames.

At day-break the next morning we entered Fouta-Toro preceded by a very bad reputation. The people of Bondou had so effectually recommended us to their neighbours, that wherever we went we met with only hostile looks and inimical dispositions; neither were we any where suffered to supply ourselves with water till the price of it had been fixed: the reader will perhaps scarcely believe that frequently it cost us six francs per bottle. If we ever deviated from the track prescribed by our convention with the almamy of Bondou, the natives immediately secured all the wells, and we were obliged to return to the route agreed upon lest we should perish with thirst. At another time, on the contrary, the people of village would have forced us to quit the road we were pursuing for another which would have taken us to a distance from the Senegal. I know not how we should have been able to withstand this fresh violence, since we were to have been allowed access to the wells only upon the dreadful condition of pursuing this latter route; as we were all reduced to extremity and our strength exhausted, two wretched blunderbusses would not have sufficed for laying siege to the wells. Fortunately, M. Partarrieu found means to gain a chief, who procured us two skinfuls of water: they cost us nearly ten francs a bottle; but having allayed our thirst we somewhat recovered our spirits and pursued our journey.

Having got out of this dilemma, we proceeded to another village, situated at a little distance from the Senegal, intending to take the first opportunity of approaching the river. Here we halted to hold council: it was resolved that we should rest there, and break up secretly in the middle of the night for the purpose of gaining the bank of the river. This resolution of M. Partarrieu's was opposed by Major Gray; he objected that we might be attacked by the way, and that, after having broken the convention we should be treated as deserters, and surely murdered; adding, that he had better take with him one attendant and make the best of his way to the French factory at Bakel, to solicit succour. In vain did M. Partarrieu strive to convince him of the imprudence of such a plan and the danger in which we should be left by his absence, "When the Foulahs," he added, "shall know that our chief is no longer with us, they will consider us as a body without head and not hesitate to attack us." All was to no purpose; the major would not listen to any remonstrance, and departed. In the morning, the Foulahs discovered his absence; they came in crowds, accusing us of treachery, and using terrible menaces; they were even preparing to fire, when M. Partarrieu conceived the happy idea of telling them that he had quarrelled with Major Gray, and that he would rather die than suffer him to come back to us. This tale was believed; the Foulahs were appeased and permitted us to go to a village situated near the river.

Major Gray accordingly repaired to Bakel, where he obtained a few blacks, with whom he set out to rejoin us; but, like ourselves he did wrong in coming off without water; having been unable to procure any by the way, he dispersed his men to seek for some. They not only found none, but lost themselves in the woods, where they fell in with the Foulahs, who, apprized of their departure, had gone in force to oppose their junction with us, and easily made them prisoners. In this affair a few shots were fired: several French negroes were dangerously wounded, and one of them had his thigh broken: Donzon subsequently performed amputation at Bakel.

The news of this disaster soon reached us; without loss of time M. Partarrieu repaired to the village where Major Gray was detained; entreaties, presents, threats, nothing could prevail upon the Foulahs to release him; and the joy we felt on being allowed to proceed at not too great distance from the river was embittered by grief at seeing the major conducted on horseback, under a strong escort, by a contrary route to ours. The Foulahs took him away solely with a view to induce us to turn back and follow him; but, conceiving that this proof of our attachment to the major would only have involved us in destruction, we took good care not to run into the snare which was laid for us, as, by so doing, we should in all probability have merely increased to no purpose the number of victims to an imprudence, which no solicitations could dissuade the major from committing.

We continued our route, still proceeding northward. After suffering at several places a repetition of the same torments, we reached Adgar, a village only a day's journey and a half distant from Bakel. Here M. Partarrieu halted and encamped close to the place, as if he intended to make a long stay there: he then visited the chief, and talked to him of sending off his sick to Bakel, that he might afterwards proceed with more ease to Fouta-Toro; but, perceiving that this plan displeased the village chief, he had recourse to a stratagem to gain his consent: he told him that, not having animals enough to carry all his baggage, he should leave part of his goods with him. The chief, perceiving in this proposition the means of subsequently possessing himself of a valuable booty, assented to every thing. M. Partarrieu immediately directed part of the chests with which the camels were usually laden to be filled with stones, and having locked these chests, he had them carried to the chief of the village; he then put aside the chests containing our goods. The camels, it is well known, are accustomed to cry when they are loaded; to obviate the danger in which this cry, the signal for our departure, might have involved us, we took care to make our camels utter this cry for several successive nights, that the inhabitants of the village might not know the moment of our flight.

All the arrangements being made, a very dark night was chosen, and as soon as we judged that every body was asleep, we started, leaving tents, huts, and palisades, standing, without extinguishing the fires which we had kindled, without even removing the pots which had been set on them for our supper, that the discovery of our departure by the inhabitants might be delayed as long as possible. The justice of this calculation of a prudent foresight was speedily demonstrated.

Part of the caravan pushed on before by a route which it opened for itself. I remained with the rear-guard, under the direction of M. Partarrieu and an English serjeant who had the superintendence of the baggage: this division set out an hour later than the other.

Such was our fear of being discovered, and so sensible were we of the imminence of our danger, that our march was more like a rout than a retreat. Forsaken chests and bales were to be seen every where; nay the very animals, as if aware of the peril and anxious to avoid it, were more untractable than ever, and scampered away across the country after throwing off their loads. It was more than two hours before we came up with our first division. Gracious Heaven! what anxiety we felt during those two painful hours! scarcely durst we ask what had become of our companions, scarcely durst we think of them; we fancied that they were taken, and had every reason to apprehend the like fate ourselves. A horn was blown from time to time: this signal of distress, amid the silence of night and the horror of the desert, had something doleful which made us shudder. Could we but have heard some answer to it! but no, not the faintest sound, not even the shriek of a night-bird enlivened the woods which we traversed in the utmost haste. Presently we perceived nothing but ambuscades on all sides; every bush, every tree, assumed to our agitated minds the form of armed enemies; every branch was mistaken for a levelled musket. At length we had recourse to a final expedient to convey to a distance an intimation of our approach. A gun was fired: echo by repeating the report several times, increased our consternation without imparting a hope that we were heard. I then compared our situation with that of the victims on the raft of La Méduse, cast upon the bank of Arquin, without hope of relief. Excessive fear gave us the courage of despair, and we made such a noise with our horns that the first division at length heard it and answered us. With what joy did we accelerate our pace to come up with it! at last we joined it just as day began to dawn. We hastily deliberated on the course to be pursued. On all sides we were surrounded with dangers; but, at any rate, the farther we proceeded from the village which we had left the preceding night, the nearer we should approach to the Senegal. This plan was unanimously adopted; and to carry it into effect with the greater chance of success, we abandoned baggage, animals, goods of all sorts; such was the panic that had seized every mind.

Day-light appeared, and enabled us to discover a village close to us; but fortunately its inhabitants had not yet risen, and we were not perceived. We soon came to a stony road which indicated the vicinity of the river; the hope of procuring water rendered our thirst more tormenting, and agitated our minds to such a degree that we kept advancing without knowing where we were: and we might have continued thus but for a negro whom we met and forced to conduct us to the river: he first led us past a field, where several negroes, who were at work, fled at sight of us towards their village. At length, at ten o'clock in the morning, we arrived at a hamlet situated on the left bank of the Senegal, at a little distance from Bakel. Without halting there, we lost no time in availing ourselves of a ford a short way off to cross the river. Though the water was then low, yet in some places it was up to our chins, so that every man was obliged to carry his things upon his head for fear of wetting them.

We were now on the right bank of the river, and it was high time we were, for some of our number were still crossing when multitudes of Foulahs appeared on the other side armed with pikes and arrows. It had been all over with us had we fallen in with them in the woods, for they were the neighbours to our camp, enraged at having been deceived by our stratagem. They durst not cross the river; but reckoning upon our simplicity, they made signs to M. Partarrieu to come to them and explain himself. The latter replied, that if they would call upon him at Bakel he would hear what they had to say. This invitation was not acceptable to them; accordingly they never came, but returned immediately to their village.

After crossing the river we were still a day's journey from Bakel: and though it would have been more prudent to push on to that place at once, we were all so overwhelmed with fatigue that we were obliged to encamp by the way before night. We went to sleep in the most complete security, under the idea that the sentinels would keep good watch; but these sentinels having undergone the same fatigues as ourselves fell asleep too. No accident, however, befel us, and early next morning we arrived at Bakel.

The reader may conceive our joy on entering that fort, especially when we observed the generous zeal with which Messrs. Dupont and Dusseault, who commanded there, hastened to relieve us. We were treated with the kindest attention and supplied with refreshments of all sorts; and our joy was at its height, when we saw Major Gray return, the negroes having released him as soon as they ascertained that he could not serve them for an hostage to bring us back to them: nay more, their envoys, more tractable under the cannon of the fort of Bakel, restored to us part of the things which we had abandoned on our flight, and which they had picked up.

The rainy season, upon which we were entering, shed its baleful influence over me as well as the others. I had the fever, which soon assumed so alarming a character that I quitted the expedition and embarked on the Senegal to descend to St. Louis. I hoped, by the aid of medicine and the effects of a more salubrious climate, to recover my health in that town; but my disorder was so violent, that my convalescence was long and difficult. To complete my recovery, I saw no other way but to return to France, and I sailed for L'Orient.

There I learned that Major Gray, after making fresh purchases of goods at the Senegal for the purpose of continuing his journey in the interior, had failed in all his attempts, not without injuring the French commerce, a species of success which can have made but poor amends for the enormous loss which he has occasioned to England: for his enterprize, and those of Peddie, Campbell, and Tucker, have, it is said, together cost England eighteen millions in French money (£750,000 sterling).

In 1824, I returned to the Senegal to try my fortune with a small venture, for which M. Sourget, a merchant of distinguished merit, made advances for me: the paternal sentiments which he manifested for me I shall ever hold in grateful remembrance.

I need not observe that, at the bottom of my heart, I still cherished my design of visiting the interior of Africa: and it seemed as if no obstacle could any longer impede me, when I saw at the head of the colony Baron Roger, whose philanthropy and enlightened understanding promised me a patron of all great and useful enterprizes.

I solicited therefore his authority for travelling in the interior, with the support and under the auspices of the king's government: but M. Roger strove in the kindest manner to damp my zeal. He represented to me that the business in which I had embarked offered chances of fortune which it was imprudent to sacrifice; and that my youth and inexperience might moreover ruin my future prospects, and perhaps endanger my life. These representations entitled him to my gratitude, but did not shake my resolution.

I was bent on going, and I declared that if the government would not accept my offers, I would carry my plan into execution with my own unaided means. This determination made an impression upon the mind of the governor who granted me some goods, that I might go and live among the Braknas and learn the Arabic language and the religious ceremonies of the Moors, in order that I might subsequently be able to lull their jealous mistrust, and thus penetrate the more easily to the interior of Africa.

CHAPTER I

Pedestrian journey from St. Louis to Neyreh — Passage to N'ghiez — Manners of the inhabitants — Miraculous stone — Departure — Robbers — Mode of fishing with nets — The steam-vessel — The author's arrival among the Braknas — Conversation with Mohammed Sidy Moctar, chief marabout to the king — Reception by the king.

On Tuesday the 3rd of August 1824, at four in the afternoon, I set out from St. Louis, accompanied by two men and a woman, all three inhabitants of N'pâl, to which village they engaged to serve me as guides. About seven, we arrived at Leybar, a village situated two leagues S.E. ¼ E. from St. Louis. We there passed a wearisome night, on account of the musquitoes which devoured us. The weather was stormy; the thunder rolled the whole night, and the rain fell in torrents. We went to bed on our arrival: at ten o'clock we were called up to supper, for which a very good fish *couscous* [6] was provided.

On the morning of the 4th we pursued our journey. My fellow-travellers met with a little incident which delayed our progress: a sheep, destined for the celebration of the festival of the Tabasky[7], escaped from the negress who was driving it; we were obliged to run after the animal, but after several useless attempts to catch it, we continued our route. At ten in the morning we arrived at Gandon, a village only one league E. ¼ S.E. from Leybar. A most delightful country presented itself to our view. I saw many fields of cotton, which the negroes cultivate with success; indigo grows there without culture; there is but little millet in the environs of the village.

We sat down under a great tree, where travellers usually rest themselves till some one comes to offer them hospitality; on that day there was a great number of them, who took me for a Moor, because I wore the Moorish dress; but, being undeceived by my guides, who told them that I was about to become a convert to Islamism, they congratulated me upon my intention.

My companions, who were much grieved at the loss of their sheep, went back to look for it. I rested myself for about an hour, and then proceeding eastward, set out alone for N'ghiez. Between these two villages the traveller who pays any attention to the beauties of nature is enchanted by the view of the groups of verdure scattered over the plain. They consist of mimosas, the thick branches of which support the slender and flexible stems of asclepias and of different species of cynanchum, which, after climbing to their tops, droop down in garlands, and by the diversity of their flowers produce an admirable effect. They frequently meet with other plants; their stems mutually entwine, and their numerous branches become so closely united and twisted together as to form an aerial canopy, through which the eye perceives at a distance other groups, frequently fantastic, but always wonderful. The plain is covered with a carpet of verdure, the pleasing smoothness of which is broken by numerous shrubs, all differently decorated by the climbing plants which grow about them.

The *parinarius senegalensis*, which is very common in the plain, also embellishes the scene, and heightens the interest of the view to the traveller reposing in the shade of its thick foliage. All these beauties, with which nature is adorned, irrestibly lead the mind up to its Creator and fill it with admiration of his profound wisdom.

These delightful plains are intersected by marshes, wherein grow a great number of aquatic plants; as the road crosses these marshes, I was up to the knees in water. I reached N'ghiez about one in the afternoon: I rested there but a very short time: then, continuing my course eastward, I passed through some fields of millet. My way then led me into a desert plain, but clothed with vegetation, and I arrived at N'pâl by sun-set, quite tired with my day's journey, which I had performed barefoot and carrying my baggage on my head. I sought a lodging with a woman of St. Louis, who had her family at N'pâl: she received me very kindly, and thanks to her attentions, I passed a good night, which made me some amends for the preceding one.

On the 5th I remained at N'pâl. I spent the day in visiting the environs of the village, which is charmingly situated, amidst an immense plain, fertilized by the rains of the tropic. The inhabitants grow in abundance all that is requisite for their wants: accustomed to lead a very temperate life, they frequently have a surplus, which they carry for sale to St. Louis, bringing back in exchange fire-arms for their defence, and amber, coral, and glass trinkets to adorn their wives. This village is reputed to be the wealthiest in the neighbourhood of St. Louis. Its population may be estimated at two thousand, all marabouts. The natural advantages of their soil and situation have a visible influence on their manners; less slothful, less insolent, and less treacherous, than the negroes of other parts, they bestow hospitality without ostentation, and always in a generous manner which heightens its value. Every stranger is sure of finding an asylum among them.

Situated between the country of Cayor and Wâlo, twenty miles eastward of Gandon, this village, entirely independent, is governed by a marabout who is its absolute master. At his death he is succeeded by his eldest son; if the latter dies without children, the supreme power devolves to his nearest kinsman. This chief levies an impost on millet, which is paid to him in kind at harvest-time, and amounts to one tenth. The inhabitants are armed with muskets and lances. When the neighbouring villages are threatened with pillage by the damel, or king, of Cayor, their inhabitants seek refuge at N'pâl, where they are not only received, but also find generous allies who take up their defence.

Throughout the whole country the huts are small, ill constructed, and extremely filthy; the door is so low that to enter you are obliged to crawl on all fours. The residence of each family is composed of several huts surrounded by quick hedges, planted at random and without taste: sometimes this inclosure is formed merely of posts and rails, or a kind of palisade of straw. The streets are extremely narrow, winding, and dirty, all sorts of filth being thrown into them. Both men and women are very uncleanly, as in all the negro villages in this country, and they rub a great quantity of butter upon their heads.

Few idle persons are to be seen among them. The men employ themselves in the cultivation of their fields during the rainy season, and in clearing the land required for fresh crops during the dry season: the women have to attend to the household concerns; they spin cotton; some dye cloths blue with the indigo which the country supplies almost without culture; and the cleverest of them traffic in the productions of the soil, which they procure in exchange for the glass beads, amber, and coral, purchased at St. Louis, whither they repair to sell the corn and cloths, by which they make a great profit.

Though better than the other negroes, their neighbours, they are not exempt from superstition: the scarcity of stones in the neighbourhood has given rise to a fable which, being generally believed, may long contribute to the security of the country. There is one, about a quarter of a mile E. ¼ S. E. from the village. The absurd stories which I heard concerning this stone made me desirous to see it. It is by the road side, about eighteen inches in length and eight broad, the top of it projecting about four inches above the surface of the ground: in colour it is ferruginous and it has a volcanic appearance: I would have broken off a piece, but the negro who accompanied me prevented it. According to an ancient custom, all the inhabitants, when they pass this stone, draw a thread from their pagne, which they throw upon it, as a sort of offering which they make to it.

The marabouts assert and firmly believe, that when the village is threatened with any danger, for instance, pillage, this stone moves thrice round it in the preceding night, by way of warning; and all the warriors arm themselves in consequence. The two following tales are related by them in proof of the virtue of their stone. The Moors, joined by the people of Wâlo, advanced to the vicinity of N'pâl with the intention of plundering the place. This was in the dry season. The stone, after making the circuit of the village in the night, caused it to rain so vehemently, and blue flames to issue from the ground in such great quantity, that the Moors, struck with terror, betook themselves to flight: the inhabitants pursued and made a dreadful slaughter among them, and took prisoners a great number of Wâlo blacks, who were sold as slaves and carried to the colonies.

On another occasion, they were attacked by two Moorish kings, who carried off some of the inhabitants into slavery. These two kings, they say, were taken suddenly ill and died by the way: they did not fail to attribute their death to the power of the stone; the slaves were nevertheless carried away and have never returned. In short, the veneration excited by this stone has always been so great, that only ten years ago it was the object of a sort of religious worship. A festival was held and all the inhabitants were obliged to attend it: in the evening, calebashes full of nicely prepared couscous were placed near the stone, and as it was always eaten by the animals, the people believed that a spirit dwelt in the stone, and considered the acceptance of the offering as a happy omen. The greatest part of the day was spent in prayer; after which, on a signal given by the chief marabouts, all present ran away. If any one, in running, happened to fall, the accident was always regarded as an indication of his speedy death.

As I have already observed, the plain through which runs the road from N'ghiez to N'pâl is not cultivated, though the soil is capable of being rendered very productive. The woods consist principally of mimosas; and the various species of grasses which cover the ground attract thither abundance of all sorts of game. The soil in the environs of N'pâl is of two kinds: you meet with hollows in which the rain water settles, and this renders them far superior to the rest of the plain: they are composed of black sand, enriched by the mud which the water deposits, and by the remains of the vegetables which rot in it: these are the most productive spots. The rest of the land, though of inferior quality, is very fertile; it contains fields of considerable extent, cultivated with the greatest care; each marabout has his own, which he tills himself with his slaves. The inhabitants grow abundance of millet, cotton, water-melons, and a sort of beans, of which they consume a great quantity. They have herds of horned cattle, sheep, and goats: they rear great numbers of poultry, wild and tame ducks, Guinea fowl, and several kinds of game, the young of which they pick up in the fields.

The water which they drink is bad: they collect it in ponds during the rainy season, for the wells are at a great distance from the village, and even these furnish water that is by no means agreeable: I meant to go to see them, but a violent storm prevented my making this excursion.

On the 6th I purposed to set out, but it was Tabasky day, and I could not procure a guide. One offered himself for the following day, when I was seized with a fever, which confined me to my bed, and had such pains in all my limbs that I was unable to move. In the rainy season all the negroes are liable to this disorder, for which, however, they employ no remedy.

At length, on the 9th I was about to depart, when I was told that my guide was a thief, and that he would certainly rob me, or arrange with some accomplice to do it. As it was impossible for me to procure another, I deferred my departure till the following day.

On the 10th I availed myself of the opportunity of some persons going to their fields on the frontiers of Wâlo, who promised to put me into the right track. We proceeded N. E. ¼ N. for three miles; there they pointed out the route which I was to pursue, and then went to their work. I stopped for a moment, and then travelled on alone in a north-east direction toward Wâlo. About noon I arrived much fatigued at Sokhogne, a village in the Wâlo country; the route which I had followed was covered with wood. The environs of this village are not cultivated.

After resting myself under a tamarind-tree, I bought some milk and couscous. I went to see the chief of the village, who offered to conduct me to Merina, whither he was going, to ascertain the truth of certain rumours which were circulated, respecting a war between his country and the Peulhs. [8] I accompanied him, in spite of the fever which had not left me, and we arrived there at three in the afternoon. This village is about eighteen miles N. E. from N'pâl. We had still to travel through woods. I was extremely fatigued, and lay down in the shade of a hut into which I had been refused admission. The man, who had acted in the capacity of guide, came and informed me that two men would set out the same evening for Mall, and he advised me to seize this opportunity. He asked me if I could walk well at night, adding that it was as far from that place to Mall as it was from N'pâl to Merina; and he assured me that on the following day I should not meet with a guide. I determined therefore to accompany those whom chance offered me: I arranged with one of them to carry my baggage; he agreed to do so for two quires of paper and four heads or three leaves of tobacco; at sun-set we started.

The direction we pursued was N. E. ¼ E. One of my guides was on horseback; we walked at a good pace. Travelling in the dark was very unpleasant; I ran so many thorns into my feet that I was unable to proceed, and I offered the negro who had the horse the same price to let me ride as I paid for carrying my baggage: the negro accepted it and made me get up behind. I found this position so inconvenient that I was as tired as if I had walked; my feet, however, became no worse.

An hour before we reached the village, we entered some very fine fields of millet, which the moon-light enabled us to perceive. We reached Mall about one in the morning: at the noise made by the dogs on our approach, some of the inhabitants rose to enquire who we were. A good old marabout offered me his hut: my feet were so swollen and so painful that I could not stir a step: the negro lent me his arm, and kindly leading me in, told me to lie down on his humble bed.

But for this attention of the humane old man's, I should not have been able to prosecute my journey on the following day.

Having extracted a great quantity of thorns from my feet, I thought myself capable of starting, when I was suddenly seized with a most violent pain in my left arm, which obliged me to halt that day and the 12th at this village. I saw the lake of Panieh-Foul or N'gher; it is at this part about a mile broad.

On the 13th at sun-rise I set out from Mall with my old marabout, who insisted on accompanying me to Nieyeh,[9] about three miles distant. The whole country between these two villages is highly cultivated. It was eight in the morning when I parted from my guide: I proceeded northward, and about ten arrived at Neyreh. I sought a lodging with the chief of the village, to whom the old marabout at Mall had directed me, and who received me very kindly. He questioned me concerning the object of my journey; I replied that I was going to embrace the Mahometan faith: he highly approved my design, and endeavoured to impress me with the notion that God was extremely gracious to me in thus delivering me from the flames to which the Christians are destined. My disguise deceived some persons; for, being in the evening at the door of the hut for the sake of coolness, I overheard a dispute between two women, one of whom asserted that I was a Moor.

On the following day, the 14th, I joined a Moor and three Moorish females who were travelling the same way as I was; they were mounted on carrier-bullocks[10]. At the distance of about three miles, we met a troop of Moors and negroes of Wâlo, who attempted to rob me. One of the Moors thrust his hand into my bundle, which was placed on a bullock, and pulled out a roll of papers, among which were letters of the utmost consequence to me, and carried them off. I ran after him, and had a long struggle with him for the purpose of recovering them, but several negroes interfered and knocked me down: at length the Moor who acted as a guide to me came to my assistance and obtained restitution of my roll. After some altercation they let me go; they nevertheless wanted, to force me to give them some tobacco, which they had seen in my bundle; I would gladly have made a sacrifice to get rid of them, but this article was absolutely necessary to me, and I persisted in my refusal to give them any thing. They left us and we continued our route, without any other accident, to the camp to which my guides were bound, where we arrived about two in the morning. By the way I had suffered severely from thirst; I appeased it with milk and water, and lay down under a tent for about an hour, after bargaining with a man to take me on a carrier-bullock to the French settlements for a hundred head of cloves.

I set out and at five in the evening arrived at Richard-Tol, where I waited for an opportunity of proceeding. On the 18th I embarked in the Active cutter for Dagana. The night which I passed on board was as harassing as that which I spent at Leybar: at this season it is impossible to get any rest on board these small vessels unless you are provided with a mosquito-curtain; the mosquitoes settling upon you in countless numbers and inflicting inexpressible torments. In the evening of the 19th I arrived at Dagana, where I sojourned eight days. During this time I took walks in the environs, especially towards the neighbouring *marigot* [11] to the east of the village, where I had occasion to notice the ingenious manner, adopted by the negroes of Wâlo to catch the fish which are very abundant in these waters. They have a net eight or nine feet square, sewed up at one end: two thick flexible sticks are securely fastened at the extremities to the lateral sides of the net in such a manner, that by means of them the net may be shut and opened at pleasure: the upper side is left open or but half sewed up; lastly, the two sticks being held together with the hand, the net has the form of a bag. The negroes drive a row of stakes into the bottom of the marigot, so as to divide it in two: these stakes are placed so close as to allow only very small fish to pass; and they fasten to them, two feet below the surface of the water, wooden cross-bars on which they stand. To catch the fish, they sink the net gently to the bottom, holding the two sticks apart, that is, keeping the net open; then bringing the sticks together, they close it and draw it out of the water: in this manner the fish are taken as in a bag. To manage it with the greatest ease, they take care to let the sticks project two feet beyond the top of the net, and support these ends upon their shoulders; then with their hands they can move it about at pleasure. They have a stick about a foot long, with which they kill the fish, and then by means of an iron hook and a cotton cord they hang it to one of the stakes, to keep moist in the water till they have finished their fishery, which is always very productive. The nets are made of twisted cotton thread of the thickness of sailmakers' twine.

The fishermen cut open the fish, dry it, and take it for sale to villages at a distance from the banks of the river; carrying on a very extensive commerce in this article.

On the 24th of August the steam-vessel, for which I was waiting to be conveyed to Podor, arrived; we started at seven in the evening of the 27th, and landed there on the 29th at two in the afternoon. It is an ancient French settlement, of which few traces only are now left. I went to lodge at the house of Moctar Boubou, the chief of the village, and minister of Hamet-Dou, king of the Braknas, to whom I wished to go for the purpose of completing my Arabic education, that I might the more easily penetrate into the interior of the country, and visit every part of that immense desert, respecting which we possess but vague and scanty information.

At this marabout's I found the agents of Hamet-Dou, who had been to St. Louis to receive the customs which the government annually pays to that prince. They were delighted to hear that it was my intention to embrace Islamism, congratulating me at great length upon it, and encouraging me to persist in my resolution. They also promised to serve me as guides in my journey to their king; but, on the 1st of September, when they set out, they refused to take me along with them, alleging that the camp was ten days' march distant, and that I should not be able to support the fatigue of the voyage. I guessed the motive which induced them to act thus: I offered two *gourdes* [12] to Boubou-Fanfale, the chief of the party; he agreed to take me with him and we started at eight in the morning.

We went back down the Senegal for two miles, towards the factory of the Cock or the Braknas. At the call of my guides, a negro brought us from the opposite bank a large canoe, into which the merchandise was put; we then went on board ourselves, ten in number. They made the bullocks swim after us, pulling them along by the cord passed through their nostrils; in this manner we reached without accident the right bank of the river. The bullocks were reloaded, and about eleven we were ready to resume our journey. The two negroes accompanied us to the marigot of Koundy. Our road lay through a black clayey soil, enriched by the relics of vegetables which cover it. Large mimosas form a thick wood under which the *zizyphus lotus* grows in abundance. This soil would be extremely fertile if it were cultivated.

Having reached the marigot the negroes began to look for their canoes which they had sunk in the water for concealment: they were very small, and could not carry the baggage across in fewer than six trips, which greatly delayed our journey.

When the negroes left us, the Moors would have obliged me to return with them, hoping no doubt to extort from me a fresh present: but I was firm, and reminding Boubou-Fanfale of the engagement which he made when receiving my two gourdes, I persisted in going along with them. At two o'clock we resumed our journey. We halted two miles N. E. of Koundy, on a pretty hill covered with verdure. The soil consisted of a reddish sand, and the ground was quite open. The bullocks there found abundant pasturage, and they were suffered to graze till five o'clock, when we resumed our route, proceeding N. E. ¼ N. We travelled in the night: the bullocks were already extremely fatigued, and one of them lay down. The Moors, unable to make it rise by blows, had recourse to a method which I have frequently seen used since, and which is always successful: they bound a cord tight round the muzzle so as to prevent respiration and left the animal to itself. It struggled for a moment, and then jumped upon its legs: the cord was immediately removed, its load replaced, and it followed the others. After we had gone nine miles in the same direction, we halted at eleven at night.

We were threatened with a storm: the firmament was on fire in the east quarter, and the thunder rolled incessantly. The Moors dug large holes, into which they put their goods to preserve them from the rain which seemed likely to be very heavy. The wind blew with violence from the east, and raised clouds of sand, which, falling again, annoyed us exceedingly. At length, the wind having ceased, the storm dispersed without rain.

The weather having become calm, the Moors prepared our supper, which consisted of a little couscous, which we took without salt, my guides having forgotten to procure a supply at Podor; but, having eaten nothing all day, appetite compensated the want of seasoning. The soil was of the same nature as at our preceding halting place.

September 2nd. At five in the morning we resumed our route proceeding N. E. Our road led through a delightful country. The ground, diversified by hills covered with verdure, presented, with its numerous valleys, rich in vegetation, a prospect of the most pleasing kind. Game is here very plentiful; the woods abound in wild boars and antelopes. I saw a wild cat, which on perceiving us, set up a loud cry, and then scampered away. The generally received opinion that ferocious beasts are numerous in the desert is erroneous; for, neither did I see any during my residence among the Braknas, nor did I ever hear of any accident indicating their presence. I have since remarked, during my journey to Timbuctoo, that these animals are not more numerous in the interior. It is the inhabited tracts, or those contiguous to the lakes and rivers, which are the haunts of lions and leopards; it is there that they attack cattle, and sometimes, but very rarely, men.

We halted an hour near a pool, by which stands a large baobab (*adansonia digitata*); the water was so muddy, that it was scarcely possible to drink it: the Moors, to render it less disagreeable, mix with it a little treacle. This forenoon we travelled nine miles. At three o'clock we stopped for prayer, and continued our journey for the space of twelve miles to the N. E. over a tolerably rich soil, covered with *zizyphus lotus* and a species of the gramineous tribe, the prickly seeds of which adhere to the clothes and run into the flesh; I had my feet full of them, and they caused me the most acute pain. This plant abounds in sandy soils; the negroes on the Senegal call it *khakhame*. No person ever visited the environs of that river without having been cruelly tormented by it. Fatigue, however, made me forget my sufferings, and I slept soundly.

September 3rd. About one in the morning I was awakened to take a little *sangleh*,[13] and two hours afterwards commenced the preparations for departure; at five we started. The heat during the day was excessive, augmented as it was by a scorching east wind. My thirst was insupportable; perceiving a group of trees, I ran to them, thinking to find water, but was disappointed; and I must have been quite knocked up had I not met by the way with abundance of *grewia*, the yellow fruit of which, of the size of a pea, is very glutinous, though far from agreeable to the taste. I kept continually chewing it, which relieved me much. At length, about one o'clock, we reached a pool, where we rested ourselves till three. Here I quenched my thirst, and my companions bathed: we had travelled nine miles to the N. E. ¼ N. over an absolutely sandy soil.

Having resumed our route to N. E. ¼ E. we came to solid ground, covered with small flints of a bright red which incommoded us much. We saw several ponds; and I remarked one on the banks of which were six baobabs of prodigious dimensions. At ten we came to a ravine where there was water: here we halted for the night. We were more fortunate in the latter part of the day than we had been in the morning; for there was no want of water, and we found in abundance a plant which I took for an *anona*, a foot high, and bearing extremely green foliage: its fruits is of the size of a pigeon's egg, and contains several seeds; the pulp, slightly acid, is very good to eat. The Moors fell upon this fruit with avidity and devoured it; I followed their example and experienced great benefit from it, for it is an excellent thing for cooling and allaying thirst.

This day's journey had greatly fatigued me; the sharp flints on which we had to walk, had cut my feet sadly. In vain did I entreat the Moors to permit me to ride for a short time on one of the bullocks; none of them would give up his place to me, so that I was obliged to follow on foot. Accordingly, the moment we halted, I threw myself on the ground, and slept in spite of the storm which came on.

September 4th. An hour before sun-rise we set out, directing our course eastward, and after proceeding three miles we found traces of a camp which appeared to have been left the same morning. We travelled about a mile to the south, to visit a small camp occupied by slaves of Hamet-Dou's, who had been sent to this place to cultivate millet. In a moment I was surrounded by the inhabitants of this camp, who thronged round to examine me, being the first European they had ever seen. An old marabout, who appeared to be the chief of these slaves, ordered them to retire, and asked me numerous questions respecting my conversion to Islamism: after making me repeat some words of the Koran he directed sangleh to be made. Each family brought us a small calabash full; but had we not been so hungry as we were, we could not have eaten it, for, it was not only without salt, but the poor creatures had not even milk to mix it with. The appearance of the camp gave no high opinion of the magnificence of the prince to whom it belonged: the huts were small and ill built, and they scarcely afforded shelter from the sun. Two very shabby tents were no doubt the dwellings of the marabouts appointed to superintend the slaves, whose only garment was a sheep-skin, which covered them from the waist to the knees: they were about fifty in number and lived in fifteen huts.

A Wolof[14] slave having heard me speak her language came up to me and inquired if I was acquainted with her country: I availed myself of this opportunity to learn some particulars concerning their occupations. She informed me that the wealthy Moors send out slaves every year to sow millet, and that after the harvest they return to the camp of their masters. I went to look at their fields and found them badly cultivated. The negroes were busy weeding the millet; they merely scratched the surface of the ground, which, from its clayey compact nature ought to be turned up to some depth and broken.

At two o'clock we pursued our route to the E. ¼ N. E. and, having proceeded eight miles, crossed a rivulet in which the water was up to our waists: its current, which is very rapid, runs to the N. N. W. I was told that this stream descends from the mountains situated near Galam, the direction of which was pointed out to me to the E. S. E.; according to the Moors, it is absorbed by a lake about three days' journey from the spot where we halted.

After crossing this rivulet, my guides changed their direction: we travelled five miles to the east over ground covered with khakames, which incommoded me exceedingly. It then became stony and hilly, and we proceeded a mile to the north that we might arrive at water; and about eleven we reached a pool, the water of which was tolerably good. We kindled a fire for the purpose of cooking our supper, but, by the time it was ready, a violent storm came on. The Moors took off their *coussabes*—a sort of tunics—and put them into the pots to protect them from the rain: I did the same, so that we were all naked. We collected wood, made a great fire, and huddled round it, and in this state were drenched with the rain, which fell for two hours in torrents: it was extremely cold, and as it may be easily conceived, we were very uncomfortable. When the storm had ceased, we again put on our coussabes, which were perfectly dry; but a mizzling rain, which lasted all night, incommoded us much. The bad weather having prevented us from getting our supper, we breakfasted at the dawn of day with a keen appetite, though our sangleh had been exposed to the rain the whole night. At sun-rise we spread out the goods to dry; all of them had got wet, the soil, composed of ferruginous rock, being too hard to allow us to dig holes to shelter them in.

September 5th. At noon we resumed our route, travelling to the N. E. for the space of twelve miles, and at ten at night we arrived at a camp situated on the bank of a rivulet: here we halted a moment, and one of our people went to apprize the marabouts of our arrival: he soon returned and we entered the camp; I was immediately surrounded. The marabouts made me repeat the usual form of prayer of the Musulmans: *There is but one God, and Mahomet is his prophet.* I was besieged, and could not obtain a moment's rest the whole evening. The females, squatted behind the men, thrust their heads between the legs of the latter to get a sight of me; but at every motion that I made they drew back their heads with loud screams, at the risk of upsetting the men, producing confusion among the throng which kept constantly increasing. Being warned by my conductors not to leave the centre of the camp, lest I should be robbed, I lay down upon the ground, and covered myself with a pagne, hoping that the Moors would retire; but this precaution was of no avail; they continued to torment me: the women, having grown bolder, uncovered me; the children, after their example, pulled me one by the leg, another by the arm, while others struck my feet or pricked me with thorns. Being unable to endure this treatment any longer, I started up in a rage, and my persecutors run away: I then went to Boubou-Fanfale, and expressed my dissatisfaction at his conduct towards me. I represented to him that I was about to turn Musulman, and that on this account he ought to protect me and to procure me a little rest. He spoke to an old marabout, who had great difficulty to keep off the crowd; I then accompanied my protector to prayers, and on my return lay down upon a mat. A calabash of milk, containing about four quarts, was given me for supper; and more was offered me in case I had not had enough. This was the season when the pastures were in the best condition; there was abundance of milk and we were supplied with more than we could drink.

September 6th. At seven in the morning, we prepared to depart. The women and children had assembled round me; for more than half an hour the rabble of the camp followed at my heels; the women, with their faces concealed by the end of the Guinea cloth which serves them for a garment, affected to take no notice of me, and turned their heads when I looked at them, while the boys pelted me with stones, crying: *Tahale ichouf el nasrani!* "Come and see the Christian!" I faced about several times, and then they all ran away; but they returned the next moment, and were more troublesome than before. At length my guides, weary themselves of these importunities, drove off the crowd, who returned to the camp.

It was nine o'clock when we arrived at the camp of Sidi-Mohammed: we stopped there to obtain bullocks, for ours were exceedingly fatigued. The whole camp thronged round me, and I had to endure a repetition of all the annoyances of the preceding night. To quench our thirst we were supplied with a large calabash full of sour milk mixed with three parts of water; this pleasant and wholesome beverage is called *cheni* by the Moors, and is common in all the Arab countries that I have visited. We hired two carrier-bullocks, and at ten o'clock resumed our journey. I had walked all the way from Podor to this place; but, as we had increased the number of our oxen, I obtained permission to ride one of them.

After travelling eight miles to the N. E. over a stony soil, we came to a small camp composed of fifteen tents and some ill built straw huts, the dwellings of slaves. The baggage was deposited in a tent, and I was invited to retire to another. To avoid disagreeable visits, I pretended to be asleep, but it was to no purpose; the whole evening I had to endure the same kind of persecutions as I had suffered in the preceding camps. We supped very late; our meal consisted of sangleh, made with fresh milk. Having observed that the grains of which this mess was composed were whole, I inquired the reason, and was told that it was not millet, but *haze* [15], and that at this season the marabouts employ their slaves in gathering it. This grain is very common, and grows naturally without cultivation. Some slaves employed in this sort of harvest were pointed out to me: they were females, provided with a small broom, and two baskets, one of which, less than the other, is of an oval shape and has a handle above. When the haze is in the ordinary state and has not been trampled by cattle, they go along swinging this basket to the right and left, so as to rub the ears of the plants against it by striking them with their hands; the ripe grains fall into the basket, and when they have obtained a certain quantity they pour it into the larger one, which is destined to receive the produce of their labour. This method furnishes the grain in a much cleaner state than the second, but the quantity obtained is smaller, for, as it may be easily conceived, the whole of the grain beaten out does not fall into the basket. When the haze has been trodden, or a first gathering made in the manner just described, they cut the plant with a serrated knife which they have for this purpose, then sweep the grain together upon the ground into little heaps, which they afterwards take up; and, as in this way they get more mould than grain, they separate them by means of the *layot*, [16] which requires a great deal of time. On their return home, they take from the quantity collected (which may be estimated at five pounds of haze in a day) as much as they need for their supper, and carry the rest to their master's tent. The haze is not pounded like millet: it is separated from the straw, washed several times to clear it from all the particles of earth and made to burst: this grain swells much and makes a very white but not very nourishing sangleh. To reduce it to flour, a little water is thrown upon it, and after steeping a short time, a few strokes of the pestle are sufficient to pound it.

In this camp we passed part of the 7th of December, because we were approaching that of the king, and my guides did not wish to reach the latter till night. We left it at two o'clock, and proceeded northward for three miles upon a soil composed of black sand, covered with ferruginous stones. The country is studded with patches of verdure, which afford pasturage for the cattle.

It was near three o'clock when we arrived at the camp of Mohamed-Sidy-Moctar, head marabout of the king, and chief of the tribe of Dhiedhiebe. He had been apprised of my coming, and had waited for me, he said, with impatience: he came to meet us, took me by the hand, and having led me to the front of his tent, made me sit down upon a sheep-skin. He appeared highly pleased, seated himself beside me, and having sent for Boubou-Fanfale, who spoke Wolof, to act as interpreter, he inquired what were the motives that induced me to change my religion; what I had been doing at St. Louis; of what country I was; whether I had any relatives in France; and lastly, whether I was rich. I was obliged to answer these questions, for I perceived from the way in which they were put, that this marabout had conceived suspicions in regard to me, which, for my security, it was of consequence to remove: I replied therefore, that, having met with a French translation of the Koran, I had there found important truths, with which I was deeply impressed; that ever since I had ardently desired to embrace Islamism, and had been incessantly engaged in devising the means of accomplishing this purpose, but that my father had opposed it; that since I had resided at the

Senegal, where I had settled as a trader, I had received intelligence of his death, on which I returned to France to secure what property he had left; and that, being then my own master, I had sold every thing I had in my country, and bought merchandise, for the purpose of carrying my design into execution. I added that, at the Senegal, I had heard the wisdom of the Braknas highly extolled, and had in consequence determined to come and live among them; but that, on entering the Senegal, the vessel which I was in was wrecked, and I had saved but a small part of my goods; that I had left them with M. Alain, who lived at St. Louis and was advantageously known to them, and intended to lay out the produce of the little pack which I had brought with me in the purchase of cattle, for the purpose of settling in their country, as soon as my education should be finished. He seemed satisfied with my answers; the intimation concerning the goods was what pleased him most, and I congratulated myself on having resorted to this artifice. It was agreed that I should remain with him, that he should undertake my education and provide for my wants; and he added, in an emphatic manner, that he already considered me as one of his children.

Several young persons, doubtless with a view to learn my business, invited me to accompany them to prayer; but the chief marabout opposed it, alleging that I was not yet a Musulman. One of the sons of my host came and asked me if I would choose meat or sangleh for supper. I replied that all dishes were alike to me; on which he left me, and at nine o'clock a large plate of meat swimming in melted butter was brought to me: I have since learned that this dish is considered as a great luxury by these people. After supper, Mohamed Sidy Moctar informed me that next day we should set out for the king's camp, and that it would be necessary for me to bathe before I was presented to that prince; to this I agreed with the greater pleasure, as a bath could not but be very beneficial to me and refresh me much after the fatigues of the journey.

September 8th. When I had risen, I took out of my sack some articles which I had brought with me, and offered them as a present to my host, who seemed highly flattered and accepted them with pleasure. A little milk was brought to us; he then made me mount a camel with him and we set out for the king's camp. We proceeded to the N. E.; the whole plain was studded with ferruginous rocks, and here and there small islands of sand remarkable for their verdure; they are cultivated by the Moors, who sow them with millet. We passed on the way several camps of zenagues, or tributaries, but at great distances from one another.

I saw some slaves employed in weeding millet; they used an instrument like a chimney-sweeper's scraper, having a handle a foot long; they knelt to their work.

The motion of the camel fatigued me to such a degree that I was obliged to dismount. The country was open, and intersected by ravines: the soil was composed of a very hard red sand, on which I saw a great number of blocks of white marble; several of these I examined to ascertain their nature. We halted at a small camp consisting of seven tents; the marabout ordered some milk and water to be given to me to quench my thirst. We remained there during the heat of the day; my marabout then desired me to perform the salam[17], and we pursued our journey still in the same direction. Before we reached the king's camp, we passed near a pond, in which my guide caused me to be again washed by a zenague Moor, to purify me, as he said.

It was three o'clock when we reached the camp of the king: we had travelled twenty-four miles, and that in a very short time, for our camel went at a great rate. The camp was situated at a place called Guiguis, near a pond which served for watering the cattle.

Every body was apprized of my coming; in consequence I was presently surrounded by a numerous concourse. There were in the camp many marabouts who expected presents from this prince; they received me kindly: one of them, the Sherif Sidy-Mohammed, belonging to the Koont nation, proposed to me to take up my abode in his camp, promising to treat me as his son. I thanked him, and told him in answer to his politeness, that if I had not promised Mohammed-Sidy-Moctar, I should have given him the preference. I desired to be presented afterwards to Hamet-Dou; but I was told that this prince was lying down and that I could not see him till he awoke: in a quarter of an hour he sent for me, and I found him with a negro who spoke a little French and served as interpreter. When I entered the king's tent, he stretched out his hand with a smile, and addressed me with the customary salutation. *Salam aleïkoom*, adding these words of French which he had picked up at the Moorish market— *"Comment vous portez-vous, Monsieur? Bien, merci, Monsieur."* He asked the question, and answered it himself, not understanding the meaning of the words, which he repeated several times; he then asked me many questions, inquiring about the merchants of St. Louis with whom he was acquainted, and lastly about my own profession. I told him the same tale which I had got up the evening before for Mohammed-Sidy-Moctar; he was perfectly satisfied with it, and I perceived (as I had on the former occasion) that what pleased them most was the account of my wealth. He reiterated his questions, to try whether I should repeat the same answers, and concluded by assuring me of his protection while I should remain in his dominions, and particularly against his great marabout. He told me not to be afraid of any of his subjects; to which I replied that I feared no one but God. This answer pleased him; he took my hand with an air of satisfaction, exclaiming at the same time: *Maloum, Abd-*

Allahi (that is right Abd-Allahi[18]) and then dismissed me, admonishing me to rejoin my mentor, and not to leave him again. As it was now dark however, and I did not know where to find Mohammed-Sidy-Moctar, I was lodged in a tent belonging to the king's suite, many of whom crowded around me.

I was not yet accustomed to the Moorish diet, and the small quantity of milk I had drunk in the morning was very little support; it was now late at night and I was ravenously hungry. I ventured at last, to ask those who were about me for something to eat. One of them repeated the request to the king, who sent for me again, made me say a prayer, and then ordered a slave to milk a cow for me. I had hoped for something a little more substantial, and I told Hamet-Dou, when they brought me the milk, that I should like to eat something before I drank, and that I was more hungry than thirsty. These words excited "laughter unextinguishable" in all those who were in the tent; the king himself laughed as if he would have split his sides, and then told me he had nothing better to offer me, for that he never took any other nourishment than milk. I drank a little, and then returned to the tent which was allotted to me. About ten o'clock at night a Moor brought me some scraps of mutton, which he carried in his hand; they were sent, as I found out, by my marabout, and the bearer sitting down on a mat very unceremoniously partook of the feast. The mutton was boiled and full of sand, but hunger gave it a relish, and I thought it good fare.

In the night between the 8th and 9th, Boubou-Fanfale arrived; they had only been waiting for him to break up the camp.

On the 9th, early in the morning, preparation was made for departure. The queen sent for me, and gave me some milk for breakfast. At sun-rise the slaves took down the tents, and loaded them upon camels, together with the stakes, each camel carrying a tent; the rest of the goods were borne by oxen, and the women were conveyed, on camels appropriated to that office. The saddles for this purpose are furnished with a sort of oval pannier, large enough for two persons to sit in, and lined with a handsome carpet; that the journey may be more agreeable to the Moorish ladies, their seat is shaded by an awning of their finest manufactures.

The queen's saddle was adorned with scarlet and yellow cloth, and her cloth housing embroidered with many colours in silk. Her bridle was enriched with three pieces of copper, which rose like pyramids from the nose of the animal. The camels of the princesses were also much ornamented; and they sit in their saddles cross-legged like so many tailors. This position is so habitual to them, that they never change it, even on the couches, where they sit all the day. On the journey, their camels were led by slaves, and that on which Hamet-Dou rode was led also. The saddles for the men are of a different construction from those used by the women; they are high, narrow seats, on which a single man sits with his legs stretched out and crossed on the neck of the beast. If several men ride on the same camel, only one sits on the saddle, the others are behind; and it was thus that I rode with my marabout.

Our party when on march resembled a routed army, all confusion. The cattle went first, driven by a few men mounted on oxen; the mournful lowing of the animals, the shouts of the men, and the shrill voices of the women, resounded on all sides. Here a camel had disburdened himself of a woman, there a refractory bullock refused to proceed, a little farther a restive horse threatened to throw his rider, and was rearing and plunging amongst oxen and camels; women losing their balance in consequence, were rolling on the ground screaming; the hurly-burly was such, that there was no hearing one's self speak. At last, after having proceeded three miles towards the north, we halted to pitch our tents, and the confusion subsided. The slaves unloaded the beasts and set up the tents, and as there was no water at this place, they went back for it to the lake of Guiguis which we had just left. Such of the slaves as took charge of the cattle employed themselves in cutting briars to make fences for the calves, and others went to seek firewood to light fires before the tents. This article is so rare in this country, that when the camp remains long in a place, the poor fellows are obliged to go a couple of miles in search of it.

The Moors always burn fires before their tents; a custom which is inconvenient, on many accounts: in the day time the heat of these fires is unpleasant, and a multitude of grasshoppers and other insects, with which the country abounds in this season, take refuge in the tents and prove a great nuisance.

On the 10th of September, the king left us to carry a present to his brother Sidy Aibi, chief of a tribe of Braknas; he took my marabout along with him. At his departure he directed that I should lodge with his aunt Fatmé-Anted-Moctar, to whom he recommended me. I had not seen her before, but she treated me with great kindness, as did also two of her nieces who lived with her. They were considerate enough to send away all the curious who were incessantly besetting me.

At noon, they gave me some sangleh, the first I had eaten since I arrived at the king's camp. I was indebted no doubt to the protection of Hamet-Dou for the peace I enjoyed here; the women also were less annoying than I had found them in the districts I had lately traversed; their curiosity was sometimes vexatious, but I was no longer tormented as I had been elsewhere.

The wind was high, and it raised a prodigious quantity of sand, which fell like rain on our heads, and incommoded us for half an hour, so that we could not stir out of doors. In the evening we had a shower of rain, and I could breathe more freely again. On the 12th, the king returned; and on the 15th, we made our arrangements for proceeding on our journey, for we had only stopped to give Hamet-Dou the opportunity of visiting his brother.

We advanced nine miles E. ¼ N. E. on a stony ground covered with briars and abounding in pasturage. At noon we encamped in the vicinity of a range of mountains which they told me were called Zirih, but, as I afterwards learnt, Zirih signifies *mountain*.

CHAPTER II

The author is forced to turn physician — Distrust of the Moors — Description of the camp of King Lam Khaté — Schools — Amusement of the women.

On the 16th the king was indisposed; he sent for me and inquired if I could tell him of any herb which would ease him. I promised to make an excursion to look for some; and accordingly I ranged the neighbourhood, and found abundance of sweet basil, a plant which grows spontaneously in a rich soil; I gathered also a number of seeds, which I concealed with care in a corner of my pagne. When I returned, I gave the sweet basil to the king, and advised him to make tea of it; he drank it and found himself better. The properties of this plant are entirely unknown to the Moors, and the circumstance made a great noise in the camp. All the princes sent for me to their tents, to consult me on their various complaints, and to ask me for remedies. A quack would have taken advantage of this event to levy contributions upon their credulity, and I do not doubt that one of their own marabouts would have played them this game; but I gave them simply the most innocent remedies, things indeed which I knew to be harmless, whenever I was compelled to prescribe. I was not ill-pleased with this transient celebrity, for it procured me the advantage of rambling about in the country without exciting suspicion, under pretence of collecting medicinal herbs.

On the 20th of September, before sun-rise, I set off to visit the chain of hills two miles east of our camp. I crossed, on my way, a plain of rich black sand, intersected by ravines covered with luxuriant vegetation. I made my way to the summit of the loftiest of this chain, which may be about three hundred feet high, and is sprinkled with detached rocks of granite. Having reached the top of this, I discovered that the chain extends far to the N. E.; the width from north to south being about three miles. The other hills of which it consists are much less considerable than that which I ascended; among the rocks I found a quantity of cotton trees, with deeply indented leaves; the husks and seeds also being smaller than those of the cotton tree cultivated in our establishments in Wâlo. I took some of the seeds of these and of many other shrubs which happened to be ripe, and hid them in the corner of my pagne; I also collected some plants. In descending the hill I was met by two Moorish hunters; they looked surprised to see me, and asked me what I came to look for so far from the camp; I shewed them my plants, and told them that I came to fetch medicines for Hamet-Dou, who was ill; they appeared satisfied, shewed me some young Guinea-fowl which they had caught and left me. I climbed another of these hills, composed of flesh-coloured quartz rocks, in smaller masses than those which I had remarked on the former. I found many resembling marble; the intermediate spaces are covered with pure reddish sand.

On my return I searched the plain for cotton trees, like those I had discovered on the hill; but I could not find a single plant. The two Moors whom I had met, had arrived at the camp before me, and given an account of my excursion: the news had come to the ears of the king and awakened his suspicions. As soon as he was aware that I had returned, he sent for me, and I had not time to dispose of my seeds. When I entered, he asked me, with an air of dissatisfaction, whence I came, and why I went to a distance from the camp by myself. There were plenty of herbs, he told me, close by, without my going so far to look for them. Some of the Moors who were present, perceived that I had a knot in my pagne, and catching hold of it, they asked me what I had got there; and then, without giving me time to reply, they untied it themselves. "What do you want with these?" said they. "These are to take to the white men when you go back to them;" and, without waiting for an explanation, they threw away the seeds. I tried to persuade them that these seeds had medicinal virtues, and that I had gathered them for the benefit of more than one of themselves; but, not succeeding, I assured them that when I came to them, my connexion with whites had ceased, and that I could never return to their country.

In the evening, being in the tent of a marabout, who gave instruction, I took advantage of a moment when I could procure some ink, and fell to work upon my journal: I had written about a page, when the Koont sherif came in and caught me; he took the paper from me, and, amazed to see no Arabic characters, asked me what I was writing. I thought at first of saying that I had set down some prayers that I wanted to remember, but recollecting that I had not learnt prayers enough to take up a page, I told him it was a song, and I began to sing to convince him. The incredulous sherif did not appear to believe it, and he accused me of coming to spy out their ways, that I might give an account of them to the Christians. It was of importance to me to drive this idea out of his head, and I succeeded, by pretending the utmost indifference as to what I had written. I put the paper into his hands again with a smile, and said, "Go to the factory and get this paper read; you will see whether I have deserved the affront you have offered me." This stratagem had the effect I expected; he gave me back my paper, and asked me to read another verse. I sung another couplet; the sherif appeared convinced, and left me, to my great joy, for his surmises alarmed me exceedingly. I thanked God that I had Come off so well, and resolved to be more prudent in future. From that time forward, when I wanted to write, I took care to get behind a bush, and at the least noise I hid my notes and took up my beads, pretending to be saying my prayers. This feigned devotion procured me much commendation from those who surprised me; but it was painful to me to perform such a part.

For three days the wind had blown hard from the east; the pastures were nearly bare, and messengers had been dispatched to the north to see if they were more abundant in that direction. In the evening a tremendous storm came on, the thunder rolled awfully, and the rain fell in torrents; all the tents were blown over, and the utmost confusion pervaded the camp. The storm had taken every body by surprise; there had been no time to take down the tents; the very huts themselves were carried away, the briars which had been used for fences were likewise torn up, and many persons were hurt. The Moors, though accustomed to scenes of this sort, seemed very much frightened. Nothing was to be heard but men and women recommending themselves to God: the tumult was increased by the doleful lowing of the cattle, which had been torn by the briars which the wind carried off, and were now wandering about at random. This was the first storm that I had witnessed in the desert, and the general consternation which I remarked, made me suppose that there was some imminent danger; for a moment I shared the terror of the Musulmans, but the wind subsided in about three quarters of an hour, and the rain ceased soon afterwards. The people then bestirred themselves to set up the tents again, and to collect the scattered cattle; the fires which the wind had extinguished were re-lighted, and every one dried his clothes, for it is the Moorish custom to have only one suit. I had a dry pagne with which I covered myself, and more than ten people asked me for it to change themselves; but I had too urgent occasion for it myself, to lend it, which drew upon me their abuse. I observed that the king himself had been exposed to the rain like the rest of us, and that he had no more change of apparel than his subjects, for he remained all night in his wet clothes.

I have already mentioned that this storm took every body by surprise; in a general way the Moors strike their tents when they are threatened by a storm, leaving only a few small ones, which almost always resist its force, and serve to shelter the king and the royal family; all the rest remain outside exposed to the rain. On this occasion the wind was so high, that the very smallest tents were thrown down, and the princes and princesses shared the common fate.

On the 21st of September, a Trarzas marabout, from Portendik, arrived at the camp: I was called to see some articles which he brought with him from that place: he showed me a pair of pantaloons, which I thought I recognized as having belonged to M. Lacaby, who was wrecked in the Rose Virginie, on the bank of Arquin; he had also a handsome little dressing-case, and seaman's boots, which he used to protect himself from the thorns and khakhames. I should have liked to ask him a few questions, but I dared not for fear of exciting suspicions. The particulars of this shipwreck I had been acquainted with before I left Saint Louis, and I had even seen some of the sufferers.

On the 23d of September, the messengers who had been sent to look for pasture returned, and said that they had found no water in the direction in which they had been: it was then determined to move to the N. E., where we hoped for better success.

On the 24th, the camp broke up. My marabout's camel was ill, so I travelled on foot. We crossed the hills; about six miles from the place which we had left we came to a lake, called Lakhadou, surrounded by a fine plain of argillaceous soil, covered with vegetation: here we halted for several days. This lake is pleasantly shaded by *grewias*.

For the last three days, Fatmé-Anted-Moctar had omitted to send me a meal of sangleh, as she had been accustomed to do; I received nothing from her but a little milk morning and night, and was tormented with hunger. The king had told me, it is true, to ask him for every thing I wanted; but I got no more for that; and the milk, instead of satisfying me, gave me the colic, and impaired my strength.

This evening a Moor, called Moxé, arrived at the camp; he is the interpreter in ordinary to the king when he goes to the coast, and speaks French perfectly well. Hamet-Dou sent for me to question me again, and I gave him the same replies as before. Moxé told me that he was come from Galam, where the agent of the commercial society had given him a piece of Guinea cloth and a gun, and that he should return very soon; he proposed that I should accompany him, adding that four or five days would be sufficient for the journey. I should have been very glad to take this trip, and alleged, as a pretext for it, the great need I had of some new clothes. I asked the king if he would lend me a camel for the journey, and he promised he would when the waters had subsided; for, he said, the roads are impassable at this season. At night he sent me a piece of mutton for supper.

On the 25th of September, while I was at prayer, I felt myself ill from exhaustion: Moxé asked me if I had a fever, and I told him the cause of my illness, adding, that I had great difficulty to support this way of living; but I hoped, nevertheless, that I should become used to it in time. After prayer the king offered me a sheep, advising me to cook it myself, because, if I trusted to the Moors, they would devour it all. I accepted the offer; but, no doubt, fearful lest I should not take his advice, and with a view to save me from the rapacity of his subjects, he took care not to send me the sheep! It is probable that I owed this good turn to Moxé; for I was told by Fatmé-Anted-Moctar, that Moxé had endeavoured to prejudice the king against me: he insinuated, as I found, that it was not the love of God, but curiosity, which had brought me among them, and that I should not be likely to remain very long. Fortunately, some of the marabouts took my part, and the king said himself, that he could not believe that curiosity alone would have induced me to come amongst them to suffer such privations, and that God must have wrought a miracle in my behalf in operating my conversion. I thought I could perceive a little jealousy in Moxé's conduct with respect to me, and he probably feared that my presence, when I should have learned Arabic, would render his own needless. No doubt this was what also induced the negro, whom I mentioned as my interpreter in the first conversation I had with the king, to tell him I had not been shipwrecked, but that I had committed some atrocious crime among the whites, who had expelled me for it. Although the king laughed at all this, it did not fail to diminish his confidence, and I could perceive from day to day that I lost something of the esteem with which I had at first inspired him. I was extremely desirous to leave the camp, not only on this account, but because I could learn nothing; it consisted entirely of warriors, who did not trouble their heads about study, and my marabout was too much engaged to give me lessons. I opened my mind to the marabout, who entered entirely into my views, and persuaded me to ask the king for a beast of some sort to convey me to his camp, where his son, he assured me, would undertake to instruct me. Hamet-Dou told me to wait a few days and he would send me thither.

On the 30th of September, the camp broke up, and we advanced nine miles to the north, over a sandy soil covered with khakham. As I wore sandals only, after the Moorish fashion, I suffered extremely from the prickles of this plant, and my feet and legs were covered with blood. I asked several of the Moors to take me up behind them on their camels, but they said that their beasts were weary, and I must apply to the king who would furnish me with one. The king was gone on before, and I had lost sight of my marabout, so I had no hope except from the pity of those who were near me. I tried again to persuade them, for I was exhausted with pain and fatigue, but in vain; I got nothing but raillery in answer to my entreaties, and I was told that I should win heaven by suffering with patience. They spoke the truth; but I am sure not one of them would have taken my place to earn heaven at this price. If they had even left me alone in my misery, it would have been more bearable; but the young princes, mounted upon their fine horses, came bounding about me, running against me, and rallying me upon my dress, which consisted only of a coussabe[19] made of coarse blue pagne, and falling to pieces. I found on the road some water-melons, which I ate to quench my thirst, and when it became still more intolerable I was forced to beg some water, with my beads in my hand, and then I sometimes succeeded in obtaining a little.

At last, about eleven o'clock we stopped near a lake called Tobaïti. I perceived the tent of the king, which was pitched, and thither I went to rest myself. Several marabouts came and took out the numerous thorns which had run into my feet, and the king appeared sorry to see me suffer; he assured me that if he had fallen in with me by the way, he would have ordered a beast for me, and he sent me some milk and some water to refresh me. When I had rested a little, I went to the tent of Fatmé-Anted-Moctar, the residence which had been assigned me. In the evening, at the usual hour, milk was distributed among us for supper, and as soon as I had received my portion, I inquired if there was any body to be found who would exchange a little sangleh for milk; upon which I was referred to an old female slave who was seldom without it. She accepted my proposition and gave me a little at the time, promising me the same quantity every day. I, on my side, promised her a reward. This poor creature was in the habit of going, when her master could spare her, to pick up haze for her subsistence; she only received the milk of one cow for her share, and care had been taken to allot her one of those that gave the least; nevertheless, in her forlorn state, she found means to soften my lot; so true it is that the wretched are the most compassionate. During the whole week that I remained after this time in the camp, she did not fail once to bring me a little calabash of sangleh.

October the 7th, I requested the king to send me to the marabout's camp as he had promised. He gave me a bullock to ride upon, and a slave to guide me. At nine in the morning we set off, but had scarcely proceeded a quarter of a mile before the bullock stopped, and would not go further, upon which we were forced to return to the camp.

On the 8th, Hamet-Dou having provided me with another bullock, I set off at six o'clock in the morning, travelling to the S. W. ¼ W. over a sandy soil covered with khakham. Our journey was very painful, on account of the thirst we endured; for there was not a drop of water to be found on the road. At two o'clock we found traces of a camp, which we followed.

Climbing some hillocks of loose sand, we perceived to the south a streamlet running from W. to S.W.; its banks were bordered with *mimosa, zizyphus lotus,* and *nauclea,* which appeared in full verdure. My guide told me that the rivulet was called el-Hadjar, and that it overflows the plain in the rainy season. I thought that it was probably the same which I had passed with Boubou-Fanfale. I saw some smoke rising from the banks of the river, which seemed to indicate the vicinity of a camp, and I rejoiced at it, hoping that I should have an opportunity of quenching my thirst; but, on advancing a few paces towards it, I perceived that the whole plain was on fire. Some person had set fire to the dry herbage, and the birds of prey were hovering around to catch the insects and reptiles as they were escaping from the flames.

When we reached the bank of the streamlet, we found a number of slaves employed in collecting haze, and some of the Moors superintending. I went up to them, and obtained a little water to drink; one of the Moors took me by the hand, and told me he was delighted to see me; he made me repeat a short prayer, and then, having called for a little pot, containing sangleh, he took me to the side of a pool, a few paces off, in the bed of a rivulet, which is dry at this season, and shaded by the green foliage of a beautiful tufted tree, which keeps the water cool. While I was sharing the sangleh with the Moor, I learned that when the grass is too short to be cut they burn it, that they may afterwards gather the haze.

We had travelled twenty-three miles since morning, and we had still three miles to go to the camp of Mohammed Sidy, *lakariche,* or prince. Having rested, and quenched our thirst, we proceeded to the N. W. The road that we pursued was crossed by banks of moving sand. At four o'clock in the afternoon we arrived at the camp.

As soon as I made my appearance, I was here, as in the other camps, the object of universal curiosity; all its inmates collected about me, and I was compelled to repeat prayers for great part of the evening. Some of the women inquired if I would accept a share of their bed; and on my replying in the affirmative, they ran off with bursts of laughter. One of them wished to examine whether I had undergone the rite prescribed by the law of their prophet, but I did not think proper to satisfy her. The site of this camp was called Lam Khaté. I had nothing but milk given me for my supper, and I was not allowed to add sangleh to it, as in the camp of the king. In the night, there was a hurricane from the east, which overthrew the tents, and prevented us from sleeping.

On the 9th of October, the guide who had been sent with me by Hamet-Dou, refused to go any further; I employed all the means in my power to induce him, but in vain; he chose to return to his master. I must stop at Lam Khaté to give a description of the royal camp.

This camp comprises the tribe of Oulad-Sidy, otherwise called the *lakariches*, or princes; and from this tribe spring all the kings of the Braknas. In some circumstances, the camp is divided into two or three parts, all retaining the original name, but distinguished also by the name of the chief who commands them. The camp of Hamet-Dou probably contained at the time of my visit about one hundred tents, and four or five hundred inhabitants. When the king receives his customary tribute, his camp is filled with strangers, who come to ask for presents. I have seen some of these gentry who had staid for three months in the hope of at last obtaining ten ells of Guinea cloth, worth, perhaps, about eight shillings. These parasites establish themselves in the first tent where they can procure lodging, and twice a day, morning and night, they sally forth, with their beads in one hand, and a tin can in the other, to beg milk from door to door. In the day time they walk about the camp, two and two, or assemble in tents to converse; and here they commonly fall asleep, while they are ridding each other of the vermin with which they are infested. I was a great source of amusement to them, and when they came about me, they were sure to pass a part of the day in questioning and tormenting me. I suffered most from the *hassanes*,[20] or warriors; fanatical, idle and ignorant they were never contented but when they annoyed me, and they added to all their other insults an insupportable ironical laugh. They were continually asking me whether I meant to be circumcised. I replied, that I had referred the affair to my marabout, who, to my great satisfaction, declared that the operation was unnecessary, that it was dangerous at my age, and that I could go to heaven without it.

The marabouts[21] do not usually inhabit the same camp with the hassanes; four of them only were to be found in that of Hamet-Dou. One of these was very poor; he was a schoolmaster, taught girls and boys, and when their education was completed the parents presented him with a coussabe or a bullock. Evening and morning the children are engaged in picking up fire-wood; it is always after dark at night, and before it is light in the morning that they take their lesson. By the light of a great fire, they recite some verses of the Koran, chanting them in a loud tone; these verses the master writes upon their boards and they have to learn them by heart. At night they meet again at the master's tent to repeat their lesson. Whilst he is hearing his class, the master walks round the fire, singing himself to give the note to his scholars, and holding in his hand a long stick, with which he lays about him, when he sees any one inattentive. When a pupil is perfect in his lesson, he goes all round the camp repeating it, and obtains great applause.

The Moors have a profound reverence for the Koran; they never lay it on the ground, not even on a mat, without putting a pagne under it. Before they venture to touch it they perform an ablution, raising their hands above their heads first, and then rubbing them over their faces and arms; any one who should do otherwise, would be despised and considered as an infidel.

The boys are not admitted into the schools till they have been circumcised, and before this epoch they are forbidden to touch the holy book. The slaves are never allowed to handle it, being regarded as impure. When the boards, on which the Koran has been written, are removed, they must be taken by the cord which serves to hang them up by, and neither be turned wrong end upwards nor trailed on the ground. When school is over, these boards are laid upon the thorn fence, and a slave who should presume to meddle with them would be beaten without mercy.

The education of the girls is very limited; they are taught to repeat the salam, and a few prayers, but seldom to write; some of them however are tolerably well informed. The boys learn the Koran by heart; but it is to the education of the marabouts that most attention is paid; some of them are very well read in the precepts of their religion, and pretend to know more than we do of sacred history. They were quite surprised that I should know any thing of the Bible, and I gained great applause by reciting some of the adventures in the lives of the patriarchs; but they were still more astonished that I was acquainted with the history of Mahomet, and this gained me their good-will more than any thing else.

Till the education of the children is supposed to be finished they go very ill clad, or even naked; the boys have only a coussabe made out of a pagne; the girls are usually naked till the age of puberty; some wearing a small guinea cloth when they have left school, or when they have made especial progress in their studies, by way of distinction.

A father seldom instructs his own children, unless there is no school in the camp, in which case he teaches the girls, because it is not the custom to send them to school in another camp. The father does not complete the education of the boys; they commonly learn the first elements from him, and are then sent to some marabout who keeps school. The parents give each of them two cows, the milk of which supplies them with food; the master does not receive his salary till the education of the pupil is finished. The hassanes seldom learn to write, and their principal ambition is to ride a horse well and to fight.

The Moors assemble to prayers five times a day, the king always attending. Amongst the Braknas the mosque is formed by an enclosure of thorns, sometimes under the shelter of a mimosa, if there happens to be one at hand. The Moors often meet here to discuss affairs of business or politics; they even pass the whole of the day in chatting on indifferent subjects; but this holy place the women are not permitted to enter; they perform the salam before their own tents. Even the men, when they enter the mosque, observe a peculiar ceremonial, which consists in putting the right foot first, and leaving it with the left foremost: on entering the mosque they perform an ablution. They have no public crier, as amongst the negroes, to call them to prayer; but, according to ancient custom, one of the oldest marabouts summons them together by calling *Allah akbar*; several of the other marabouts repeat this cry on entering the mosque; the practice is not obligatory, but they seem to consider it as a duty.

The king's tent differs in nothing from those of his subjects; it is twenty feet long and ten wide, and covered like all the others, with a stuff made of sheep's hair;[22] at each end are eight leather straps, and as many stakes, upon which it is stretched. Two upright poles ten or twelve feet long, crossing at top and fitting into a cross-piece a foot long and six inches wide, are placed in the centre to raise it; this cross-piece rises above the uprights, and prevents their ends from piercing the awning. A carpet of sheep's hair manufactured in the country surrounds the interior of the tent; four stakes are driven in at one end, supporting two cross-bars, over which a cord or string is passed in the form of a net, and upon this is placed their baggage. Their things are stowed in square leather sacks shaped like portmanteaus with an opening at the end; and these bags have a lid secured by a padlock.

The harness of the horses and camels hangs up round the tent. The king's bed is after the same fashion as that of the negroes, consisting of a hurdle covered with mats, and raised by stakes and cross-bars about a foot from the ground. A mat spread on the ground covers the unoccupied part of the tent, and serves the king's attendants for a bed. The common people lie on the ground on mats, under which they *sometimes* spread a little straw. A matting is put round the goods at the end of the tent, to preserve them from thieves. The store of water is kept in skins upon stakes in the inside of the tents; it is reserved for the masters and the calves, and refused to the slaves; and even she who has had the trouble to fetch it cannot obtain a little but by dint of entreaties and after enduring all sorts of mortifications.

The king's table service consists of six or eight deep round wooden dishes, each containing about three quarts, and used to hold milk and other articles; three metal pots and two of earthen-ware, which they obtain from the Fouta, form the cooking apparatus, and complete the list of the furniture. This description will serve for all other tents as well as the king's, except that the poorer class have mats instead of a carpet.

Hamet-Dou is almost always surrounded by *guéhués* or strolling singers, who abound among the Moors, and are always to be found in the train of the princes, from whom they obtain whatever they want, sometimes by threats, at others by the basest flattery. Every prince has one of these men in his retinue, and Hamet-Dou's *guéhué* follows him wherever he goes. When they are seated together in the tent, he sings the king's praise, and loads him with such outrageous panegyric, that none but an African monarch could hear it without blushing; the king's wife and children usually join and repeat in chorus all the absurdities he can invent. These parasites have contrived to make themselves as much feared as despised by the Moors; they understand the art of persuasion in perfection; and though they are noted impostors and consigned to everlasting fire by public opinion, their calumny is so ingenious that it always injures the character of those against whom it is aimed. The marabouts have the greatest contempt for the guéhués, but they always receive them politely when they make their appearance, for fear of the false reports which they would raise if they were offended. The instruments which the guéhués use to accompany their songs are of two kinds. One, in the form of a guitar, is nothing but an oval gourd, covered with a well dried sheep-skin; this is crossed horizontally by a stick a foot long, upon which the strings of the instrument, five in number, are fastened: these strings are made of twisted hair, and the tone of this instrument, which is touched by the hand, is pleasing enough. The second is a sort of harp with fourteen strings of sheep's gut, mounted upon a stick two feet long, and placed obliquely in a round calabash of much larger dimensions than the other. A leather thong, stretched horizontally over the skin which covers the gourd, serves to fasten the lower end of the strings, or sometimes they are attached to a bit of wood placed across. At the edge of the calabash and under the last string is a piece of iron, flat and oval, about five inches long, and set round with small iron rings, which tinkle when the harp is played upon, and add to the effect. The musicians never fail to ask for presents from the princes whose praises they sing, and as they are seldom refused they have numerous flocks and good beasts of burden. Sometimes they make presents to the marabouts to conciliate their esteem; and the marabouts accept the gift and despise them nevertheless.

During the month that I passed with the king, I never once saw him take any solid food, or drink any thing but milk. When I asked him why he took neither sangleh nor meat, he replied that he preferred milk to all other food. To distinguish themselves from the common people, the king and his nobles always drank camel's milk, and said they preferred it; but I always suspected that their only motive was the difficulty of procuring it, which prevented the slaves from drinking it also; a sort of distinction of which they are jealous. I have seen the queen several times eat meat swimming in melted butter.

In the rainy season the Moors seldom take any other food than milk, which they have in abundance at that period of the year. The rich sometimes kill a sheep, but not often. The king's guéhué killed a sheep one day, and was roasting it on the embers while I was in his tent; presently as many as thirty Moors collected, having found out what was going on by the smell of the meat; and they watched like so many ravenous beasts for the moment when they could satisfy their voracious appetite. The guéhué hoped to have got rid of them by distributing some small pieces among them; but no sooner had he sat down to the feast with his wife, than the Moors fell upon it and carried it all off, tearing the scraps from one another's hands and mouths; they even fought for the bones, and dispatched the poor guéhué's sheep without giving him a taste. I could only compare them to dogs fighting for a piece of meat that one of them had stolen; and I, who had been invited to partake with the lawful proprietor, was not more fortunate than himself. This was a great disappointment to me, as I was very hungry. I was told that this scene could not have taken place except at a guéhué's, and that they would not have dared to behave so to a person of more importance.

I sometimes suggested to the Moors that they would improve their fare by sending their slaves to collect haze, and making it into sangleh, but this hurt their pride: "It is food for the common people," said they, "and for slaves; we do not condescend to eat it." Those who have a little millet left from their stock save it for the return of the dry season, when milk becomes scarce.

The Moors have large herds of oxen and camels; and they have also a number of fine horses, of which they take great care; giving them milk when it is plentiful, morning and night. When a horseman arrives at a camp, he goes about inquiring for milk and for water for his beast.

The care of the camels is committed to the Laratines[23] or the zenagues, and very seldom to negro slaves. As soon as a camel is foaled, its legs are tied under its body, to habituate it from the first to the posture in which it is to receive its burthen. When it is old enough to carry a load, a month is sufficient to teach it to rise with its burthen, and to balance itself. When it is to be weaned, they thrust a splinter through its nose, and fasten some thorns to the splinter, that it may prick its mother whenever it comes near her, and she may prevent it from sucking. They also tie a cloth round the teats of the mother, and fasten it over her back. The black slaves attend on the bullocks, driving them to pasture at seven o'clock in the morning, and bringing them back at sun-set. The cows are not milked till ten o'clock at night, after the last prayer; those who took care of them in the day time performing the office. The wooden vessel which they use to milk into is never cleaned except by holding it over the fire for about ten minutes; by this method of purification, it contracts a smoky taste, which it imparts to the milk, and this renders it very unpleasant. The Moors let the calves suck, because they fancy that the cow would cease to give milk if they did not. A boy is employed to lead them out one after another, as soon as they are milked. The calf runs to its mother, and is suffered to suck for a few minutes; they then tie it to one of its mother's legs, and she permits herself to be milked without perceiving the change. The calves are left for a short time with their mothers, and are then shut up again in the thorn enclosure, where they remain the rest of the night and all day.

The favourite female slaves of the princes receive the milk in calabashes, and distribute it again to their masters. Beauty amongst the Moors consists in enormous embonpoint; and the young girls are therefore obliged to drink milk to excess; the elder ones take a great quantity of their own accord; but the younger children are compelled by their parents, or by a slave whose office it is, to swallow their allowance. This poor creature commonly takes advantage of the "brief authority" that is granted her, to revenge herself by her cruelty for the tyranny of her masters. I have seen poor little girls crying and rolling on the ground, and even throwing up the milk which they had just drank; neither their cries nor their sufferings making any impression upon the cruel slave, who beat them, pinched them till they bled, and tormented them in a thousand ways, to force them to take the quantity of milk which she thought proper. If their food were heavier, such a system would have fatal consequences; but it is so far from hurting their constitutions, that they grow visibly stronger and fatter. At twelve years old they are enormous, but at twenty or twenty-two they lose their embonpoint; I never saw a woman of that age who was remarkably corpulent.

The largest women are reckoned the handsomest. The Moors have no taste for beauty of form or mind; on the contrary, what we consider a capital defect is an attraction with them; they admire women who have the two front teeth of the upper jaw projecting from the mouth; and ambitious mothers employ all possible means, to make their daughters' teeth grow in that direction.

The men, as I have said, feed also on milk; but they drink less than the women. The slaves live upon cows' milk, and in the season when milk is scarce, they are allowed a small portion of grain, about three quarters of a pound, without milk; at that season they eat only at 11 o'clock at night, when their masters are in bed. Such of the Moors as have young slaves ten or twelve years old, send them to the enclosure where the calves are, at milking time; and from every cow they let them drink a mouthful of milk; which is all the food they receive, so that they suffer much from hunger.

When supper is over, the milk which is left is put in a leather bag, called *soucou*, to curdle. In the morning, after the cows are milked, they breakfast as they supped over-night, that is to say upon milk; the difference being that they have less of it, because the calves are allowed to suck in the morning.

At noon, a slave churns the milk to make butter; filling the soucou which holds it with wind, and then shaking it on her lap for a quarter of an hour. When the butter is made, they work it into little balls of the size of a walnut, and add three parts water to the milk, which is set by in calabashes to be distributed at dinner. The balls are put into the portion destined for the women, and they swallow them in drinking; this beverage of milk and water is called *cheni*.

The Moors are naturally filthy; and they seem to chuse the dirtiest slave on purpose, to make the butter and apportion the cheni. I have seen the women making the balls of butter with their hands wipe their fingers on their hair, and then plunge them again into the calabash containing the butter and milk. They disgusted me to such a degree by their uncleanly ways, that I have often suffered hunger, rather than accept a drink which they had prepared so filthily.

If the slaves are ill treated by the hassanes, those who belong to the marabouts fare still worse. I have mentioned that the hassanes allow them to gather haze for themselves, which tends much to alleviate their condition; the marabouts, on the other hand, make them collect it for them, and give them a very small quantity of it, and that without milk.

The herds of the hassanes are less numerous than those of the marabouts; they have hardly ever any thing in their camp but a few cows and oxen; the rest of their cattle, the camels excepted, are entrusted to zenagues, or tributaries, who are responsible for them, and bring them back when they are wanted. Each tribe has a distinct mark for its herds, to which the proprietor adds his own counter-mark. The wooden vessels which they use for milking are made by their workmen; they take a piece of the trunk of a tree of suitable size, cover it with cow-dung except where they mean to hollow it out; then putting fire under it, they blow up the fire with bellows, driving the flame towards the wood; and thus, the dampness of the cow-dung on the outside preventing it from burning too far, the vessel is hollowed. They make wooden funnels also by this process, which is very tedious, but the only one with which they are acquainted.

I have already mentioned that I was on the point of continuing my journey, and that my guide had left me at Lam-Khaté. On the 10th of October, one of the sons of Mohammed-Sidy, lakariche, gave me a slave for a guide; we set off at seven o'clock in the morning, and advanced a mile to the west along the bank of a large lake, where I saw plenty of ducks, teal, and coots. The soil in the neighbourhood of the lake is argillaceous and rich; I observed there some stems of millet of the preceding year. After having passed this lake, we directed our course to the S. W. and proceeded fifteen miles on stony ground covered with doggrass. I had nothing to hold water, and suffered from thirst. On the road we met a marabout riding on an ox; I begged him to give me a little water, and accompanied my request by a short prayer in Arabic; he gave me some rather grudgingly, and told me that I should have had none if it had not been for the prayer. At noon we arrived at the camp of Boubou-Fanfale, situated on the bank of the Hadjar; he seemed pleased to see me, and gave me a bit of mutton for dinner. My guide returned and Boubou sent one of his sons to conduct me to the camp of my marabout. At two o'clock we set off again, directing our course over a stony soil. At six in the evening, having travelled about ten miles, we arrived at Ténèque, the camp of the zenagues belonging to the king; we passed the night there. My host gave me for supper a bowl of sangleh, which I enjoyed very much. In the evening, I was visited by all the women of the camp.

On the 11th, at five in the morning, we continued our journey still in the same direction. One of the marabouts was going the same way, and we travelled in company. The soil, consisting of yellow sand, was covered with khakhames. We passed near eight or ten tombs, and as soon as my fellow-travellers descried them at a distance, they exclaimed: *Salam aleycoom; la allah ila allahou!* (Peace be with you; there is only one God.) We stopped to pray, which gave me time to examine the tombs. Mounds are raised upon the bodies, and at the head of each is a flat stone, on which is written the name of the deceased. After a short prayer, we each threw a small branch of a tree on the tombs; my companions then went to the grave of a celebrated marabout which had a hole a foot deep at the head; they took earth from this hole, and rubbed their foreheads, breasts, and backs with it, and then invited me to follow their example; from which I inferred that all passers-by were expected to perform this ceremony.

At eleven o'clock, we arrived at the camp of the Dheio-lebere tribe, of which my marabout was the chief; we had then travelled ten miles. We rested here during the heat of the day, and they gave us water to refresh ourselves. At two, we continued our journey towards the west, over a rich black argillaceous soil. We came again to the rivulet, and at six o'clock we halted at el-Khara Hett-Louhed-lahi. A little before we reached the place, we were espied by a troop of women, who were gathered around a drum; two youths, with each a stick, were beating this drum; and the women kept time, clapping their hands, singing, and making a thousand contortions without changing their places. As soon as they perceived me, they left their amusement and came to torment me; gathering around the bullock on which I was seated, they pulled me by the legs, pinched me, and screamed frightfully whenever I moved. In vain the marabout who was with me attempted to drive them away, and assured them I was a Musulman; they pursued me, shouting *el-nasrani! el-nasrani!* (the Christian! the Christian!) while the children threw stones at me. A girl struck me with a stick, and fairly exhausted my patience; I snatched the stick from her, and gave her a such a stroke on the face, that all the rest were frightened and ran off. We visited a friend of my guide's, where I was well received, and had some couscous given me for supper which I thought delicious; for it was the first time I had eaten any since I had been amongst the Moors. I was afraid that I should have been tormented again in the evening, but the stick had frightened the curious, and I was left in perfect quiet.

On the 12th of October, at six in the morning, we resumed our route to the south. The soil, though stony in some places, is good. I remarked on the road some indigo plants of great beauty; the Moors are not aware of its properties. We travelled for six miles, and towards nine in the evening arrived at the camp of my marabout, where I was received with great joy by the inhabitants.

On the 13th, the youngest son of Mohammed-Sidy-Moctar cut off my hair, and made me a pair of breeches out of my coussabe, and a coussabe out of a pagne which I had with me.

On the 14th, we went to visit his aunt, whose camp was not far from ours. All the marabouts welcomed me politely, and I was happy to find that I should be less tormented than I had been by the hassanes. One of the marabouts brought me a slave who had a cancer in her breast, and begged me to tell him of some herb which would cure her, offering me six oxen as a reward; I bade him observe that vegetation was all dried up at this season, and that it was impossible to procure any herbs. After him, came a multitude of invalids, all entreating that I would cure them; some I remarked were suffering acutely, and it grieved me extremely that I could afford them no assistance. In vain I told them that I was not a physician, and that I had no medicines with me; they renewed their entreaties, and I could only escape from this scene of woe by leaving the camp. It was one o'clock when I returned to my marabout.

I have observed that the Moors in general are not subject to severe illnesses, an exemption which they probably owe to their temperance; but they are very susceptible of pain, and the least suffering unmans them. I have seen a Moor with a slight head-ache cry like a child. The remedies most in vogue amongst them, are the following: when ill, they diet themselves and take nothing but milk, and as soon as they are convalescent, they feed upon flesh only, that they may recover their strength the sooner. When they have a head-ache they bind a cloth round the forehead, as tight as they can. For a cold, they introduce melted butter into their noses, by means of a pipe fitted into a vessel, and they pretend that they derive much benefit from this, especially for a cold in the head. When troubled with pain in the stomach, they make a drink of half a glass of camel's urine mixed with two bottles of water; the bark of mimosa burnt and reduced to powder serves for all sorts of cuts, burns, contusions, &c. They make an ointment of it, by mixing it with butter, and rub it on the part twice a day. The leaf of the *bauhinia* pounded, and mixed with powdered gum and water, is a recipe for aches; they lay it like a poultice on the part affected, and the gum when dry forms a crust, which they leave to fall off of itself; they sometimes burn the gum before they make use of it. For pain in the face occasioned by cold, they have a special remedy in a certain very hard red stone, which they find on the mountains; they reduce it to powder by grating it against a flint, and rub the powder in a dry state upon the part. It is common to see people with half the face red—sometimes an eye, or part of the cheek: this stone is called *lahmiri*; I consider it to be a sort of red lead, and the Moors make ink of it by mixing it with gum water. I wished to have brought home a specimen of this stone, but I looked for it in vain, and could never persuade any one to give me a bit. The Moors are subject to fever, for which they have no remedy, but they drink gum and milk when they are attacked with it. I saw a woman, who had had a fever for a month, rub her head with very hot butter, in which pounded cloves had been steeped.

Aperients are seldom employed, although they are acquainted with the use of them. They collect senna, and call it *falagé*; when they mean to make use of it, they bruise it in a mortar with the fruit of the *ziziphus lotus*, and dilute the powder in a considerable quantity of water, which they give to the patient to drink. They have another plant which they use as an aperient, which is less potent in its effects.

The itch, so common among the negroes, is rare with the Moors. Whoever is attacked with it is shut out from society; he is forbidden to enter the mosque; a mat is spread in one corner of a tent for his bed, and nobody drinks out of the same vessel with him till he is cured. Gunpowder steeped in water is the remedy, and with this the patient rubs his body all over. Such is the medical practice I have seen in this country, from which the Moors appear to benefit very little. I saw during my stay, one case of elephantiasis, one blind man, but not a single leper; with the last disease they seem not to be acquainted; I never once met with a cripple.

When I returned to the camp, I asked the marabout's son, who was about eighteen years of age, to repeat some verses of the Koran, which I wanted to write down, that I might learn them by heart. At the second line, however, he stopped and refused to proceed, telling me that it was unlawful to write the words of God with a profane hand; he afterwards consulted one of the marabouts on this point, who was wiser and bade him to continue.

Walking about in the camp, I remarked some heavy black stones lying loose on the soil; one of these I broke; and found that it contained a great deal of iron; a specimen of these stones I have sent to the governor. The Moors smelt this ore, and make locks, fetters, and other things, of the iron. To smelt it, they dig a hole in the ground, a foot and a half deep, over which they build a furnace in the shape of a pyramid five feet high, leaving at the bottom four holes for the bellows. They fill the furnace with ore broken into small pieces, and heat it with sheep's dung, which when dry makes a very strong fire. Four men, placed at the apertures of the furnace, blow the fire, till the iron is melted, after which they leave it to cool without giving it any form, which renders it very difficult to work, so that they prefer what they buy of us.

On the 15th of October, the pasture being exhausted, we broke up the camp, and removed four miles to the S. W. ¼ W. to a peninsula formed by the bed of a rivulet, and called by the Moors Guigué; it was then covered with pasturage, which is inundated in the rainy season, and the trees are finer there than elsewhere.

On the 21st, I suffered much from the colic. One of my marabout's sons repeated prayers, and then spat on my stomach, assuring me that it was an excellent remedy; he did the same to the milk which I was to drink, and I let him have his own way, disgusting as it was, rather than contradict his opinions.

In the evening, a caravan on its way to Fouta, to exchange salt for millet, stopped at our camp, and took up its quarters in the midst of us; mats were brought to serve as beds for the travellers. At ten o'clock at night, milk was brought to the marabout, from all sides, and calabashes full of sangleh and milk, which were distributed among the *ziafis*, or travellers.

When a caravan is small, only a part of the camp contributes to the supply of its wants, and the inhabitants take their turns to do so: if it is large, every body furnishes his quota. If it arrives in the day time, the chief of the camp, when he goes to the mosque to prayer, makes a collection for the ziafis, and each person sends a measure or two of grain according to the number of the strangers. A slave is appointed to pound the corn and prepare the sangleh. When a traveller arrives alone, he goes to any tent he pleases, and the owner supplies him without having recourse to his neighbours. As strangers always prefer the best-looking tents, the same tent is often visited five or six days in succession. Travellers frequently stay some time in the camp; for the first three days they are fed as a matter of right, after which the master of the tent is at liberty to refuse them provisions. The hassanes when they travel are always unwelcome guests, on account of the arbitrary manner in which they exact what they want. If they are not waited upon as quickly as they expect, they clamour and threaten, and call their host an infidel—the most opprobrious epithet that can be bestowed on a marabout. If a stranger arrives amongst them, he is ill-treated, and ill-fed; hence their camps are always avoided, and the burden of entertaining travellers devolves in consequence upon the marabouts.

The Moors, as has just been observed, afford one another hospitality, but they do not deserve to be called hospitable, for nothing annoys them so much as the sight of strangers. They receive them not out of humanity but from fear, particularly when they happen to be hassanes, who would not fail to plunder, if they were not treated as they liked. They seldom afford assistance to travelling negroes; if any such pass through a camp, they beg morning and night when the cows are milked for a draught, going about with a jotala in their hand, and receiving so little, that they are obliged to traverse two or three camps before they obtain sufficient for a meal.

Many negroes from Fouta-Toro come amongst the Moors to study the Koran; they often remain five or six months, and have no other means of subsistence but alms. Though Musulmans, they are in bad repute, and very generally despised amongst the Moors, who say they are fit for nothing but slaves. The negroes take nothing with them, because they would be sure to be stripped by the hassanes; they always travel on foot, and carry at their backs a small board, on which they write passages of the Koran.

There are amongst the Moors a sort of vagabonds called *Wadats*; these are the very poorest hassanes, who have often neither tents to lodge in, nor cattle to feed them; and being too idle to work, which indeed they consider as a disgrace, they like better to run from tent to tent and beg for a living. The insolence of these troublesome parasites is without bounds; when they arrive at a camp they throw it into confusion: nothing is heard on all sides but the disputes which they cause by their importunities. Impudent as they are, they get whatever they ask for; because, if they were to complain to their tribes that they had been ill received in a camp, the hassanes would carry off the herds belonging to that camp while feeding in the woods, and the marabouts would be obliged to give many head of cattle to redeem them. The parties of Wadats are chiefly composed of women and children; there are seldom any men amongst them: they travel on foot or mounted on asses, and always apply to the chief of the camp, who is obliged to find them provisions. To get rid of them, it is common to give them food enough for three or four days, and send them off; they then go to another camp, where they beg again, and as they know that they shall always obtain as much as they want to eat, they sell what they can spare for Guinea cloths, often to the very people who afford them hospitality. If they have no beasts to carry what has been given to them, they borrow some to go as far as the next camp. They visit only the marabouts, for the hassanes and zenagues refuse to receive them.

At the time when the gum is collected, these vagabonds beset the marabouts, and follow them into the woods, requiring to be fed, and worrying them till they can get a good share of gum, which they carry to the markets. The marabouts dare not refuse them, for the Wadats would join together if they did, beat them, and steal their gum. Such is the life of these people. It is worthy of remark, that when they are with the marabouts they are very exact in performing the salam; but they trouble themselves no further about it when they are out of their sight.

I had now been nine days with Mohammed-Sidy-Moctar, and not a word had been said about teaching me. I applied to the eldest of Mohammed's sons, who wrote the Arabic alphabet upon a board for me, and told me to learn it by heart; I could not do it alone and begged him to help me; and I afterwards applied to his brothers, but seldom found them disposed to take the least trouble with me: they liked better to loll in their tents and to chat or sleep. In other respects, my situation was more agreeable than in the king's camp; I never suffered from hunger, for I had commonly sangleh twice a day with a little milk to it. At noon and at ten o'clock at night they gave me my allowance. At noon I had sometimes cheni instead of sangleh, and sometimes my sangleh was moistened with cheni and butter; but this mess was always so filthy, that I often went without my dinner on account of the nasty way in which the butter is made; nevertheless it is a great luxury amongst the Moors—none but the rich eat it, and they very seldom. The marabouts live better than the hassanes because they employ their slaves in gathering haze; the men eat sangleh once a-day, and drink milk at night; the women live entirely upon milk. In the dry season, when milk is scarce, the marabouts go to Fouta to buy millet in exchange for cattle and Guinea cloth. Those who have no means of buying it, content themselves with what milk they have; and to a certainty they are very ill off, for in the months of February and March the best cows do not give above two bottles a day. The poor who have no herds of their own are maintained by their tribe, every inhabitant of the camp in turn giving them the milk of one cow; this however is only amongst the marabouts.

Those who have large herds and flocks kill a cow or a sheep, but it is a rare event: during the seven months that I spent in Mohammed-Sidy-Moctar's tent, only ten were killed, and those during the dry season, for they are never killed when milk is abundant, or after the millet harvest.

The wealthiest hassanes eat meat once a day; some, however, from economy, refrain from it for several days. They are great gluttons, and if they were to eat as much as they liked, their flocks would not be capable of supplying their wants. They never eat to their heart's content except on a journey, when they can levy contributions upon their hosts.

CHAPTER III

Method of cultivating and using millet — Character of the hassanes or warriors — The balanites ægyptiaca, its fruit, method of extracting oil from it — Quarrel excited by a woman — Manner of protecting oneself from cold in the tents — Method of collecting gum — Marriages of the marabouts, and of the hassanes — Inheritance of property — Method of tanning leather — Dress of the Moors.

The millet is reaped at the end of May; at that time the marabouts receive it from their slaves and the hassanes from their zenagues, or tributaries. This millet supports them till the month of July when the rainy season commences; they then withdraw from the banks of the river, and live entirely on milk. If any millet remains, it is laid by till the next dry season.

In the month of November, when the waters begin to subside, the Moors send their slaves to sow the ground which has been flooded by the rains, or by the overflowing of the river. It is at this season also, that the zenagues come down to the banks of the river to cultivate millet. The slaves of the same camp lodge together, and cultivate the same district; each field is marked out, and the produce carefully kept in a separate place. Their method of cultivation is exceedingly bad, but it gives them little trouble. With a thick stick they make holes in the ground six inches deep, and into these holes they drop three or four grains of millet, covering them with sand or light mould. They never prepare the ground in any way, and only weed it after the millet has come up. To save themselves trouble they select a poor soil, because a richer would require more weeding, and they are naturally lazy. When the seed is sown, they wait quietly till the millet makes it appearance, then thin it a little, and weed round the roots to give it air; many do no more than this, and suffer the grass to grow up between the roots.

When the ear begins to show, they stay in the field to drive away the birds, which would devour the grain before it is ripe; and this occupation does not allow them a moment's rest: they walk about the field incessantly, shouting and throwing stones, and at night they lie down among it to protect it from gazelles, porcupines, and wild boars, which would make great havoc.

When the millet is ripe, they cut it, and thrash it with sticks. The grain is put into sacks, and carried to the camp, and those who have reaped more than they are likely to want carry the surplus to the markets, and sell it to the dealers.

On the 4th of November, the son-in-law of Mohammed-Sidy-Moctar came to the camp. As he did not lodge with his father-in-law, I conclude that they were not on good terms. I went to pay him a visit; he was very polite, and asked me many questions about the resolution which I had taken, congratulating me upon it, and telling me that he was very much afraid the Christians would detain my goods, or, if I returned to fetch them, would detain me by force. I endeavoured to correct a mistake which proceeded from his religion, and assured him that the Christians would leave me at perfect liberty to do what I pleased; and that as to my goods they would be as safe in their hands as in my own. "The whites," said I, "rob nobody; their laws punish such crimes with severity, and they would do justice to the poorest Musulman exactly as they would to a Christian of the first importance; both are equal in the eye of the law." I seized this opportunity to ask him, why the Musulmans pursued a conduct with regard to christians, so contrary to religion; and why they ill-treated and made slaves of those who ventured amongst them for commercial objects, without having committed any offence. "I cannot believe," added I, "that a good and merciful God approves of such conduct. If you want to convert the Christians, it can only be effected by intercourse with them, and by excelling them in justice and kindness—not by ill-treating them. For my part, I am a Musulman, but I shall never approve of doing ill to those who have done us no harm." The marabout allowed the truth of what I advanced; but he said it was unbearable, that when a Musulman spoke to a Christian about the prophet, the Christian should laugh in his face; that none but an infidel would do so; and that it would be a good action to kill him, that they might both go to heaven. I wished to enter into some particulars respecting Christianity; but I durst not let my zeal run away with me, and I contented myself with telling him that the Christians adored the same God as the Musulmans. "Yes," said he, "I know that; but they never pray; they drink wine and spirituous liquors, which is displeasing to God; and the religion of Mahomet, which alone is agreeable to him, condemns to everlasting fire those who do not adopt it." He asked me afterwards if I meant to make a journey to Mecca; to which I replied that it was the duty of every good Musulman, and that I hoped to discharge it. He took me by the hand, and answered: "That is right, Abdallahi, you love God and the prophet." Boubou-Fanfale served as interpreter in this conversation.

The same day, a young Moor invited me to accompany him into the woods, where I was to meet a number of other young men from the same camp. When we came to a very thick part of the wood, he sat down, and a moment after a slave brought a sheep; he then picked up wood, and lighted a fire, after having made a hole in the ground, in the form of an oven; a marabout then killed the sheep,[24] and the slave skinned it. The marabouts took the intestines, which they emptied by squeezing them between their fingers; and then, without washing, they made puddings with them; these were put over the fire, and eaten when they were half cooked. When there was a large quantity of embers, they were removed from the hole, and the sheep put in their place; embers and ashes were then spread over it, and fire kindled above. In half an hour's time, my companions considered that the sheep was sufficiently dressed; they took it out of the hole, gave the head and a scrap of the neck to the slave, and divided the rest into as many portions as there were persons present; lots were cast after this to determine to whom each share should belong. Feasts of this kind are much in vogue with the Moors; five or six young men join, and furnish each a sheep in their turn, which they eat in the woods, that they may not be beset as they would be in the camp. When they have had as much as they can eat, they carry the rest to their relations; but there is never much left for this purpose, and sometimes none at all. Of the skins of their sheep and goats they make leather bags, and use them to keep and carry water in; for that purpose, they slit the skin of the animal from the knee nearly to the shoulders, loosen it with their hands and turn it back, and then take out the flesh through the opening.

On the 6th of November, the camp broke up; we then marched three miles W. ¼ N. W. along the bank of a stream, where pasturage was abundant. Part of the camp remained behind, and rejoined us on the 8th. I was informed by a marabout that Mohammed-Sidy-Moctar was then on the road to his camp.

The ground in the vicinity of el-Hadjar is rich, and covered with fine vegetation. The periodical inundation of the river deposits a slime which improves the soil, and it is also enriched by the numerous flocks and herds which are attracted by the pasturage. This virgin soil wants nothing but the hand of the husbandman to produce in abundance all the plants which it might be desirable to cultivate; but it would be in vain to suggest such a thing to the Moors, and the distance from the coast will never admit of a European establishment. Half a league from the banks of this stream, the nature of the soil changes, and it becomes ferruginous; vegetation is to be found only on little patches of very hard yellow sand, where the rain brings forth a few species of grass.

On the 9th of November, some Moors came and asked me to shew them the proper way of taking sweet basil; Mohammed's eldest son advised me not to tell them till they had given me a new coussabe; but I replied that if I was fortunate enough to have it in my power to render any service to the Moors, I would do it for the love of God, and not to gain a reward. I mention the fact to shew how little idea those people have of generosity. I have already said that the sons of my marabout gave me very few lessons; I did not, however, neglect any opportunity of gaining instruction; I applied to the other marabouts, who taught me some verses of the Koran, and I also learnt from them the Arabic letters. The news of their father's speedy arrival rendered my hosts more attentive; they now furnished me with a regular scholar's board, and I was set morning and night to sing the praises of God and his prophet, by the light of a small fire.

On the 10th, as I was boiling a little milk for my breakfast, two hassanes, who had lately arrived at the camp, came to me; one of them threw a dirty rag into my milk, and then began scolding his companion, as if *he* had done it, and pretending to take my part. This anecdote will give a correct idea of this class. Both these men were still with the camp on the 12th, when we were preparing to remove. They had found a poor wretch, a *haddad*, or blacksmith, and wanted to force him to give them a coussabe: the poor fellow had not one for himself, for he was naked; they struck him, threatened him, and at last put a cord round his neck, and tied him to a camel to take him off with them; but, at this moment, a marabout interfered, and obtained his release after many entreaties. When I inquired the cause of this cruelty, I was told that the hassanes always treat the zenagues, or tributaries, in this way when they want to extort something from them; they make them run to keep up with their camels, beating them unmercifully, and do not let them go till they get what they want.

The artizans are always zenagues; they are generally despised by the other classes, and perpetually exposed to the rapacity of the hassanes. When they have earned any thing by their labour, they give it to a marabout to keep, for it would not be safe in their own hands. They are either shoemakers or smiths; the shoemakers do all kinds of work in leather, make shoes, portfolios, saddles, etc.; the smiths make locks, fetters, poniards, and other iron articles; they are also goldsmiths, and are extremely ingenious; though they have few tools, they produce astonishing pieces of workmanship. Those who employ them commonly supply them with metal, and pay them with millet, milk, or stuff for clothing.

It was eight o'clock when the camp broke up. We travelled six miles N. N. W., on a soil covered with iron-stone, and three miles over yellow sand. The tree named *balanitis ægyptiaca*, grows here in great abundance; the

Senegal negroes call it soump. The Moors collect the fruit of this tree, from the kernel of which they make a kind of sangleh, which they relish much, because it is very greasy.

This kernel contains much oil, and the inhabitants of Senegal extract it for their use when they are short of olive oil. I tasted it at St. Louis, and found it tolerably good, but I think it might be better if more care were taken in gathering the fruit, and expressing the oil. If government were to afford encouragement to this culture, this fruit might become an important article of commerce. The tree grows every where near the Senegal. To extract the oil, the inhabitants pound the kernels in a mortar; when reduced to a paste, they make a hole in the middle, into which the oil flows speedily and abundantly; they lade it out by degrees, until no more runs; they then squeeze the paste in their hands, and it yields a little more oil, but not so clear as the first. A quart of kernels produces about a bottle of oil; hence it might be inferred, how much might be obtained by a better process. The negroes eat the pulp of the fruit, either raw or baked in the ashes. The trunk of the balanite furnishes yellow wood, easily worked, and firm; the Laobés[25] make mortars, pestles, baganes (large wooden bowls) and many other things of it.

On the 24th of November I was witness to a scene which diverted me extremely. I saw a number of women outside the camp, who were uttering shrill cries, and some children who were throwing stones; I approached to see what was the matter, and found a woman in tears, muffled up in her garments, and supported by her friends. While I was inquiring the cause of her affliction, I espied some men and a crowd of women at a distance, quarrelling about the loads of two oxen; three slaves with leather straps attacked the women when they came near the oxen, and the women in their turn laid on with sticks, and pitched off the loads. While the men were engaged in replacing them the women snatched what they could reach, and carried it off towards the camp in triumph, singing as they went. This contest lasted more than two hours, and the baggage was perceptibly diminished, when the wife and daughter of the great marabout interfered; they seated themselves on the remainder of the baggage, and the two parties began to listen to one another. The distressed female was born in this camp, and had married a marabout of a distant camp. Wishing to see her relations again, she had persuaded her husband to accompany her; some days after their arrival the husband was desirous of returning, he put off his journey however, at the request of his wife. At last, his business required it, and he was determined to return; but his wife who was bent upon keeping him, got up a quarrel, struck him, and collected all the women of the camp round him. The women flew at the husband like furies; the husband was supported by some of his friends; they tried to load the oxen again with the goods which the women had thrown on the ground; the women pushed and pulled, and sent them rolling with the bales; and the oxen were four times loaded and unloaded in my presence. In vain did three strong negroes, slaves of the husband, lash the women by the order of their master; they could not keep off the crowd, but were beaten themselves; and the boys, who are always fond of mischief, threw showers of stones upon them and the marabouts. At last, the wife and daughter of the grand marabout having taken possession of the baggage, a capitulation ensued; the women were desired to disperse; and the marabouts promised to take the goods back to the camp till the morrow. When every body was gone, they loaded the oxen again and set off, taking with them about a fourth of their goods; and in the evening the lady departed to rejoin her husband.

The Moorish women have great influence over their husbands, which they frequently make a bad use of. Polygamy is not practised by the inhabitants of this part of Africa, and their wives would not permit them even to have concubines. The king himself has, like his subjects, only one wife.

On the 25th of November, an hassane stole some oxen belonging to a marabout of our camp, which caused a great bustle; every body was on foot all the evening, and two friends of the injured man went to the hassane's camp to demand the oxen. I was told that if the king had been there the thief would have been severely punished. The same evening Mohammed-Sidy-Moctar arrived; I expected to see his family very joyful upon the occasion, and was surprised that nobody went out to meet him. He entered his tent, and saluted them all; his greeting was very coldly returned; his daughter alone rose, and laid her hands respectfully upon his head, without any demonstration of affection. I have never seen the Moors embrace each other; even a lover does not kiss his mistress; he lays his hand on her lips, and then puts it to his own, no doubt to convey to it the kiss which she has impressed on it. The next day the marabouts who went to demand the oxen returned; but without success.

On the 28th, the grand marabout went himself to claim them, and they were given up; he had much difficulty in prevailing, and did not return till the 6th of December; the oxen arrived shortly after him.

The Moorish laws are very severe against theft, but they are hardly ever enforced. If the thief is taken in the king's presence, the king may order him fifty or sixty stripes on the back, or have his ears cut off, without any form of trial. Capital punishment is sometimes inflicted upon the tributaries, but never upon hassanes or marabouts. By the law of Mahomet, a thief is to have his hand cut off; but every body has an interest in mitigating this clause, for the Moors would all be one-handed if it were rigorously enforced. The law does not apply to those who pillage christians; on the contrary, that is considered a meritorious action, and they lose no opportunity of plundering them.

On the 10th of December, the camp moved twelve miles W. ¼ N. W. to a spot three miles east of lake Aleg, whither a party went to fetch water for the use of the camp. The women are charged with this labour; they fill the skins and load them upon asses; at nine they left the camp, and they were back again in an hour.

It was now beginning to be cold; the north wind blew violently, and rendered the nights very unpleasant. At this season the Moors set up the *varroi*, a large covering made of tanned sheep-skins sewed firmly together; they stretch it over stakes in their tents, with the sides hanging down, so as to keep off the wind during the night. They have also woollen counterpanes, or cloaks, which they buy from the Koont traders, who bring them from Wâlet, or other great towns in the interior. They wrap themselves up in these counterpanes at night, and also in the day, when the cold is severe. The slaves sleep also under the varroi, upon the ground, with no other covering than the sheep-skin which serves for their clothing.

On the 11th, I saw an ox killed: the four feet were first tied by slaves, who knocked the beast down, and thrust a stake through the skin of his throat to prevent him from moving his head; a marabout stuck him, and the slaves took off the skin. The flesh was cut into thin slices and hung upon cross-bars, fastened to poles, to dry. A fence of briars was formed round it to keep off the dogs, and it was covered with mats to preserve it from being spoiled by the sun. A slave slept by it till it was dry, and kept up a small fire at night to counteract the effect of damp. The meat thus dried was put in leather sacks to preserve it. When it is well dried, it will keep a long time, and has no disagreeable taste. The Moors generally eat it without further preparation or cooking. The slaves who flay the ox receive the neck and some bones; the head is given to the haddads, and the other bones are distributed as presents.

The Moors never invite their friends, not even their relations, to eat meat; what they have they keep for themselves. Sometimes a number of them join together, each furnishing his ox, which they kill in turn, and eat the flesh in common, as I have before said respecting the young men and the sheep. This is a sort of carnival amongst them, and they give it a name which signifies "a party to eat flesh."

On the 12th of December I went to lake Aleg, it was surrounded by camps of marabouts, for it is the rendezvous of all those who travel on the banks of the river. The environs are broken by little hillocks covered with iron-stone. The *voscia integrifolia* grows abundantly in the plain; the Moors collect the fruit, which they call *iré*, and eat it cooked with meat. The banks of the lake are covered with *mimosa, zizyphus lotus,* and *nauclea africana*. Its breadth does not exceed three miles; it stretches from south to north, and terminates in a north-westerly direction; the circumference may be about twelve leagues. It overflows periodically, like the river, and inundates the contiguous lands for a mile round. These lands are particularly productive, and are cultivated by the Moors when the waters have subsided. The lake is fed by the el-Hadjar, and by an immense number of ravines, which collect water during the rainy season.

The season for collecting gum had now arrived, and every body was employed in making preparations; I intimated a wish to accompany those who were going out for that purpose, but I could not get leave. I attribute this refusal to distrust; for the Moors conceive that the Europeans wish to take possession of their country as being the finest in the world. Not being allowed to gratify my wish of observing these operations, I tried at all events to obtain accurate information on the subject.

On the 13th the slaves destined to this labour set off under the direction of several marabouts; it was not till some days afterwards that I learnt from my host's wife the particulars which I am now about to relate. It has been believed, but without foundation, that there were forests of gum-bearing trees in the desert; travellers have fallen into this error from the inaccurate accounts of the Moors, who, to do honour to their country, always profess that every thing is to be found there in the greatest abundance. The acacia which furnishes gum grows singly in all the elevated parts of the desert, never on argillaceous or alluvial soil, but on dry sandy ground; it is very rare on the banks of the Senegal. The tree is not the same with the *mimosa gummifera* of the botanists, which I had seen in our settlements; its leaves are regularly pinnated; the folioles are broader, thicker, and of a darker green; in its shape and appearance it more nearly resembles the acacia cultivated in France.

The wells which have been dug in the interior, where the operation of collecting the gum is carried on, have given their name to the neighbourhood, and such has been the origin of the names that have been given to the fictitious gum forests. Near these wells the marabouts take up their abode, and the slaves cut straw to make huts; a single marabout superintends the slaves of his whole family, or of several of his friends; and he assembles them all, sometimes to the number of forty or fifty under the same hut. Every marabout sends as many slaves as he can spare, and they are sometimes joined by a few wretched zenagues. The superintending marabout takes with him two cows, and carries a bag of millet for his food.

When a zenague joins the slaves, he applies to the marabout, who gives him a cow and what else is needful, and at the end of the gum-harvest he receives half of what he has collected. The zenagues are only permitted to gather upon this condition; if they were to attempt it on their own account they would be plundered by the hassanes. Every detachment is provided with a pulley and cord to be used at the wells, and a leather bag which is to serve as a bucket for drawing up water. I have been assured that those wells are very deep, and the ropes which I saw were thirty or forty fathoms long. The pulley is fixed, to two stakes driven into the ground on each side of the well, and meeting at their extremities; the end of the rope passed through it, is tied round the neck of an ass, which, driven by a marabout, draws up the bucket; another marabout receives it, and pours the water into a wooden trough for the use of the cattle. The superintending marabouts are charged with this duty. The slaves fill their leather bags with water every morning, and, furnished with a great forked stick, they traverse the fields in search of gum; as the gum-bearing trees are all thorny, this stick is used to knock off from the higher branches the lumps of gum which could not be reached by the hand. As they pick it up they put it in their leather bags; and thus they spend the day, without any thing but a little water to refresh them. At sun-set they return to the hut; a woman prepares sangleh for the marabout's supper; another milks the cows; and each drinks the milk of that which is allotted for his subsistance. When the gum is plentiful each person employed collects about six pounds a day, which proves that the trees are detached; for if they grew in forests, as some say, and no time were lost in running from one to another, the quantity of gum collected must be much greater.

The superintending marabout receives a proportion of the gum; the slaves work five days for their master, and the sixth for the superintendent, who thus comes in for the greater part of the produce. The Moors have neither vessels nor bags to carry home their gum; when they have collected a certain quantity, the slaves make holes in the ground and there deposit what they have collected. When these holes are full they are covered with ox-hides, straw, and earth; care is also taken to give the surface of the soil above the same appearance as it has round about; for, if discovered, the treasure would be carried off by other Moors; when they remove from the spot, they make a mark on some tree or stone near the hole, and the gum is left there till it is taken to the markets to be sold: it is then put into large leather bags; and carried by oxen and camels.

There is no private property in gum-trees; every marabout has a right to send as many slaves as he likes, without asking leave, or paying any additional contribution. It would assuredly be a great source of wealth to them, if they consulted their own interest better, but they are so indolent that they not only do not try to augment the number of their slaves, but do not even send as many of those they possess as they might do. Their wants however are limited; a single garment suffices them.

On the 14th a young man belonging to a neighbouring tent, having a mistress in the camp of the Oulad Biery tribe, invited me to accompany him, with some other friends, to pay her a visit; this camp was a mile to the north of ours. I accepted the invitation, for I sought every opportunity of obtaining an insight into the character and customs of these people. I was politely received; all the women collected around me, talked to me a great deal, and asked me many questions; our conversation was pretty lively; for they asked me amongst other things if I intended to marry, and on my replying in the affirmative, they desired me to chuse one of them, and pressed me to say which I liked best. I told them that the choice was too embarrassing, and that I would rather marry them all, for I thought them all equally beautiful and agreeable. This joke amused them; they were very much pleased with it and even thanked me. Perceiving that the marabout lover was absent, I inquired what had become of him, but could get no information except that he would come again towards night. Several of the women were employed in adorning the betrothed lady, and they had just put on the *henna* to render her more lovely in the eyes of her admirer. This henna, *lawsonia inermis*, is found in great plenty in the interior; the Moorish women bruise the leaves, and obtain from them a pale red tincture which they rise to brighten their charms. The leaves being bruised and reduced to pulp, this pulp is applied to the various parts of the body which they are desirous of staining; it is kept covered, to preserve it from the action of the air, and moistened at intervals with water in which camel dung has been steeped. The colour is five or six hours in fixing; after that time the pulp is removed and the flesh to which it has been applied is stained a beautiful red. Henna is applied to the nails, the feet, and the hands; upon which last they make all sorts of patterns; I have never seen it applied to the face. The colour remains a month without changing, and does not disappear entirely in less than twelve months. It is not only an ornament with the Moors, but a religious ceremony for women who are about to be married. When a woman has used henna she takes care to show it, and to attract attention to her hands and feet, that she may be complimented; women are coquettes all the world over!

The toilet of the Moorish ladies is not confined to the use of henna; the lady in question had her hair dressed; her tresses, which hung on her shoulders, were smeared with a sort of ointment, made of butter, pounded cloves, and water; and adorned with amber, coral, and bits of glass of different colours. I had never seen a Mooress so bedizened before.

In the evening I went to look for the lover; a young Moor accompanied me. We met him close to the camp, and I concluded that he was going to his intended; but he told me, on the contrary, that he did not chuse to pass by her tent, and that he was on the way to one of his friends. I expressed my surprise, and he told me that he wished to avoid the lady's relations; on this subject we had a long conversation, the substance of which is as follows.

When a young man becomes attached to a girl, and wishes to marry her, he seeks her in secret, and obtains her consent. That point secured, he commissions a marabout to treat with the girl's relations, as to the presents which he is to make, the number of oxen he is to give to the bride's mother &c. This being arranged, the marabout who has undertaken the negociation informs the other marabouts, when they are assembled to prayer, the lover himself being present. From this moment the lover is not to see the father and mother of his future bride; he takes the greatest care to avoid them, and if by chance they perceive him they cover their faces, as if all the ties of friendship were broken. I tried in vain to discover the origin of this whimsical custom; the only answer I could obtain was, "It is our way."

I did not like to suppose that a connexion of this kind could destroy the esteem and affection which had previously subsisted between the two families, and I took some pains to ascertain whether it was so or not; I often talked to a father of his son-in-law and *vice versa*; and I found that the indifference was only feigned, that they felt the same affection as before, and in conversation extolled one another's merit.

The custom extends beyond the relations; if the lover is of a different camp, he avoids all the inhabitants of the lady's camp, except a few intimate friends whom he is permitted to visit. A little tent is generally set up for him, under which he remains all day, and if he is obliged to come out, or to cross the camp, he covers his face. He is not allowed to see his intended during the day, but, when every body is at rest, he creeps into her tent and remains with her till day-break. This indiscreet method of courtship lasts for a month or two; after which the marriage is solemnized by a marabout. The mother of the bride gives a feast, and kills an ox if she can afford it; providing abundance of couscous and sangleh for the guests, who are sure to be numerous. The women collect round the bride, singing her praises and amusing themselves the whole of the day; I have seen some of them dance.

The hassanes are not obliged to conceal themselves from their new relations; they meet as usual both before and after the marriage: their feasts are also more gay and brilliant, and they admit the guéhués to them. Whatever may be the difference between the ceremonial however, the woman and her husband are in all cases subjected to the parents of the latter.

When the marriage is celebrated, the husband may take away his wife forthwith if he has a camel; in that case the mother-in-law supplies the equipage for the beast, the cradle, and the carpet which lines it; she adorns the daughter with her finest ornaments, gives her a mat to lie upon, and a sheep-skin for a coverlid; the husband leads the camel, and keeps his face covered till he is out of the camp. If he has no camel, he leaves his wife in the camp till he can procure one, for it would be a terrible disgrace if the woman were brought home to her husband's camp on a bullock. Sometimes he settles in his wife's camp, sends for his flocks and herds, and ceases to hide himself.

It often happens that the husband and wife cannot agree, or are desirous of a separation; one of them then quarrels with the other, and they part without having recourse to the marabouts who brought them together. The one who wishes for a divorce makes a present to the other. If there are children, the boys go with the father, and the girls remain with their mother; if she is pregnant at the time, and brings forth a boy, it is sent to the father who has it nursed by a zenague.

When the husband dies, his wife goes into mourning and wears it four months and ten days; during this time, she puts on her worst apparel, receiving nobody into her tent but her nearest relations, and covering her face when she goes out. The husband, on the other hand, does not wear mourning for his wife, and may marry again the next day.

The law of inheritance is as follows: when a man dies his wife receives one fourth of his goods; the mother of the deceased has a tenth of the three other fourths, and the father a fourth of the remainder; the children's share, which is thus reduced to one half, is so divided, that each boy shall have twice as much as each girl. When the husband inherits, he takes half the property of his wife, and the other half is divided among the grand-parents, and the grand-children, in the same proportions. At the death of husband and wife without offspring, the property goes back in the ascending line; for collateral branches never inherit.

At the death of husband or wife, the uncle of the deceased becomes guardian to the children, until they are eighteen, which is the age of majority; the oxen which they are to inherit are confided to the grandfather until that time. Children who are still at the breast are sent to the zenagues, till they are two years old, and then return to their uncle.

The Moors never grieve for any body's death, and would think it very improper to shed tears over the deceased, being persuaded that his soul has ascended straightway to heaven! They shave the whole body with the exception of the beard, and wrap it in a white shroud, after having washed it with care; it is then left exposed in the tent for four days, during which time the marabouts assemble round it and sing verses of the Koran.

If the relations of the deceased are rich, they kill an ox to regale the singers; if they are poor they only give a little sangleh every evening. On the fifth day, they dig a grave about two feet and a half deep, and the body is laid in it on one side, with the face towards Mecca. Briars are placed upon the grave to protect it from wild beasts. If the deceased was a person of consequence, the grave is lined with mats; when it is filled up, an inscription is placed upon it; the marabouts perform the salam and return to the camp.

The hassanes and zenagues do not bury their own dead, but have recourse to the marabouts, who undertake the business for a small remuneration. The women are not present at the interment of a man, nor the men at that of a woman.

When a child is born its body is rubbed all over with fresh butter, which is also given to its mother to take; her face is likewise rubbed with it; she eats nothing but meat till her complete recovery. The husband takes care to be absent himself when his wife is in labour, for no sooner does a woman feel her pains coming on, than she screams in the most frightful manner, and assails her husband in the most abusive and indecent language. This is another of their customs! When the child has acquired a little strength, it is slung in a pagne, tied at the four corners to serve as a hammock. The mother usually suckles the child herself.

The country of the Braknas is situated about sixty leagues E. N. E. of St. Louis; it is bounded on the south by the Senegal; on the east by the country of the Douiches;[26] on the N. E. by that of the Koonts;[27] and on the north, by the tribe of Oulad-Lame,[28] which is united with another neighbouring tribe; these two compose a nation formidable on account of the depredations which they commit; they are not Mahometans. The tribe of Labohs[29] is on the N. E., and to the west of the Trarzas. This nation is composed of several tribes, some hassanes, and others marabouts.

The principal tribes of hassanes are: Oulad-Sihi, Oulad-Aly, Oulad-Hamet, Oulad-Makhso, Oulad-Abdallah, Oulad-Baicar, Oulad-Pis-nem-Nematema; of the marabouts, Dhie-dhiebe-Touaryk, Oulad-Tandora, and Oulad-Biery-Togat. Each of these tribes has its separate and independent chief. Hamet-Dou is recognised as king by the French government, and the duty on the trade in gum is paid into his hands; he receives also the tax which is levied on merchant ships; but the goods derived from these sources are divided amongst all the chiefs and princes. The marabouts receive nothing from the princes.

These tribes are often engaged in war with one another, which they undertake without the king's consent. The crown is hereditary only when the king leaves a son who is of age; if he leaves no children, or minors only, it devolves to his brother, who enjoys it during life; after his death, if the sons of the preceding king are of age to inherit, the eldest succeeds to his father's rights. The population of the Braknas is not very numerous; it is divided into five classes, which have been already mentioned: *hassanes, marabouts, zenagues, laratines,* and *slaves.*

The hassanes may be considered as the aristocracy of the country and its warriors; their armies consist of themselves and their slaves; the zenagues join also, in the hope of pillage; the common people, that is, the poorer hassanes, are attracted by the same hope, but they serve only as volunteers, and the princes have no power to compel free men to enlist in their armies.

When the chief of a tribe is cruel or unjust towards his subjects, or even deficient in liberality, it is at every man's option to remove with his flocks, and to join any other tribe which he pleases; hence nothing is more uncertain than the population of a tribe, which increases or diminishes according to the reputation of its chief; even the king's own tribe is not exempt from desertion.

When the Moors make war upon one another, they take no prisoners; if any of their enemies fall into their hands, they kill them immediately, and the spoils of the slain belong to the conqueror. They fight from a distance, and only attack by surprise. The chiefs fight like their subjects; I have been told, however, that when Hamet-Dou goes to war, he is always accompanied by one of his ministers, whose business it is to hold him by his coussabe and to keep him at a safe distance: report says the coussabe has never been torn; but this may be a calumny. It is the hassanes who always make excursions against the negroes to pillage them, and carry off slaves; and on these occasions they are seldom accompanied by the zenagues. The hassanes are idle, mendacious, thievish, envious, superstitious, and gluttonous; they combine in short, all possible vices. An hassane who possesses a horse, a gun, and coussabe, thinks himself the happiest of mortals. Filthiness they seem to consider as a virtue. The men swarm with vermin, of which they take no pains to rid themselves. The women are disgusting; lying always upon their couches, with their heads besmeared with butter, which, being melted by the heat, runs down their faces and their whole bodies: they exhale in consequence a perfume which to Europeans is any thing but agreeable. In idleness they surpass the men, for they will not even rise to take their food, but rest on their elbows while a slave gives them their milk.

The commerce of the Braknas is carried on by the marabouts. It is they who collect all the gum, for which they pay no tribute; and when they have disposed of it to Europeans, they travel into a distant part of the country, to sell the guns and Guinea cloth which they receive in exchange. They often stop at Adrar, seven days' journey north of lake Aleg; this town gives its name to a small kingdom, and is inhabited by a number of marabouts who are wholly engaged in agriculture, and keep numerous herds of cattle. Dates are plentiful in this part; the fields are surrounded by date-trees. These marabouts do not live in tents, like the Braknas; they have mud houses one story high, and flat at the top. They barter their dates and millet, for the guns and Guinea cloth of the Braknas; of the Guinea cloth they make garments, for they grow no cotton. They have many slaves, who are employed in the cultivation of rice and millet, and in the tending of the cattle. Pasturage is not abundant in the neighbourhood of the town, so that they are obliged to send their flocks to a distance to graze: it is said that the slaves who take care of them are sometimes absent for one or two months. This nation is peaceful, and only takes up arms to defend itself against the depredations of its neighbours. It is during the rainy season that the Braknas undertake their trips to Adrar, in which they are compelled to cross a desert of four days' journey. These particulars I received from some marabouts who have visited that country several times. I intended to accompany those who were going the following spring, if I had remained among them.

The Brakna marabouts are as idle as the hassanes; they take no other exercise than walking to the mosque; and their only diversion is reading the Koran. They sometimes converse together as they lie on the sand, and go to sleep while talking over religion and politics.

Of all the classes of Moors the marabouts give the least and require the most; their quality of priests causing them to be considered as the dispensers of favours, they are never refused any thing, especially as the Moors are persuaded that they shall gain heaven by liberality. It is not to the hassanes alone that they apply; they harass one another also, and they torment the poor zenagues more especially. This class, despised by the others, is oppressed by them all. If the marabouts do not maltreat them as the hassanes do they threaten them with everlasting fire; and the poor zenague, in the hope of a happier life hereafter, strips himself to comply with the demands of his insatiable masters in this. Those marabouts who have no slaves to collect gum, being far too lazy to work for themselves, would be without clothes if the zenagues did not supply them with the means of procuring them. In the same way they obtain bags of butter to sell at the markets for Guinea cloth.

It may be thought, perhaps, that the marabouts are grateful, and know how to appreciate the sacrifices which the zenague makes to please them; but ingratitude is one of their vices, and scarcely have they obtained what they want before they slander their benefactors, curse them, and devote them to eternal fire.

Some of these wretches, who have no other means of subsistence, settle amongst the zenagues to instruct their children: besides their food, they receive in payment sheep, butter, tanned hides, and stuff for tent-covering.

The marabouts are not more susceptible of friendship than of gratitude. I told Mohammed-Sidy-Moctar one day, that I should like to go and see his son-in-law; he tried immediately to dissuade me. "He is a good-for-nothing fellow," said he; "he ought to have given you an ox the first time you went to his tent, and he only gave you a coussabe; he never gives *me* any thing; he does not like me." I asked him if he liked Hamet-Dou, who had made him presents before my eyes: "Oh," said he, "Hamet-Dou is rich."

I recollect, that when I was leaving the camp, I gave a pagne to a slave who had taken care to supply me with sangleh; my marabout, who was near, took the pagne from her, and gave her a severe scolding. I insisted that the pagne should be returned, but he would not hear of it, and he scolded me in my turn, and told me that a marabout ought never to give, but always to receive. At last he handed the pagne to my guide, and bade him put it with the rest of my goods. This trait conveys a good idea of their character.

If they are ungrateful, they are also inhuman. They treat their slaves with barbarity; calling them by insulting names, beating them, and requiring a great deal of service in return for very little food, and having no other garment than a sheep-skin. I sometimes protested against the cruelty with which these wretches were treated, "They are slaves, they are infidels," was the reply; "you see that they never pray; they know neither God nor the prophet," I have seen slaves however who prayed with the utmost regularity, and were no better treated for it; neither did it save them from the degrading appellation of slaves.

The office of the marabouts renders them more dissembling than the hassanes; they are less cruel, and more hospitable; but I have found repeatedly that they receive strangers unwillingly, rather from the fear of insult or pillage than from humanity.

A European traveller who should not make up his mind to dissemble, as I did, if he were to escape the fanatic fury of the hassanes, would probably not be murdered by the marabouts; but they would forbid him to enter their tents; and they would afford him no sustenance; or if they gave him a little milk to save him from dying of hunger, it would be in the hope of being well paid. If a Christian were to fall into the hands of the hassanes or zenagues, there is no kind of torture to which he would not be exposed.

The marabouts wander less from the banks of the river, than the hassanes; they remove their camps less frequently, and never change their place except to seek pasturage.

The zenagues, or tributaries, are the most wretched of the Moors; they are the serfs of the hassanes, and every hassane has more or fewer under his command, They exact from them annual contributions, consisting in general of a mator (about a quarter of a barrel) of millet, a calabash of butter, a few sheep-skins, and a *laize* of stuff for a tent; or a cow and a calabash of butter from each. The tributaries pay with the utmost exactness; but their unjust and grasping lords always claim more than is due, and inflict the most horrible tortures to extort what they want. I have already mentioned how they drag them at the camel's tail; but their cruelty goes still farther; if nothing can be got by torturing a poor zenague, his barbarous master not unfrequently stabs him. They are never safe from these tyrants, who pursue them even into their camps; where they sometimes take up their abode for days, and call for whatever they like.

The zenagues possess few oxen, but large flocks of sheep and goats, of whose milk they make butter, which they can exchange at the markets for Guinea cloth. They are allowed to keep a few slaves, who are employed in taking care of their flocks; but they must not send their slaves to collect gum, or the hassanes would take it all for them. They seldom go far from the river, and usually encamp in a thick wood, to avoid as much as possible the troublesome visitations of the hassanes and other travellers. They prefer marshy land, because it affords most food for their cattle. They have a great deal of milk, but its flavour is unpleasant, owing to the many rank herbs which the ewes and goats feed upon; it is so bad indeed, that the hassanes and marabouts who come amongst them will hardly drink it, and never if they can procure any other.

Immediately after the waters retire, the zenagues come down to the banks of the river to sow millet; they work in the fields themselves with their slaves. The women, laborious through necessity, spin and weave the hair of the sheep and camels, to form coverings for their tents; they also sew them together; tan leather, make the varrois and every thing else except iron-work. Their method of tanning is as follows: if it is an ox-hide, they cut it down the middle; they then make a pit in the ground and plaster it with cow-dung; after having moistened the hide, and rubbed it with ashes, they put it into the pit, and cover it carefully with ashes. Having thrown water upon the ashes so as to wet them thoroughly, they close up the pit with a layer of cow-dung. The hide is left in this state for six or eight days, at the end of which time they scrape it with a knife to take off the hair, and then wash it well to cleanse it from the ashes. When cleaned it is put into a large calabash with the bark of the boscia and the seed of the mimosa, (the same that is known in commerce by the name of babela, and on the Senegal by that of nem-nem,) taking care to rub and mix them well. Water is poured upon it to soak it thoroughly; in this state it is left for four days or more, then taken out again and scraped, to remove any hair that may have remained after the first operation. When thoroughly cleaned, it is again put into the calabash with an increased quantity of seed, reduced to powder and sufficiently moistened. Four days suffice to tan it completely. At the end of this time, it is well washed, and scraped with sharp-edged shells, which the Moors bring from the sea-shore. Sheep and goat skins are tanned in the same manner, only more quickly, from being thinner. The leather which is tanned by this process, is exactly of the same colour as ours, and very good. For common purposes it is used without further preparation, and a little butter is applied to grease it, when it is required to be particularly supple. The women also make soap of beef-tallow and ley; but the soap is very bad, washes ill and gives an unpleasant smell to the linen.

When a tributary is unusually oppressed by his master, he can choose another. He takes his flocks and all he possesses to him to whom he wishes to subject himself, and tries to cut off his ear, if he finds him asleep, or to kill his horse; from that moment he is tributary to this new master, who has immense power over him, while the former loses all his authority. If the fugitive should be taken again before he has cut off the ear or killed the horse, he is beaten, stripped of all he possesses, and driven away without mercy. He is then extremely wretched; few people will grant him hospitality; his life is only protracted suffering, and he frequently sinks under the weight of his misery, while none of his fellows deigns to bestow on him a look of pity. I saw one in the camp where I was, who came stark naked to beg alms and shelter; instead of awakening the least symptom of compassion, he was driven away with blows, and they even set the dogs at him. What would become of this unhappy creature? And what cause could there be for such cruelty? Had he lost the attributes of humanity because he wished to change his oppressor? With what pleasure would I have gone without my supper, to give it to him! but his relentless countrymen would not allow me this satisfaction.

I have been told that in times of scarcity the zenagues eat grasshoppers, drying them first in the sun; this, however, I suspect to be only a fiction to degrade the zenagues in my estimation; for, as they cultivate millet, and possess flocks, they are usually better provided with food than the other classes, and must suffer less in a scarcity than the less industrious orders. In the whole course of my peregrinations, though I have been among very needy tribes, I have never seen the Moors eat grasshoppers.

The haddads (or blacksmiths) belong to the class of tributaries, and are, perhaps, still worse off than those who are employed in agriculture and the care of flocks. They cannot inhabit a separate camp, if they did, the hassanes would plunder them; they are obliged, in order to avoid their rapacity, to dwell in the same camps as the marabouts, and make them the guardians of all they possess.

Notwithstanding the pains I took, I never could learn the origin of this race, nor how it had been reduced to pay tribute to the other Moors; when I made inquiries on the subject, I was always told that it pleased God it should be so, and that they were infidels who seldom performed the salam. Can they be remains of conquered tribes? And, if so, why is there no tradition left about them? This can hardly be; for the Moors, proud of their ancestors, never forget the names of those who have been a credit to their race; and the zenagues, forming the majority of the population, and being, moreover, accustomed to war, would have revolted under the conduct of some descendant of their former chiefs, and recovered their liberty, by exterminating their oppressors. It is in their power to do so, for they are very numerous.

The fourth class of the Moorish population is composed of the offspring of a Moor and a black slave; they are called laratines. Though slaves by birth, they are never sold, but have land of their own, and are treated almost like the zenagues. The laratines, whose fathers are hassanes, are warriors; those, whose fathers are marabouts, receive instruction and embrace the profession of their fathers. Proud of their birth, they are not very obedient to their masters, and it is only by force that the latter can compel them to pay the tribute which is due to them. They possess few cattle, for they are not allowed to increase their herds, lest they should enfranchise themselves if they were to become wealthy. The laratines and the zenagues have the care of the herds which the hassanes possess out of their camps.

The slaves form the fifth class, and are all negroes. They are charged with all the labours of the camp—the care of flocks, the providing of water and wood, and the culture of the land. The women pound millet, prepare food, wait upon their mistresses, water the calves, fetch water, and if they belong to marabouts, collect haze and gum. On a journey, the slaves carry on their heads whatever cannot be laid upon oxen. They are, as I have already mentioned, ill treated, ill fed, and beaten at the caprice of their masters, whether they have committed any fault or not. They are seldom addressed by any name but that of *slave*. In short, there is no species of vexation, which they are not obliged to endure.

The Moors leave the banks of the river, when the rainy season commences, that is at the beginning of August; for not only would they be greatly incommoded by the inundations, but they would also be exposed to many diseases which they occasion, and their cattle would be devoured by the mosquitoes. They remove to the N. E., to the confines of the great desert, where they find plentiful pasturage, and a salubrious climate, and are free from the inconveniences which they would suffer in the vicinity of marshes. They return towards the river when the waters retire, and reside there from March till August.

The dress of the wealthy Moors consists, in a *drah*, or tunic of Guinea cloth, which reaches nearly to the knees; the sleeves are as wide as the body and hang down to the ground. Loose drawers containing six or eight yards of Guinea cloth come down to their knees; a pagne completes the dress; this is put on over the tunic, and sometimes on their heads also, like a turban. Those who cannot afford a tunic, wear only a coussabe[30] made of two or three yards of Guinea cloth.

The Moors shave all the hairy parts of the body except the beard, which they suffer to grow and hold in great veneration. A fine beard is the greatest ornament of a Musulman.

The dress of the woman is half a piece (about seven yards) of Guinea cloth, which they wrap three times round them. With one end, consisting of about one third of the stuff, they make a kind of coussabe, doubling the stuff down and sewing it so as to leave three holes, one for the head, and two for the arms. The openings are not at the side, as they are in the men's dresses, and the stuff falls in drapery so as not to obstruct the motion of the body; where it is sewed together at each shoulder, there is a silver clasp, which serves to support the second round of the stuff; the third passes over the head, and forms a head-dress.

In mourning, or in the presence of strangers, of christians especially, they put it on so as to show nothing but their eyes. This dress is called *malafé*; they have no change of apparel, but wear it for two or three months without washing, and are often two years without being able to procure a new one.

They have fine hair which they lay in tresses round the head in an oval form, two smaller tresses which unite under the ear, are ornamented with pieces of glass, and hang down on each side of the head. Some of them have, on the sides, two other longer tresses, from which they suspend strings of amber, coral, and glass beads, hanging down upon the breast; others again have an immense number of tresses, but always loaded with ornaments. Those who do not suspend their string of beads from the hair, attach it to the clasps of their dress; they are not in the habit of wearing it round the neck. A strip of Guinea cloth, five feet in length, and five or six inches wide, completes their head-dress; they wrap it several times round the head. They grease their hair daily with butter; this custom preserves the hair extremely well, but communicates an insupportably rank smell. The young girls have a large gold ear-ring in the lower part of each ear, and four others in the upper part, which is bent down by their weight. Women of twenty-four wear only one small ring in the upper part of the ear.

Children go quite naked till the age of twelve or fourteen; their heads are shaved and figures drawn upon them, or tufts of hair left; but sometimes only half the head is shaved. At twelve the hair of the girls is suffered to grow, and the boys are completely shaved at eighteen. The opinion of some travellers, accredited in Senegal from popular stories respecting the manner of cutting the hair of the young people and leaving tufts to be cut off by degrees as they may distinguish themselves by brilliant actions, is absolutely false, at least in regard to the Braknas. I have had many occasions to know that these tufts of hair are a mere matter of fancy and that the number depends upon the will of the shaver or of the young man himself. It is a fashion which varies with individual taste; it is rare to see two heads trimmed in the same manner, excepting amongst the men above eighteen years of age, who closely crop the whole head.

I have already observed that the Moorish women have great influence over their husbands; I repeat it here, to correct an error into which M. Durand has fallen, and which he may have communicated to his readers. The husband has no authority over his wife but what a superior understanding gives him; I should even say that the Mooresses possess more influence over their husbands than our French women. They rarely wait upon them; and only for want of slaves; even then I have always seen that in this case a neighbour would lend a woman to pound the millet and make the sangleh. I except the zenague women; but if these perform menial offices for their husbands, it is because the slaves are occupied; and besides they are in the habit of working. M. Durand says also that wives are never admitted to the meals of their husbands: I have witnessed the contrary; I have seen them eat with their sons and husbands, not often, indeed, but I have remarked that it was owing to the custom which the women have of taking nothing but milk, which is set before them in small calabashes.

It is likewise incorrect to assert that the mother pays any deference to her son; or that the father and mother affect indifference to their daughters; the son is always submissive to his mother and pays her the utmost respect;

and if the parents shew some preference for the boys, they do not love their daughters with less tenderness. Besides, I have never witnessed rejoicings at the birth either of a boy or a girl.

The greater part of the Moors believe that we live upon the sea, and that we have only a few little islands like St. Louis: under this impression they imagine that we wish to possess ourselves of their country, which they consider as the finest in the world. The marabouts are better informed, and know that we inhabit a country far superior to theirs. They often expressed their regret that they had nothing good to offer me; observing that God would recompense me for my voluntary privations, in relinquishing the happy land of the christians to live amongst them. They have however no idea of our arts or manufactures. They often inquired what use we made of gum and and were always persuaded that I was deceiving them; they would not believe any other than that we transform it into amber, which it somewhat resembles in colour, and into other merchandise of great value, and that we could not dispense with gum nor even exist without it. I could not undeceive them on this point; and in like manner when discussions arise at the settlements or at the markets, or if they are refused what they ask, they threaten to bring no more gum.

CHAPTER IV

Difficulty in going to market — Oxen stolen by a neighbouring tribe — The Ramadan — Circumcision — The feast of Tabasky — Gum trade with the Europeans — My return to St. Louis.

We sojourned upon the shore of lake Aleg till the 20th January. The north winds blew with violence and were very cold; part of the time they lasted, I was kept in my tent by fever. In the course of the month, slaves were sent to a distance with part of the cattle, because the grass diminished around the camp; they only kept the milch cows, as indispensibly requisite for the support of the inhabitants: they pursue this plan to avoid removing the tents elsewhere.

The 21st January, 1825, the pastures being entirely exhausted, we broke up the camp and went two miles to the east, over a soil covered with ferruginous hillocks. The place at which we halted was of the same nature, and yet covered with herbage. The slaves set out in the morning to fetch water from the lake and did not return till night; the camp was without water till sun-set, but fortunately the weather was not hot or we should have suffered severely.

On the sixth of February, we returned towards the west: at the distance of three miles W. S. W., we crossed the rivulet, and it was not till we had gone nine miles further that we encamped upon a sandy soil, very hard and covered with forage. I had remarked on the banks of the rivulet the *zizyphus lotus*; here we found only the *balanites ægyptiaca*. People were again sent to the lake for water; it was very scarce in the camp on account of the distance; there was often not enough for cooking the meals.

Until this time I had only seen some single Wadats; I had not seen them in numbers. On the 10th a great number arrived, and came in front of the tent of my marabout. This band was entirely composed of women: they asked to see me; and were refused, but unfortunately I was not apprised of it and went out of my tent. They then surrounded me and tormented me worse than ever.

I would have withdrawn to my tent, to avoid the insults of every kind which they offered; but this they opposed, and it was with difficulty that I escaped and hid myself in a neighbouring tent. They had treated me so ill, that the inhabitants were indignant at their conduct, and would not allow them to stay; they gave them some millet and dismissed them. On the 19th, the men and baggage of the king's camp passed us on their way to the banks of the Senegal, and on the 21st we removed again, provided with water for two days, as we should be that time without finding any on our route.

We traversed a sandy country, where I saw some beautiful balanites and some mimosas. Our allowance of water was not abundant, and the greater part of our stock was reserved for the calves, so that we suffered dreadfully from thirst during these two days. On the first we travelled fifteen miles W. S. W. The cattle remained behind us, and we all went without supper. On the 22d we advanced twelve miles in the same direction, and arrived at three in the afternoon at the place where we were to halt; we were then three miles S. E. of the el-Awanil, a lake to which we sent for water. On the 29th to amuse myself, I went to visit this lake, following the slaves, who were dispatched thither for water; the soil which surrounds it is slightly argillaceous, and produces a great quantity of the *ziziphus lotus*, *mimosa*, and *nauclea*. In this excursion, I was pleased to see the slaves, for the first time, enjoying themselves a little. These poor creatures, so sad and gloomy in the presence of their cruel masters, profiting by the first moment of freedom from constraint, give themselves up to their natural cheerfulness, and passed the time in dancing, singing, and amusing themselves. I was as pleased with their mirth as they could be themselves, for I was weary of seeing them tormented. When their gambols were over, they filled their skins again, and took the road towards the camp, which we reached in an hour.

I hoped that the camp would continue to approach nearer to the river; but I was informed that we were not going further westward. I was in a state of complete destitution; my clothes were in rags, and it was extremely unpleasant to me to live upon alms, as I had done since I came amongst the Moors. I wished to inform the governor of the Senegal of my condition, and to request assistance from him; but this I could not do without going to the mart. I communicated to my marabout the desire I felt to make this journey, assigning as a reason, that I wanted to get new clothes, and to send for my goods. He consented at first, but after a moment's reflection, he proposed to conduct me to the king's camp, where I might write, and whence I might send my letter by one of the sons of Moctar-Boubou, chief of Podor, who would bring back the goods. This plan did not suit me: I told him therefore that they would not deliver my goods to a messenger, that I must write to the settlement, and that I must moreover go myself to procure some clothing. He raised some additional obstacles, which were the result of suspicion.

Perceiving the cause, I assured him that if he objected to my journey I would give it up, and I would rather renounce my goods entirely than do any thing to displease him. This inspired him with confidence, and he promised to provide me with the means of undertaking the journey, but it was only after much hesitation and tardiness on his part that I was enabled to set off on the 9th of March. The preparations for this journey did not occupy much time, but they were embarrassing, for I had no means of hiding my notes, the seeds which I had collected, and some mineral specimens which I wished to take with me. I bethought myself of borrowing from my marabout's wife two leathern bags, which I told her were to hold the merchandise that I should bring back from the settlement; when I proposed to take my own, Fatme objected, and told me I should not want it; I took out some of my notes, and told her that all these papers were the inventory and receipts for my goods, so that they were indispensible for me to establish my claims; upon which she allowed me to take them. I put over them the bags she had lent me and a pagne, and when any body was inquisitive as to my baggage, I shewed them the bags and pagne, without letting them see the rest.

On the 9th of March, at nine in the morning, I set off, accompanied by one of the sons of my marabout. Six miles to the west, we came to the marigot of Koundy, which I had passed eight months before with Boubou-Fanfale; we forded it and continued our journey through a thick wood, followed by a valley, magnificent from the vegetation of the plants by which it was bordered.

All the inundated lands situated between the marigot and the river are sown with millet among the trees, without any previous preparation of the ground, and even without the dead branches being removed. All the low grounds are argillaceous, and in many places I have seen ferruginous rocks.

We had travelled three miles from the marigot when we perceived smoke rising out of the wood; some travellers who had joined us went to see whence it arose, and told us, on their return, that some zenagues had made a fire to cook their victuals. They regretted extremely that they had not arrived in time to levy a contribution upon these poor wretches, traces of whom only had been found, and who had no doubt, hidden themselves at our approach. We quitted the valley and proceeded to a camp half a mile to the south, in a place so woody that there was scarcely room to pitch the tents; this spot is called *Teneque*. We passed the night there, and were supplied for supper with some ewes' milk of a detestable flavour; but we were forced to drink it, for we had no choice and were dying of hunger, not having tasted a morsel that day. We had still nine miles further to go to the bank of the river; and the next day, at dawn, we continued our journey. We met many travellers who were coming from Podor and from the settlement.

At two o'clock we reached the bank of the river, which we crossed in a canoe, and proceeded to Moctar-Boubou's, where I had lodged when I first came amongst the Moors. We remained there three days, during all which time my guide endeavoured to dissuade me from going to the mart; being apprehensive that, on my arrival there, I should leave him and return to the christians.

The Braknas do not eat fish but hold it in the greatest abhorrence; it is not, however, forbidden by the laws of Mahomet, but they dislike it on account of its strong smell. The marabout who accompanied me abstained for three days from couscous, rather than eat what had been boiled with fish. This dislike is not universal amongst the Moors; I have seen the Trarzas eat fish, and have been told that those who live on the coast are fishermen. I mentioned this to my companion; he replied, that the Trarzas, being nearer neighbours to the christians, easily learn to eat any thing, and even to drink wine, and that they are infidels.

On the 14th, my guide at last resolved to take me to the mart; we arrived early in the day. I went on board la Désirée, belonging to a merchant of St. Louis, and borrowed of his agent a piece of Guinea cloth, some sugar, tobacco, and a little paper; I then wrote to the governor to acquaint him with my situation, and to beg him to give orders for the delivery of some goods, of which I had urgent need. As it would have been too long to wait at the port for an answer, and the anxiety of the Moor, my guide, increased daily, I resolved not to stay, but to return to the camp; I told him so, to his great surprise, but he begged me to wait till the next day; we passed the night on board. On the 15th of March, we returned to Podor for our beasts; and at two o'clock crossed the river again. An hassane, of the tribe of Oulad-Sihi, joined us; on the road we met a laratine, whom he asked for tobacco, and the hassane wanted to take his coussabe from him, but the other resisting, the hassane drew his poniard to stab him. This behaviour disgusted and incensed me the more, because we had just finished our prayers, and I did not comprehend how a man, who pretended to be a Musulman, could pass immediately from an act of devotion to robbery. At my intreaty, my companions went to the assistance of the poor laratine, and I could not restrain myself from reprimanding the offender, and threatening to report his conduct to Hamet-Dou; he replied, in an insolent tone, that I might tell him if I pleased, for he was not afraid of him. This fact shows how completely persons of his class despise authority; they acknowledge no law but that of the stronger. My reprimand irritated him, and I verily believe that, had it not been for my character of marabout, I should have suffered for my imprudent zeal. This event gave rise to many painful reflections: I said to myself, if they behave thus to their own countrymen, what would they not do to a stranger, a christian, without protection, in a country where no laws shield the indigent, and where the very circumstance of their being poor seems to expose them to greater persecution? What would become of me if my secret were discovered? A speedy death would be the greatest favour that I could expect, from their hatred to christians.

On my return, however, I was welcomed with many and hearty salutations. The Moors were persuaded when I went away that I should never come back, and that I should escape from the port; many of them had advised Mohammed-Sidy-Moctar not to let me go. When they saw me again they all testified their great joy, and no longer doubted my conversion; they vied with each other in doing me honour.

We passed the night in a camp of marabouts who were superintending the cultivation of the lands. I remarked a great many seeds of *nymphœa* which were drying, and I was told that this seed is used to flavour the sangleh. I ate a little of it, but its taste was unpleasant. They also eat the bulbous root of this plant boiled in water, it has a pleasant flavour and is slightly astringent. This plant, the greatest ornament of the lakes and marigots, grows in profusion in all the lands which have been inundated, and is of great service to the Moors who live on the banks of the river. I have since learnt at St. Louis that the negroes also make use of this plant; they eat the root, boiled; and employ the seed more particularly to season their fish.

On the 16th we arrived at our camp, where I was received with fresh congratulations. The grand marabout especially was proud of my return, and seemed to attribute it to the effect which his superior wisdom had produced upon me; it was not my business to undeceive him, and it was very easy to confirm him in his error.

Hamet-Fal, his eldest son, took me aside to question me as to the reception I had met with on board the vessels. I told him, and his brother could witness the truth of what I said, that persuasions had been used to induce me to return to the whites, and that I had rejected their propositions; that I liked better to eat a little sangleh with Musulmans than to return to the christians to live in luxury; and that I hoped this sacrifice would be well pleasing to God. He took my hand, lifted it to his forehead, and then exclaimed in extacy: "Do not doubt it, Abdallah; all the good things of this world are not to be compared with those which you may expect in Heaven; in this life all is transitory; but the riches which God reserves for the faithful are eternal. The christians are rich; they have abundance of every thing; they eat a great deal, they drink wine, and spirituous liquors; they will not acknowledge the prophet: they will go to hell; this world is their paradise. As for us, we have nothing but oxen and sheep; we eat nothing but a little sangleh and drink nothing but milk and water; but we pray to God who will reward us in heaven. Nothing is to be compared with the bliss which is there enjoyed; it is renewed every hour, every minute; you have only to wish in order to obtain in abundance whatever you desire. Four great rivers flow through Paradise; one of water, one of milk, one of honey, and the fourth of brandy; but this brandy is far superior to what the christians drink and what God forbids: it is the most exquisite beverage that can be drunk. There, are to be found bowls of butter, of dates, of sangleh, in a word, all that renders life agreeable; and beauties the freshness of whose bloom never fades. Look at this fruit," said he (holding in his hand a fruit of the *zizyphus lotus*); "on earth it is very small; but in Paradise it is as big as a very large liquor bottle." (He chose this comparison because he had seen some very large liquor bottles on board the vessels at the port). "You Abdallah," continued he, "you will occupy the first place; you will have more merit in the sight of God than all other Musulmans together, because you have renounced the comforts of life, and all the advantages which you were called to share, in order to come amongst us, subjecting yourself to privations which you never had suffered before."

Such was the address of my marabout's son. This man was about forty years old; he had been at St. Louis, was able to appreciate the sacrifice which I had made, and became in consequence one of my warmest friends. All doubts as to the sincerity of my conversion were now dispelled, and from this moment I was considered as a true disciple of the prophet. I was in the highest esteem with all the Moors, and hoped that this esteem would enable me to put into execution a project which I had long ago formed, of visiting all the most interesting parts of the desert; travelling as a merchant and pilgrim to Mecca, and there effecting my return through Egypt into France. My proposition however, as will hereafter be seen, was but ill received.

On the following days, I went to visit the marabouts of the camp; they all received me equally well. I will mention an anecdote which I think characteristic. One of them had killed an ox during my absence, and he knew that I had brought back some goods; he offered me a meal on condition of my giving him some tobacco; I consented. He brought a little bit of meat on a board, and began eating it with me. While he was swallowing it as fast as he could, he preached to me about abstinence, and assured me that he who eats little is beloved by God, because he likes better to pray than to satisfy his hunger (which they call being *koran-stomached*); and that he who thinks only of satisfying his appetite is an infidel. He flattered me much and told me that I had a Koran stomach. I gave him to understand that his device was easily seen through, and told him that though I ate little it was because I had little to eat, and that I believed other Musulmans were abstinent for the same reason. I pointed to an old man who was seated near us, and seemed half-famished; "Look at this good old man," said I, "he has eaten nothing to-day: I will answer for it, that if you will give him some sangleh, he will show no Koran stomach, but eat it up directly." The poor man replied; "It is true that I have tasted nothing since last night, when I had a little milk for my supper; and I shall bless him who gives me a good dinner to-day." I told my host that if he himself made but one meal a day, it was for want of means, and not for the love of God; and I added, that if he could meet with any body who would give him as much as he liked, he would not require much pressing to eat it. "Ah," said he, "the hassanes would perhaps take advantage of such a circumstance to eat immoderately; but a marabout would never do so." I mentioned an occurrence which took place at the port, on board the Désirée, and to which Mohammed-Sidy-Moctar's son was witness. Four marabouts came on board to sell a package of gum; as it is the custom to supply them with food till the goods are delivered, a supper was prepared for them. An enormous dish of rice boiled with meat, on which was poured a great quantity of butter, of which they are very fond, though they rarely eat it at home, was handed to one of the party who seemed to be the leader; he hid himself in a corner to devour it, and presently after came back and asked for supper for his three companions. The astonished agent inquired what he had done with the dish of rice which contained supper for four. "Pooh," said the Moor, "I have eaten it all, and I am not half satisfied." Supper was brought after this for the three others; but the greedy fellow was punished, for he had like to have died of an indigestion. My host censured the want of moderation which his colleague had shown, but I am convinced that he would not have been more discreet in a similar situation.

On the 24th of March I set out again for the port hoping to find an answer from the governor as it was now thirteen days since I wrote. We travelled W. N. W. that we might proceed direct to the port without going through Podor. On the way I was shown some of the genuine gum-trees, from which the gum had been gathered. On the 31st I arrived at the vessels. The pinnace which had taken my letter to St. Louis had returned without bringing me any answer, and I concluded that she had not waited, I took up some goods belonging to M. René Valentin, a resident at St. Louis, and I cannot speak too highly of this gentleman's generosity towards me. On the 3rd of April I set out on my return to the camp. We wished to keep the same course which we had taken in coming, but the woods were so thick and the road so ill defined, that we lost ourselves. We travelled on at random without knowing whither, till ten o'clock at night, when we met with a marabout who was tending his flock. We requested him to direct us to the camp; he gave us equivocal answers, and told us first one way and then another, leaving us more uncertain than ever as to which we should take. We suffered terribly from thirst, for we had found no water on our journey, and followed the marabout for a long time, begging him for the love of God to show us the way; the holy man amused himself at our expense, and purposely kept back his cattle. We perceived that he was afraid lest we should attend him home, and oblige him to give us a supper; we were very hungry but we assured him that we did not want any thing to eat, and cared for nothing but a drop of water. He hesitated a long time, and at last, yielding to our entreaties, he gave us a cow to serve as our guide. As soon as the poor animal was set at liberty, she ran towards the camp, lowing; and we soon heard her calf answer: the cow proceeded to the thorn enclosure, and we to the tents, where we were better received than the behaviour of the marabout had led us to expect. All the marabouts welcomed me with great politeness, and made me recite prayers that they might judge of my progress by the number I could repeat; after this the marabout's son and I had sangleh for supper, but our companions had nothing but milk.

On the 5th of April, we arrived at the camp; it had removed three miles to the east since we left, and was now near a marsh named Tiartiaka.

On the 6th, I was told that the governor had passed the port on his way to Podor, and that on his return he would stop to have an interview with king Hamet-Dou; I was informed also that he had expressed a wish to see me. I desired most ardently to have an interview with him and did all that lay in my power to set off again immediately. But it was not till the 8th that I could set out again for the port, where I arrived on the 10th, two days after the departure of the governor for St. Louis. I expected to find a letter, but had the mortification to learn that he had not left one for me; he had however authorized the officer who commanded the brig on that station to make some advances on my behalf; but when I applied to this officer, he told me that he had no government effects on board, and that the advance which he was ordered to make was very trifling. My wants however were urgent, and I asked for two pieces of Guinea cloth; they gave me two pieces of burham pooter,[31] but so very bad that I could not have exchanged them for millet. I wrote again to the governor, but received no answer. I suspected from that time that opposition would be made to my scheme, and my fears were afterwards realized.

Before I left the mart, I took up some more goods belonging to M. René Valentin, who had the generosity to let me have them without security. I set off on my return to the camp with a heavy heart and a head wearied with the thoughts that crowded upon me, on losing the hope which I had cherished of assistance from government for the completion of my design. I scarcely noticed what was passing around me; it was not till we halted near a lake called Tichilite el Bedane, that I perceived that my companions had purchased a sheep with the Guinea cloth which I had received on board. Two zenagues, who had followed us in the hope of coming in for a share of the sheep which they had sold, were charged with the business of dressing it. When it was cooked, the two marabouts were very generous at my expense, and we found about fifteen persons ready to partake of it: they had the precaution, however, to reserve a piece uncooked for the morrow; the marabouts took their share apart, and did not eat with the rest. On a journey they always affect to be people of prodigious importance, and shew a great deal of pride in all their actions.

The next day, when we wanted to cook the part we had saved, we were rather embarrassed by having neither gun nor flint to strike fire. I was then witness to an operation which I had never seen before, though I had heard of its being practised; the Moors took two pieces of wood, and rubbed them violently together, till they took fire, which was not for some time; the wood which they used was very hard.

The camp had again changed its situation; it was a mile further to the east, near a rivulet called Rekiza. On our arrival, we were informed that Hamet-Dou was at war with the Oulad-Hamets, and that the latter, who were greatly inferior in number, were flying from their enemies. The cause of hostilities was this: the laratine slaves of the tribe of Oulad-Hamet had quarrelled with those of the king, and had ravaged their fields of millet; the slaves complained to their master, who went with his people to seize the flocks of the Oulad-Hamets, in order to make them pay for the damage done in his territory. All the women of the tribe came to implore the king's mercy, and he restored the cattle without insisting upon any indemnification for the damage. So far from being thankful for the goodness of the prince, these wretches attacked Hamet-Dou's people again, surprised them in their tents, and killed four of them; they met with a vigorous resistance, however, for they retired with the loss of seven men. This atrocious conduct on the part of the aggressors excited the indignation of the king; he swore that he would be revenged, and declared war against the whole tribe. The Oulad-Hamets, knowing that they should have nothing to gain in this contest, entered into a negociation, and the king pardoned them once more.

The tribe of the Oulad-Hamets is the most perfidious of all the Braknas; they spare nothing, not even the people of their own tribe. When they meet travellers, they strip them if they can; and if chance conducts a stranger to their camps, he never escapes till he is plundered of every thing he has with him; of course care is taken to keep out of their way. Their atrocious character causes them to be detested by all the other tribes, and they are never spoken of but with horror.

The same day, word was brought that the Trarzas[32] had fallen upon the oxen in the woods, and were driving them off. Our people were greatly embarrassed, for there were very few men in the camp, most of them having left it at the approach of the Ramadan; seven or eight only were at hand to pursue the robbers. I observed that they had no guns, but I was assured that the Trarza hassanes would make no use of theirs, and that the matter would be decided with sticks. During the absence of the men, the women collected in groups, and discussed the probable result of the affair; there was much quarrelling amongst them, for some asserted that the Trarzas would carry off the oxen, and others maintained, on the contrary, that they would be beaten, and that the marabouts would oblige them to relinquish their prize. Towards the end of the day, these disputes were decided by the return of the marabouts, who reported that the robbers had fled at their approach and abandoned their prey.

At night, the new moon appeared; it was that of the Ramadan; and the fast was about to commence: long prayers were said, and a great quantity of sangleh was made. We supped later than usual, because we were to fast the next day. Before light I was roused to drink, for it is not lawful to take any thing while the sun is above the horizon.

The truly devout Moors observe a most rigorous fast; they make only one meal in the middle of the night, and not only take no food in the day-time, but neither drink nor smoke. As the Ramadan often happens in hot weather, and the fast is more painful on account of the dreadful thirst which is experienced, the less zealous take the opportunity of travelling just at this time, because they are excused from observing the fast when they are on a journey. It was for this reason that there were so few men in the camp, when the oxen were carried off; they had all set out on their travels a few days before. This emigration does not exempt them from fasting altogether, but it affords them the advantage of chusing their own season; they always fast in preference in cold weather, because they are not then liable to suffer so much from thirst.

The first day I bore the fast pretty well, but I suffered severely from thirst, and sighed for the setting of the sun; it was only a quarter of an hour after sun-set that the *cheni* was brought, and this quarter of an hour appeared as long as a day. Impatience increased my thirst to such a degree, that I could not restrain myself, and drank more than was prudent. My body was covered with a violent perspiration; my legs failed; I fell motionless upon the mat, where I remained for half an hour, but without losing sensation. At last my strength returned by degrees, and I was able to get up to go to prayer.

At eleven o'clock at night, some sangleh was brought for supper; I remarked that a greater quantity had been made than usual, but I ate very little, for thirst had taken away my appetite and I felt feverish. The women had all intended to fast, but at noon they were obliged to drink, and their fast was broken. For my part, I persevered for the next few days, and my sufferings increased, as my strength diminished. On the sixth day, I thought that I could no longer endure these privations. The east wind blew violently; the heat increased; my throat was parched, my tongue, dry and chapped, was like a rasp in my mouth, and I thought I should sink under my sufferings. I was not the only one who was in this state; every body around me was tormented in the same way. The marabouts, at last, bathed the face, head, and part of the body, and I was allowed to do the same; but I was watched very closely, and could only have deceived my Arguses at the risk of my life, in case I had been seen to swallow a drop of water. When my sufferings were excessive, and a murmur escaped me, they told me, for my encouragement, that when I died Mahomet would receive me into heaven, present me with a vase of delicious liquor to quench my thirst, and reward me for the pains and privations I had endured. One day I contrived to enjoy this treat beforehand, as the law permits you to wash your mouth, and to snuff up water through the nose, provided you spit it out again; I seized the moment when my marabout, being engaged in washing himself, could not observe me, to swallow part of the water that I had in my mouth: it seemed to me as if the prophet was that moment opening the gates of heaven to me, for I had never tasted any thing so delicious. This was the only time that I could elude their vigilance, and I did it then with fear and trembling. I fasted thus for seventeen days, and on the eighteenth I was attacked with a fever; a dispensation from fasting was then granted me, if a man can be said not to fast because he drinks a little water in the course of the day: they gave me absolutely nothing to eat.

Besides being compelled to observe a most rigorous fast, I had to bear the insolence of a number of travelling hassanes, with whom my sufferings were a subject of ridicule. If they found me lying upon my mat, and expiring of thirst and exhaustion, they pulled me by my clothes, and pinched me, and tormented me in a thousand ways to force me to answer their questions, which were all intended to insult me. They commonly concluded by asking me if I would not drink a little brandy and eat pork, and whether I did not intend to be circumcised. At each of these questions, to which I refused to reply, they laughed violently, and answered for me, affecting the most cutting contempt. The marahouts did not like this, but they could not protect me from the annoyance, and it was not till after the departure of the hassanes that they censured them and called them infidels.

I observed, that the marabouts were not so strict with their countrymen as they were with me, for I often saw young men who were eating in the day-time. When I asked why they were not obliged to fast like the rest of us, I was told that they could not have got through the day without eating. This pretext they employed whenever they were disposed to break the fast.

To amuse themselves, and make the days seem less tedious during the Ramadan, the Moors have a game called *sigue*. It consists of six flat pieces of wood, rounded at the ends in an oval form, white on one side, and black on the other. The game is played by two, four, or six persons, but always divided into two parties. Three rows of holes are made in the sand, twenty-four in each; the outside rows are taken by the different parties, who cover each of the holes with a straw, taking care that the straws of the two parties shall be of different colours, so as to be easily distinguished; the middle row of holes is left open. One of the players takes five bits of wood in his hand, shakes them and drops them on the ground; if all the pieces of wood are of the same colour, or all but one, this is called *making the sigue*, and counts for one: the player continues with six pieces until he fails to make the sigue; then another plays, and so on. Every time a player makes the sigue he puts a straw into one of the holes of the middle row, and moves it forward as many places as he has thrown pieces of wood of the colour adopted by his party. When a player has reached the last hole in the middle row, he leaves his straw there; if his adversary arrives at it also, the first straw is thrown out, and the player begins again as before. When all the holes in the middle row are taken, the player begins upon his adversary's, and they go on with the game, taking straws out of all the holes which they win from him; when either party has lost all its holes the game is over.

They have another game which they seldom play because it requires more exertion. They set up several small flat bones in a row, and a number of men with four stones each throw at the bones from a distance; he who knocks down the greatest number fillips the noses of his companions. The princes sometimes play at this game. The boys, who are not so lethargic as the men, and love running about, have a game which really gives them some exercise. They form a large circle; one of them places himself in the middle, and all the others annoy him as they run round; one strikes him, another pushes, or pulls him by his coussabe. The one in the middle endeavours to catch his assailants, and when he succeeds they change places. This is a very noisy game, for they all shout and scream as they run round. The girls also play at this game amongst themselves.

It is during the Ramadan that the boys are circumcised, between the ages of four and twelve; a marabout always performs the operation. The child is not to shew any sign of pain, but is required to hold a bit of wood in his mouth, and pick his teeth with it during the operation. Nothing is applied to the wound but some ass dung mixed with water, and this plaster is allowed to drop off of itself. The boys who have been circumcised run off into the woods, armed with bows and arrows, and amuse themselves with shooting at birds; they do not return to the camp till two o'clock, when they eat sangleh; at night they have nothing but milk for supper. To prevent them from hurting themselves at night while asleep, stakes are driven into the ground about the place where they lie, so that they have not room to turn. The interval between the operation and their entire cure is a privileged time, when they play all sorts of roguish tricks on their parents; but I have been assured that they do not steal, as I have seen the children do amongst the negroes. The girls are circumcised at a year old; the hassanes, like the zenagues, always employ a marabout to perform the operation.

At the end of the fast, they celebrate a feast (the Tabasky) which is considered as a great solemnity. All put on their best apparel; a ram is killed, and plenty of sangleh is made: every one has abundance to satisfy his hunger, and it is perhaps the only day in the year when their appetite is completely satisfied. They present one another with millet; but it is rather an exchange than a gift, for they always give to those who have the ability to give to them and not to the poor.

This is purely a religious festival amongst the marabouts, and the greater part of the day is passed in prayer; it is a sort of Easter, when custom permits them to eat more than usual. The hassanes make it a day of rejoicing; the men fire off their guns, and perform evolutions on horseback, and the women, assembling round the guéhués, sing to their music, and accompany it by clapping their hands. The feasts of the hassanes are usually gayer than those of the marabouts, because the guéhués, who are present at the former, enliven them by their songs, their music, and their tricks.

On the 18th of April, my marabout's sons returned from the port, whither they had been carrying gum, and told us that Hamet-Dou was going to St. Louis. Mohammed-Sidy-Moctar advised me to go thither too and look after my goods. "They would not dare," said he, "to detain you while the king is there, and if they should refuse to deliver your goods, the king will take you under his protection. This proposal suited me exactly; for I could no longer remain among them in the state in which I was, and I wanted to solicit from the governor the means of finishing my education and completing my journey. I did not betray my eagerness however, but, pretending to be guided by his advice, set off for the port with his second son Abdallah; we arrived on the 20th. On our way we passed the night in a camp of zenagues, and I heard a Moor who was talking of me say, "I should like him to die in my tent when he comes back with his merchandise." "Do not say so," replied a woman. "Why not," rejoined the Moor, "would not he be very well off? He would go to paradise, and I should have his goods." I heard all this distinctly, but I did not take the trouble to thank him for his good intentions towards me.

The king had set off from St. Louis two days before we arrived at the port, and we had to wait for an opportunity of following him. In the mean time I visited all the supercargoes on board their vessels; my guide followed me every where and made inquiries about me, my shipwreck, and my goods. He seemed very uneasy, but as I had cautioned all these gentlemen, they took care not to contradict my story. His curiosity nevertheless annoyed me a good deal, because I knew that he would find people at St. Louis who might undeceive him, even without intending to injure me; and, as I foresaw that I should have difficulty in obtaining what I meant to solicit from the governor, I did not wish that any thing Abdallah might hear should destroy the good opinion which his countrymen had formed of me, and induce them to thwart my schemes hereafter. I should for this reason have been very glad to get rid of my companion, and I had some hopes of being able to do so, for a short time, after a conversation which passed between us.

Every time that we left a vessel he reproved me for not begging of the christians, and when I told him that I was not in want of any thing he replied: "That is nothing to the purpose; you should always ask for something. If they give, so much the better; if they refuse, so much the worse. They are infidels, and you should always get as much as you can from them. Do you think that the Musulmans who are here come to see the whites? No such thing; they come to get their Guinea cloth whenever they can. Perhaps you imagine that I am going to St. Louis to see the town, and the christians?" I replied that I concluded he was, as he had expressed a wish to that effect, before we quitted the camp; "Besides," said I, "what else should you go for?" "What should I go for?" said he, "do not suppose that I go to see the infidels and their country. I go to try if I cannot get some goods out of them, and that you may pay me three or four pieces of Guinea cloth and a gun for my company." Though I was no stranger to the rapacity of his countrymen, yet this confession really surprised as much as it incensed me; I durst not give vent to my indignation, so I contented myself with saying, that if he had reckoned upon my generosity, he would find himself mistaken, because he had no claim upon it; that I thought myself indebted to his brother, and that he alone should receive the presents which I intended as a return for his kindness. He was disconcerted, and told me that if that was the case he should return to the camp and I might go to St. Louis by myself. I should have been heartily glad to do so; but when he saw me about to embark, he joined me. Before I leave the port, I must give a short sketch of the mode in which the gum trade is carried on.

At the appointed time, the government of St. Louis sends a king's ship to the port under the command of an officer, who is charged with the police of the port, in all that concerns navigation, and the stationing of the different vessels; he is also empowered to decide all disputes with the marabouts and the Moors. The Moorish king on his side sends his plenipotentiaries, who remain at the port to settle the customs[33] and which are to be paid by the merchants. Any difficulties which arise are settled between them and the commander of the vessel on the station. When a merchant ship arrives at the port, she remains at anchor in the middle of the river till the duty is fixed; a point which is seldom settled without a long discussion, for the Moors always persist in the hope of gaining some advantage, though the tax is governed by the tonnage of the vessel; it is often necessary to have recourse to the king to terminate the dispute. It is not till the agreement has been signed that business can be transacted, and the *aloums* (or Moorish agents) watch on the shore, to see that no gum is taken on board. These same agents watch the vessels when their right to trade is suspended.

The duties which the merchants pay are considerable. A vessel capable of carrying from twenty-five to thirty thousand pounds of gum pays in general one hundred and twenty or one hundred and thirty pieces of Guinea cloth[34] in fixed customs; to this may be added three or four pieces more in the shape of presents to the princes, which they call their *supper*, and two or three for the aloums, who, if they were not feed, would give the preference to other vessels.

All the preliminaries being settled, the ship begins to trade; she approaches the shore, to which a bridge is thrown to facilitate the communication; the trader has a hut built on the beach where the women whose business it is to pound the millet are lodged; where all cooking operations for the ship's crew are performed; and where the master may repose when he comes on shore. He must now have an interpreter to carry on conversation between himself and the marabouts, and this interpreter is paid and fed on board; the aloums are also fed at the joint expense of all the merchants. The princes and princesses who come to the port must also be fed, and any one who should refuse to conform to this practice would lose his right of trading.

When a prince arrives, he sometimes takes up his abode on board one of the ships, where he is politely received, and allowed to be as troublesome as he pleases, for fear he should interrupt the traffic. He takes possession of the cabin, throws himself on the master's bed, calls for treacle and water to drink, and worries his host with incessant questions. At dinner, he sits down at table without invitation, thrusts his fingers into all the dishes, tastes all the victuals, and puts back what he dislikes after it has been in his mouth; he touches every thing with his dirty hands, takes bread, sugar, and whatever he pleases, pretending all the time, that he likes nothing, and boasting of the good cheer that is to be found in his own camp.

It may seem possible that a Mulatto born at Senegal, accustomed from his childhood to such behaviour, and having but an imperfect notion of European manners, should put up with this treatment; but how a European, and a Frenchman, can endure it, is what I never could comprehend, though I have seen it. It is true that it is in general the clerks of traders at St. Louis who are forced to submit to these customs, for fear of compromising the interests of the houses by which they are sent. They have only one chance of avoiding the annoyance of such guests, and eating their meals in peace; and that is, to have every thing cooked with bacon or pork; the Moor, in that case, will eat what has been prepared for him in a corner by himself; but he exercises the same rapacity upon bread, sugar and every thing else that pleases his gluttonous palate. Sometimes, the dealers, wearied out, attempt to dismiss the princes; but they avoid coming to a quarrel, because, if a blow should be struck, the right of trading would be suspended; fresh negociations must take place, and they would only terminate in the payment of a fine of several pieces of Guinea cloth. When the zenagues come on board to walk about, there is no such thing as getting rid of them without making them some present, or at least giving them a calabash of molasses and water.

The traffic generally commences in the month of January, and ends the 31st of July. Towards the end of May, the king comes to the port; he sometimes lodges on board the station-ship, but more commonly on shore in a hut that the dealers have built for him. During his stay, which sometimes lasts two months, the dealers are obliged to feed all his attendants, and to pay a daily tax of two or three pieces of Guinea cloth; this is called, as I said before, *the king's supper*. He visits one or other of the ships every day, receives presents, and never forgets to call for an enormous calabash of sugar and water for himself and his suite. He is always received with the greatest politeness on board all the ships, for he would break off the traffic if any dealer were not to behave well to him. In this way he is sure of obtaining whatever he desires.

Whilst he stays at the port, he levies another tax, which has been established for some years under the name of a "forced present." He requires from each dealer one hundred pieces or more of Guinea cloth, and if this quantity is not delivered to him within a fixed time, he breaks off the trade. The dealers then contribute each of them according to the tonnage of his vessel, and when the quantity required is made up, it is delivered to the king, who permits them to resume their traffic. A whim, or the slightest complaint made to the king, is enough to interrupt it; nay, I have known it to be broken off because Fatme-Anted-Moctar (the king's aunt) complained that one of the supercargoes had given her some coffee which she did not like.

It may be supposed perhaps, that the price at which the gum is bought makes amends for all these annoyances by the profit which it affords. No such thing! the profit might indeed be immense if the dealers understood their own interest; instead of which they enter into a ruinous competition with one another, to the advantage of the Moors. If they know that a caravan is on the way to the port, each dispatches his interpreter to meet it and make offers to the marabouts. They go on shore themselves to try to gain the chief by promises and presents, and to get him on board their own vessel. The consequence of all this eagerness is that the Moor becomes more and more greedy and obstinate; he suspects that he is selling his gum too cheap, hesitates a long time before he closes the bargain, runs backwards and forwards to all the ships, and decides at last in favour of the highest bidder.

From the arrival of the caravan to the delivery of the gum, all the marabouts belonging to it are fed by the dealers; and every time a Moor goes on board a ship to sell the smallest package of gum, he and all who are with him are treated. Five or six of them will often go about with twelve or fifteen pounds of gum, hawk it about for two or three days, and at last, when they have sold it, require a dinner into the bargain. The bargains are usually made very slowly; the marabouts, for fear of being cheated, measure their gum before they expose it for sale, with a small measure, the weight of which they know, that they may ascertain beforehand the quantity of Guinea cloth which it ought to produce them. In general a certain weight in gum is agreed upon as the value of one piece of calico. This price varies according as the season is more or less productive; when I was at the Cock station a piece would fetch fifty or sixty pounds of gum, sometimes it is up at one hundred, and sometimes down to thirty or even lower.

When the price of the piece of stuff is fixed, the bargain is not concluded; it is still to be settled what presents shall be made to the marabout. These presents consist in gunpowder, sugar, small trunks, looking-glasses, knives, scissors, &c.; and this last part of the bargain is often longer in being concluded than the first: after all, when the things are delivered, and every thing settled, he stays a longer time, teazing the purchaser for further presents. However outrageous his demands, he always thinks that he receives too little for his gum; so valuable do the Moors suppose it to be to us.

These expenses and these presents, added to the price paid for the gum, raise the price to such a height, that it costs more at the port than it will fetch at St. Louis. The dealers endeavour to cover themselves by practising a thousand tricks on the Moors; the latter, however, being always on their guard, are not often deceived. The Europeans frequently suffer considerable losses, and will continue to do so as long as the trade is founded on fraud. Their leisure moments are all employed in devising some new cheat; and the successful inventor conceals his scheme from the other dealers, and, reckoning upon his ingenuity, offers his cloths at a low price to attract the marabouts. His rivals all the time watch him narrowly, and set their wits to work, so that they are never long in finding out his contrivance, or inventing one of their own that may enable them to sell at the same rate. It is evident that people are not all equally qualified for a traffic of this kind; we may even assert that it requires a particular course of study to make a good gum-merchant.

It would certainly be doing a great service to the inhabitants of Senegal to put this commerce on a more honourable footing; but, if such a thing is suggested, they take fright and protest that it is impossible to deal honestly with the Moors. Government alone could set matters right, by forming a company, in which each member might hold a share proportionate to his capital, and then appointing two agents to traffic at each port, subject to the inspection of a government-officer, whose business it would be to see that the conditions on each side were fulfilled. By these means, competition would be annihilated, and the expenses considerably reduced, because a single ship would be sufficient at each port, and the gum would be conveyed to St. Louis in boats. The Moors would be unwilling to submit to any alteration at first, but when they should have ascertained that there was no other intention than that of dealing fairly with them, a mutual confidence would soon take place between them and the dealers, which would permit the latter to behave in a manner more suitable to the dignity of the French character. The merchants allege that the Moors in this case would take their gum to Portendick; but they would not take it all thither; and government would have it in its power to adopt measures for diminishing the competition which the English are creating at that port.

During the traffic, many camps of the zenagues establish themselves near the port, to be ready to sell the produce of their herds and flocks. Morning and evening the women bring milk and butter to barter for Guinea cloth, gunpowder, glass wares, etc. A pound of butter sells for about seven pence halfpenny, and a calabash of milk for two pence halfpenny.

Those Moors who have no gum, and who cannot procure the means of subsistence at the port, force themselves into the camps of these poor creatures, live upon them, and devour the profits which they have made by the sale of their commodities. It is indeed an established principle, that this class should be continually plundered by the others.

As commerce attracts to this spot a vast number of dealers and visiters; there is a perpetual bustle. While the trade lasts, the port is like a tumultuous fair; on one side are the camels and oxen of the caravans, driven out to graze or to the river to water; on another a flock of sheep, which a zenague is endeavouring to sell; here a caravan just arrived from the desert, with dealers besetting it and quarrelling with one another; laptots[35] fighting, and women squabbling; further on, hassanes on horseback, or mounted on camels, running to and fro, and heightening, by their violence, the confusion of all the groupes which were already too turbulent.

On the 31st of July in the evening, the station-ship fires a gun, which is the signal for the close of the traffic and the departure of the vessels. Such of the Moors as have not sold their gum take it away, and dig holes in the ground, where they keep it till the next season. The remainder of the customs is paid at this time; for the dealers never pay in advance, lest the Moors should send off their gum to some other place, in order to obtain double dues. Neither is it till after the return of the station-ship to St. Louis that the king receives the allowance granted by government to insure the protection of the trade. She sails on the 1st of August, and all the merchant ships usually follow.

On the 11th of May I embarked for St. Louis; my guide accompanied me, and we arrived on the sixteenth. I took every possible precaution on the way, to prevent him from having an interview with Schims, the chief of the Dawalache tribe;[36] but my efforts were frustrated, and they met in a village not far from his post. They had a long conversation together, in which Schims informed my marabout that I had been with him before I went to the Braknas, and that I had proposed to receive my education from him; entering at the same time pretty fully into his motive for not receiving me, which he said was founded upon the accounts he had heard of me. As soon as Schims perceived me, he dropped the subject and congratulated me on my conversion; I reproached him for his refusal to take me into his camp, and he then repeated what he had just said, and laid great stress upon the bad account that the *children of the Senegal* [37] had given him of me; but for this, he said, he should not have hesitated to receive me and to treat me as his own son.

I strove during the rest of the conversation to counteract the bad impression which these imputations had made upon my marabout; but I saw that I had lost all his confidence, and that it was only by a speedy return, and an apparent resolution to settle in his country, that I could impose upon him or his nation.

CHAPTER V

Disappointments experienced at St. Louis — The author takes up various occupations — He departs once more — Particulars respecting the environs of Kakondy — The Nalous, Landamas, or Lantimas, and Bagos.

When I reached St. Louis, I heard, to my great mortification, that Baron Roger had returned to France; I requested, nevertheless, an interview with the governor; which was not granted till several days afterwards. In the mean time, I was indebted to the hospitality of one of my friends; for although I had made known my forlorn condition, the administration of St. Louis did not offer me any assistance. I could not but be much hurt by this insulting reception. Was I then estranged from my country by the pains I had taken to serve it? Could I be suspected of being a mere adventurer? And had I not eight months before received instructions from Baron Roger, who promised me the protection of the government?

I still hoped, however, that the governor, when he had read my journal, would do me justice and appreciate my zeal. When I delivered it to him, I apprized him of my plans for the future; it was not long before I discovered how much I had lost by the departure of my true patron; not that his successor was deficient in talents, or in the love of science, but he did not enter into his views; in short, it was not he who had sent me amongst the Braknas. The substance of my plan was as follows:

I asked of government the moderate sum of six thousand francs, (£250) with which I intended to buy a flock and two slaves, and take them with me to the Braknas. Here I proposed to establish myself for some time, and to continue my studies; and I reckoned upon dispelling, by these means, the suspicions which had been excited about me, and which were no doubt known to my marabout. Returning to them in this way, with means of subsistence analogous to their own, I could easily have obtained leave to accompany them on their commercial expeditions. I intended to visit Adrar this year, to penetrate as far as possible towards the northern part of the desert, and, when I had a favourable opportunity, to direct my course to the east, under pretence of a pilgrimage to Mecca, passing through the towns of Wâlet and Timbuctoo. I hoped to traverse this immense tract of desert, in more senses than one, to collect all the information I could of a commercial or geographical nature, and to return to Europe through Egypt.

I know not whether this project appeared too vast, or whether the governor suspected me of imposition, but the scheme which I had adopted of pretending to be converted to Islamism insured the success of a journey which would have been impracticable to a christian. Whatever might be the reason, I obtained neither money nor the countenance of government; but M. Hugon apologised speciously enough for his refusal.

"My strength," he told me, "was inadequate to such an undertaking; besides, government had not authorised him to dispose of so large a sum for such a purpose; moreover, M. Beaufort had already received twenty thousand francs to enable him to carry into execution a similar project. "Would it not be unfair," he added, "to commission another person to undertake the same journey as that officer, and to furnish him with the means of outstripping him? M. Beaufort is at Bakel; he has almost attained the goal; let him follow his fate, and if he should unfortunately fail, we will then see what government can do to facilitate your design."

This reply, prudent and proper as it might be, cast me down to the ground. My situation became critical: I had come to St. Louis with several Moors, particularly a marabout who was to have accompanied me to Mecca; I was now compelled to dismiss him, and, more than that, I was forced to hide myself for many days, because the Braknas, who had brought me to St. Louis, having heard of my secret intentions, and enraged at being imposed upon by my feigned zeal for their religion, determined to do me a mischief.

I should have deemed myself fortunate if the vengeance of the Moors had been all I had to fear; but every thing concurred to overwhelm me. The coldness of my patrons, the ridicule of all kinds to which I was exposed: nay; some went so far as to assert that I had undergone the initiatory operation of Islamism.

One of my friends, seeing me reduced to the allowance of a common soldier, which had been granted to me out of compassion, warmly exhorted me to give up my plan, to relinquish my costume, and to return to business; but he was not aware of my persevering disposition, and doubted my courage. The taunts of Europeans only rendered my African costume more dear to me: I was proud of wearing it; I braved raillery and despised calumny, and, slighting the advantages which trade would have afforded me, I persisted in my projects. Besides, I knew that Baron Roger was to return, and I calculated upon the support of that excellent governor; with his aid I had no doubt that I should at last reach Timbuctoo.

In the mean time, however, it was needful that I should be kept alive. In spite of my repugnance, I so far conquered my pride, as to apply to the governor *ad interim*, requesting him to pay for my board at the inn. My petition was granted more speedily than I expected, and I was offered a salary of fifty francs a month, as overseer of the negro workmen at one of our settlements on the river.

This favour vexed me exceedingly, by postponing the possibility of undertaking my journey. I felt that I possessed energy enough for something better than a negro driver and in my despair, instead of going to Richard Tol[38], according to my instructions, I set off for N'pâl, a village near St. Louis, without any other design than that of catching and stuffing birds for my livelihood. One of the grandees of the colony, from whom I had sent to beg the necessary instruments, replied to my messenger: "By all means; and then he will be of some use." This reply, which was repeated to me, put me in a rage, and in the utmost indignation I left N'pâl to go to Richard Tol.

On my arrival at this settlement, I was consoled by the kindness of M. Lelièvre, the gardener, who had the kindness to add some other provisions to the regular soldier's allowance, which was all I could claim as overseer.

Whilst I was discharging this office, with all the mortification of a man who feels that his business is beneath him I learnt the arrival of Baron Roger. At this intelligence I was transported with joy; I ran about in all directions in search of a vessel to take me to St. Louis, and if I could I would have swum thither. On landing, I hastened to present myself to our former governor; I delivered into his hands, the same day, the notes which I had taken during my stay with the Braknas; I accompanied them with a fresh application for assistance, or for an appointment, to enable me to perform my great journey—it was not granted!

To any other person this would have been a thunderclap; but my resolution struck deeper and deeper root every day, and I had the courage to return to the charge. Then indeed, I was kindly promised a sum of money on my return from Timbuctoo.—On my return from Timbuctoo! And what if I died on the way? this idea so dreadful to a man, who in case of this misfortune would leave a sister whom he adored in a state of want, suggested my answer. I refused to make any arrangement; and I determined that, were I destined to die, I would at least leave an incontestable legacy to the friend of my childhood—the merit of having done all without help. I changed my plan, and asked for nothing but the hundred francs that were due to me as overseer. I had disdained to receive them before, but my poverty and the way in which I was abandoned rendered them indispensable.

Attired as I was in my Arab costume, I did not care to ask for letters of introduction to Albreda,[39] whither I resolved to go, knowing that I should have been refused because I was not dressed in the French fashion. As if my heart had ever ceased to beat for my country!—as if I had been more guilty than Aly-Bey, whom government had so warmly patronized! I set off then without passport and without letters of recommendation. I crossed over to the main-land in a canoe, and then pursued my way alone, and with no resource but my hundred francs, towards Goree. Eight years before, I had followed the same route, poor, dejected, and ready to renounce the scheme which might then perhaps have met with encouragement; I was no richer the second time, but I had all the ardour and energy of riper age, and I was resolved, were it only out of pride, to undertake what I had been supposed incapable of accomplishing.

On landing at Goree, I called to see nobody, for I was afraid of being subjected, in this insular dependency of St. Louis, to the same insults with which I had been loaded at the capital of our settlements. I took my passage in a French brig, which was about to sail for Albreda; and thence I proceeded to Sierra-Leone. General Turner, governor of this English establishment, received me with kindness, and, in order to keep me in the colony, he offered me the superintendence of an indigo-factory, and attached to the situation (which he created for me,) a salary of 3600 francs, (£150).

This governor had no notion of the passion for activity which stimulated me, and he fancied he could gratify me with money—a generous mistake, for which I was grateful to him. Shortly after, in 1826, he was succeeded by Sir Neil Campbell, to whom I applied for 6000 francs to enable me to undertake my journey; I met with the refusal which the meanness of my appearance, and what was called the extravagance of my scheme, had already procured me. Sir Neil Campbell did not mention M. Beaufort, but he spoke of Major Laing, from whom he said it would be unfair to attempt to snatch the glory of first arriving at Timbuctoo, and on this ground he rejected my proposal.

The refusal of the French governors had distressed me, but that of the English governor did not affect me at all; I felt myself the more free; I thanked heaven that I was now able to break off my engagement with foreigners, to whom I was indebted for their generous hospitality, but who might perhaps in return have laid claim to the glory of a discovery, with which I hoped to do honour to France. I gave in my resignation, therefore, with as much eagerness as I had felt in giving up my little allowance of fifty francs a month. The sacrifice was so much the easier as I had saved nearly two thousand francs, and this treasure seemed to me to be sufficient to carry me all over the world. Lastly, there was a hope which tranquillised my mind as to the fate of my poor sister; I had just heard of the premium offered by the Geographical Society of Paris to the first European who should reach Timbuctoo, and I said to myself; "Dead or alive, it shall be mine, and my sister shall receive it."

These hopes, these visions of glory, of patriotism, and of fraternal affection, left me no rest; and I had nothing like peace till the evening before I left Sierra-Leone. Not having been able any where to obtain the necessary assistance for a journey to Timbuctoo, I determined to undertake it entirely at my own expense. I hoped also that when I returned, the French government, ever just in its appreciation of courageous exertion, would reward the service which I should have rendered to geographical science, by making known the new countries which I intended to visit.

Encouraged by these hopes, I gave in my resignation without regret; I was afterwards actively engaged in procuring the goods I was likely to want, and laid out my savings in the purchase of paper, glass, and other articles.

During my residence at Freetown, the capital of the colony of Sierra Leone, I became acquainted with some Mandingoes and seracolets.[40] I won their confidence, and availed myself of it to gain information about the countries which I intended to visit. At last, to make sure of their friendship, I gave them a few trifles; and then I told them one day, with a very mysterious air, and a charge of secrecy, that I was born in Egypt, of Arabian parents, and that I had been carried into France, in my infancy, by some soldiers of the French army which had invaded Egypt; that I had afterwards been brought to the Senegal by my master, who in consideration of my services had given me my liberty. I added that, as I was now free, I felt a natural inclination to return to Egypt, to seek my relations, and to adopt the Mahometan religion. At first the Mandingoes did not seem to credit my account, and especially what I said of my zeal for their religion; but their doubts were removed when they heard me repeat many passages of the Koran, and saw me join with them in performing the salam; at last they said to one another that I was really a good Musulman. Need I say that in secret I addressed my fervent prayers to the God of the christians to favour my undertaking?

The Mandingoes, deceived by my apparent anxiety to observe all the ceremonies of their religion, confided in me entirely. Our acquaintance ripened into intimacy, and they seemed as if they could never be happy without me; every day I was invited, to my great annoyance, to dine with them upon boiled rice and palm-oil. It will be seen by what follows how far these effusions of friendship were to be trusted.

One day, when I was going home, I was accosted in the street by one of my new friends, the Mandingoes, who asked me if I had not taken a silver toothpick which he had lost; the rogue added, aside, "Do not make a noise; give me back my toothpick, and I will say nothing about it." Imagine my surprise and indignation! I had no difficulty in understanding what the fellow meant; I reproached him for this shameful behaviour to a brother, without protection, in a foreign country; then, transported with anger, I followed him home and appealed to the merchants who were assembled there; but they all refused to interfere in the business. I then went to fetch a negro who spoke English, and Mandingo, that we might the better understand one another. When my accuser saw the interpreter, he was alarmed, and said I had mistaken his meaning, and that he only came to inquire whether by chance I had found the article which he had lost, adding, that he should be miserable to have any dispute with me. I was satisfied with this explanation; but I left my former companions with looks of scorn, and told them that they had taken the wrong way to gain any thing from me. Recollecting very soon that I might meet some of these Mandingoes on my journey, I thought it best to appear to forget the offence, and I made a few presents to their chief, after which we were as good friends again as ever.

This little incident served as a lesson to me. I found that I must use greater caution, and that above all I must pretend to be very poor, that I might not excite rapacity.

Notwithstanding my reconciliation with the Mandingo merchants, I did not think it prudent to set out with them, and I sought a better opportunity of travelling through the Fouta-Dhialon. I thought that I had found one when I made acquaintance with a Mandingo, a very devout man, according to his own account, who was honoured with the title of sherif. I did not hesitate to ask leave to accompany him to Tembo, the capital of Fouta-Dhialon: he consented very readily, and, when I offered him a reward he replied, with downcast eyes, that whatever he did would be for the love of God and the prophet, and that there was only one thing which he should beg of me, and that was to obtain a passport from the governor of Sierra-Leone. In spite of my entreaties and all I could do, the governor had given me no answer on the day before that which we had fixed for our departure. I went to inform Ibrahim (for that was my guide's name) of this unlucky circumstance, and he did not chuse to wait any longer for me. He hastened his journey, and took with him an Arabian dress that I had had made and left with him the evening before. As soon as I recollected this, I ran after the devout sherif and asked for my bundle; he pretended to be greatly surprised at first, and then, rubbing his forehead, exclaimed, with the air of a man who is vexed: "O, good God! those rogues of slaves have gone on before, and taken your clothes along with them; but be not uneasy, I will send them back to you." The safest way would have been to have detained the thief by way of hostage; but it was dangerous for me to make enemies, and I allowed him to continue his journey, reflecting sorrowfully, as I returned home, upon the knavish disposition of my new African friends.

Since I had been at Freetown I had resumed the French costume. Perhaps, said I, these Moors have found out my imposture; I give myself out for an Arabian and a Musulman, without forsaking my European dress and habits I cannot act my part completely unless I renounce them. I could not well effect this change at Sierra-Leone; for the white inhabitants, who were all acquainted with my person, would not have been more indulgent to me than those of St. Louis. I thought therefore of leaving Freetown, and proposed to go to a place where I might land in my Arabian dress without inconvenience. I fixed upon Kakondy, a village situated on the Rio Nuñez, fifty leagues to the north of Sierra-Leone, where I knew that there was no European establishment.

Before I set out for Kakondy, I converted my two thousand francs partly into specie and partly into merchandise. This was my whole fortune, but I meant to devote it all to the accomplishment of my project. I expended seventeen hundred francs in the purchase of gunpowder, paper, sundry glass wares, tobacco, amber, coral, silk handkerchiefs, knives, scissors, looking-glasses, cloves, three pieces of Guinea stuff, and an umbrella. All these goods formed a bundle of no great bulk; they did not weigh one hundred pounds, for I had bought but a small quantity of each article; the price of European goods being then high in all the colonies. I put into my girdle the rest of my two thousand francs, half in silver and half in gold. Thanks to the kindness of my friends at Sierra-Leone, I had no need to buy medicines; they furnished me with cream of tartar, jalap, calomel, and different kinds of salts, sulphate of quinine, diachylon plaister, and nitrate of silver.

Provided with all these useful things, and with two pocket compasses to direct me, and dressed in my Arabian costume, with my pockets filled with leaves torn out of the Koran, I embarked at Sierra-Leone on the 22nd of March, 1827, for Rio Nuñez, on board the schooner Thomas. The wind being foul we did not arrive at the mouth of the Rio Nuñez till the thirty-first of the month. I had here the good fortune to meet with a Frenchman of the name of Castagnet, who, though not acquainted with me, took me home with him, and promised that he would do all he could to forward my undertaking. He was then going to Rio Pongo, and as he was to be absent a fortnight, he begged me to defer my journey till he came back. I was glad to accede to this obliging request, for I was told that M. Castagnet owned one of the principal factories at Kakondy, where caravans from the interior were arriving daily, and particularly from Kankan, a part of the country which I was particularly anxious to visit. I must confess that this meeting with M. Castagnet was a most fortunate circumstance for me, and that the generous hospitality which I enjoyed in his house during my stay at Kakondy merits my everlasting gratitude.

On the 5th of April, I was conducted to Rebeca by Mr. Bethman, an English merchant, the proprietor of an establishment near M. Castagnet's residence, and who had the kindness to introduce me to the presumptive heir of the Landamas, whose name is Macandé. The king had been dead for some months, and they were waiting for the rainy season to chuse a successor.

Mr. Tudsberry, who possesses a noble factory at the foot of the mountain, was so good as to accompany us to see the prince, who received us without ceremony in the corridor belonging to his house. This corridor is supported by pillars, and goes all round the premises.

The prince was informed in the Landamas language of the object of my journey, and my wish to visit the almamy of Fouta-Dhialon. The prince of the Landamas is not a Musulman; he drinks spirits, and so do his subjects. My visit did not appear to interest him much; he told me jokingly that he thought I was a christian; but they assured him of the contrary, and added, that I was a real Arab. He did not speak to me, but he could not take his eyes off my Arabian costume, which seemed to surprise him.

The news of my arrival, soon spread in the neighbourhood, and some of the inhabitants, attracted by curiosity, came to visit me. They all shook hands with me in token of peace. Amongst the crowd was a Mandingo, who had been settled for some time in that country; he had travelled amongst the Moors of the Senegal, and acquired some knowledge of the language, in which he asked me several questions. I answered them, and begged him to tell the prince that I had been taken prisoner by the christians when very young; that I had been long away from my native land; and that, being now free, I was returning to my relations. This Mandingo interpreted my words very faithfully, and told the prince and his ministers that they were very fortunate, and ought to thank God for having sent to them an Arab from the prophet's own country, to open to them the gates of heaven; and lastly, that they had that day seen what their ancestors had never beheld. After this short conversation we took leave of the prince and returned to Mr. Tudsberry's.

A few days before this time a caravan had arrived at Rebeca from Kankan, with a large quantity of gold. I soon made acquaintance with the chiefs; they were not a little surprised when they beard the object of my journey, and congratulated me on my attachment to Islamism, assuring me that the chief of Tembo would be happy to see me, and anxious to forward my plans. I said prayers with my new friends, after which they received me as a true Musulman, and gave me part of their supper, which consisted of boiled rice.

As it was then the time of the Ramadan, I pretended not to eat before sun-set. I did not sit down to table till towards night, and took nothing but some dried beef, which a Mandingo brought to me. As it was late, I spent the rest of the night at Mr. Tudsberry's, who was extremely polite, and promised to do all in his power to assist me in penetrating into the interior.

On the 6th, we went to see Mr. Bethman's factory, situate at the foot of a mountain, not far from Mr. Tudsberry's. Here are deposited the remains of Major Peddie and four of his companions, victims, as I have already mentioned, to the unwholesome burning climate. Their graves, which are on a little terrace near the house, are shaded by two superb orange-trees. A little to the east is a rivulet, the clear waters of which form a cascade, and keep up the freshness of the vegetation around them. The grounds, which are delightful, are planted with orange-trees, citrons, banians, and fine bombaces, which afford an agreeable shade. From the top of the mountain a great extent of country is visible; with the windings of the Rio Nuñez, the picturesque banks of which heighten the effect of the landscape.

After this little excursion, I returned to the Mandingoes. The kindness which these worthy people had shewn me made me forget the vexations I had endured at Sierra-Leone, and inspired me with the hope of travelling in safety, and accomplishing my object without any serious obstacles.

The Ramadan obliged me to wait a few days for the great caravans which were to arrive after the fast, and with which I hoped to penetrate more easily into the interior. To make the best of my time, I endeavoured to gain information about the manners and habits of the Bagos, a small tribe who inhabit the isles at the mouth of the river, and of whom I had heard some very curious particulars; but before I give any account of them, I must take some notice of the Landamas and Nalous, who live in the neighbourhood of Rio Nuñez.

These tribes are entirely idolaters, or worshippers of fetishes. The Foulahs of Fouta-Dhialon have subjected them to their dominion, but they have chosen rather to become tributaries to the almamy,[41] than to renounce their ancient superstition and adopt Mahometanism.

The tribute is received by the chief of Labé, who forwards it to Tembo. The chief of the Landamas receives himself the tribute which his subjects destine for the almamy, every one contributing according to his means. The sovereignty remains always in the same family, but the son never succeeds his father; they choose, in preference, a son of the king's sister, conceiving that by this method, the sovereign power is more sure to be transmitted to one of the blood royal; a precaution which shows how little faith is put in the virtue of the women of this country.

Amongst the tribes on the banks of the Rio Nuñez there is a secret society, not unlike that of the freemasons. It has a head, who is called the Simo; he makes laws, and they are executed under his authority. This Simo lives in the woods, and is never seen by the uninitiated; he is attended by pupils who are partly initiated in the mysteries. Sometimes he assumes the form of a pelican, sometimes he is wrapped up in the skins of wild beasts, and sometimes covered from head to foot with leaves, which conceal his real shape.

Novices may be initiated at several different times of the year. The families in several different villages, who wish to have their children admitted, collect all the boys between the ages of twelve and fourteen, and send for the Simo. He comes to the place in disguise, to circumcise the children, none but candidates being present at the operation; the ceremony is accompanied by a great feast, at the expense of the parents, who contribute according to their respective means. The feast lasts sometimes for several days; after it is over, the Simo withdraws to the woods, and takes with him the boys who have been initiated; from this time forward, they have no further communication with their relatives. They lead a pleasant idle life; provisions are bestowed upon them in abundance, and they dwell in huts made of the branches of trees, with no other clothing than a few palm leaves skilfully arranged, from the loins half way down the thighs, the head and the rest of the body being quite naked.

I have often seen them go by with two calabashes of palm-wine slung at the two ends of a stick, which they carried on their shoulder. They walk at a prodigious rate, and seem afraid of being seen. When the Simo or his disciples meet a stranger in the wood, they ask him for the watchword of the order; if the answer is correct, the stranger is admitted amongst them; if not, the master and his pupils, all armed with sticks and rods, attack him, and, after beating him severely, exact a high ransom. If an uncircumcised boy falls into their hands, they circumcise him and keep him, for the purpose of initiating him. They have no mercy upon women, whom they beat most cruelly, and, as I have been told, they are sometimes barbarous enough to kill them.

The young persons thus initiated lead this idle and vagabond life for seven or eight years; this period, it is said, is necessary for their instruction.

When the parents are desirous of getting them back from the woods, they collect all the pagnes they can, and make with them a fine girdle, which they adorn with copper bells, and send it to their children with a present of tobacco and rum for the master. It is only at such times that the son shows himself in public.

The eve of this festival is celebrated in the woods, near the spot where he is to make his appearance, and he gives notice by his loud shouts that he means to be visible.

Without this notice no person excepting the uninitiated durst look at him, for they are foolish enough to think it unlucky, and if they were to feel ill after it, they would not fail to ascribe it to the unfortunate glance.

On the festival day, the Simo again announces his approach by frightful howlings, which are imitated by his pupils with cows' horns. They are all armed with whips, in token of their authority. Those who have been formerly initiated, and reside in the neighbouring villages, collect and join in the rejoicings. They dress themselves in their best apparel, and, preceded by the music of the country, march at the head of the troop. After having complimented the Simo, they make him a little present, and conduct him in triumph to the village, with the sound of the tomtom. Those who are present accompany the music with their monotonous singing and fire off guns. The women also assemble, singing, and bearing each a calabash of rice, which they fling at the Simo, by way of offering, amid dances and shouts of joy.

These festivals are usually very gay: much palm-wine and rum are drunk, sheep and oxen are killed, and there is great feasting, which lasts several days. When all this rejoicing is over, the children whose parents cannot afford to make presents to the Simo return with him into the woods, and continue the same course of life for seven or eight years longer. When they are old enough to be serviceable, however, they are allowed to help their parents, at the approach of the rainy season, to work in the fields; after which they return to the woods and the master employs them in cultivating his land.

When the initiated return to their families, they set up before their doors a tree, or merely a stake, at the end of which is suspended a small piece of stuff, most commonly white. The tree or stake, whichever it may happen to be, is a gift from the master, in return for the handsome present which he has received.

They give the name of Simo to this tree or stake, and it becomes their tutelar deity; they respect and fear it so much, that, to prevent any one from going to a particular spot, it is only necessary to set up a Simo before it. They also swear by it, and believe that a false oath would draw upon them the vengeance of this mysterious demon; they are even afraid of lying lest they should provoke its interference.

If any thing is owing to them, or if any one has taken from them some article which they cannot recover, they piously address their prayers to this bit of wood, and offer it a sacrifice of rice, honey, or palm-wine, firing off a gun at its foot. This is a species of complaint which they make to the Simo, to petition for redress. From this time, if any of the debtor's family should fall sick, it is ascribed to the agency of the Simo; the relations in a fright hasten to discharge the debt, to return what has been stolen, or to make reparation if any insult has been offered.

They believe in sorcery and witchcraft; whoever is suspected of sorcery is forthwith delivered to the Simo, who acts as chief magistrate. The accused is questioned, and if he confesses, he is condemned to pay a fine; if, on the other hand, he maintains his innocence, he is compelled to drink a liquor made with the bark of a tree which gives to water a beautiful red colour. The accused and the accuser are obliged to swallow the same medicine, or rather poison; they must drink it fasting and entirely naked, except that the accused is allowed a white pagne, which he wraps round his loins. The liquor is poured into a small calabash, and the accuser and accused are forced to take an equal quantity, until, unable to swallow more, they expel it or die. If the poison is expelled by vomiting, the accused is innocent, and then he has a right to reparation; if it passes downwards, he is deemed not absolutely innocent; and if it should not pass at all at the time, he is judged to be guilty.

I have been assured that few of these wretched creatures survive this ordeal; they are compelled to drink so large a dose of the poison, that they die almost immediately. If however, the family of the accused consent to pay an indemnity, the unhappy patient is excused from drinking any more liquor; he is then put into a bath of tepid water, and by the application of both feet to the abdomen they make him cast up the poison which he has swallowed.

This cruel ordeal is employed for all sorts of crimes. The consequence is, that though it may sometimes lead to the confession of crimes, it also induces the innocent to acknowledge themselves guilty, rather than submit to it.

It is not lawful either to quarrel or fight near the places which are inhabited by the mystical magistrate. When war is to be carried on in the neighbourhood, notice is given to the Simo and his retinue to retire. If two adversaries were to fight while he was near, they would be forced immediately to take him a present as a reparation for having disturbed him;

if they were to omit this, they would fancy that some great calamity was continually impending over them.

When they carry their gift to the Simo, they are obliged to turn their backs to him, and put their hands over their eyes; he receives the offering, pronounces a long prayer, and picks up a little earth, which he throws at them in token of absolution. After this ridiculous ceremony, the disturbers of the Simo's peace returned perfectly satisfied. During the few days that I was at Kakondy, I heard the Simo and his attendants howling horribly while dancing.

Polygamy is practised amongst the Landamas and Nalous, who may be said to inhabit the same country; the husbands have not only many lawful wives, but as many concubines as they can afford to keep. I have been told that the rich have sometimes so many as two hundred which I should think is a great exaggeration. This custom among these idolatrous nations proceeds no doubt from this, that the mothers do not suffer their husbands to approach them till their children are able to walk. It is very remarkable, that good order and perfect harmony prevail among all these women who are called to share the same conjugal couch.

They are not all faithful to their husbands; but when a man suspects that one of his wives is false he compels her by the fear of the Simo to confess who has been the partner of her guilt. The woman seldom holds out long against his questions and threats; the fear of being subjected to the ordeal of the magistrate of the woods forces her to confess her fault and to discover her paramour. From that moment the latter becomes the slave of the husband, who sells him without pity to the negro merchants, or to any other negroes of the country.

A young man has no need of the consent of the female whom he loves to obtain her hand; he takes care to gain over to his interest an old woman and an old man, whom he employs to convey a present to the parents of the girl, in order to incline them to give a favorable reception to his proposals. Should this offer be accepted, he continues to pay his court to the relations of his intended by these means, until, having obtained their consent, he sends a final present of rum, tobacco, stuffs, and colat-nuts,[42] which are very common on the banks of the Rio Nuñez, and which must always be of different colours. The father of the girl takes two of the colat-nuts, one white, the other red; he cuts them in two and throws the half of each into the air, to draw thence a favourable omen. After having examined the manner in which they have fallen, and being satisfied upon this point, he calls his daughter, who is not yet informed of the steps, taken to obtain her, and indeed very often does not know the lover who has applied for her. He makes her eat a little of each of the colat-nuts from which the omen has been drawn, and informs her, before the persons present, that she is to become the wife of him who has sent the presents; and the same day, without consulting her inclination the unfortunate creature is led to the home of a husband whom she will, perhaps, never love.

She is conducted thither by the old people who were charged with the preliminary negociations, and followed by a crowd of her young friends, who rejoice and sing her praises. The old woman is appointed to prepare the hut in which the new-married couple are to dwell. After taking away every thing belonging to the master of the cabin, she puts upon the bed a pair of very white pagnes to receive the happy pair the first night of their marriage; next day these pagnes are presented to the bridal party, who pass them from hand to hand, singing and dancing in honour of the chastity of the young bride. This ceremony always takes place to the sound of rustic music and lively songs which render the spectacle more animated. These festivities generally last two or three days. The parents of the new couple never attend them; they do not visit their children till a week after the marriage.

On the seventh day after the birth of a child there are great rejoicings; it is not till then that the mother begins to go out of the house. During this interval she remains shut up to bestow all her attentions on the new-born babe. That period being elapsed, the parents sacrifice an ox, and both night and day are passed in dancing.

Amongst the Landamas and Nalous, death also claims its sacrifices. On the day of interment, the relations kill a sheep and sprinkle the grave with its blood. This ceremony is proceeded by several discharges of musquetry at the grave; the sheep is afterwards divided amongst the neighbours. A month after the decease a second funeral ceremony is celebrated; such of the relations as are rich in herds kill several oxen, and all the inhabitants of the village are admitted to the feast, which often lasts several days.

These festivals are enlivened alternately by the wild music and the simple dances of the natives, and also by the fumes of palm-wine. The Landamas and Nalous take great pleasure in these amusements, and they will even deprive themselves of the necessaries of life to support the expense of their sacrifices.

The food of these uncivilized tribes consists chiefly of rice boiled in water, to which they sometimes add the fruit of the palm-tree, from which they are too idle to express the oil. They seldom eat fish, for they have not skill to catch it; but they rear poultry, sheep, and goats. They have few cattle, and still fewer horses; I saw only a single ass whilst I was at Kakondy.

These tribes carry on very little trade, for they sell nothing but salt, which they buy of the Bagos. For the rest, they are extremely indolent, and consequently work very little. Most of them do nothing but clear the ground for the purpose of sowing rice, or planting cassava, and they do not even take the trouble to break it up, though it would be more productive, if they would bestow a little labour upon it.

As they are not disciples of Mahomet, they drink a great quantity of spirits; and the palm-trees which abound in their country supply them with abundance of a very sweet wine. The fruit which they call *caura* also affords an agreeable beverage, when bruised and fermented with water; it is intoxicating, and I have been told that it very much resembles cyder. They sometimes eat the pulp of this fruit; for the idle (and these form the majority of them) have no other resource for satisfying their appetite. They have another liquor, called *jin-jin-di*, made with the root of a plant of the same name; this they burn, and then mix with the bark of a tree (which I could never get any body to shew me); the whole being pounded together, they pour water upon it and stir it briskly for a couple of hours: after having left it to ferment for two or three days, they draw it off into another vessel; it thus acquires a sweet and agreeable flavour. It is always drunk at feasts and entertainments, because it promotes digestion. The root jin-jin-di is also used, without any admixture, as an excellent aperient medicine.

The Landamas and the Nalous inhabit straw huts, like those of other negroes in the interior of Africa; these huts are small and dirty. Their costume varies much. I have seen numbers of them in the neighbourhood of Kakondy with breeches like Europeans, a pagne over their shoulders, and a hat on their head; others again without breeches, with a vest and a coussabe. The women wear pagnes.

The soil near the banks of the Rio Nuñez is fertile; all the trees which flourish in the colonies would grow there if they were cultivated. The natives, accustomed to live in idleness, in their hot and even scorching climate, do not trouble themselves with any thing of the kind; the Europeans alone have gardens.

Bees are very common in this part of the country, and the inhabitants are fond of honey, which they obtain by placing hives in the trees. To get at the honey without accident, they let down the hive, by means of a rope, to a certain distance from the ground, and light under it a great fire of damp herbs; the smoke drives away the bees, and the negroes are left masters of the hive. The wax which they make is sold to the Europeans.

Bees are so numerous, that it is not uncommon for them to swarm into the huts and drive out the inhabitants; recourse is then had to smoke to dislodge them. The short time that I passed at Kakondy not permitting me to visit the Bagos, I shall just relate what I was told of those people.

These negroes are idolaters, and they have hitherto preserved their independence. Their vicinity to the islands off the coast, and the facility with which they can transport themselves thither, may have prevented the almamy of Fouta-Dhialon from disturbing their tranquillity. They dwell near the mouth of the river; and this country, which is flat and fertile, affords abundance of rich pasturage for their numerous cattle. It is singular that this tribe, who are in many respects stupid enough, have never found out the great advantage there would be in milking their cows and ewes; their cattle however prosper, and they do not lose as many as the negroes who are accustomed to milk them.

The Bagos are very different in their manners from the Landamas their neighbours. They are more industrious, and consequently more prosperous; they inhabit a fertile country, which they cultivate with care; their principal produce is rice. They contrive to plough their fields in the European manner; and, the instrument which they use for this purpose is a kind of wooden coulter two feet long, with a handle of six or seven feet.

As the country is flat, they take care to form channels to drain off the water. When the inundation is very great, they take advantage of it to fill their little reservoirs, that they may provide against the drought and supply the rice with the moisture which it requires.

They are also accustomed to sow the rice close to their villages, and then transplant it into their fields when it has risen to the height of six inches. This is the business of the women, who also weed it. The men get in the harvest which is very abundant. In this lovely country, so rich in natural advantages, the women are in the habit of going naked all their lives; young and old, without distinction, have no other dress than a single strip of calico, seven or eight feet long, and five inches wide, which they wind round their waist, and pass between the thighs. These poor creatures perform all the work of the house; they cook, and labour in the fields and at the salt-pits.

The Bagos buy salt, and sell it with a profit to the Europeans who trade with Kakondy, receiving in exchange piece-goods, tobacco, rum, glass-ware, and other trifles.

The women who are employed at the salt-works collect, at the ebb tide, the earth which is most impregnated with salt, and make heaps of it. After this first operation, they make large vessels or jars, of the earth mixed with straw, and pour into them water, which, in filtering through the earth, carries off all the saline particles. This water is afterwards poured into large coppers, in which it is boiled till nothing remains but the salt. Being collected into heaps, it is then sold to the inhabitants of Kakondy, who have a great market for it in the Fouta.

The rain, which falls in torrents in the wet season, does not prevent the Bagos from attending to their affairs. Both men and women have a little mat, two feet and a half long and one foot wide, through which they pass a string which they tie round their heads, and this serves as a protection from the rain: this species of umbrella also skreens them from the sun. The women use it also to shelter their children, whom they carry constantly on their backs, from the burning heat of the sun. They take part of the strip of cotton which covers their loins to tie the child to their bodies: and this troublesome burden does not prevent them from working. Whilst they are young they shave their heads entirely. When they are taken in labour, they lie down on the ground even before a stranger, and bring forth without a groan. As soon as the child is born, they go and wash it in the river, and then resume their usual occupations, as if nothing had happened.

The Bagos are accustomed to marry their children at a very early age; they are sometimes contracted at seven or eight years old. From the moment when a marriage is agreed upon, the father of the boy is obliged, if he has a daughter of his own, to exchange her for the girl who is promised to his son; if he has none, application is made to the lad's relations, who never refuse to comply with the demand.

When the young people are once engaged in the manner I have mentioned, they live in the same house, and are brought up together, with the knowledge that they are designed for one another; from that time the lad brings his intended every morning a large calabash full of palm-wine, with which his parents supply him till he is capable of making the wine himself.

The children naturally live very happily together, and the marriage is not celebrated till the girl is eleven or twelve years old. Great rejoicings are made on the occasion, and an ox is killed to regale the guests, who are always very numerous.

From the time that the children come together to the celebration of the marriage, the lad furnishes the relations of his future wife with two calabashes of palm-wine every day, one in the morning, the other at night.

The girl, who on such occasions is given in exchange to be useful to the parents who have lost their daughter, leaves them when she is to be betrothed to go and live with her future husband; the adoption is, in fact, only as a compensation for services. Men are not obliged to find substitutes: like the Landamas, they have many wives; but they marry them after considerable intervals.

The Bagos also offer sacrifices at the birth of a child and at the death of a relation. When the head of a family dies, it is very common to burn every thing that is in the house. The goods are packed in boxes, and, before they are thrown into the fire, the virtues of the deceased are enumerated, with some such addition as the following: "See how industrious he has been; how well he has managed his affairs! try to imitate him, that you may be as fortunate as he was." The riches, all the while, may probably consist of a European hat, trowsers, shirts, and a few other articles of the kind, which he never wore in his life. The bed of the deceased is held in great reverence, and at the foot of this wretched pallet a hole is dug, six feet deep, in which the corpse is buried upright; a fire is kindled over his head every night, and his relations come and talk to him under the idea that he hears what they say.

The family of the deceased, who are ruined by this act of superstition, are supported till the next harvest by the inhabitants of the village; for even their rice is not saved from the flames.

This beautiful and fertile country produces abundance of palms, from which they obtain a great quantity of oil: this they are very fond of, and use in their cookery. It is with this oil also that they anoint their bodies and heads; they even besmear their clothes with it: they are, consequently, very filthy, and smell of palm-oil to a great distance.

They wear nothing but a pagne round their loins; and though they have all the materials for clothing at hand, they will not take the trouble to use them. They wear a copper ring suspended from the cartilage of the nose, and ornament their ears with several rings of the same kind. The women have no other ornament than a few beads.

These people are considered thieves by their neighbours; and yet they are very hospitable, which seems scarcely compatible with the vice of which they are accused. They never see a stranger without inviting him to share their repast, and it would be almost an insult to refuse them; they consider it as a kind of contempt, and are much hurt at it. They are warlike, and are often at war among themselves. Whole families sometimes fight to settle their own quarrels, or even those of their ancestors. They are armed with poniards, and defend themselves very skilfully against the blows of their adversaries with large shields made of elephant's hide. I have been assured that they are not accustomed to make slaves, but kill their prisoners without mercy.

The Bagos have no king; each village is governed by the oldest of the inhabitants, who settles their disputes, though they have, like the Landamas, a Simo, who performs the functions of chief magistrate upon important occasions.

They are a jovial people, and fond of drinking; persons of both sexes often assemble round a large calabash of palm-wine, and do not leave it till it is empty. They are great eaters, and their diet principally consists of dried fish, swimming in palm-oil, which renders it so disgusting, that a European could not touch it. When they kill a sheep, they mix the skin and entrails, unwashed, with the stews which they make: they also eat snakes, lizards, and the monkeys which they catch.

The Bagos never visit their neighbours, neither have they occasion to do so, for their own country produces abundance of every thing requisite for the subsistence of any really temperate man. They cannot imagine that any nation is better off, and believe themselves superior in every respect to all others. I could not gain any information as to their ideas of the Deity; that they have some idea of a Supreme Being, however, is certain; for when they hear thunder they dance and sing, to a drum, and say that God is rejoicing, and that they rejoice with him.[43]

Their houses are large and convenient; many families live together, and the members of each sleep upon the same bed; with the exception, however, of the head of the family, who has a bed to himself. The women never eat with the men; each has her own dish and eats in private; the boys also eat by themselves. The men are very good swimmers, and they have canoes made out of a single tree, which serve them for crossing from one island to another.

The Bagos are quite black, with curly hair; they shave the front of the head, and let the hair grow at the back; anointing it with palm-oil, which makes it look very much like sheep's wool. When the men go to Kakondy on business, they put on trowsers and a European hat; but, as soon as they return, they lay this costume aside, and resume the pagne.

CHAPTER VI

Departure of the author on his great expedition — Manners and customs of his travelling companions, and account of the caravans in this part of Africa — The Caura — Mountains of Lantégué — River of Doulinca — Smelting of iron — Rio Pongo — Mountain of Touma — Description of Irnanké and its inhabitants — Telewel — Cataract of Cocouo — Orange trees.

The information which I have just been communicating to the reader was acquired in M. Castagnet's absence, and by the help of some excursions that I took with Mr. Bethman and Mr. Tudsberry in the neighbourhood of Kakondy. I was endeavouring to arrange the notes that I had made respecting the Nalous, the Landamas, and the Bagos, when M. Castagnet returned. He was so good as to turn his attention immediately to my journey, and gave me much useful advice respecting my conduct amongst the tribes whom I intended to visit. He furnished me with all the particulars that had come to his knowledge concerning their manners, their jealousy, and their distrust of Europeans; and thinking that this was not sufficient, and that he had not done enough to oblige me, he sent for some Mandingoes, who deservedly enjoyed a considerable reputation in the neighbourhood for their probity, experience, and wealth. He endeavoured to persuade these Mandingoes to accompany me to Timbuctoo; and he communicated to them the object of my journey, with many encomiums upon my love of my country; he had expatiated on the courage displayed by so young a man in braving such dangers to return to his kindred: then, gradually unfolding the tale of my Egyptian origin, he endeavoured to interest their feelings in my behalf, and to secure their assistance. In vain did M. Castagnet exert his eloquence; they were perfectly indifferent till he promised to reward them for any thing they should do for me; then indeed, they showed great zeal to serve me, and protested, every one of them, that they would treat me like their own son.

They made some remarks upon the difficulties and fatigue which I should have to endure and which I might not have strength to sustain; but, upon my reply that I was determined to bear every thing, that I might return to my country, they fixed a day for our departure. M. Castagnet gave them the value of an ox in merchandise, and the Mandingoes, as they had promised, procured a slave to carry my small bundle. These arrangements were speedily terminated.

On the 19th of April, I took leave of M. Castagnet; and—shall I confess it?—I shed tears at parting from this generous friend; my regret at leaving him, however, sincere as it was, could not damp the joy which I felt in undertaking a journey upon which my mind had been bent for so many years.

Our caravan consisted of five free Mandingoes, three slaves, my Foulah porter, my guide, and his wife. All except the last two and myself carried enormous burdens.

We travelled along the left bank of the river Nuñez, and in two hours arrived at Mr. Bethman's factory. I again saw the graves of Major Peddie and other officers of the same expedition, and was seized with an involuntary shudder at the thought that the same fate perhaps awaited me; these sad forebodings vanished however on leaving the tombs, and gave way to hopes of a happier issue.

At nine in the morning we directed our course S. S. E. Ibrahim my guide, to whom I had given several articles stopped all of a sudden, and told me, by means of a negro who could speak English, that he should be obliged to make a great many presents on the way, and that he was afraid after all I should never get safe to Fouta-Dhialon, on account of my fair complexion. This reflection appeared to come a little too late, but I understood the purport of it, when he added in good Arabic that I must give him a piece of cloth.

It would have been dangerous to encourage his importunity, so I pretended that I did not know what he said, and went on in the same direction without giving him any thing. We found the soil composed of red earth, and rather stony, but covered with most beautiful vegetation; the nédé [44] in particular is very abundant. We came to a group of Mandingoes and Foulahs seated under some large trees; they were quarrelling with one another, and looking out for the customary presents. There is such a competition in the Kakondy trade, that the proprietors of each factory send couriers before the caravans to make presents to the dealers and to draw them to themselves; if they are numerous, an ox is killed on their arrival at the factory, and they are supplied with rice all the time the traffic lasts: when they are about to return a present is made them, and they are furnished with provision for the journey. So great is the competition that the merchants will even sell their goods without profit.

As I proceeded, I found the face of the country broken by stony hillocks, covered with large trees which formed a most picturesque and varied landscape. The heat was beginning to be painful; our porters were fatigued, and we halted near a pretty rivulet, with the limpid and delicious water of which we quenched our thirst. We had then travelled nearly twelve miles to the east. We kindled a fire; the negro slaves went in quest of wood, and my guide's wife prepared to cook our dinner.

Throughout all Africa, the merchants have adopted the plan of taking one of their wives with them to cook for the caravan. These unhappy creatures are loaded with earthen pots, calabashes, salt, &c.; in short, they are compelled to carry the heaviest burdens, whilst their husbands walk at their ease.

On our way we joined many Foulahs loaded with salt, who were going to Fouta; we afterwards met others carrying leather, wax, and rice; they were going to Kakondy to buy salt. I was very much surprised to see these poor Foulahs and Mandingoes, who were carrying nearly a hundred weight on their heads, walk with the greatest rapidity, and climb the Irnanke mountains with the utmost agility. They carry a staff in their hands to assist them in supporting their burden, which is packed in a long basket made of thin and flexible pieces of wood; this basket is about three feet long, and one foot wide and deep. When the goods are stowed in it, the lid is put down, and the whole tightly secured with cords made of the bark of trees. If the bearers are weary, they rest one end of the basket upon the branch of a tree, and support the other with their staff; thus loaded, they travel to the Kankan to sell their salt. We seated ourselves under the shades of a superb bombax to take our slender repast, consisting of boiled rice, and pistachio-nuts parched and pounded, to which they added a little palm-oil. The six free Mandingoes and I placed ourselves round the calabash containing our dinner, and each in turn took a handful of rice; the slaves and my porter ate together, and the women dined alone.

When they halt, as well as on the road, the women have all the labour; the husband lies down on dry leaves or straw, which his slaves carry for his accommodation. After this frugal repast, I lay down too for a few moments. Several of the Foulahs, who had joined us on our road, gave me some of the fruit of the *nédé*, which is very common in this part of Africa, and very useful to travellers; it has a great deal of nourishment in it, and helps to save the rice which is destined for the purchase of salt.

About half-past two we were again on our way, proceeding to the S. E. over the same kind of soil as in the morning. After travelling about seven miles in this direction, we arrived near a deep ravine, where we halted to pass the night. One of the slaves, went to fetch water, and our cook fell to work.

The Foulahs, who had been told that I was an Arab, shewed a sort of veneration for me, and were never weary of looking at me and pitying me: their extreme devotion renders them very charitable: they came and sat by me, taking my legs upon their knees and rubbing them to relieve my fatigue. "Thou must suffer sadly," said they, "because thou art not used to such a toilsome journey." One of them went and fetched some leaves to make me a bed. "Here!" said he, "this is for thee; for thou canst not sleep upon the stones, as we do." Lying upon my bed of leaves, I felt as happy and as much at my ease as if I had been in my own apartment.

The sky was serene. The heat of the day had been succeeded by a refreshing breeze, and every thing was exceedingly pleasant.

Several Foulahs gave me a little rice, and I was the more grateful for it as this was all they had to give. The Mandingoes too were exceedingly kind and attentive to me, and endeavoured to anticipate all my wishes.

Prudence required me to retire to the woods to write and arrange my notes. I observed this precaution throughout the whole of my journey; for every observation that dropped from those by whom I was surrounded convinced me how dangerous it would be to rouse their suspicion.

My guide, Ibrahim, though of a touchy disposition, was, upon the whole very kind to me. He conducted me in safety through the Fouta, notwithstanding his repeated threats to take me back to Timbo, where he knew that the almamy would have me arrested.

At five in the morning of the 20th of April, we resumed our journey, directing our course eastward. We passed near a charming rivulet, which ran in a southerly direction, between two hills, over a bed of rocks. After proceeding nine miles we halted, about eleven o'clock, on the banks of the Tankilita, a rivulet which my companions gave out to be the Rio Nuñez.

About half past one in the afternoon, we set out and travelled E. N. E. We passed near the little village of Oreous, which is inhabited by Foulahs, who rear a considerable number of sheep. This village is situated on the slope of a high mountain, which is covered with beautiful vegetation. We proceeded eastward seven miles, over a stony mountainous tract of country, interspersed with large trees. The nédé and the bombax grow here abundantly. At sun-set we halted at the foot of a stony hillock, where there is a very deep ravine, on the margin of which are some extremely agreeable spots: there we passed the night. My companions again made me a bed of leaves; but I declined the accommodation, being fearful of the ill effects of the coolness and damp, proceeding from this couch of verdure after the excessive heat of the day. I therefore preferred lying on the stones, enveloped in my wrapper.

At five o'clock on the morning of the 21st, we again started. We proceeded seven or eight miles amidst stony hillocks, which rendered our journey exceedingly fatiguing. At length we passed near a village inhabited by slaves who are employed in agriculture. All villages of this kind receive the general denomination of *ourondé*: the particular name of the one which we passed is Sancoubadialé.

About ten in the morning, we halted near a little spring shaded by lofty trees, which seemed to rear their majestic heads to the very clouds. The spring is in a ravine, forty or fifty feet deep, and surrounded by huge masses of quartz. The neighbourhood is inhabited by numbers of red apes, who come to the spring to drink. Two of these animals, which spied me, suddenly stopped and began to bark like dogs. They advanced upon me and as I was unprovided with any defensive weapon, I must confess that I felt somewhat alarmed. Fortunately, however, at this moment I perceived two Mandingoes of our party, who were coming to fetch some water. At their approach, the apes ran off to the woods, and we were left in undisturbed possession of the spring. About noon, we again resumed our course, proceeding to south east. Our road was less stony than it had been during the morning, but it was interspersed with hillocks, which obliged us to make frequent windings. The country was covered with large trees, the shade of which skreened us from the excessive heat of the day. I observed many wild fig-trees, and a sort of plum-tree, which the negroes call *caura*. This tree bears a very good fruit, it is shaped like a plum. The pellicle is reddish and marked with somewhat lighter spots. Beneath the pellicle is a pulp, which is very agreeable to the taste. It is not more than four lines thick, and it envelops a kernel as large as that of the peach. The negroes are very fond of this fruit.

After proceeding about nine miles, we passed the ruins of a village, and then continued for a mile and a half in the same direction. The road became more stony than hitherto; and at three in the afternoon, we arrived, greatly fatigued, at the village of Daourkiwar, or Daour-Kiwarat, where we passed the night. This village contains about four hundred inhabitants, partly Foulahs and partly Mandingoes. It is situated near a lake, the water of which is very good. This lake is surrounded by bombaces, plum-trees, and a few *naucleas*. We gathered and ate the plums, which we found delicious.

On the 22d, at five in the morning, we continued our journey in the direction of E. S. E. On the slope of a mountain, about three hundred and fifty, or four hundred feet high, we discerned the pretty Dhialonké village, called *Lom-bar*, which lay to our right. We next reached the little hill, on which is situated a second Daourkiwar village. The soil here is very good and susceptible of much higher cultivation. We proceeded onwards to some distance, and, having descended a mountain, we found a little stream, on the bank of which we halted. The stream flows through an extensive plain, which is surrounded by well wooded hills. These hills are composed of a red kind of earth, which might be rendered highly productive by cultivation. The road during the morning had been exceedingly stony and fatiguing; and, as my sandals galled me, I was obliged to take them off and walk barefoot; but the stones hurt my feet still more. I remarked that all the trees and shrubs were scorched with the heat of the sun. The environs were covered with reeds, which the natives use in building their huts. Some rice was boiled in water for our dinner; and after this frugal repast we again started about half-past twelve o'clock. We ascended the mountain, proceeding eastward; the path was very stony and nearly blocked up by the roots of trees. On reaching the level top of the hill we rested a little, and afterwards pursued our journey to the S. E. The road now became more agreeable than it had been during the morning. We found many caura trees, and amused ourselves in gathering the fruit; and, after travelling six miles, we arrived, at five in the evening, much fatigued, at Coussotami, a pretty little village, situated on a hill. Bananas were brought to us; we purchased them for a few glass beads. Some Foulahs of the village, being informed of my arrival, came to see me, and, as it was night, they lighted a taper made of a kind of wax, which is found in great abundance among these hills. During the night we lay down beneath some trees, upon the stones which covered the ground.

On the 23d of April, about five in the morning, we left Coussotami. Proceeding eastward, we passed a dry ravine, surrounded by trees, forming the most romantic groups. The aspect of the country was generally pleasing. Advancing to the S. E., we arrived in a beautiful valley covered with rich pasture, and next reached a deep ravine, the passage of which we found exceedingly difficult, owing to many large blocks of granite which we were obliged to climb over. This ravine brought us to the foot of a mountain, five or six hundred feet high, which we ascended by a circuitous route, and, after journeying about four or five miles, we reached its summit. Here, being greatly fatigued, we made a halt. About one in the afternoon we again started, and proceeded about four miles in the direction of E. S. E. We now reached a pretty little stream, whose limpid waters flow over a bed of granite: its course is from south to N. N. E. The natives call it Naufomou, and they informed me that it emptied itself into the Rio Nuñez. We seated ourselves for a short time on the margin of this stream, and ate some little cakes made of rice-flour, mixed with honey and allspice, and baked in the sun. I thought them very good. The Mandingo and Foulah traders always take care to provide themselves with these cakes for their journeys. We next passed Dougué, a pretty village, containing three or four hundred inhabitants, Foulahs and Dhialonkés. It is situated in a plain of grey sand, which might be rendered very fertile by cultivation. This plain is surrounded by high hills, which afford fine pasturage. We stopped near a spring to pass the night. The little village of Mirayé is situated on the declivity of a high mountain, a mile S. E. of Dougué. Several Foulah shepherds who were tending their flocks in the neighbourhood came to see us, and sold us what they call *cagnan*: this is a sort of small loaves or rolls, made of pistachio-nuts, baked and pounded, then mixed with maize, and sweetened with honey. These loaves form a portion of their provision when travelling. I observed a young Foulah who gazed at me very stedfastly: he invited me to go with him to his camp, where he said he would give me some milk. As I did not like to go alone, he requested some of my fellow-travellers to accompany me, which two of them readily consented to do. The young man walked before to shew us the way, and he took the trouble to remove some large pieces of stone which obstructed our path. On reaching his camp, which was not far from the place of our halt, he spread out a bullock's hide, upon which he begged me to seat myself. The camp consisted of five or six straw huts of a roundish form, and so exceedingly low that it was necessary to stoop nearly double to get into them. The furniture consisted of a few mats and sheep-skins, and calabashes to hold milk: the bed was composed of four stakes fixed in the ground, supporting long planks of wood, which were covered with a bullock's hide. He went to fetch his old mother and sisters to see me. He told them that I was an Arab, a countryman of the Prophet's, going to Mecca. They looked at me with great interest, and, making several gestures, exclaimed, *La allah il allah, Mahommed rasoul oullahi* (There is no god but God, and Mahomet is his prophet) to which I replied according to the usual form. They seated themselves at a little distance from me that they might view me at their ease. The young Foulah went to fetch me some milk in a calabash, which he washed, an extraordinary ceremony in this part of the world; and he afterwards brought me a little fried meat: I requested him to eat with me, but, pointing with his finger to the moon, he said, smiling, and with an air of timidity, "I fast; it is the Ramadan."

From this little camp we discerned the village of Mirayé, situated on the declivity of a high hill, apparently thickly wooded. The village is inhabited partly by Foulahs and partly by Dhialonkés, all Mahometans. We took our leave of the hospitable young Foulah, and returned to our halting place, where we found some of our party returning from Dougué, whither they had been to purchase rice for our journey. We slept in some little huts, made of branches of trees, covered with straw. These huts served to shelter travellers in rainy weather, for the village of Dougué lies at some distance from the road.

At four in the morning of the 24th of April, our caravan again moved forward. We proceeded eastward, along a pleasant road covered with fine gravel, and soon reached a stony mountain, which we ascended. In turning another mountain, seven or eight hundred feet high, we almost made the round of the compass. We then came to a beautiful valley, watered by a large rivulet, which the natives call Bangala: it runs from N. to S. We proceeded E. S. E. for the distance of half a mile. We then ascended a mountain of the same height as that just mentioned, and exceedingly steep. On reaching the summit we descended the other side by a very rapid slope, and, at eleven in the morning, we halted in a fine valley, near a spring surrounded by hillocks. We took our dinner beneath the shade of a bombax. At one in the afternoon we proceeded to the S. S. E. still across mountains. We passed near the huts of some Foulah herdsmen. When we were about four miles from the place where we had stopped to dine, we were overtaken by a violent storm. The thunder roared tremendously, and the rain poured in torrents. We took shelter in the herdsmen's huts. The storm lasted nearly two hours and a half. When it was over we journeyed onward to Dougol, a small slave village,[45] about a mile and a half from the herdsmen's huts.

It was about three in the afternoon when we reached this place. The hospitable chief of the village received us very kindly. He sent me, a supper of rice and sour milk, to which he added a little melted butter. The village contains about three hundred inhabitants, and it has a mosque of the same form as the huts.

At five in the morning of the 25th of April, we took leave of our host; to whom my guide, Ibrahim, gave a little salt. Our road lay to the S. E. We descended the hill on which the village is situated, and then crossed a very fertile plain. We arrived at a chain of mountains called, by the natives, Lantégué. It extends from N. E. to S. Each of these mountains rises perpendicularly to the height of nearly two hundred fathoms, and they exhibit scarcely any trace of vegetation. We soon found ourselves surrounded by large blocks of grey granite of a pyramidal form, resembling the ruins of an ancient castle. Having penetrated into the gorges of these mountains, which are composed of beautiful grey granite, we forded the rivulet called the Doulinca, which flows rapidly over a bed of granite from east to south. The water was more than knee-deep. We next proceeded to the distance of a mile over a fertile and very beautiful plain, surrounded by large rocks of grey granite. Large bamboos grow in the clefts of these enormous rocks. We again crossed the Doulinca, near a point where it falls in a cascade, the pleasing murmur of which charms the ear of the weary traveller. I seated myself for a few moments on the banks of the rivulet, while the poor negroes were reposing at a little distance, and I contemplated with admiration the beautiful scene around me. Though interspersed with mountains this district is fertile in the utmost degree, and it is watered by numerous streams and rivulets, which keep the verdure constantly fresh. The mountains are inhabited by Foulah herdsmen, who live secluded from all other society. The milk of their cattle, together with the rice which they cultivate, suffices for their support. I did not see a wild beast among these mountains. The country, which seems to be favoured by nature, is inhabited by numerous birds, whose plumage exhibits an endless variety of colours. I saw many of the same species as those found on the banks of the Senegal. We resumed our journey, and passed the huts of some Foulahs, who brought us milk. I bought some for a few glass beads. They looked at me with manifestations of earnest curiosity, and they said they had never seen a Moor so white as I was. On leaving them we found ourselves in a valley formed of two hills of granite. The soil, which consists of grey sand, is fertile and covered with good pasturage.

We were obliged once more to cross the Doulinca, and, about one in the afternoon, we halted among some Foulah herdsmen. Their huts were built beneath the shade of large trees, a most enviable situation in this part of the world. Since my departure from Kakondy, I had not seen so beautiful and fertile a tract of country. Instead of rocks, I now beheld on every side delightful plains, which required only the labour of the husbandman to produce every thing necessary for human life. The day had been excessively hot, and about two in the afternoon we heard thunder in the direction of N. E. The sky was overcast with black clouds, and the rain fell abundantly. We repaired for shelter to the huts of the herdsmen, who at first scrupled to admit us. The thunder rolled in terrific peals; and I expected every moment that we should be struck by the lightning. The flashes rapidly succeeded each other, and the sky appeared to be one sheet of flame. We lay down on the herdsmen's beds, consisting of round pieces of wood placed upon posts which raised them a little from the ground, and we patiently awaited the termination of the storm. When the rain ceased, we left the huts, and the freshness which now pervaded the atmosphere added new charms to the surrounding scene. We ate a little rice, and then proceeded eastward. We crossed a little rivulet which flowed over a bed of granite. The road was wet and muddy, which rendered our journey fatiguing. After travelling half a mile to N. E. and another half mile to the east, we arrived at night-fall at an ourondé, or slave village, called Lantégué. We were again overtaken by rain on the road, and I had recourse to my umbrella which, however, did not entirely protect me. The chief of Lantégué gave us a hut. Before it there was a beautiful orange-tree, beneath which I sat down on a sheep-skin. Thunder was again heard. The sky was covered with clouds, the atmosphere warm and damp, and it continued raining the whole of the night. The incessant flashes of lightning continually illuminated our hut, the door of which would not more than half shut.

We stopped at Lantégué the whole of the 26th, for one of the slaves of our caravan, who was heavily laden, had bad feet. I spent a part of the day in visiting the village and its inhabitants, who were about one hundred and fifty in number. Many of them thought me too white for a Moor.

I observed round the huts some fine bananas, pineapples, cassavas, yams, and various other useful plants. They were well cultivated. It is the women's business to attend to them. The men labour in the rice fields, &c. The heat was very great during the day, which denoted a storm in the evening. We were now approaching the rainy season which in these mountainous districts commences in April, and continues six consecutive months. In the course of the day a little dispute arose between my guide Ibrahim and two Mandingoes of his village, who insisted on having their share of the value of a bullock, which had been given to them by M. Castagnet, at Kakondy. The two Mandingoes came to me, and wished me to decide their difference. However, my decision only made the matter worse, and so irritated my guide, that he threatened to leave me, which would, of course, have thrown me into no little embarrassment. At length, a young negro, who had been to Sierra-Leone and spoke a little English, came to my aid. He helped to interpret what I said, and thus peace was restored among us.

The merchants spent the remainder of the day in examining their goods and I amused myself in looking about the neighbourhood of the village. I saw several furnaces for smelting iron, a metal which is found in great abundance among the mountains. These furnaces, which are from five to ten feet high, and eighteen or twenty feet in circumference, have a chimney at top, and four holes at the base, in the direction of east, west, north and south. At a little distance from the village, there are some small streams, which descend from the mountains and run rapidly over beds of granite. Here I took the opportunity of bathing, and some of the Mandingoes washed their clothes.

At half-past five, on the morning of the 27th, we left the village of Lantégué, to cross the chain of mountains of that name, proceeding to the S. E. Some of these mountains appeared to be three hundred and fifty and four hundred fathoms above the elevated plain on which we were. I observed some very beautiful granite of a whitish-grey colour. We passed not far from a little village, where the Foulahs were tending their cattle. As we crossed the chain of mountains, I saw the poor negroes, with loads on their heads, leaping from precipice to precipice, and every moment expected to see them fall into the yawning gulphs beneath. From the depths proceeds a dull murmur, produced by the numerous springs which rise among the mountains. They fall into the plain beneath, where they form a sort of river. When we descended we saw nothing but mountains on every side, though none appeared so high as those which I had seen in the morning. At the part where we crossed the chain, it extends in the direction from N. E. to S. S. E. I did not perceive any snow. I saw some very beautiful black granite, both in strata three or four feet thick and in blocks. I also saw grey, white, and pale rose-coloured granite of a very beautiful grain. We travelled on in an eastern direction until we reached the banks of the Kakiriman, a little river which runs from north to south, over a bed of granite. Its current is very rapid and its width may be about seventy or eighty ordinary paces. I could trace with my eye the course of this river to the distance of three or four miles and along that space its breadth did not appear to vary. At the point where we forded it the water came up to our waists. Having deviated a little from the course taken by my companions, I was carried to some distance by the current, and the water came up to my arm-pits. The negroes, perceiving me, called out, desiring me to make the best of my way back again. They all exclaimed with one voice, *La allah il allah, Mahommed rasoul oullahi,* and appeared very much alarmed at my danger. A little further down, the river becomes deep, and, as I could not have contended against the current, I should have sunk. At length, by managing to ascend a little, I gained the left bank in safety, but my baggage was completely wet. About eleven in the morning we halted not far from the banks of the river, in a place covered with hillocks of black sand, on which grew numbers of large bamboos. We seated ourselves beneath the trees. The poor slaves were dreadfully fatigued, and though I had no load to carry I was almost as tired as they. I bought some cagnan, a sort of bread which I have already described. This was the first food I had tasted during the whole of the day. Several Foulahs made me little presents. The negroes told me that the river we had just crossed was the Rio Pongo. Want of rice obliged us to pack up our baggage and proceed to Pandeya, a little village inhabited by Foulah herdsmen. On our way we met two negroes, each of whom had on his head a calabash of *foigné* (a small kind of grain), which they would not sell to us. After travelling eleven miles E. S. E. we reached the village about half past twelve. Our road had been level and well wooded, but covered with stones.

Pandeya is situated at the foot of a mountain, and contains from one hundred and fifty to two hundred inhabitants. They all came to see me, and each brought me a little present of milk. After we had reposed for a short time in the shade of some large nédés, and refreshed ourselves with the milk, for which we were indebted to the generosity of the Foulahs, my guide Ibrahim and his comrades proposed to buy a bullock, to celebrate the festival of the Ramadan, which happened on the following day. He asked me, through the medium of the young Foulah, who spoke English, whether I would pay my share of the price. This I declined doing, alleging that I had a long journey to perform with very scanty resources; and Ibrahim said no more on the subject. They purchased the bullock for four bars of tobacco; about the value of two gourdes, the joint contribution of about twelve or fifteen of our party, including the travelling Foulahs.

On the 28th of April, which was the grand festival day, we staid at Pandeya, and about eight in the morning the merchants all ranged themselves in a line to repeat the prayer. I took care to be among them and even affected greater devotion than any of the rest. The prayer being ended, the bullock was killed. The Mandingoes spent nearly an hour in equalizing the lots of meat. They each took a little bit of wood to serve as a measure, and after mingling them all together, the lots were distributed. Some of the meat was dried and smoked, that it might keep for the journey; but a considerable portion was immediately boiled with rice for the festival.

I received numerous visits from Foulahs, who brought me their usual presents of milk and rice, which were all they had to give. The festival was celebrated with considerable gaiety. The Mandingoes, in particular, indulged in tumultuous manifestations of joy. They fired several discharges of musketry, and afterwards all the negroes assembled round my guide's hut and sang songs in his praise. He was, as I have already mentioned, the chief of the caravan; and it was he who furnished the gunpowder for the rejoicings. These people have a bad habit of putting too great a charge of powder into their muskets, and on this occasion one of them burst in the hands of a negro; but fortunately, the poor fellow was not hurt. About eleven in the forenoon Ibrahim, accompanied by the two Mandingoes who were engaged in the dispute to which I have already alluded, came to invite me to partake of their dinner, and they again requested me to forget what had passed. I accepted the invitation. On entering Ibrahim's hut, I saw a large calabash full of boiled rice, upon which was laid a considerable quantity of the beef. We sat down and each helped himself with his hands, according to the negro custom. When the rice was finished, Ibrahim distributed the meat. I observed that the Mandingoes ate an unusual quantity that day. Eating, indeed, seems be the highest pleasure they are capable of enjoying. During the rest of the day they were very merry, and they exchanged the bullock's hide for some rice, which we ate during our journey.

On the 29th of April, the remainder of the meat which had been smoked all night was put into leather bags, and we resumed our journey at six in the morning. Opposite to the village, about half a mile to the north, there was a small chain of mountains, with level summits; and at each extremity of the chain one rises to a considerable height above the rest, like the turret of an ancient castle. These mountains have no vegetation. We proceeded for a mile eastward, upon rocks level with the surface of the ground, of a reddish colour and porous nature, and we next ascended a mountain composed of blocks of beautiful black granite, among which grew various large trees particularly the nédé, which abounds throughout all this part of the country. The road was very bad; we had to walk upon black calcined stones, which had the appearance of being of volcanic origin. After crossing several little streams that flow over beds of rock, we came to a mountain about five or six hundred ordinary paces high. It is called by the natives Touma, and it separates the country of Irnanké from the Fouta-Dhialon. We rested for a short time on its summit. My companions assured me that the road thence to Cambaya, my guide's village, would be better than the preceding part of our journey. I observed in this neighbourhood some very fine indigo, and some bombaces which rivalled in size the enormous baobabs on the banks of the Senegal.

The country of Irnanké lies to the west of the Fouta, and to the east of Kakondy. It has on the north the negroes who inhabit the neighbourhood of Casamance; and on the south the Timannee negroes, who occupy a tract of country not far from Sierra-Leone. Irnanké is studded with lofty mountains, and inhabited by pastoral Foulahs. They possess fine flocks, which are their principal wealth. The complexion of these Foulahs is a lightish chesnut colour; they have good countenances, high foreheads, aquiline noses, and thin lips, and their heads are somewhat of an oval shape. The only point in which they resemble the Mandingoes is their curly hair. They hold themselves very upright, and walk with an air of dignity; for they think themselves far superior to the other negro tribes. Their dress, like that of the Mandingoes, is exceedingly simple; it consists of a coussabe, or shirt, of white cloth, of their own manufacture, and a pair of trowsers. The trowsers are made of coarse cloth; they are very wide, and confined round the waist by means of a buckle; they reach about half-way down the leg, where they are left loose. A cap of the same material completes the costume. When these negroes travel, they are armed with bows and poisoned arrows, and they also carry lances. They rub their bodies all over with butter, and they put a great deal upon their heads, which occasions a very disagreeable smell. The women take remarkable pains in dressing their heads. They plait their hair and adorn it with various glass trinkets. They wear amber necklaces, and their whole appearance is animated and pleasing. In these mountains there are many Dhialonkés, the ancient possessors of the country of Fouta-Dhialon, which was conquered long ago by the Foulahs, who compelled part of the population to embrace Mahometanism. Those who refused to forsake idolatry became tributaries to the almamy, or chief, of Irnanké. They pay their tribute in cattle. These people are very mild and hospitable to the strangers who are continually travelling through their mountainous country. They have a particular dialect, which the Foulahs do not understand.

After resting for a short time, we continued our journey eastward. The road was interspersed with small masses of rock, which incommoded me exceedingly; for, as I could not walk with the sandals of the country, I was obliged to go barefoot. We passed Courgin, a little village containing a population of about one hundred and fifty or two hundred. The masses of rock were succeeded by stones, apparently volcanic. Proceeding nine miles further, to the east, we arrived at three in the afternoon at Comi-Sourignan, a pretty village, situated on a hill, and containing about one hundred and fifty inhabitants. The aspect of the surrounding country was beautiful; it was interspersed with fine hills, covered with brilliant verdure. The soil, which is of a yellow colour, is very productive. The village, enclosed by a quick-set hedge, is very clean. The huts are surrounded by gardens, containing plantations of pistachio-nuts, cassavas, caribbee cabbages, and other things. These gardens, which are cultivated by women and children, are kept in very good order, and the little paths leading to the huts are cleanly swept. The chief, in whose presence we said the prayer, invited Ibrahim and me to his hut, where he made us partake of his dinner, consisting of boiled rice with a little sour milk. We seated ourselves on a mat, near a little fire; for fires are always kept burning here, on account of the humidity of the climate. When our repast was ended, the wife of the chief came and sat down beside us. She listened in silence to our conversation: we were speaking of the christians, who are always objects of contempt among these people. The wife of the chief kindly asked me to take a little milk, and then she went to gather some figs and bananas, and put them into a clean calabash, which she gave to me and my guide. This woman had a pleasing countenance, and her dress, which was very clean, consisted of two breadths of cotton cloth of the manufacture of the country. She had not the offensive smell of the women of the roving Foulahs of Irnanké. The hut was large and in good order; the floor was adorned with handsome designs, made of earth. We passed the night in this pretty village.

At half-past five, on the morning of the 30th of April, we took leave of our kind hosts, and proceeded to the S. E., crossing an extensive plain, apparently susceptible of high cultivation. In descending, we turned an elevated plain, situated in the province of Timbi. The plain in this part is covered with red rocks, level with the ground; the country is, generally, very open. We saw several hillocks within the distance of seven or eight miles round us. We met a Bondou negro, who said that he had come from Boulibané, the capital of the country, and was going on a trading expedition to Kakondy; he had nothing with him but gold. I was very much astonished that this man should undertake so long and difficult a journey on foot, when he was within reach of our establishments at Bakel, which are provided with all sorts of merchandise. We proceeded eastward, crossing a pretty valley, situated between two hills, and containing three villages; the largest is Telewel: its population is, at most, five hundred. I was overtaken by a Foulah, accompanied by one of his wives, carrying on her head a calabash full of milk, which he begged me to accept. Ibrahim, my guide, having stopped for a short time, had informed this Foulah that I was an Arab from the neighbourhood of Mecca, and related to him my adventure at Alexandria. The zealous disciple of the prophet thought that he was performing a meritorious action in the eye of God by giving me a little milk. When he left us he extended his hand to me, and wished me a speedy return to my country. The road now became somewhat more stony, and we halted for a short time beneath the shade of some trees to wait for our companions. Several women brought us bananas and figs, fourteen of which I purchased for three glass beads.

We pursued our journey across a plain, composed of a yellow fertile kind of earth, and we next arrived at Bouma, a village situated near a pretty little stream; the silvery waters flow over a bed of granite in a S. E. direction. This stream falls in cascades, the murmur of which is heard at a considerable distance. After passing this place, we came to enormous rocks of granite level with the ground; our road was interspersed with those little hillocks with which all this part of the country is covered. When we approached Bouma-Filasso, a village on the declivity of a mountain, I saw a great deal of indigo growing spontaneously; I also saw some cotton plantations. The country is clothed with superb vegetation, and has a very beautiful aspect. I remarked several spots recently cleared for planting. We descended a hill, at the foot of which runs the river Cocoulo, which at this part is about forty or forty-five paces wide; it flows rapidly over a bed of granite from N. N. E. to S. W.: where we forded it, the water was more than knee-deep. In several places its bed is dry, and it is necessary to walk over large masses of granite covered with mud, which renders the passage slippery and dangerous. At a little distance from this place it falls over a precipice to the depth of sixty feet, making a terrific noise. I stopped for a short time to contemplate this cataract. The Cocoulo runs among high mountains covered with large trees, among which the native plum-tree is very abundant. After crossing the river, we proceeded S. S. E.; we passed near Marca, a small village, containing from two hundred and fifty to three hundred inhabitants, and situated on a very fertile soil. About three o'clock we passed Dayeb. The road was stony from this place to Tin-foulasso, a village surrounded by cotton plantations, in a plain of grey fertile sand. At five in the afternoon we halted, much fatigued, at Gnéré-temilé, having travelled twelve miles in the course of the day. During our halt a violent storm arose. As I was an object of general curiosity, the inhabitants came out in crowds to look at me; some brought me little presents of milk and smoked meat. Many of these poor creatures had ulcers in different parts of their bodies: I became their physician; and I gave them some caustics (nitrate of silver) and lint. They evinced their gratitude by sending me a good supper. Ibrahim, fearing that I should consume all my stock of medicaments, strongly advised me not to give them any more, alleging as a reason for this uncharitableness, that they might take me for a christian.

At six o'clock in the morning of the 1st of May, we left the village of Gnéré-temilé, the population of which is about two hundred and fifty. The rain of the preceding evening purified the atmosphere and added new charms to the surrounding scenery. We journeyed on cheerfully to E. S. E. I saw an ouroudé, or slave village, surrounded by good plantations of bananas, cotton, cassavas, and yams. We passed Maraca, after which we found ourselves in a sandy plain, containing several small slave villages, and sat down beneath a tree to wait for some of our party, who were lingering behind.

The negroes of the village of Bourwel brought us some delicious oranges: after eating them we pursued our journey along the side of a deep valley adorned with large trees. Having descended a rapid slope, we came to very fertile land. About two in the afternoon We halted at Popoco, situated in the plain, having travelled eight miles since morning.

CHAPTER VII

Popoco — Granite mountains — We cross the Bâ-fing (the principal tributary of the Senegal) near its source — Great cataract — Fouta-Dhialon. — Langoué — Couroufi — Schools — Albinos — Industry of the inhabitants — The traveller obliged to turn physician.

The 2nd of May was employed in procuring carriers for our luggage, as those who had come with us from Kakondy would not proceed any further. About three in the afternoon some of our fellow-travellers left us, and amongst the number was my young interpreter. I confessed that I was sorry to part with him, for his conversation sometimes helped to while away the weariness of the journey. He talked of his country, to which he appeared fondly attached. He was sorry, he said, to see it desolated by the civil war which had existed since it had had two sovereigns, each supported by a formidable party. I shall treat of this subject more at length hereafter.

We escorted our companions out of the village. As we could not procure porters, we were obliged to stay there the whole of the 3rd of May. The inhabitants, having learned who I was from my guide, Ibrahim, thronged to see me, and our hut was all day full of visiters. They overwhelmed me with troublesome questions, and some of them made me little presents. I sent to buy some cassava with glass beads; but the people who sold it would not take payment. The news of the arrival of an Arab, a countryman of the prophet's, spread through all the neighbouring villages. I was visited by several great marabouts, or priests, who in that country receive the name of Tierno. The chief of Tiéléri, a village two miles north of Popoco, sent me a present of some milk, and a colat-nut, a mark of very high respect. The women in this country have an unusual share of curiosity. They came to see me, and gave me cassava. Some of them knelt down when they presented it to me.

Popoco is situated in a fertile plain. The soil is a kind of black sand. The village is large, containing between one hundred and fifty and two hundred slaves, who are employed in agriculture. I saw cassava, yams, and pistachios, thriving well. The inhabitants also grow a considerable quantity of rice and millet. At a little distance from the village there are some orange-trees.

I learned here that the Fouta-Dhialon had been divided by two parties since the death of the almamy Gadry, whose reign had been tranquil. Tierno-Boubacar, and Tierno-Yayaye, each claimed the right of succeeding him, and they were at war. Yayaye, whose party was at first the stronger, withdrew for some time to wage war against the infidels. This hazardous expedition proved very unfortunate for him, as it afforded his adversary time to ingratiate himself with the people. When Yayaye returned from his expedition, in which he sustained some loss, circular letters were distributed throughout the country, proclaiming the elevation of Boubacar to the dignity of chief of the state. Yayaye retired, but without renouncing his pretensions, and still retaining a very formidable party.

Damasisya is situated to the north. We proceeded four miles E. S. E. over a gravelly soil, and at two in the afternoon halted at Dité, where we changed our carriers. I met with a very kind reception in this little village, where I found a negro who had seen me at Kakondy; he eagerly related to the inhabitants the story which I had invented, and which produced a good effect, and was of great advantage to me. Timbo, the capital of the Fouta, is two days' journey S. E. ¼ S. of this village, which is surrounded by a quick-set hedge.

On the 5th of May, at five in the morning some new milk was brought for my breakfast; I drank it, and was soon seized with a violent retching and pains in my stomach, which continued during a great part of the day. This illness obliged me to stop in the village with my guide. I must confess, that I entertained some apprehension of having been poisoned; but the conduct of the Foulahs, who came to inquire after me, and who appeared greatly concerned for my illness, removed this suspicion. One of them made me a present of a large fowl, which was eaten by my guide and his slaves; for my part, I could not touch food. The caravan set off, leaving me behind; but, about three in the afternoon, finding myself better, we started with the intention of overtaking it. Proceeding over a gravelly tract in a S. S. E. direction, we passed Foucouba, a village containing a population of five or six hundred. We next reached the village of Diqui, containing three or four hundred inhabitants. Here we halted a little before sun-set, and went to visit a friend of my guide's, who gave us a very kind reception. The chief invited me and Ibrahim to his hut, and asked us to partake of his supper of rice and sour milk. I ate a little of it; but this sort of food was not calculated to restore my disordered stomach. The chief proposed that I should go and see the almamy, who, he said, would receive me well, and make me handsome presents. I was not inclined to put his generosity to the test, being fearful that he might detain me. My guide answered for me, and observed, that when we should arrive at Kankan-Fodéa, his country, he would conduct me to the chief of Timbo. Our host sent us a supper of rice with roasted pistachio-nuts.

The morning of the 6th was rainy. I was visited by several women, who brought me little presents of milk, rice, oranges, &c. A shoemaker gave me a pair of sandals, which were very acceptable, mine being out of repair. About nine o'clock, the rain having ceased, we departed. Several of the inhabitants escorted us out of the village. Our course was E. S. E. The rain had purified and refreshed the air. We passed Courou, a village situated at the foot of a hill, twenty-five or thirty fathoms high. We passed through a fertile and picturesque plain, thickly bespangled with small white flowers. I saw a number of slaves employed in preparing the ground for sowing rice and various kinds of grain. After crossing a little stream, we arrived near Bady, a village agreeably situated on the banks of a rivulet which we forded, the water being nearly as high as our waists. This village contains a population of three hundred and fifty, or four hundred; it is situated in a plain, and overlooked by a hill. I saw in the neighbourhood some good plantations of a small species of tobacco.

At five o'clock in the afternoon we arrived at Doudé, a village of the same size as Bady, and about a mile and a half to the E. S. E. of it. The chief came to receive us at the entrance of the palisade, by which his grounds were surrounded. I remarked some cotton very badly cultivated. They sow it broad-cast, as we do corn, so that it grows too close, which prevents its thriving. I saw a young negress gathering the cotton, which appeared to me to be of inferior quality. We were lodged in a large and handsome hut with two doors, situated on the left of our route. Our host felt highly honoured in having beneath his roof a countryman of the prophet's; for my guide had related to him the pretended events of my youth. He came up close to me, stroked my head with his hands, and then rubbed his own face, as if this contact with a countryman of the prophet's had in it something holy or salutary. We performed our devotions together. The old man had collected near an orange-tree a great number of small flints, on which, in the spirit of penitence, he knelt to prayer. This greatly annoyed me; for I was obliged to follow his example. He afterwards presented to me a child of four or five years of age, who had sore eyes, and begged me to cure him if I could. I was much embarrassed, and told him that I had no remedy for the disorder; but my guide had assured him of the contrary, and the old man, supposing there was a want of inclination on my part, offered to pay me. I told him that my baggage had been sent forward, and that I could not overtake it till next day. He was silent, but appeared not to be best pleased with my answer. In all my life I never saw such a disease as that under which this child laboured. It suffered no pain, but it was almost deprived of sight. I have since thought that it might be a kind of cataract. The marabouts, who officiate as doctors in this country, had ineffectually exhausted all their skill in grigris, or amulets, for the patient. They could do nothing more, and the child was abandoned to its fate. I advised the pa rents to wash its eyes with a decoction of baobab leaves, which might serve as a substitute for mallows, and to take the child to Sierra-Leone for medical assistance; but they shrunk with horror from the idea of placing it in the hands of christians.

Our host gave us rice and sour milk for supper, which we ate seated under an orange tree.

At seven o'clock in the morning of the 7th of May, we prepared for departure. On going out I observed that the goats had been put for the night into a loft, ten or twelve feet high. We set out in an E. S. E. direction, and proceeded four miles down hill, by a very stony road, which brought us to Couraco, a village situated near a hill, at the foot of which flows a pretty stream. We seated ourselves on the margin of this stream to take our breakfast of rice, which we had saved from the preceding evening. Our repast being ended, we proceeded gaily on our way, in the same direction, over a very good sandy soil. We passed near Coulinco, a village containing from five to six hundred inhabitants, and surrounded by a quick-set hedge. Farther on we came to Cagnola, a fine village, situated near a hill, below which runs a stream, that we had to cross. After we had ascended the hill, the road was covered with ferruginous stones. We found ourselves on an elevated plain, whence we could perceive a chain of very high mountains, extending further than the eye could reach, from N. E. ¼ E. to S. W. They appeared to be covered with fine vegetation. The Bâ-fing has its source there; and there are likewise numerous ponds of beautiful limpid water. These mountains give rise to several large rivers and streams, which fertilize this fine country and clothe it with a verdure, that is incessantly renewed. On the slope there are to be seen many small slave villages, surrounded with plantations of cotton and the fruits which are to be found in our colonies. These charming and picturesque spots delight the eye and help to relieve the monotony of the journey. Rice and many other articles are cultivated here.

A violent storm came on from the east. We rapidly descended by a declivity, covered with large blocks of black granite, and red sand mixed with stones of the same colour. We proceeded three miles E. S. E. over a stony road. I observed some ferruginous rocks, and numerous springs issuing from among them. The storm approached, and we were overtaken by the rain, which fell in torrents. I used my umbrella, but it was of little service. On every side the rain water came pouring down the hills, and swelled the streams. We hurried forward to some huts, situated near a little hill, and there we halted. This hamlet is called Bâfila, a name probably derived from its vicinity to the Bâ-fing (black river). We entered the hut of an old woman, who cheerfully afforded us hospitality. She gazed earnestly at me, and told me that she had never till then seen a Moor. Her little dwelling was surrounded with cassavas, caribbee cabbages, giraumons, pistachios, and gombos.

I likewise observed many kinds of herbs, with which I was unacquainted. As soon as the rain ceased, I went out to walk round the garden. The sun was not visible, and the clouds which had gathered upon the tops of the mountains, rendered the atmosphere gloomy and damp. I saw, at some distance in the plain, a stream running over a bed of pebbles, and producing a soft murmur. I might almost have fancied myself in some romantic region of fairy-land. I returned to the humble habitation of the old woman; she was gathering herbs for the supper of her little family, which consisted of two lads, who, she told me, were working in the field. I went back to our hut and roasted in the ashes some pieces of cassava, which the old woman had given me. Shortly afterwards the two young negroes entered. They had no clothing except a small piece of cloth fastened round their middle. As soon as they learned that a Moor proceeding to Mecca had become their guest, they came to me, and asked me how I was, in a very kind tone. They invited me to their hut, which was much larger than ours; and they fetched a large mat to cover me. The rain, which had begun again, continued all night, accompanied with dreadful claps of thunder and flashes of lightning, in quick succession. When I entered their hut, the kind negroes seated me near the fire upon a sheep-skin, and offered me a little sour milk, which probably they had intended for their own supper; but I should have offended them by refusing it. The mother cooked a little foigné, which grows in abundance in these mountains, for the family's supper. She placed a small pot on the fire, by the side of a large one, for boiling the herbs which she had gathered that evening. I recognized among them the calabash, the giraumon, allspice, brette, sesamum, and many others;—to these she added a little gombo. The foigné, when cooked, was placed in calabashes to be eaten. I now perceived two little girls, whom I had not before remarked. They ate their supper apart, and the old woman reserved her own portion in the pot. Ibrahim sent me my supper of rice and milk which the negroes had given me. They would not partake of it although I pressed them. They invited me to take some of theirs, which I at first declined; but, as they urged me, I took a handful and withdrew, I really wondered how the poor creatures could eat this rice; for it was without either salt or butter. They, did not like to touch my supper because they were slaves. We said prayers together, and lay down upon mats; but I was kept awake all night by the thunder.

On the 8th of May, at six in the morning, after eating a piece of the cassava which was cooked the evening before we took leave of our hostess; for the lads were already gone to the fields. We proceeded eastward; then turning into the mountains, we were obliged to climb from rock to rock. There is, however, some very good soil. We arrived on the banks of the Bâ-fing (the black river) so called because its bed consists of enormous rocks of black granite. Some of these rocks are pointed and very sharp, so that they often cut the feet of the negroes in crossing the river. The Bâ-fing is the principal tributary of the Senegal: it runs from south to north among the mountains. The masses of granite, of which its bed is composed, form several islets. Its current is astonishingly rapid and white with foam, which I supposed to be occasioned by some cataract. I questioned the negroes on the subject and their answers verified my conjecture. They told me they had seen the cataract in going to Timbo, and assured me that it fell from a great height with a loud noise. We were very near the source of the river, which in this part might be about a hundred feet wide and a foot or eighteen inches deep; but its depth varies. We crossed it not without some difficulty and with the assistance of poles. I saw with some alarm a poor negro tottering beneath his load; however, we all reached the left bank without any serious accident. Several of our party had their feet cut by the sharp rocks, and although I had nothing to carry I did not escape unhurt. A great number of persons were assembled at the place where we crossed. They took no notice of me, supposing me to be a Moor.

On the right bank of the river I observed some wretched huts occupied by smiths. We continued our route to E. S. E. The soil consisted of very good red mould covered with the finest vegetation. We arrived at Langoué, a village containing between three and four hundred inhabitants. It is situated on a somewhat elevated plain, whence high mountains are to be seen in every direction. Here a storm overtook us. The inhabitants gave us a hut and sheep-skins to sit on. We made a good fire, for the atmosphere was damp. The Foulahs soon came to visit us. Not having observed me enter the place, they were much surprised to see me and took me at first for a white. They asked my guide in the Mandingo language whither I has going, and what was the object of my journey. Ibrahim very promptly informed them how I had been taken by the Europeans. The Foulahs congratulated me on my zeal and my attachment to my religion. They presented me with some rice, milk, cassava, and a fowl. They urged me to go to Timbo, assuring me that the almamy would be very happy to see me, and that he would most willingly give me a horse and a guide to take me into my own country, because, as they said, he held the countrymen of the prophet in high estimation. They added that the almamy had at that moment gone to make war against Firga, an idolatrous country, but that doubtless he would soon return to Timbo.

Seated round the fire we made a cheerful breakfast on what the Foulahs gave me. The storm having ceased, we left them, and about nine o'clock proceeded to the S. E. The sun was obscured by clouds, and the atmosphere gloomy and cool. The country, refreshed by the morning's rain, presented a most beautiful prospect. I perceived in the distance some pretty hamlets, watered by a multitude of small clear streams, flowing over beds of pebbles. They wind among the small hillocks, and seem to quit those enchanting scenes with regret. The hamlets are inhabited by agricultural slaves.

We entered the passes of the mountains, which are five or six hundred feet high, and covered with large trees, among which I observed the nédé and the caura, or plum-tree of this country. The soil is composed of very rich grey sand, mixed with gravel. I remarked likewise some blocks of white quartz. My attention was arrested alternately by the cries of large red monkeys from two feet to two feet and a half in height, and the warbling of a multitude of birds whose plumage exhibits an endless variety of colours. We descended into a plain composed of very productive black mould, watered by a little stream, which, I was told, after many windings empties itself into the Senegal. The natives call it the Telonco. It takes its rise in the neighbourhood of a high mountain, which we had much trouble in ascending. Having crossed it, we arrived at Bougnetery, a slave village where we rested a short time, having proceeded four miles and a half to the S. E.

Continuing our journey, we turned a little mountain composed of beautiful black granite, and destitute of any kind of vegetation. A little to the E. S. E. we saw some villages in the distance: the country was covered with pasturage, which being watered by small streams grows luxuriantly. These streamlets flow on into the valleys amongst blocks of beautiful black granite. We met a Moor, with whom I conversed for a short time. He asked me some questions respecting the whites, and congratulated me on my determination to return to the religion of my fathers. We descended into a plain and proceeded three miles to the E. S. E. The country still presented the same aspect. At half past four in the afternoon, we arrived very much fatigued at Foudedia. We passed the night at the village and there found the people of our caravan who had gone on before. The chief gave us a good hut and sent us a supper of rice and milk. Several men belonging to the village, who had formed part of the expedition of the almamy Yayaye against Firga, arrived. They said that the almamy had received a check and had lost some of his troops in battle; and that one of the inhabitants of Foudedia was among the number of the slain. This intelligence occasioned great grief. The wives of the deceased, accompanied by many of his relations and friends, paraded the village, singing in a shrill tone and alternately clapping their hands and striking their foreheads. Having continued this ceremony some time, they returned to their huts, followed by a crowd of women imitating their gestures. Their cries seemed to augment their grief: they rolled on the ground striking their bodies and uttering dreadful groans. The children shed sincere tears, but the women merely made a noise; deep as their affliction seemed to be it lasted only half an hour. They then appeared clothed in white; they had a calm and resigned air, and immediately resumed their usual occupations. The men were assembled round the mosque, and seated on the ground. They appeared really afflicted at the death of their comrade, and loudly censured the conduct of their sovereign.

On the 9th of May, at six o'clock in the morning, we pursued our route in an E. S. E. direction. We went two miles, over a soil at first rather stony but which afterwards changed to black sand covered with gravel, till we came to some rocks of white quartz, and crossed a little stream the waters of which reached up to our knees. It flowed to the north over a sandy bed. Its banks were thickly wooded. I observed many tamarind-trees. The soil continued level and covered with gravel. We met many persons going to the market of Labé, to sell calabashes and earthen pots manufactured in the country. These pots appeared to be of good materials and of much better workmanship than those made on the banks of the Senegal. I even saw some that were very well glazed. We proceeded three miles towards the east, crossing very deep ravines.

Along all the road I saw troops of monkeys, which leaped from tree to tree, and barked after us like dogs. We arrived at Dimayara, the first village of the Fouta-Dhialon, inhabited by Mandingoes. It contains a population of from seven to eight hundred. It is situated at the foot of a chain of mountains extending from N. to S. S. E. These mountains are not very high. They are composed of granite, and are destitute of vegetation. The village of Faramansa is a little to the left of Dimayrara. We proceeded for three miles to the east among the gorges of the mountains. Near the village of Sela I saw many Mandingoes engaged in tanning hides. Pursuing the same route, we arrived near an ourondé, or slave-village, where I bought some pistachios. At the distance of two miles and a half from Sela, we descended a hill covered with large rocks of granite. We sat down for a moment, to wait for some of our comrades who had lagged behind. We afterwards proceeded over a level soil, composed of very hard sand. I passed near an enormous rock of black granite, from a hundred to a hundred and twenty-five fathoms in height, without any kind of vegetation, except upon the summit, where

I saw some slender bamboos. This rock rises in the midst of a plain of very fertile grey sand, producing rice, maize, millet, pistachios, yams, onions, and giraumons. We passed near Kouroufi, which has its name from the rock that I have just described. It is a large village, containing between five and six hundred inhabitants, Foulahs and Mandingoes. This village forms part of Kankan-Fodea, a little province of Fouta-Dhialon. At five o'clock in the evening we arrived at Sanguessa, a little village, five miles from the place where I had bought the pistachios. We had constantly travelled over a very level soil composed of grey sand, in a S. E. direction. Two of our companions were natives of Sanguessa. They were moreover friends of my guide's, which procured us the advantage of becoming the guests of the chief. He gave us a good hut, and ordered a number of mats to be spread in his court-yard, on which we seated ourselves to converse till supper time. The conversation turned chiefly on me, and afterwards various questions were asked respecting the journey of the Mandingoes to Kakondy. About ten at night, our two friends sent us some supper, at which I played my part, for I had eaten nothing all day, excepting some pistachios and a little of the fruit of the nédé steeped in water. The chief also sent us a supper of rice and sour milk, to which he added by way of luxury a little butter. During the evening Mamadi, one of our companions, introduced me to his wife, and brought all his little children to see me. The neighbours were also admitted. They crowded round me and gazed at me with curiosity. Mamadi, being acquainted with the story which I had invented, took pleasure in relating it to them, and added that I was a *Souloca-tigui* (a real Arab.) He then showed me over his little habitation. In the garden I observed some feet of ground planted with tobacco and gombo, which his wife had cultivated in his absence. This little village contains from three to four hundred inhabitants.

The whole of the morning of the 10th of May was occupied in paying visits to the friends of my guide. About ten o'clock I was sent for by the elders of the village: I was taken in front of the mosque, where I saw a great assemblage of Mandingoes; they were seated on the ground around two large calabashes, filled with little cakes, or handfuls of bruised rice, moistened with water, and covered with red and white colat-nuts. I seated myself on a sheep-skin which was offered me. I thought, at first, that the generous Mandingoes intended to make me a present; but I was egregiously mistaken. The conversation turned on my residence among the christians, concerning whom they entertained very erroneous ideas; they overwhelmed me with troublesome questions, and wandered widely from their subject. At length a marabout pronounced some prayers over the little cakes, which were thus converted into a sort of holy bread; they were then distributed among all present, and even the absent were not forgotten, their share being sent to them; two pieces were given to me, which, however, I did not eat. I knew not what was the occasion of this kind of treat, but conjectured that it was to celebrate the safe arrival of the traders who belonged to the place: on inquiry, I learned that it was in honour of two boys whose heads had been shaved for the first time. After the ceremony, a good breakfast was sent to us. About eleven in the forenoon we took leave of our companions, who promised to come and see me at Cambaya, where I intended to stop for some days. I was indebted for this mark of attention to the promise which I had made to give them a pair of scissors.

We continued our route to the S. E., over the mountains of granite, which extend in that direction, and amongst which there are some very fine plains of sand. We arrived near the Tankisso, a large stream which flows from W. S. W., and runs to the east, making a thousand windings amongst the mountains. The Mandingo negroes, who had made many journeys to Timbo, told me that this stream issued from the Bâ-fing, a little below that capital; that it emptied itself into the Dhioliba; and that Bouré, a country rich in gold, is situated on the left bank of the Tankisso, about half or three-quarters of a day's journey from the Dhioliba. My companions bathed whilst waiting for Ibrahim, who had stopped behind. Continuing our route, we descended a little mountain of pale pink quartz, the strata of which are eighteen or twenty inches thick. This road brought us into a beautiful extensive plain of firm sand, completely surrounded by high mountains, apparently of granite. In this plain was situated the village to which Ibrahim, my guide, belonged. We proceeded three miles to the east. In some places the soil consisted of grey clayey mould, mixed with small gravel. The Tankisso, after flowing among the mountains, falls in a cascade, and winds through the plain, which it fertilizes by its inundations. We advanced slowly, waiting for night to make our entrance into the village. We recrossed the Tankisso, the water of which was up to our waists. A little after sun-set we stopped to offer up our prayers; my companions then prepared to announce their arrival by a discharge of musketry, which they fired as they entered the village, about three miles eastward of our last station. When we entered the court of my guide's hut, we were greeted by a second discharge of musketry. Joy was painted in every face; the negroes embraced their children, taking them up in their arms, and inquiring after their health and that of their friends. The women also appeared equally pleased at the return of their husbands, but they did not give way to that natural and sincere joy which would be manifested on similar occasions in Europe: they approached their husbands with an air of timidity, and lowered the knee to the earth, in token of salutation, but without asking any questions. The neighbours ran in crowds to congratulate their friends on the happy termination of their journey; bullocks' hides were spread in the court-yard, and we sat down upon them in a circle, while the moon shone brightly above our heads. Much conversation took place respecting the circumstances of the journey, and the price of different commodities, especially salt. No notice had as yet been taken of me, but, as soon as I was observed, every one looked at me with astonishment, and the question, "Who is this man?" was repeated from mouth to mouth. Ibrahim was glad of the opportunity to relate my whole history, as I had told it to him; which rendered me still more an object of curiosity: I was importuned with questions, to which my guide had the kindness to reply for me. The court-yard was filled the whole evening, and about nine o'clock, a supper, consisting of rice and meat very well cooked, was brought to us: two of our travelling companions added theirs, and our party consisted of about twenty, for many of Ibrahim's relations remained without waiting for the ceremony of an invitation. All ate with great avidity, and yet no one seemed satisfied. When the company had retired, my guide sent for me to partake of some couscous, made of very good cow's milk, and then invited me to retire to rest on a bullock's hide, which he had ordered to be prepared for me in the hut of one of his wives. Although the weather was very hot, a fire had been lighted in the hut, and I found myself very much annoyed by the heat, and particularly by the smoke, which had no vent but through the straw-covered roof. My guide's wife lay in the middle of the hut, surrounded by her children.

On the 11th of May, at eight in the morning, Ibrahim came to pay his respects to me, and asked me to go and see his father, the chief of the village of Cambaya. He was an old blind man, and we found him lying in his hut, on a kind of platform of earth, raised six inches from the ground. It was three feet broad and six and a half or seven feet long, and was covered with a mat. At one end of this couch, a smooth plank was fixed, and above that was laid another piece of wood six inches thick, intended to raise the head and serve the purpose of a pillow. The old man appeared to be at least eighty years old. He had been informed of my arrival on the preceding evening, and his son introduced me, saying that I had come to salute him. He raised himself with some difficulty from his couch, and stretched out his hand to me, with the usual salutation, *Salam alekoum*. He passed his hand over the whole of my person, saying *el-arab, el-arab acagnie* (Arab, thou art good). He appeared to regret that he could not see me, and asked me if I was quite determined to return to my country, promising me a safe escort thither, and every now and then asking me in a jocose manner to remain among the Mandingoes. He treated me with great kindness, and made me a present of two colat-nuts which Ibrahim ate, for they were too bitter for me. My guide introduced me to several of his friends, who received me kindly.

My hut was all day filled with people who came to visit me out of curiosity, and who asked me a thousand questions. Several of them informed me that they had been at Sierra-Leone, where they had seen many whites; adding that I was very like them, and that they did not believe I was an Arab. They said to each other *Lo forto, forto,* (he is a European). Some said this merely in jest; but others sincerely believed it. However, Ibrahim manfully took my part, asserting that I was a *souloca-tigui, tigui* (a real Arab) and that a christian would never perform the salam and study the Koran.

In the course of the day Ibrahim desired one of his wives to prepare a warm bath for me. He lodged me in company with an old marabout of Bondou, who had come to this part of the country to officiate as a schoolmaster. He taught the children of the village the Koran. The method of teaching adopted among all the Musulmans of the interior of Africa is to write on small boards verses of the Koran, which are chanted by the scholars as they sit round a large fire. The lesson is written by the master himself, until the scholars are sufficiently advanced to write it themselves. At Cambaya this sort of public, school is very well managed: the master maintains the most rigid discipline. The school is attended by girls as well as boys; but the education of females is much neglected. It is thought enough if they know the first verses of the Koran: boys, on the other hand, are required to learn it all by heart, after which a more able master is found for them, and he explains to them the most difficult passages of the sacred book. The scholars, are, in some respects, the servants of their master. They fetch wood and water for him, clean his hut, cultivate his field, and gather in his harvest. The parents of the children make the tutor some little presents of cloth, tobacco, and seed to sow in his garden. The schoolmaster of Cambaya had a high reputation for piety. He was poor and took his meals at the house of the chief, who also sent for me to partake of all their repasts. In the hut of the Bondouké (man of Bondou) I slept on the ground, upon which was spread a mat which Ibrahim had given me. The old marabout every night kindled a fire in his hut, the smoke of which I found exceedingly unpleasant. His religious zeal led him to rouse me every morning at three o'clock, to go to the mosque and return thanks to God; for the old man exercised the two-fold functions of priest and schoolmaster. The Mandingoes were far from being so very devout. They said their prayers in their huts at five or six o'clock. We were often the only persons in the mosque, though the old man used every endeavour to summon the faithful. He complained that the Mandingoes were not sufficiently attentive to prayer. On returning to our hut, I lay down on my mat to rest; but my companion, instead of following my example, spent the rest of the morning at his prayers. The good old man was very kind to me. Ibrahim was not the only person who invited him to eat with him. Many others did the same, and thus, though the old man was poor, he lived very well. I found myself extremely comfortable in the village. The people had become accustomed to my person, and my assiduity in fulfilling my religious duties, banished every suspicion of me. There was, however, one man who persisted in asserting that I was a white. He pretended to speak Arabic, of which he only knew a few words, and those he pronounced so ill that it was with difficulty I could understand him. This vexed me a little, though nobody paid much attention to what he said.

On the 13th, I was sitting at the door of my hut, holding in my hand a small board and some leaves of the Koran which I had brought with me. I was going to write down a souriat, or charm, which I wished to learn by heart, when I saw this Mandingo, who always seemed ill-disposed towards me. I beckoned to him, and, having invited him to sit down beside me, I asked him to write the souriat which I wished to learn. He was flattered by this mark of my confidence, and immediately did what I wished. From that time he became my best friend, and proclaimed through the village that there was no doubt of my being an Arab. When about to take my departure, I went to see him accompanied by my guide. He gave me a grigri, which he said would preserve me from all danger. I accepted the precious talisman with warm expressions of gratitude.

A white infant, the offspring of a negro and negress, was brought to me. The child was about eighteen or twenty months old. Its mother placed it in my arms and I examined it attentively. Its hair was curly and white, and its eye-lashes and eye-brows of a light flaxen colour. The forehead, nose, cheeks, and chin, were slightly tinged with red, and the rest of the skin was white. The eyes were light blue; but the pupil was of a red flame colour. The lips were of a rather dark red. I remarked that the child had very defective sight. I endeavoured to make it look up by drawing its attention to my beads; but it appeared to suffer pain, cried, and held down its head. It was just beginning to cut its teeth. Its lips were rather thick, and, indeed, it had altogether the Mandingo physiognomy. The infant appeared to be in good health. The negroes have no dislike to a white skin; they merely consider it as a disease. I was informed that the children of parents of this kind, that is to say, Albinos, are black.

On the night of the 13th, a gale, blowing from the east, brought us rather a violent storm. We had no rain, but a great deal of thunder and lightning. Next day the sister of the almamy Yayaye came to see Ibrahim's wife. Sho in formed me that a French christian, named Lesno, had come to Timbo, whither he had been sent by the chief of the Senegal. She spoke highly of the generosity of the stranger, and told me that he had solicited the almamy's permission to visit the sources of the Dhioliba. This permission, however, was not granted, and, indeed, he was not allowed to go further than Timbo, and had, in consequence, returned to the Senegal. This was said to have happened about a month before I heard of it;—no doubt the name had been corrupted, but I have not yet ascertained who was the traveller alluded to.

On the morning of the 14th of May, Ibrahim fired several musket-shots, as a signal for his friends to come and receive some little presents of tobacco which he destined for them. The court was soon crowded with old men, and as the portions had been made up on the preceding day, there was nothing to do but to distribute them; he also gave some blue Guinea cloth to each of his three wives for their dresses. After this distribution, Ibrahim was overwhelmed with benedictions. The women danced, and sang his praises, and the men offered up prayers for his prosperity. The good old schoolmaster was not forgotten. After our breakfast, which was always equally frugal, Ibrahim and I walked to the ourondé to see the slaves employed in preparing the ground for sowing. The poor slaves work entirely naked, exposed to the heat of a burning sun. The presence of their master intimidates them, and the fear of punishment expedites the work; but they make themselves amends in his absence. The women, who had very little clothing, had their children tied to their backs. They were employed in collecting the dry grass, which, being burnt, forms a kind of manure, indeed, the only kind they use.

Ibrahim assured me that rice in these fields grows to the height of four feet. The soil, which is composed of a very hard grey sand, is fertilized by the inundations of the Tankisso. The uplands, which the inundations do not reach, are planted with yams, cassava, maize, small millet, and foigné, which is much cultivated here. The foigné is sown in the course of May, and gathered in the month of July, at which time the rice is no more than four inches above the ground. Two harvests of foigné may be gathered during the year. But for the foigné, which grows very rapidly, this country would frequently be subject to famine, for the people are accustomed to sow no more rice than what they absolutely need, and very often less; in which latter case they have recourse to the foigné. I sat down for a moment under the shade of a tree, to watch the slaves work. They appeared to perform their tasks much better than the negroes employed by the Europeans on the western coast; They use but one agricultural implement, which is a hoe, made in the country, six inches long by four broad; the handle from eighteen to twenty inches long, is very much bent. Previously to sowing their rice the ground is broken up to the depth of about a foot, but the same preparation is not made for sowing the foigné. They merely cut the grass, and sow the seed broad-cast, before the ground is properly prepared, then draw the grass over the seed, which thus becomes covered. It is the business of the women to perform this simple operation. When the foigné rises above the ground, no pains are taken to remove the weeds which impede its growth. Greater attention however, is bestowed on the rice; the ground in which it grows is carefully cleared of noxious weeds. In the Fouta, I observed that the Foulahs spread burnt dung over the ground which they intend to sow: they also burn all kinds of roots and grass for the same purpose. I approached the Tankisso, the banks of which are well covered with trees: indeed, I saw the branches of several extend across the river, the navigation of which could only be attempted in the rainy season. I bathed, and found the water up to my arm-pits. The banks of the river, I observed, are composed of grey argillaceous earth, mixed with fine sand.

I rejoined Ibrahim, and we went together to see the huts of the slaves. An old woman was employed in preparing the dinner of the husbandmen, who provide their own food. Behind their huts there are small plantations of caribbee cabbage, which the women cultivate. As we were sitting near the labourers, the old woman gave her master a portion of the dinner, which she had just prepared; consisting of a calabash of foigné boiled without salt, with the addition of a sauce of different herbs and gombo, which the want of butter and salt rendered very unpalatable. I ate about a handful of it; but my guide, a little more dainty than I, refused to take any; the poor slaves, however, seemed to relish it. I was informed that, in the Fouta-Dhialon, the negroes are allowed two days in the week to work in their own fields, that is to say, the ground which furnishes their subsistence. One of Ibrahim's women brought for our dinner a calabash full of rice and milk, which she had carried on her head. We did not return to the village until a short time before day-break. My guide behaved very kindly to me, and in the evening, sitting with him in his court-yard, I amused myself by playing with his children. However, at my departure, I thought to penetrate to the east, and learned, with regret, that Ibrahim would not accompany me to Bouré, according to his promise. He alleged that he was prevented from going with me by the necessity of attending to his plantations; but that if I would wait for him, he would fulfil his promise. This proposition was far from being satisfactory to me, for I was very anxious to see myself to the east of the Fouta. I was afraid of being discovered by the Foulahs, and wished to reach Kankan before the rains, which already began to be very frequent, should have fairly set in.

On the 17th of May, I went with Ibrahim to the village, to see a drum made, which is used by these people in time of war. There were twenty Mandingoes employed in making it. The drum consisted of a large bowl, formed of the trunk of a tree, three or four feet in circumference, and from six to eight inches deep, covered with a piece of untanned bullock's hide. At the bottom of the drum were pasted a great many bits of paper, inscribed with Arabic characters. These were amulets, to preserve them from their enemies. They were employed a whole day at this work, which they regarded as an amusement.

The day was hot and stormy, and the sun was several times obscured by dark and thick clouds. In the evening a violent south wind rose, followed by thunder and lightning. Thick black clouds gathered on the summit of the mountains, surrounding the beautiful plain of Kankan-Fodéa. About eight in the evening, a heavy rain set in, and lasted all night. I could not sleep, and passed the time in reflecting on the difficulties which I should have to surmount, in crossing a country intersected by rivers and large streams, which in this season overflow their banks. I travelled on foot, for the appearance of humility which I had imposed upon myself during this journey did not allow me to purchase an animal to ride on, which would have awakened the cupidity of the various tribes that I had to visit; thoroughly persuaded that the success of my undertaking depended on this appearance of poverty.

The old schoolmaster fell ill, and I became his physician. He had a fever, and I gave him some doses of sulphate of quinine, and, afterwards, a dose of salts as a purgative; I then advised him to buy a fowl to make broth, seasoned with brettes, a sort of herb which grows in that country, but the poor old man had not the means of buying a fowl. I begged Ibrahim to make him a present of one, but he replied coldly that he had none, though I saw twenty running about in his yard. I gave the old man five tobacco leaves, to purchase a fowl, which Ibrahim found for that price; he gave it to one of his women to cook, and the schoolmaster speedily recovered. I had given Ibrahim some doses of jalap, which he had asked me for, and though nothing ailed him, he took a dose of it, with the view of having a claim on some of the broth, which he saw preparing for my patient. It was rumoured among the inhabitants that I possessed medicines for all sorts of disorders, and I was much importuned and harassed for them: Some had ulcers on the arms or legs, others, fever and bowel complaint; I was teazed all day long by demands for medicine. To cure the ulcers, I washed them with a caustic, and then dressed them with lint; and to those suffering from fever I administered a few doses of quinine, and directed a regimen, which did not always please my patients. To act up to the character of doctor, I sometimes grew angry, and threatened to abandon to their fate those who did not follow my directions. The only medicines I had were those few with which the English doctors of Sierra-Leone had been kind enough to furnish me, and I was anxious to keep them for myself, presuming that I might need them; but the Mandingoes imagined that my stock was inexhaustible, and that it might be beneficially employed in all kinds of distempers. They were continually asking me for physic, and though I was obliged to refuse them, yet they continually renewed their applications, observing that they were Musulmans as well as I, and that no Musulman ought to withhold a service which he can perform. Wearied by their importunity, I sometimes left them in an ill humour and went to lie down. They then cried out "He is a Christian! See how he behaves to us! He has medicine, and will not give any to us Musulmans." In these dilemmas, I was always much indebted to Ibrahim, who told his countrymen that I had been brought up among christians, and had learned their manners. But they constantly renewed their entreaties, and, in the end, succeeded in getting what they wanted. During the whole period of my residence at Cambaya, I was teazed in this way by the inhabitants, who were not satisfied with obtaining my medicines for nothing, but also expected tobacco, scissors, and Guinea cloth, to make coussabes. Several children used to come into the yard and ask me to dress their sores. At length, after innumerable importunities of this kind, which I omit to mention, these Mandingoes, more selfish and ignorant than deliberately wicked, began to accommodate themselves to my character, and ceased to regard me as a white. In fact, they never could conceive it possible that a European should undertake so long a journey on foot, and alone, merely from philanthropic motives. As they live in a state of ignorance and simplicity, similar to that of our first parents, unacquainted with wealth and luxury, the existence of learned societies in Europe, formed for the purpose of meliorating their condition and extending to them the advantages of knowledge and all the benefits of civilization, is to them a thing quite incomprehensible.

Ibrahim was not more sagacious than the other negroes. He did not solicit me directly, but pretended that he wished to purchase every thing; he coveted in particular, my baggage. He had brought a quantity of Guinea cloth and tobacco from Kakondy, but that did not prevent him from continually proposing to buy what I had. He alleged that my Guinea cloth was finer than his, and that the flavour of my tobacco was superior, though they were both of precisely the same quality. Sometimes he hinted to me that he was without trowsers, or that his coussabe was quite worn out; and in this way he suggested the necessity of purchasing what he wanted from me, in the hope that I should make him a present of it. While we were at Popoco, he took a fancy to a fine piece of muslin, which served me for a turban. He begged that I would sell it to him when we arrived at his village. I made him a present of it, and in return, he overwhelmed me with endless thanks.

I shall here relate an anecdote relative to my character of physician, which the Mandingoes made me assume in spite of myself.

On the 17th, I gave to a man, who had long solicited me, a dose of jalap for his wife, who he said, had the colic. He begged me to call and see her; I visited her and found her really in great pain. I made the husband promise to kill a fowl and make a refreshing broth of it, which she was to take after the jalap had operated. He came to me next day and told me that the medicine had operated very well, but that his wife still suffered from swelling of the abdomen, and begged me to give her a second dose. I supposed that this distension of the abdomen was the effect of irritation, in consequence of the jalap having been given in too great a quantity, and I told him that a second dose would probably do her a great deal of harm, and that it was necessary to let the patient have rest, and to give her the broth as I had directed. But I could not convince him. He alleged that there was a want of good-will on my part, and reiterated his request so earnestly that, for the sake of peace, I was obliged to substitute for the jalap a dose of cream of tartar, which I knew could do no harm; but the Mandingo perceived the difference, and would have jalap, insisting that it was better. Being unable to convince him, I again visited my patient. I was uneasy about the consequences of my jalap. However I diluted the cream of tartar, which she drank, and I ordered a mess of gruel to be made for her. Thus I became a physician, without having had for a moment the idea of assuming that character.

I was extremely desirous to set out as soon as possible for the country of Kankan, as I feared that I should be obliged to go to Timbo, to visit the almamy, and that I might there be discovered and arrested. It is true my skin had became so swarthy, by exposure to the sun, that I might very easily have passed for a Moor; I was nevertheless not disposed to incur the risk. My guide was employed in his husbandry labours, which were likely to detain him a month or two, and I by no means wished to wait for him so long. I therefore resolved to take advantage of the first opportunity which might occur for crossing the country which separates Fouta-Dhialon from the Kankan.

CHAPTER VIII

Bridge over the Tankisso — Departure for the Kankan — Description of Fouta-Dhialon — Character, Manners and Customs of the Foulahs — Country of Kankan-Fodéa — Butter-tree — Course of the Dhioliba— Countries of Couranco, Sangaran, and Kissi-kissi — Mandingo marriages — River of Bandiégué — Bagaraya — Saraya — Bacocouda — Warlike dances.

On the 24th of May, I went with Ibrahim to a Mandingo who was shortly to set out for the Kankan. My guide strongly recommended me to him, and I determined to avail myself of the opportunity of accompanying him. I promised that on our arrival in that country I would make him a handsome present. In the course of the day, a Mandingo asked me for medicine to cure impotence in his own person; his wife, he said, complained of him and was even guilty of infidelity. He added that a little boy who was running about was her son by one of her lovers, "But," said he, with a sigh, "I cannot blame her since I cannot do as much for her." As ginger grew in the environs, I advised him to eat plenty of it and assured him that it would do him good; but this prescription did not satisfy him. He wished for a dose of jalap, which I gave him to get rid of him.

I went to the evening prayer where, contrary to custom, I found a great number of Mandingoes assembled. On leaving the mosque they all formed a circle round the old chief. He made a short speech, informing them that a messenger had arrived from Timbo with a circular letter, which should be read to them, and to which he requested them to pay attention. A marabout who was seated beside him then read the letter aloud. It stated that the almamy Yayaye was deposed, that Boubacar had succeeded him, that he had declared himself the protector of islamism, and enjoined the people to be faithful to him. The letter was written on both sides of a piece of paper, which was about three inches broad and five long. After it had been read, the messenger, without losing a moment's time, took up his dispatch, and proceeded in the direction of Baléya, whether he was to carry it. This precipitate departure prevented me from copying the letter, to enable me afterwards to ascertain more precisely its contents. The chief said a prayer and invoked the favour of Heaven on the reign of the new almamy. Several Mandingoes followed his example, after which a long conversation took place on the divisions which distracted Fouta. Yayaye had retired with a party, in a way which gave reason to presume that peace would not continue long. After we had reached home, Ibrahim informed me that Yayaye on his return from Firya had not been well received by the leading men of Timbo, who had deposed him, in consequence of their disapprobation of the useless war in which he had engaged, and which had cost the country a number of men.

In the morning of the 25th of May, after giving some cream of tartar to a negro, who had teazed me for several days with applications for medicine, I went with Ibrahim to see a bridge that was building over the Tankisso. On the road, I saw some Mandingoes beating the great drum, of which I have already spoken, to summon the labourers to their work. When we arrived at the bridge, I observed six or eight men lying by the side of the water, waiting for the arrival of others. I was informed that in the rainy season the water rises to the height of twenty-five or thirty feet. The branches which bar the passage are covered by this extraordinary swell, and I was assured that the bridge is often demolished and carried away by the current. The stream inundates the plain, from which a harvest of foigné is gathered before the rice is sown. All the workmen having arrived, they set about their labours singing. They were very gay and seemed to amuse themselves much, for it was a party of pleasure to them. All the inhabitants of Cambaya, being sensible of the necessity of the bridge, had resolved to assist in the labour. The bridge was about forty or forty-five feet long, six or seven feet broad. It was formed by driving a number of thick poles close together in the middle of the stream, to which were attached cross-pieces of timber, and these in many places were supported by branches of trees which overhung the stream. On the traverses pieces of plank, firmly bound together by lianes, a very flexible kind of wood, were laid lengthwise. Pieces of wood were then laid on crosswise at the distance of a pace from each other, to afford a secure footing to passengers over this unsteady bridge. I was assured that if it were not supported by branches of trees it could not resist the rapidity of the current. It was finished in a few days, for there was abundance of workmen. The whole population of Cambaya contributed to forward the work. Several women brought calabashes of rice and foigné to their husbands for dinner. I was invited to partake, and, having all sat down without distinction in a circle, every one helped himself. We then returned merrily to the village.

On the 26th of May, I went with Ibrahim and Lamfia, who had undertaken to be my guide to the Kankan, to inform the chief of the village of my intended departure. My old guide asked me, in his presence, whether I would not, before leaving them altogether, go to Timbo to see the almamy. I told him that I should be happy to do so, but that the road from Cambaya to Timbo was intersected by high mountains, which it was difficult to cross, and the passage of which would greatly fatigue me: I stated besides, that I was anxiously desirous to continue my journey to the east before the rains became more frequent, as it would then be impossible to travel without encountering great difficulties. He acknowledged the justice of my observations, and agreed that I should set out with Lamfia, to whom the worthy chief particularly recommended me, directing him to deliver me to the chief of Kankan, who would take care to have me conducted to Bouré in safety. During my residence at Cambaya, I was extremely attentive to my religious duties, and to impress more strongly the idea of my piety, I studied the Koran day and night. I settled with my new guide that he should carry my baggage to the Kankan, and our agreement was, that he should be rewarded with four yards of Guinea cloth, which I gave him before our departure. To Ibrahim, with whose conduct I was well satisfied, I gave a handsome present, consisting of amber, printed calico, Guinea cloth, gunpowder, paper, scissors, and silk handkerchiefs. He begged me not to mention this present to any one: he was desirous of passing for a generous Musulman, though avaricious, like all his countrymen. Their generosity towards me never went further than two or three colat-nuts, while the Foulahs, who came to Cambaya to sell salt or other merchandise, always made me little presents, and never looked for any thing in return.

In two days our journey was to commence, and we set about making arrangements for it; that is to say, Lamfia provided a supply of rice for our subsistence on the road. Ibrahim promised to give me some provisions, but when the time for setting off arrived, his promise was forgotten. Our neighbour, a worthy old Foulah, who had settled in the country, caused a large loaf of cagna to be prepared for me; this kind of bread is a compound, as I have already mentioned, of pistachio-nuts, maize, and honey. The name of this Foulah was Guibi. He gave me the loaf, he said, to amuse me on the road, and assured me, that were it not for the necessity of attending to his husbandry labours, he would himself accompany me to Kankan. Ibrahim also offered to have a cake of the same sort made for me if I would buy the honey, and I thanked him for his kindness. He seated himself beside me, and told me that, in the countries through which I should have to travel on my way home, I should often be troubled by the Mandingoes, and advised me as a friend not to shew any ill-humour when they applied to me for medicines, because in these parts the people might not be so easily managed as in Cambaya. I thanked him, and promised to follow his counsel. In the course of my conversations with the Foulah Guibi, he often observed that the Foulahs were the whites of Africa, and the Mandingoes, the negroes; by which he meant to impress upon me the superiority of the former.

Fouta-Dhialon is governed by an almamy, appointed by the chiefs of the country. They assemble to elect him, and have also the right of deposing him if he does not give satisfaction. The government is theocratic.

The Foulahs of Fouta are in general tall and well made; their manner is noble and dignified; their colour is a bright chesnut, somewhat darker than that of the wandering Foulahs: they have curly hair like the negroes, a rather high forehead, large eyes, and aquiline nose, thin lips, and the face a little elongated. In short, as to their features, they approximate to the European physiognomy. They are all Mahometans, and extremely fanatical. They hold the christians in horror, and are fully persuaded that they wish to obtain possession of the gold mines, situated to the east of Fouta. It is for this reason they take such precautions to prevent the christians from penetrating into that part of the country. They do not travel like the Mandingoes to distant places, but prefer remaining quietly at home, and superintending their slaves, who form an important part of their property. They are jealous and envious; they often impose rigorous exactions on foreign merchants passing through their country, especially when they are rich. They are, nevertheless, very hospitable, and generously assist their countrymen. I never saw a mendicant among them. In their mountains they cultivate rice, maize, and millet; and also cotton, of which they manufacture stuffs in pieces only five inches wide. These narrow strips are used for covering their nakedness. The principal trade of the country is in salt and cotton cloth; they go to Kakondy to barter leather, rice, wax, and millet, for salt, with which they afterwards purchase stuffs at Kankan and Sambatikila. Some Foulahs likewise travel to Bouré to procure gold, which they barter on the coast for muskets, gunpowder, glass trinkets and other articles, with which they purchase slaves. The Foulahs are warlike and ardently love their country. When at war they all take the field without distinction, leaving only the old men and women at home. Many are armed with muskets and sabres, but the bow and the lance are the weapons of the majority. They all carry a poniard the blade of which is in general straight, though I have seen some of them curved. These poniards are made in the country. They are dressed in a coussabe, which is commonly made of white stuff, and breeches, the fashion of which I have already described, of the same. They also wear a pagne, which they pass round the body, sandals and a red cap. Their hair is plaited, and greased with butter. A Foulah seldom goes out without taking several lances in his hand. I remarked that their dress was always very neat and clean. They often wash the whole body, and always with tepid water. In every village there is a public school for the children. The classes meet in the morning and evening in the open air beside a large fire. When they are able to read the Koran, they are considered well instructed. I observed that in this country the parents are always very indulgent to their children, who in their turn are always docile and obedient. The Foulahs of this part of Africa do not let their children run naked. They have always a coussabe. Those who come to our establishments are not so neatly dressed, because when they travel they put on their worst clothes. They keep their salt in the leaves of trees very ingeniously arranged for that purpose. They take a great deal of snuff, but do not smoke; and the tobacco purchased in our settlements is preferred by them to that which grows in their own country. The women are lively, handsome, and good tempered. They clean their teeth with snuff. Their dress, though simple, is always neat and clean. Like the whole of their sex throughout every part of the interior, they are completely subject to the will of their husbands. They never venture to take the slightest liberty with their lords and masters. On the other hand, I cannot say that I ever saw the husbands beat their wives. Like the Mandingoes, they may have four; the Koran does not permit them to take more. This privilege is however only exercised by the rich; the poor never have more than two wives. These women cultivate a little garden adjacent to their huts; they have detached sleeping places, and they also take their meals separately, seldom eating together. Each in her turn prepares the husband's supper. He gives to each wife a cow, which she milks, morning and evening. Their domestic utensils consist solely of some calabashes, to hold milk and the food prepared for consumption, two or three earthen pots, and a large jar, in which their dry rice is deposited. Around the inside of the hut a little elevation is formed, about six or eight inches high and a foot broad, upon which these utensils are placed. At the farther end there is a kind of bed, similar to that in the hut of the chief, which I have already described. In the floor of each hut are fixed four poles, supporting a kind of ceiling made of bamboo, serving as a protection against the soot with which the roof is covered. In general, the women appear very happy, and by no means jealous of each other, except when the husbands make a present to one without giving any thing to the rest. They often asked me for amber and coral, and did not appear much offended when I refused to comply with the demand. The Foulahs keep a great number of black cattle sheep and goats. They have horses of a small breed, a few asses, some dogs, and abundance of poultry. They make frequent journeys to Sierra-Leone, where they sell their cattle for the supply of the colony. The soil is prolific of all the necessaries of life; as rice, millet, yams, cassava, caribbee cabbage, oranges, bananas, &c. The diseases which I noticed in the country are leprosy, swelling of the neck, or goitres, fevers, and ophthalmia. I never observed any venereal malady. The Foulahs are haughty, distrustful, and of very questionable veracity. They are also accused of indolence and of a disposition to pilfering. They are however sober and support the greatest privations with fortitude. Like all Musulmans they are very superstitious, and have great confidence in their grigris, and when they go to war they are covered with these charms. They are naturally brave, and compel the surrounding tribes either to embrace Mahometanism or to become their tributaries. During my residence at Cambaya, I did not observe that there was any particular judge or tribunal established there for settling differences, such as Mungo Park has described in treating of the Gambia; disputes indeed often arose, but they were settled by the elders of the village. They do not even go before the chief unless when the complaint is of a serious nature, and in that case they often refer it to the decision of the almamy of Timbo, which is two days' journey to the W. S. W. of Cambaya.

Every married Mandingo is in his own family a respected chief. His hut stands in the middle of the huts occupied by his wives. On entering it, no domestic utensil is to be seen except two large jars containing the stock of grain for the year, which he deals out in portions to his wives. The bullock's hide on which he sleeps is the only furniture of his hut, and its only ornaments are his weapons when he puts them out of his hands.

When the master goes to the fields to superintend his slaves, the women bring his dinner to him. When they sit down to their meal, it is their custom to invite all who are near, or who may be passing at the time, to partake with them. If the person invited does not sit down beside the calabash, the owner takes up a handful of rice which he turns about for a long time in his hand, then dips it in the sauce, and presents it to his guest; after this act of politeness the offer cannot be refused without giving offence to the host. If strangers sit down to partake of the meal, the Mandingo plunges his hand into the dish, and stirs the rice to cool it. This also is an act of politeness. The master pours the sauce on the rice himself, eats the first handful, and invites his guests to follow his example. In beginning to eat they always say *bismillah*, (in the name of God &c). People often leave these repasts only half satisfied, for a number of idlers stroll about in every direction for the purpose of obtaining a share of their neighbours' dinners. I shall have occasion hereafter to speak more fully of the manners of the Mandingoes, which somewhat differ in every country.

Kankan-Fodéa, of which Cambaya forms part, is a small district, inhabited by Mandingoes subject to the almamy of Timbo. It is situated in an immense plain, composed of grey sand mixed with some gravel. The soil is fertilised by the inundations of the Tankisso, which makes a thousand meanders through this beautiful country. After winding to the south, it flows to the N. E., then turns to the N. N. E, and finally, after numberless sinuosities, discharges itself into the Dhioliba. Bouré is situated on the left bank of the Tankisso, at the distance of a day's journey from its junction with the Dhioliba. All the Mandingoes of Cambaya concur in describing that country as being rich in gold mines, and possessing an extremely fertile soil, which however is not cultivated by the inhabitants, who purchase every thing, even pistacho-nuts, with gold. The plain of Kankan-Fodéa is surrounded by mountains about one hundred fathoms in height. They are inhabited by pastoral Foulahs who rear numerous flocks. The butter-tree grows in the mountains as well as in the plain. Some of the fruit was brought to me and I liked it; but as animal butter abounds in the country it is preferred. This vegetable is applied as a remedy for pains and wounds, and some of it is sold to the European settlements on the coast.

Five days' journey S. ¼ S. E. of Cambaya commences the kingdom of Couranco. According to the reports of Mandingo travellers, the Dhioliba has it source in that country. I questioned them on the subject, and they at first told me that it rises between Bouré and Yamina. I observed to them that they were asserting what was impossible; but I discovered afterwards that they meant the cataract, which they called *Sourondo*, and that I had erroneously understood this word to signify source in their language. I drew on the ground a line to represent the river, and, pointing to its origin, asked them how they named that part. They answered *folou* (beginning) and intimated that they had no other word for *source*. They assured me that the *folou* of the Dhioliba is in Couranco; only the Bâ-fing and some other small rivers, they said, rise in Fouta. The Bâ-fing passes through the country of Bondou and runs to N'dar (St. Louis in the Senegal). A journey of a day and a half southward brings the traveller to Fryia, or Firya, which consists of several small villages united. They informed me that the Dhioliba passes that place and is of considerable size there. The first villages of Sangaran lie five days' journey to the S. S. E. Sangaran and Couranco are large countries like Fouta; the inhabitants are idolaters. These countries, I was told, are divided into a number of small districts, which have their separate and independent chiefs, who are often at war with each other. Some Musulmans are settled among them. Couranco extends from east to west and to the south of Sangaran, which also stretches from west to east. I was informed that these countries are mountainous and very fertile. The small country of Kissi-kissi lies to the west of Couranco, at the distance of ten or twelve days' journey from Cambaya, and in the environs of Sierra-Leone.

In the evening of the 28th of May, a caravan of saracolet merchants passed, on its route from Cambaya to Kankan, where it was to divide into three parties, for Bouré, Ségo, and Yamina. The merchants visited the *mansa* or chief, and that worthy old man recommended me to their care. They went on, and halted for the night at Bagaraya, about two miles to the east of Cambaya.

The 29th of May was employed in making our preparations. I arranged my baggage, which since my arrival had been left in Ibrahim's hut, because, that in which I slept was not within the inclosure and had no fastenings. I often examined it, and several times suspected that it had been meddled with; I thought so from the manner in which it was tied up; I had some pieces of stuff which had been cut, some tobacco, and some glass ornaments, which seemed to please the people greatly. I could not however ascertain whether they had robbed me or not, and I chose rather to presume that they had been induced by curiosity to examine my property than to suspect them of theft. I made a little present to the Foulah Guibi, in return for the pistachio bread which he had given me.

In the evening I took leave of the chief who had been so kind to me; I made him a present of some gunpowder, which pleased him much; he gave me his blessing, and offered up prayers for the prosperity of my journey.

On the 30th of May, 1827, I took leave of my friends, (at least, such friends as a white can have among negroes,) and we set out, about ten in the morning, after eating a little rice, which Ibrahim had prepared for me. Lamfia, my new guide, was accompanied by one of his wives, who was to cook for us on the journey: she carried on her head a bag of salt, some calabashes, and an earthen pot. Our caravan was composed of eight individuals. Ibrahim and the Foulah Guibi came with me as far as the bridge across the Tankisso; my old guide carried my umbrella and my satala; the latter contained seven or eight rice loaves baked in the sun, which had been given me on my departure: Ibrahim thought proper to appropriate to himself two of these loaves without my knowledge. I mentioned the circumstance to Lamfia, who censured Ibrahim's dishonesty, and asked me whether he had eaten much of my merchandise, a phrase employed to express any fraud or breach of confidence. Ibrahim and Guibi parted from us at the bridge: they again recommended me to the care of Lamfia, telling him that, as my resources were but scanty, he must be moderate in his demands upon me, and that God would reward him. They seemed sorry to leave me, and after we had separated they turned round and called loudly after me, *Salam alékoum, Abd-allahi:* (Abd-allahi was my assumed name). They repeated this salutation three times, and then they exclaimed, *Allam-Kiselak!* (May God preserve thee on thy journey!) But though both uttered the same words, yet I could easily perceive that Guibi's regret was more sincere than Ibrahim's.

We soon reached Bagaraya, which is situated two miles east of Cambaya; our road was covered with butter-trees.[46] The chief of the village received us well: he gave us a good hut, and sent me a supper of rice. He said he had not heard of me all the time I was at Cambaya. The saracolets, to whom I was recommended by Ibrahim's father, had set out in the morning to cross the woods which separate the Fouta-Dhialon from Baléya. The evening was rather stormy, the sky dark and cloudy, and the heat oppressive. I went to the mosque with my new guide, who shewed me great kindness, and seemed anxious to anticipate all my wishes; he even carried his attention to the length of servility. As I was leaving the mosque the people all thronged round me, and looked at me with great curiosity; Lamfia replied to their questions, and informed them of the circumstances which occasioned me to visit their country: he told them I was a sherif of Mecca,[47] doubtless with the view of rendering me an object of greater respect than I should otherwise have been. The village of Bagaraya is inhabited partly by Dhialonkés and partly by Mandingoes: its population is between three and four hundred. There is a mosque approriated to the women, who, according to the Mahometan custom, cannot enter that which is attended by the men. On our return to our hut, we had a visit from the chief, who sat a short time with us; he talked very much, and asked me many questions about the way in which I had been treated by the christians: I endeavoured to remove the bad opinion he entertained of us: he imagined that I must have been beaten and ill-treated by the infidels.

We were obliged to stay at Bagaraya the whole of the 31st of May, having to wait for some Mandingo merchants, who proposed travelling in our company; our road to Baléya led through woods which are infested by robbers, and, as our party was not sufficiently strong to resist an attack, we thought it prudent to wait for the merchants who were to join us.

In the course of the day I had many visiters, and received a present of a fowl, together with some rice and milk, which we had for supper. The Mandingoes of Cambaya, to whom I had given medicine and advice, were not by any means so grateful as the Dhiolonkés of Bagaraya. These good people told me they were highly gratified in having among them a sherif on his way to Mecca, which place they call *Maka*. I gave the chief a little cream of tartar, for Lamfia informed him that I had some very good medicines. He sent us a supper, consisting of foigné boiled without being bruised, and a little milk. In the afternoon I observed that two sheep had been killed. I was astonished at this preparation for feasting, and asked the cause of it. I was told that it was to celebrate the marriage of the chief, which was to take place that evening. The chief was a man about fifty or fifty-five years of age, and this was his fourth wife. Several women of the neighbourhood kindled a large fire, for which the friends of the chief sent their slaves to collect wood. On this fire were placed two enormous earthen pots, eighteen or twenty inches in height, and twelve or fourteen in diameter; in the one was boiled rice, and in the other a sheep. Several other women of the village, who came to assist their companions, kindled other fires for cooking a distinct supper for the female friends of the bride. The cooking was performed in the open air; and the cooks were each provided with a large spatula with which they stirred the rice and meat, performing that office by turns. When the rice was sufficiently boiled, it was placed in calabashes of such enormous size, that there were at least a dozen women to each. They arranged the rice in the form of sugar-loaves, smoothing it with their hands, and slightly sprinkling it with cold water. There were provisions enough for at least two hundred negroes, for almost all the inhabitants of the place were to attend the feast, which was to commence at night. The calabashes of rice were removed to a hut belonging to the chief.

Among the Mandingoes, marriages are contracted without much ceremony. When a man sees a woman whom he wishes to marry, he gains the good graces of her parents by sending presents to them as well as to the daughter. The price which the bridegroom is to pay for the bride is agreed upon: it consists of one, two, or three slaves, according to the beauty and other recommendations of the bride. These slaves are given to the mother, who, if satisfied with the price, consents to her daughter's marriage. The husband defrays all the expence of the nuptial feast, which usually takes place at night, and when it is over, the marriage is consummated, without the observance of any religious ceremony.

It rained a little during the evening, and some thunder was heard, but the storm did not last long. In the course of the night, I heard the joyous songs of the negroes and negresses, who were dancing to the sound of a small drum. Their dance was more decorous than that of the Wolof negroes in the neighbourhood of the Senegal: it was little more than walking in measured time accompanied by motions of the arms and head. The women all wore two pagnes, and their head-dress consisted of a piece of cloth passing over the forehead, and fastened at the back of the head. They plait their hair and grease it with butter. I had not the pleasure of seeing the bride. I was not even invited to the feast; but this I had no reason to regret, for, from what I saw of it, it was not very tempting.

At six on the morning of the 4th of June, we set off and travelled four miles to the S. E. among the gorges of mountains of granite. Our caravan consisted of fourteen men and one woman carrying a burthen. We proceeded three miles over a tract of country covered with trees and fine vegetation: the cé or butter-tree was growing in profusion, and I also saw the indigo and nédé. We met a party of Foulah traders returning from Kankan. They took me at first for a christian, and exclaimed with astonishment:— "A white going to the east! Surely, the great men of the Fouta do not know this, or they would not suffer it." They even wished to prevent me from going further; but Lamfia, my guide, who had lingered a little behind, came up and put a stop to the discussion, which might have become serious, for I could not explain myself very well in the Mandingo language. My guide related the manner in which I had been taken by Europeans, and assured them that I was a real Arab, a sherif of Mecca; for these people had never heard of Alexandria, my pretended country. Lamfia informed them that I had crossed the Fouta in safety, that all the inhabitants had received me well, and even made me presents; that I read the Koran, a thing which a christian would never do. "Besides," added he, "the christians never travel alone and on foot. They only go by rivers in vessels." The prevailing idea of the people in the interior of the Soudan is, that we inhabit little islands in the middle of the ocean, and that the Europeans wish to get possession of their country, which is the most beautiful in the world.

One of these Foulahs addressed to me a few words in Arabic, to which I replied. This quite ingratiated me with him; as it afforded him an opportunity of proving to his companions that he spoke that language, which flattered his vanity; for the negroes are, in general, fond of shewing their superiority over their fellows. The Foulah then assured his companions that I was a real Arab, and they allowed me to continue my journey.

After proceeding a little distance, we halted and entered some huts made for sheltering travellers from the rain. These huts are very simple. A row of poles is driven into the ground, and branches of trees are laid in a slanting direction, that is to say, resting against the tops of the poles, and sloping gradually to the ground. They are covered with straw, and defended from the wind by pieces of wood, placed transversely, forming a sort of hedge sloping very much towards the ground, and to the west.

My guide's wife prepared our dinner. Lamfia provided food for some of the negroes of the caravan, for they had brought no women with them, and they had no pots for boiling their rice.

We caught a sheep which had, no doubt, strayed from its owner. The Mandingoes held a council to deliberate whether they should kill it. They agreed that there would be no impropriety in doing so, since they did not know the owner. The animal was accordingly killed, and we had a good supper to help us on our way. In all negro countries meat is a great luxury and, in general, it is only eaten on festival days. The sheep we caught was with lamb; but we nevertheless found the meat very good.

The place where we encamped was called Sokodatakha, a name derived from the trees by which it is shaded. It is a large sandy plain, covered with trees and beautiful verdure, and surrounded by granite hills, nearly three hundred feet high. These hills have no vegetation. We passed the night in the huts which I have above described, on the outside of which large fires were kindled, though the weather was very warm. In the middle of the night our rest was disturbed by a storm. I could not sleep on account of the rain, for our huts were by no means weather-proof.

At half past six on the morning of the second of June, we again set off in high spirits, though our clothes were very wet. Our course lay to the east. The country was woody and our road rather gravelly. The cé and the indigo are abundant in this part. After we had travelled about fifteen miles over a hard sandy soil, covered with gravel, we found the trees, though still numerous, neither so large nor so high as before. We were overtaken by a violent storm from the east: the wind was cold and the rain fell in torrents. In a moment, the whole plain was flooded with water, through which we waded, ancle-deep. I opened my umbrella; but it was impossible to hold it on account of the wind. I was drenched to the skin. Fortunately, I had taken the precaution to keep my notes in a little portfolio of untanned calf-skin. We took shelter under some huts similar to those in which we passed the preceding night. About three in the afternoon the rain ceased, the sun re-appeared, and the surrounding country was clothed in new charms. We prepared to kindle a fire; but this was no easy task, on account of the wetness of the wood. However, we at length succeeded and dried our clothes. We burned a great deal of straw; for it was scarcely possible to make the wood burn, even after we had dried it at the straw fire. We met some travellers coming from Baléya, who, like us, had braved the storm. They were laden with white cloth of the manufacture of the country, which they were going to exchange for salt in the Fouta-Dhialon.

I had seated myself for a few moments behind a bush in order to make some notes, when I saw the wife of Lamfia advancing towards me. I immediately hid my paper and took up my trowsers which were drying at the fire. She returned to her husband, who asked her whether I was writing: — "No," replied she, "he is putting on his clothes." I was near enough to hear this conversation, which sufficiently indicated that they suspected me. I therefore became doubly cautious, and shewed a greater assiduity in the study of the Koran. When, on the road, I sometimes withdrew a little from my companions, I saw them looking at me and endeavouring to discover what I was about; but I always took care to hold in my hand a leaf of the Koran, on which I laid my note paper, and when I saw any one advancing towards me I concealed my writing and pretended to be reading a verse of the sacred book.

We had a little of our mutton left, of which we made a good supper: Lamfia and I ate together, and the other Mandingoes took their meals apart. In spite of the distrust which he appeared to entertain, from his having sent his wife to watch whether I was writing, he was, nevertheless, very kind to me, always taking my part against those who doubted my conversion, alleging that I was a sherif, which seemed to be a satisfactory answer to every objection. He was older than the other individuals of the caravan, and, therefore, had some ascendancy over them. This respect for age is universal among the negroes, who never undertake any thing without consulting the elders of their villages. At the place where we were now encamped the soil was good, consisting in some places of black, and in others of red, mould, like that of Sierra-Leone, mixed with stones. I saw some palm-trees growing here.

At seven on the morning of the 3rd of June, we resumed our course, proceeding a mile eastward along some hills, about one hundred and fifty or two hundred feet high, composed of red, porous stone, like that of Sierra-Leone. These hills extend north and south, and they are the last of the Fouta-Dhialon towards the east. From their summits we discovered a beautiful sandy plain, into which we descended by a very rapid declivity. We now found the surface of the soil covered with reddish sand. Further on, our road became gravelly. We continued our course eastward through a level and very open part of the country. To the north, however, I observed many trees and plants, namely, the bombax, the cé, the mimosa, the nédé, the *nauclea africana*, and the indigo. We met many travellers on the road. Having proceeded thirteen miles, we halted about four in the afternoon, much fatigued, near a rivulet, the wide and shallow bed of which consists of argillaceous sand. It is dry in some places. The natives call it, the Ba-ndiégué (fish river). It waters Baléya and flows into the Tankisso: two of our party went to buy smoked fish from some fishermen, who were near the place where we stopped. We dried our merchandise which had got wet by the rain of the preceding day, and I was sorry to be obliged to display my pieces of printed calico which attracted, in no small degree, the notice of my companions. In the place where we halted there were not many trees; but I perceived some clumps of nauclea. The ground was covered with a dry kind of grass. I think this place must be inundated in the rainy season by the overflowing of the Ba-ndiégué, the banks of which are well wooded.

On the 4th of June, at six in the morning, we left the banks of the Ba-ndiégué, and found the plain covered with a beautiful white narcissus. We took a very pleasant road to the south-east. About eight o'clock we seated ourselves under a large bombax to breakfast. In this part huts are erected for the accommodation of travellers, and I saw many cés in the neighbourhood. We now heard the sound of a drum proceeding from Saraya, the first village eastward of Baléya. After a good breakfast of rice and smoke-dried fish, we proceeded nine miles eastward over a sandy soil. The country is very open, and its uniform level is not broken by a single hillock. Having crossed the

Ba-ndiégué by a tottering bridge made of the branches of trees, we reached Saraya about three in the afternoon.

In the plain in which this village is situated I saw some slaves at work preparing the ground. They had a drum to stimulate them at their labour. It was the beat of this drum that we heard in the morning. In some parts of Africa nothing is done except to the sound of music. Lamfia called to see a man of his acquaintance, who gave us one of his huts to lodge in. On hearing that an Arab sherif had arrived, the inhabitants thronged to see me. They gazed at me with great curiosity, and said that they had seen *Soulocas* [48] before; but none so white as I was. Lamfia told them my history, and our hut was full of visiters the whole evening. My umbrella, which I shewed them, strongly excited their curiosity. Those who went away, described the wonder to their friends, who came in their turn to get a peep at it. We made a good supper, which I purchased for about three charges of gunpowder.

We stopped the whole of the 5th of June at Saraya, in order to recover a little from our fatigue. My feet were very painful, for my sandals galled me.

I surveyed the village and its neighbourhood. It is surrounded by two earth walls, nine feet high, and eight or ten inches thick. The entrance gate is surmounted by a close range of loopholes for muskets. I also remarked a little sentry box, round which there were holes looking in every direction. This village, which is on the frontier of Baléya, is situated in a sandy plain, level, open, and fertile. I saw in the neighbourhood large bombaces, baobabs, nédés, and cés. Indigo grows here without cultivation, and is employed by the natives for dying their cloths. I shall hereafter describe the way in which they use it. Water is procured here from wells, two feet deep, and though rather thick, it is very pleasant to the taste. The negroes of Saraya, who are all Dhialonkés, came to see me during the day, and brought me little presents of milk, and the chief gave me a fowl, which we ate for supper. I gave Lamfia some glass trinkets to purchase rice and honey, as I wished to treat the people of our caravan. I observed that Lamfia kept some of the glass for himself; but this was a trifle which I did not think worth while to notice to him. I asked him to get the rice pounded, and made into cakes with the honey which I had bought and that which the people had given me. Lamfia and his wife mixed with their dirty hands the flour, honey, and powdered allspice. They made it into little cakes, which, after a great deal of kneading, were baked in the sun, and put into a little bag to be eaten on our journey. To add to my stock of provisions, I bought some salt, an article which was beginning to be very scarce and dear. I learned that the village of Foho, the residence of the chief of Baléya, was a day's journey E. N. E. of Saraya. The people advised me not to go to Foho, "For," said they, "the chief is not a Musulman, and he will make you pay transit duties." In the neighbourhood of the village, I saw some ferruginous stones. I broke one, which contained many particles of iron. These stones are found on the surface of the soil. The inhabitants smelt them to make their agricultural implements, which consist merely of hoes, seven or eight inches long, and three broad. The ends are rounded, and the handles, which are two feet long, are much bent.

The village of Saraya contains a population of about seven or eight hundred. The inhabitants keep many cattle which at night are driven within the two walls that surround their village. I was informed that the great river flows at the distance of a day's journey south of the village. Fish are caught in it, and, after being dried and smoked, they are used as sauce, and eaten with rice: they make them also an article of trade. The whole evening the young people of this village amused themselves by dancing to the sound of a tambourine, and a small instrument made of bamboo; their dances are sprightly and decorous. My guide and I paid a visit to the chief, who received us very kindly, and offered me a sheep-skin to sit upon. The door of his court was shaded by two bombaces. He afterwards sent us a very good supper of rice and gombo.

At half past six o'clock in the morning of the 6th of June, we proceeded four miles E. S. E., over a fine plain of sand. We passed Fausimoulaya, a village surrounded by a mud wall. The country was covered with cés and nédés. We crossed the Ba-ndiégué, which flows through a fine plain clothed with perpetual verdure. We advanced for two miles in the same direction, over a level plain, composed of red earth, with a great deal of gravel, and some red stone of the same kind as that of Sierra-Leone.

We entered the village of Sancougnan, in order to visit the chief, a ceremony which all travellers are obliged to observe. We found him lying on a large bullock's hide, with his head resting on a log of wood. My guide told him that I was a sherif going to my native country, near Mecca. This chief, who was said not to be a very pious Musulman, gave us a very kind reception. He assigned to me a very good hut, and asked me to pass the next day in his village. Lamfia met with the son of the chief of Kankan, a zealous Musulman, who had come to Baléya to sell a horse. I was desirous of making acquaintance with him, and with this view I gave him a sheet of paper. He spoke favourably of me to the chief of Sancougnan, who, he said, was a great warrior, and not over-devout, and therefore might make me pay a considerable tribute for liberty to pass. After our interview, which took place in a stable, where he was lying beside his horse, we went to the hut which was destined for us. The mansa, or chief, soon sent me a calabash full of rice, mixed with milk and butter, and sprinkled with salt, which we ate for dinner. I took the precaution of circulating in the village a story calculated to serve my purpose. I said that Mr. Macaulay, a merchant at Sierra-Leone, well known through all this country, had wished me to remain in the English settlement, and for that purpose offered to advance me money to carry on trade; but that I rejected the offer on account of my strong dislike to live among infidels. When in the presence of the chief, I drew forth some leaves of the Koran, which I read aloud, to induce a belief that I was a very zealous Musulman. An old man of Bondou, who was settled in the village, took the leaves of the Koran out of my hands, and wishing to show his learning, he mumbled some words in a low tone, holding the leaves sometimes sideways, and sometimes upside-down. I was so imprudent as to remark upon this, and laugh a little at his ignorance. He was offended, and immediately returned me the leaves of the Koran. He remained with the chief until we were gone, and then he asserted that I was a christian, and not a sherif, as my guide had stated.

In the evening a storm came on, and it rained heavily all night. The chief sent us a supper of rice, cooked like the last. On the morning of the 7th of June we prepared to depart. Lamfia and myself, accompanied by the son of the chief of Kankan, went to see the mansa of Sancougnan, to whom I presented seven or eight charges of gunpowder and some leaves of tobacco; Lamfia added some colat-nuts, which we distributed among the relations of the chief. They were all in their smoky hut, on the walls of which were suspended bows, arrows, quivers, and lances. A jar for water, a bullock's hide, and some mats, composed the whole furniture of the place.

We left the village about eight in the morning, and were soon after overtaken by the mansa, accompanied by the Mandingo of Kankan; the latter proved very serviceable to me on this occasion. The chief told us that the old Bondouké had assured him that I was a European, and not a Moor; that, moreover, I was too white for a Moor; and, that we certainly intended to deceive him, in order to evade the payment of the passage duties. Here my guide behaved exceedingly well: he assured the chief that I was a real Arab, a countryman of the Prophet's, and a great sherif, supporting his assertions by the arguments which he had already employed to convince other incredulous persons whom he had met with. The Mandingo of Kankan strongly confirmed the declarations of Lamfia, who manifested much zeal, and asked the chief whether he had ever seen a christian read the Koran; the mansa concluded by saying, that he perceived the old Bondouké had spoken falsely, and that he had no longer any doubt of my being a sherif; then, offering me his hand in token of peace, he wished me a pleasant journey, and returned to the village. We continued our route to the east, over a soil composed of gravel and volcanic stones, black, brittle, and porous. As I went along I reflected on my imprudent behaviour to the old Bondouké, which had irritated him and induced him to seek revenge. I resolved in future to be more circumspect in my intercourse with the negroes, who, being ignorant, are naturally irritable and vindictive.

After travelling two miles, we arrived, at half-past nine in the morning, at Courouman-Cambaya, a village surrounded, like Sancougnan, with a double wall. It contains between five and six hundred inhabitants. My guides who had many acquaintances in this village, assured me that I had nothing to fear: "These people," said he, "will not take you for a christian, as they did there," meaning at Sancougnan: "they wanted to get at your baggage, for they are Kaffres,[49] and but for the son of the chief of Kankan, we should not have come off so well." We went to one of his school-fellows, who lodged us in a good hut. It was soon filled by people, attracted by curiosity to see a sherif. I was visited by a saracolet, who was on his way from Ségo to Kakondy: he addressed me in the Moorish tongue. I made him a small present of tobacco-leaves. We stopped at this village the whole of the 8th; Lamfia exchanged some salt for cloths. The heat, which had been suffocating throughout the day, was at night succeeded by a violent storm and heavy rain. On the 9th, we had to wait for several travellers who were to join us. Some persons brought me small presents of milk and a fowl, which served for our dinner. Our host was particularly attentive to us. The inhabitants were kind and hospitable: every evening by moon-light they assembled under a bombax to dance. I was much amused by seeing them caper to the sound of a little tambourine and an instrument made of bamboo, resembling a flageolet, and producing a very melodious tone.

On the 10th of June, at seven in the morning, we took leave of our host, to whom at parting I gave a sheet of paper and some tobacco, for which he loaded me with thanks. We proceeded three miles towards the east, over a plain of grey sand, covered with the most beautiful indigo, growing spontaneously. On reaching Siralia, a large village, containing from seven to eight hundred inhabitants, we went to visit the chief, who fortunately was absent: my guide assured me, that if I had seen him, I should have been obliged to make him a considerable present.

The country around the village is well cultivated. We advanced nine miles to the S. E. over a road which was partially flooded, owing to the frequent rains. On our way we saw many neat little ourondés, surrounded by quick-set hedges, which are very ornamental. We crossed, up to our knees in water, two streams which flow to the northward, and discharge themselves into the Niger. On the N. E. of our route, a chain of small mountains was pointed out to me. This chain extends from north to east, and separates the Baléya from Bouré. The woods are infested by robbers, who stop travellers, and pillage them without mercy. We proceeded three miles to the S. E., over fine, level, and well cultivated ground, and arrived, at three in the afternoon, at Bacocouda, which contains between five and six hundred inhabitants. This is the last village east of Baléya. I and my guide waited on the chief to ask him for a lodging. We found him seated in a large hut on a bullock's hide, and surrounded by some saracolet merchants, who had arrived the preceding evening. I confess that I was not quite at my ease at sight of these merchants, for they were the same who had passed through Cambaya, in the Fóuta, on their way from Gambia. One of them spoke to me in the Moorish language; I answered his questions, the chief immediately rose and conducted me into one of his huts; he gave us a sheep-skin to sit upon. My guide presently gave him an account of my adventures, to which he listened with pleasure, and approved my resolution. We retired, and went to our hut, where the saracolet, who had spoken to me in Arabic, came to see me. He told me that he had at first taken me for a christian; but that now he saw he had been deceived, and that I certainly was an Arab. He talked very much, and endeavoured to flatter me. I saw that he wanted something, and gave him a little tobacco, promising that on my arrival at Kankan I would present him with a pair of scissors: he proposed to conduct me to Ségo, whence he said I could go to Jenné by water: I told him that was just what I wished, and he took his leave. The chief sent us something for supper, and one of the inhabitants gave us some white yams boiled. The people of this village spent their evenings and great part of the night in performing martial dances. They came to borrow my guide's musket. The men dance to the sound of two tambourines. These tambourines have each a stick about fourteen inches long, one end of which is fastened to the bottom, and the other to the rim of the instrument, by strings made of sheep's gut, resembling those of the guitar; at the ends of the stick are a number of small bells, rings, and bits of iron, which make a jingling accompaniment to the sound of the tambourine, and produce a very agreeable effect. The musicians sing, and strike the tambourines with the hand; their songs stimulate the courage of the warriors, whom they exhort to fight bravely, and destroy the infidels. The actors in these mimic wars are armed with sabres, bows, and muskets; they leap and dance to the sound of the instruments, assuming menacing attitudes, as though they would destroy their adversaries: they discharge their muskets, and shoot their arrows, and afterwards, as if they had been victorious in battle, they leap and dance in token of rejoicing, and make a thousand other grimaces of that sort. This spectacle collected together almost all the inhabitants of the place. After looking on for a short time, I returned to my hut, for I was afraid of being insulted. When Lamfia joined me, he told me that the dance we had just witnessed was a representation of the way in which these people make war against the infidels.

CHAPTER IX

Description of Baléya—Arrival on the banks of the Dhioliba — Courouassa — Sambarala — Bouré, a mountainous country, rich in gold — Crossing the Dhioliba — The river Yendan — Kankan — Description of the town — The market — Gold of Bouré — A religious festival — Ordeal of fire — Critical situation of the traveller — Diseases of the country.

The soil of Baléya is an argillaceous sand, compact, but extremely fertile, producing all the necessaries of life in abundance. It is bounded on the west by the Fouta; on the south by Sangaran, through which runs the Dhioliba; on the east by the little country of Amana; and on the north by forests. All the villages in this part are surrounded with a double wall of mud, surmounted by battlements. These walls are from ten to twelve feet high. The villages contain each from a hundred to a hundred and twenty-five huts, made of straw.

The inhabitants of Baléya were subjected to the laws of the Prophet by the Foulahs, since which they annually present some cattle to the almamy of the Fouta. They are warriors and husbandmen, and have abundance of the necessaries of life, which they obtain by the cultivation of the earth, while their cattle supply them with butter and milk. They manufacture white cloth, which they exchange with their neighbours for salt. Earthenware is made in almost every village. The people of Baléya are Dhialonkés. Though Mahometans, they are, by no means, so zealous as the Foulahs, and drink in private a sort of beer made of millet and honey. Lamfia told me that formerly they possessed Fouta-Dhialon. The women are lively, pretty, and coquettish, and bestow much attention on dressing their hair, which is arranged in two tufts, one on each side of the head: many have four tufts. They ornament their heads with coloured glass beads, tastefully disposed; they wear necklaces of small black glass beads, interspersed with a few gilt glass ornaments. The necklaces, which are about three inches broad, encircle the neck like a cravat. The head-dress of these women would be becoming, if their hair was not covered with a layer of butter, with which they also grease their bodies: it renders their skin glossy, but gives them an unpleasant smell. Most of the females have no other dress than a piece of cloth, five feet long and two wide, which they fasten round their waists. On holidays they throw another piece of cloth over their shoulders, and cover their bosoms; they also wear sandals. This is nearly the general costume of the women of Negroland. Their dispositions are gentle and cheerful; their colour is very black; their features handsome, with curly hair, noses slightly aquiline, thin lips, and large eyes. They do all the household work, and are obedient to their husbands.

On the 11th of June, after taking leave of the chiefs to whom I presented three leaves of tobacco, which seemed to please him, we proceeded in a S. E. direction. The saracolet merchants, who had asses to carry their merchandise, went on first, having to pass several streams which would retard their progress. The heat was excessive, and a storm came on. The atmosphere was heavy and obscured by clouds. I was attacked with a fever on the journey, and, notwithstanding the heat, I had shivering fits, from which I suffered greatly. After crossing the streams, where the water was knee-deep, we overtook the saracolets. They had bargained with some Mandingoes to carry a part of their baggage, for they were heavily laden. I observed that the country sloped towards the east. We continued in the same direction. The eldest saracolet, having traced some Arabic characters on the ground, and muttered some prayers, assured us that we might pursue our journey without apprehension, as no misfortune would happen to us. The country is a little wooded. The nédé and the cé grow here in abundance. Our road was gravelly. About two in the afternoon we arrived at Courouassa, a village of Amana, situated on the left bank of the Dhioliba. Shortly before our arrival a storm arose. My umbrella and some trees, beneath which we sought shelter, protected me a little. We had travelled fourteen miles in a S. E. direction, and were all much fatigued. Lamfia took me to lodge with the chief, who gave us a kind reception. He provided us with a good hut, and offered us a hide to sleep upon. I bought a fowl for two charges of gunpowder, and we had it cooked for supper. The fever had left me, and I now suffered only from a severe head-ache. I hastened to take a view of the Dhioliba, which had so long been the object of my curiosity. I observed that it flowed from S. W. ¼ S. proceeding slowly to the E. N. E. for the distance of some miles, and then turns due east. A little to the north of the village I saw a sand-bank lying very near the left shore of the river. The channel for canoes is near the right bank. I seated myself for a moment to contemplate this mysterious river, respecting which the learned of Europe are so anxious to gain information.

On the left bank, and pretty near the northern part of the village, there are hills between one hundred and fifty and two hundred feet high, covered with young trees. The soil appeared to be red, and of the same kind as that of Sierra-Leone. Some smiths have established themselves near these hills:

they smelt and work up the iron which in found there in great quantities. These hills extend in a N. E. direction. There are some also on the right bank, but they are not so high. The air became cool, and I returned to my hut. During the night it rained a great deal.

We remained at Courouassa during the 12th. A storm came on accompanied by an east wind, which occasioned a suffocating heat. The rain poured in torrents. When it ceased I again visited the banks of the river. I watched its current, which flowed at the rate of about two miles and a half or three miles an hour. At this period it was about nine feet deep. This I calculated by the long pole which the boatmen used to push along the canoes.[50] In this part it appeared as broad as the Senegal at Podor. The right bank is lower than the left, on which the village is situated at an elevation of nearly a twentieth part of a mile above the water. I observed in the village many large bamboos, under the shade of which the old men assemble and spend part of the day in conversation. These people use much snuff; but they do not take it as we do in Europe, with the fingers; some use a small brush, and others a little iron spoon like an ear-pick. The negroes told me that the river begins to overflow in July, and that then they can go three miles over the plain in canoes. A great quantity of rice is grown on this plan. The sand-bank which I had seen plainly on the preceding evening was now no longer visible.

Courouassa is a neat village, surrounded by a mud wall, from ten to twelve feet high and from eight to ten inches thick. It contains between four and five hundred inhabitants. I observed that thousands of swallows, of the same kind as those seen in Europe, had built their nests in this wall. They were collected in flocks upon the trees, and I concluded that they were preparing to depart.

Courouassa is entered by several low and narrow openings which are closed by a thick plank made of a single tree. The town is shaded by bombaces and boababs, and it is the principal of five small villages situated on the banks of the Dhioliba. This country is called Amana; the inhabitants are called Dhialonkés, and are chiefly idolaters. They do not travel, but occupy themselves peaceably in the cultivation of their little fields, which are fertilised by the inundations of the river. They catch many fish with hooks, which they obtain from travellers coming from our settlements on the coast. They likewise fish with the fouène, an instrument consisting of three branches with darts having teeth like a saw. A large piece of wood forms the handle of this instrument, which the natives use with great address. I saw a species of fish with a number of small bones like the carp. The people dry and smoke this fish, and sell it to their neighbours and the traders who pass through their country.

Bouré is situated at the distance of a five days' passage down the river, in a canoe. The voyage is thus divided: from Courouassa to Cabarala one day; from Cabarala to Balatou one day; from Balatou to the village of Dhioliba one day; from Dhioliba to Boun-Bouriman, one day; from Boun-Bouriman to Bouré, proceeding a little way up the Tankisso, one day.

Bouré is a mountainous country, containing a number of rich gold mines, according to the account given to me by the natives. I shall speak of it more at length in the proper place. I went, accompanied by my guide, to pay a visit to the chief, who I was told, was a great warrior and dreaded by his neighbours. We found him alone in his hut employed in fastening a point to an arrow. A number of bows, arrows, and quivers, were hung up in various parts of the hut. He asked us to sit down on a bullock's hide, and Lamfia conversed with him. The conversation turned on me. He promised that we should cross the river next day. Travellers are rowed across by his slaves. He levies duties which are paid in European merchandise, such as gunpowder, tobacco, knives, scissors, &c. He also receives salt in payment of these duties, which render him tolerably rich. He told me that, out of respect to my rank of sherif, he would allow me to pass duty free. The chief was a man about fifty years of age, five feet and some inches high. His countenance was mild, nay even pleasing.

On returning to our hut, we bought some fresh fish for supper. It was of the kind resembling the carp, which I have already mentioned. It measures about eight inches long and four or five broad, and is very bony. The general food of the inhabitants is boiled rice without salt, but seasoned with a sauce made of dry fish minced. They also eat fresh fish. With the foigné they make a sort of thick pudding, which they call *tau*. This is the sangleh of the Senegal. They eat this tau with a sauce made of herbs or pistachio-nuts; the latter they cultivate very abundantly. As salt is beginning to be dear, they use it on festivals and rejoicing days only. They gather the fruit of the cé and nédé, from which they obtain butter. I saw some heaps of the seeds of these trees freshly gathered and exposed to the rain. They were already beginning to germinate.

On the 13th of June, we crossed the river in canoes, twenty-five feet long, three wide, and one deep. A great number of people were going across, and they were all disputing, some about the fare that was demanded, others about who should go first. They all talked at once and made a most terrible uproar. The saracolets had a great deal of trouble in getting their asses on board the canoes, and the parties who had crossed fired muskets in token of rejoicing, which augmented the tumult created by the disputes of the negroes. I was obliged to remain exposed to the sun the whole morning; for the banks of the river are very open. Along the left bank but one tree was visible. This was a large bombax, under which so many people had crowded for shade that I could not find room. I saw a number of women and girls bathing in the river. They were quite naked, but they seemed to care very little about the presence of the men. Having finished their ablutions, they returned to the village, with pagnes round their waists and calabashes on their heads. There were only four canoes for conveying between two hundred and fifty and three hundred persons, besides luggage. We were not all landed on the right bank until near eleven o'clock. The excessive heat had brought on me a severe head-ache accompanied with fever. We proceeded onwards to the S. E. over good land, leaving behind us a few merchants who bad not yet crossed the river. I was so ill that I experienced great difficulty in walking. The heat was intense, and I opened my umbrella to shelter me from the scorching rays of the sun; but some of my travelling companions advised me to shut it on approaching the villages, lest, as they said, it should excite the cupidity of the Kafirs (infidels). We proceeded eastward. The road was flooded, and in several places the water was ancle-deep. We passed Sambarala, a village situated on the bank of the river and surrounded by nédés and cés. We next pursued our course over a sandy soil, clothed with beautiful vegetation, among which I observed tamarind-trees. About three o'clock we arrived at Counancodo, where I saw some fine orange-trees. We had travelled nine miles in the course of the day.

I told Lamfia that I wished to procure a few tamarinds, as I was very feverish. He immediately sent his brother to gather some in the neighbouring wood; but the brother, not understanding what I meant, brought the leaves instead of the fruit. We could procure no milk, for the saracolets had gone before us and bought all that the village afforded. My fever had continued without intermission the whole of the way. For a little powder I bought a fowl, in order to recruit my strength. Our caravan consisted of sixty or eighty men, some carrying loads, others leading asses, and very few walking free from all encumbrance. One of our companions had a slave, whom he said he had procured at Sierra-Leone. He feared that he intended to desert, and begged me to write an amulet to prevent him. The man was very earnest in his request, and offered immediately to furnish me with ink and paper. However, as I did not wish to write European characters, for fear of exciting suspicion, I observed that having left my country very young I did not know how to make grigris, and I begged him to apply to some one more learned than I. Next day I saw the poor slave bearing on his head a burthen which he could scarcely carry, fastened to a rope the other end of which was tied round his leg, so that it was out of his power to run away; for his prudent and suspicious master took care that he should not have a knife to cut the rope.

Our host sent us a good supper of rice, which I added to my fowl. All the evening, and indeed till night was pretty well advanced, the young negroes and negresses amused themselves by dancing to the sound of the tomtom. Their dancing was more decorous than that of the Wolof negroes in the neighbourhood of the Senegal.

On the 14th of June, at seven in the morning, our caravan proceeded onward in the direction of E. S. E. After travelling three miles, we passed near the river, and advanced six miles eastward. We then turned half a mile to the north, to reach the village of Fessadougou, where we halted about noon. This village, which contains a population of about three or four hundred, is situated on the bank of a river, about half the width of the Dhioliba at Courouassa. I at first conjectured that it was a branch of that river; but I observed that the direction of its current, which flowed at the rate of about three miles and a half an hour, was from south to north. The Mandingoes informed me that it falls into the Dhioliba, not far from this place. The river is called the Yendan; its banks are for the most part low and open, but, about six miles from the village, there are, on both sides, some little hills. Fessadougou is a part of the Sangaran.

Our road, during the day, was partly sandy, and partly covered with red porous stones. The country is thickly overgrown with large trees, which renders it exceedingly pleasant. In the neighbourhood of Fessadougou, the cé and the nédé are very abundant; indeed, they are the only trees reared by cultivation, and they are highly useful to the inhabitants. In the vicinity of the village I saw tilled land in very good order. Our host sent us a supper.

On the 15th of June, after paying our reckoning in a little tobacco and salt, as we had done all along the road from Cambaya, we crossed the river in canoes. It was near ten o'clock when we reached the right bank. We then proceeded four miles to the S. E., over a gravelly soil. I had not yet got rid of the fever, but I had enjoyed a little rest during the night.

The heat was excessive, and my guide insisted on my using my umbrella to shade me from the scorching rays of the sun: he himself took the precaution of letting it down, whenever we approached any inhabited place. It was near half-past eleven when we halted at Farancou-Manbata, a village containing between three and four hundred inhabitants. Our road, next day, lay through a tract of country, in which we should have to travel a considerable distance without coming to any villages. A storm arose soon after we entered Farancou-Manbata, and it rained heavily. At seven, on the morning of the 15th of June, we resumed our journey, travelling twenty-two miles in the same direction, and crossing several little streams. The surface of the ground was covered with red stones and gravel. The country was generally level, but some hills were visible to the east and west.

About half-past four in the afternoon we stopped to rest in some huts, made of branches of trees, covered with straw. We had travelled at a great rate during the day: indeed, we might be said to have run rather than walked, for we were anxious to reach Kankan next day. On the road we met many Mandingo merchants going to the Fouta-Dhialon. They looked at me with great astonishment, but did not inquire whether I was a Moor, or a christian. The saracolets travelled even faster than we: they were going to the ourondé (slave village) of Kankan. On my expressing a wish to go thither also, my guide observed that it was too distant: it is true, we were greatly fatigued by our forced march. I had now the good fortune to be free from fever. In the evening it thundered and lightened, but without rain. We ate our supper with a good appetite, and, though our bed consisted only of a little straw scattered over the stones, we enjoyed a good night's rest.

At half-past five in the morning of the 17th of June, we proceeded southward, and after travelling three miles and a half, we halted near the ourondé, and joined the saracolets, who were going to Kankan. I saw some well cultivated fields of yams, pistachios, and maize. The foigné was already in a pretty advanced state. We next entered a fine plain. I saw in the distance some little hillocks, and I remarked that the ground sloped gently to E. N. E. Many negroes ran after us to see the caravan. We had gone four miles and a half S. S. E. In some places the soil was red, mixed with gravel, and very fertile. The country is covered with cés and nédés. We crossed a little stream, and about ten o'clock arrived at the town, which is the capital of Kankan. My guide insisted upon my opening my umbrella, to make my entrance into his native place. On the road we had met some Mandingoes on horseback, very neatly dressed, and wearing large straw hats, made in the country, and of a round form, like those worn by the French peasantry. I was told that these Mandingoes were going to the fields to superintend their slaves. Lamfia lodged me in one of his huts, with a Foulah, who travelled with us, and had come to Kankan to exchange cloth for salt. On Lamfia's arrival, all his family ran to greet him, for he had been absent a considerable time. He called for milk, some of which he gave to me. During the whole of the evening, people thronged to Lamfia's yard to see the Arab sherif. I was visited by several Mandingoes of rank, and by a good old Moor, who had been settled in the place for some time. I did not go out of my hut for three days, as I wished to recover from my fatigue. I also took some doses of sulphate of quinine.

On the 10th, I went, accompanied by Lamfia and some old men, to wait upon the chief, whom the Mandingoes of this part of Africa call Dougou-tigui. He had already been informed of my arrival. He received me kindly, and made me sit down on a bullock's hide. I solicited his permission to pass through his country on my way to Jenné, and he replied that he would order me to be conducted thither on the first occasion. I allowed Lamfia to speak for me, for I could only express myself very imperfectly in the language of the country, and he related very circumstantially the stories I had circulated respecting the way in which I had been taken by the christians. The old chief, whose name was Mamadi-Sanici, was the father of the Mandingo who had so kindly helped me out of my scrape with the Bondouké at Sancougnan. After taking leave of the chief we returned home. My guide had ordered a bull's hide to be laid down in my hut. This served for my bed, and, besides a jar containing foigné, it was the only furniture in the place. When any suspicious persons in the village asserted that I was a christian, and that I was not at all like a Moor, Lamfia warmly took my part, and became very angry with those who sought to injure me. He was particularly kind to me. We ate our meals together, and twice a day we were served with a good mess of rice, with a sauce composed of pistachio-nuts, and a good quantity of onions, which thrive well here. Every evening Lamfia ordered a fire to be lighted in my hut, a custom which is very general throughout all the country. The negroes, indeed, burn fires at all seasons of the year, and keep them up the whole night. On the day of my arrival I made my guide a present, as a reward for his attention to me on my journey. This present consisted of a yard of blue Guinea cloth, which he had expressed a wish to have, three yards of printed calico, and six sheets of paper. He seemed much pleased, thanked me gratefully, and promised to conduct me to the Wassoulo, where I subsequently learned that he had to go on business of his own. He passed part of the day with me in my hut, because he said he did not wish to leave me alone with the strangers who came to see me. He employed himself in sewing together pieces of cloth of the country.

On the market day, the chief of Kankan sent for me. I obeyed the summons, accompanied by my guide. On entering the hut of Mamadi-Sanici, I found assembled a number of old men all well dressed. I must confess that I felt no small degree of uneasiness and anxiety to learn what decision they would pronounce on the fate of an Arab, whom several among them declared to be a christian. First of all a short prayer was said. My guide was questioned as to the way in which he had become acquainted with me. Lamfia spoke a great deal, and said that the chief of Cambaya had directed him to conduct me to Mamadi-Sanici, at Kankan; that I wished to go to Jenné, with the intention of proceeding to Mecca, my native country. He particularly dwelt on the circumstance that Mr. Macaulay, the king of the whites at Sierra Leone, for so the negroes style him, had wished to establish me in trade, at that place;

but that I had repelled the odious idea of remaining among infidels. I was then asked the names of my parents; whether they were still living; whether I had any other relations, and whether I should know them again on my arrival in my native country. I replied that having left Egypt very young, I was quite ignorant of the condition of my parents, if, indeed, they were still living. After this examination, the old men deliberated together for a short time and then dismissed me, telling me that I must remain with Lamfia, to whose care the chief, Mamadi-Sanici, had recommended me. On leaving the assembly, I asked my guide what decision had been formed relative to my journey. He told me it had been determined that it would be better for me to go by the way of Wassoulo instead of Bouré, as the latter place was then at war with Kankan, and that one of their men had already been killed on that road. He added, that I was to be conducted by the first opportunity to the Wassoulo, whence I might proceed to Jenné, either by way of Ségo, or Lambatikila, whichever I preferred. I was very well pleased with this decision, and returned to my hut to get a few glass ornaments, with which I went to the market to buy some milk.

On the 22nd of June, I went to the mosque accompanied by my guide. The mosque is a square building of earth, with doors on three of its sides looking west, north, and south. It contains several avenues formed by large posts, or pillars, which support the roof. It is not near so neatly built as the straw mosques of the Fouta-Dhialon. The prayers were very short; but the almamy, or spiritual chief, read some passages of the Koran. All the people present were very clean in their dress. The women have a mosque to themselves, for they are not permitted to enter the men's place of worship. The women's mosque was not much frequented. Our religious service being ended, I saw some well-dressed old men proceed to the women's mosque, which is built of straw, and very airy. Thither I was summoned, together with my guide, and we were both desired to sit down in the middle of the assembly. Lamfia was again questioned respecting the circumstances which had induced me to travel through the country. The answers of my guide were repeated aloud by a crier, in order that they might be heard by those who were outside. When his examination was ended, one of the old men asked me whether I had any more to say, or whether all that Lamfia had said was true. I replied that it was. The saracolet, who spoke Arabic, and had travelled with us from Baléya, was then called in; I repeated in Arabic all that my guide had first stated. The saracolet was desired to put many questions to me; but he got rid of this task by saying that the Arabic spoken in my country, was not at all like that which he understood. Lamfia was then praised for the manner in which he had treated me, and the whole assembly unanimously agreed that I was a true Musulman. The meeting had only been held to make all the inhabitants acquainted with my journey through the country, and the circumstances which occasioned it. Thus, I had nothing to fear from those who might take me for a European. The assembly consisted of between a thousand and twelve hundred persons, all very well dressed, and there were many more outside than in the mosque, which is very large. We were informed that we might retire, and we did not wait to be told so a second time. After this examination, I regularly attended the mosque in order to lull suspicion, and when any one entered my hut, I took care to be holding in my hand a leaf of the Koran. I frequently saw the saracolet, to whom I gave the pair of scissors, which I had promised him on the road. He professed a regard for me, and wished to take me with him to Ségo. I thought he wished to extort further presents from me; but, perhaps, I was somewhat prejudiced against him. He and his comrade rested for some days at Kankan. I did not wish to go by the way of Ségo, being apprehensive of detection there, and, besides, had I gone thither, I must, on account of the continual war between the two countries, have renounced all intention of visiting Jenné, whither I wished to go. I must confess too, that I did not like the assiduous attention of the saracolet. His officious kindness appeared to me suspicious, and I determined not to put his honesty to the test, feeling pretty certain that if I did, I should have reason to repent it. I, therefore, allowed him to depart for Kankari, where he was to embark on a river which flows into the Dhioliba, and on landing, to take the road to Ségo. Following the advice I had received from the good old Moor Mohammed, who was perfectly acquainted with the country, I resolved, to go by way of Sambatikila, whence I could proceed to Jenné in greater security. I was assured that those who performed the pilgrimage to Mecca always took that road, and that a Foulah of the Fouta-Toro had even crossed the Bondou, a part of the Fouta-Dhialon, Baléya, and Kankan, to reach Jenné, by the way of Sambatikila, rather than go by Kaarta and Ségo. I had, therefore, only to wait for a guide, and a favourable opportunity of availing myself of his services.

On the 23rd of June, my friend, the saracolet, came to inquire after my health. He asked me why I did not call to see him in his hut. He seated himself beside me on a sheep-skin, and after the usual compliments he gave me a small piece of paper, on which there was some writing in Arabic characters. This was a grigri, and he assured me that as long as I kept it about me, I might travel in safety and without fear of illness. I gratefully accepted this precious talisman in return for which I gave a few charges of gunpowder.

On the 24th of June, the saracolet again paid me a visit. He begged me to write him a charm which would make him as rich as the whites. I told him that, having left my country very young, I did not understand the art of writing charms; but if I did I should of course employ my skill for my own advantage. However, I told him that I could give him a piece of advice, and if he followed it he would certainly grow rich. I reminded him that he had often spoken to me of the gold mines of Kankari. "Now," said I, "when you get there, make your slaves dig up the ore, and when you have got a certain quantity of gold, take it to the christians, and with that talisman you can obtain whatever you want." He laughed and said he knew of that talisman before, but that it was a piece of advice which it would be very difficult to follow. I thus got rid of this troublesome fellow, and also took my revenge for the falsehood he had trumped up with the view of tempting me to go to Kankari with him; for I was assured that there was no such thing as a gold mine in that place.

On the 25th of June, I inspected my baggage, which I did not keep fastened up. I found that I had been robbed of part of my paper. Lamfia continued to show me so much kindness, that I could not possibly suspect him. When I mentioned the circumstance to him, he seemed greatly astonished and protested that he was not the thief. He went and fetched the things which I had given him, and desired a negro, who was in my hut, to return them to me. But I refused to accept them, observing that I placed too much confidence in him to suspect that he had robbed me. He then told me that he had seen the Foulah, who was my fellow-lodger in the hut, rummaging among my things for which he (Lamfia) had been very angry with him, and desired him never again to touch the Arab's property. The poor Foulah, whom he thus accused, had been gone three days on his return to his own country. I passed over this little dishonesty in silence. In the evening I went with Lamfia to see a negro just arrived from Jenné: this man's hair was indescribably filthy, but in spite of this disadvantage he had an air of pretension about him and appeared perfectly self-satisfied. He moved his head from one side to another, and shook his dirty hair, which was long and platted. I and my guide sat down beside him, and he began to scrutinize me with great curiosity, appearing to doubt whether I was an Arab. He was told whence I came and that I wished to go to Jenné. I inquired of him the distance from that town to Kankan, and begged him to inform me what sort of people I should meet with on the road. He assured me positively that it was a journey of three months and ten days, and when I remarked that it would consequently be necessary to rest by the way, he told me that, on the contrary, the caravans travelled every day. He said that most of the tribes between Kankan and Jenné were idolaters, and that there were very few Musulmans among them. He assured me that I should have many difficulties to encounter; that the negroes would take me for a white; and that they had no great liking for people of my colour. As for the difficulties, which he spoke of, I had made up my mind to meet and to surmount them but I was somewhat startled by the length of the journey which I should be obliged to perform on foot; I soon bethought myself, indeed, that the negroes never count the time which their journeys take and that this man could not know for certain how long he had been on his. I was desirous of setting off as soon as possible, before the rains became heavier, but I wanted a guide, and I could not find one willing to accompany me to Sambatikila, though I promised a handsome present as a reward. I was therefore persuaded to wait for an opportunity, which would, I was told, soon occur; and I was glad to hear, that there were numerous communications between Kankan and the country to which I was bound.

On the 29th of June, the saracolets and some Mandingoes prepared to set out on their journey through the woods Which separate Kankan from the Wassoulo. My saracolet friend came to see me, and asked me if I was ready to go with him, observing that I should not, for some time, meet with so favourable an opportunity for traversing the woods of the Wassoulo, which were infested with robbers. I informed him of my resolution of going to Sambatikila, and thence to Jenné. After inquiring of some Mandingoes, whether that road, with which he was not acquainted, would answer my views, he bade me adieu. I confess I was heartily glad to be rid of him. Perhaps, as I have said before, I was prejudiced against the saracolets, in consequence of what I had seen of their conduct at Sierra-Leone. This man certainly appeared to be very obliging, and possibly might not have been as great a rogue as the rest; yet I could not prevail upon myself to trust him.

Being resolved to take advantage of the first opportunity for departing, I disposed of part of my merchandise, in order to lighten my baggage, and sold a flask of powder, and a piece of Guinea cloth; the rest of my property, consisting of silks, glass trinkets, amber, and coral, I kept to carry with me. I sold the gunpowder and cloth at a profit of sixty per cent.; for I would take nothing in payment but gold, which had became extremely scarce in the country since the communications between Bouré and Kankan had been interrupted by the war. I did not speak the Mandingo language sufficiently well to dispose of the things myself, and I commissioned Lamfia to transact the business for me. He told me that, to make sure of a good sale for his commodities, he was in the habit of writing a grigri on a board such as school-boys learn to write on; then washing off the writing, he sprinkled with the water the articles he wished to dispose of: by this method he said he was sure of a good profit. I believe, however, that an understanding existed between him and the person who bought my powder and Guinea cloth, and that he gained some little advantage himself by the transaction.

He expressed a desire to purchase my tobacco for some trumpery glass trinkets, which he could not otherwise dispose of. To persuade me to strike the bargain, he assured me that, in the countries through which I was about to pass, tobacco would obtain no price, but that glass ornaments, on the contrary, had a very ready sale. In order to get rid of his importunity, I made the exchange, and I observed that he cheated me, setting a very low value on the tobacco. I made a similar exchange with another Mandingo, who treated me better. I was told that there was at Wassoulo a saracolet merchant, going to Sambatikila, who must set off in a few days. It was determined that Lamfia and I should go and join him, and that I should travel the rest of the way with him. We agreed to set out after the festival of the Salam, which would take place in a few days; but it was ordained otherwise as will be seen presently.

I went several times to the market, which is held twice a week in the town of Kankan. I observed in it several people from the Wassoulo, Sangaran, and Toron, who come to trade in this place. They bring cloth, honey, wax, which is carried to our establishments on the coast, cotton, cattle, and gold. The inhabitants of Toron are distinguished by their dress. It consists of a short yellow coussabe, wide trowsers of the same colour, and exceedingly dirty, a large round straw hat, and occasionally sandals. They are all armed with sabres, which they procure from the Mandingo merchants. They have also bows and quivers filled with arrows, and they carry lances in their hand. A linen band is passed round their waists, to fasten the coussabe, which is very short and narrow. They wear beards like the Musulmans, but pay so little attention to cleanliness, that their faces appear covered with filth. They use great quantities of snuff, and smoke still more; habits which increase their natural dirtiness, They do not smoke while travelling, but when they halt they make amends for their self-denial. I was told that they meet and pass whole days under the shade of large trees, in smoking and conversing with one another. They are idolaters. All whom I saw were tall, well made men, and of a warlike appearance. They are as black as the Mandingoes, whom, however, they do not resemble in features. Their faces are rather round, their noses short, though not flat, and their lips thin. I never saw any women of that nation, but I presume that their dress is neither more elegant nor cleaner than that of the men, consisting, I suppose, of a piece of their own cotton cloth fastened round their waists. These people have woolly hair, and wear it platted. The custom of the country allows a man to take as many wives as he can support, but the obligation of giving a large present to the bride's mother deters them from taking so many wives as they would otherwise do. This custom prevails generally among all idolatrous nations. Toron is subject to numerous petty chiefs, all independent of each other, and possessing despotic authority. The dignity of chief is hereditary. The people rear large herds of oxen and sheep, and keep a great quantity of fowls. Their mountainous country furnishes them with honey, of which they are extremely fond, and which they bring for sale to the market of Kankan. Their fertile soil produces all the necessaries of life; and I was told that they bestow great care on its cultivation. They grow rice, yams, cassava, pistachio-nuts, foigné, maize, and millet. They manufacture a great deal of cotton stuff, not more than five inches broad. I have seen them wear poniards of their own making, and they also make their agricultural implements, but where they get the iron I did not learn. The inhabitants of Toron are often at war with the people of Kankan, who wish to make them embrace the religion of the Prophet. They are naturally brave, and vigorously repel the attacks of the Musulmans, who are not sufficiently strong to keep up a continual warfare.

But to return to the market. It is always well stocked with European goods, brought from the coast by Mandingo merchants, consisting of muskets, powder, printed calico, blue and white Guinea cloth, amber, coral, glass beads, and hardware. I also saw a good deal of white cloth, manufactured in the Wassoulo; earthen pots made in the country; all kinds of provisions, such as rice, foigné, yams, cassava, &c. Fowls, sheep, oxen, and horses, are brought by the inhabitants of other countries. Fire-wood is also sold in this market by slaves, who by this traffic procure for themselves a little salt, which is very dear, but is the principal article of barter. I observed that several merchants had gold, but they attached great value to it, and exchanged it for none but the choicest articles. All the dealers are provided with small scales made in the country, and which appeared to be tolerably accurate. The seeds of a tree which grows in the Fouta-Dhialon, the name of which I have forgotten, are used for weights. These seeds are black and of the size and shape of corossol seeds, but rather heavier. A piece of gold of the weight of two of these seeds is worth six francs. The dealers are never deceived by their weights, which are as accurate as ours. The gold, which I saw in the Kankan, and which I was told came from the mines of Bouré, was made into ear-rings of the value of six gourdes. There are also some worth twenty-five gourdes. I saw likewise gold in small grains, of the size of shot, and even less. These grains were usually kept in quills. Lamfia told me in confidence that the merchants, who possess gold, conceal it in grigris covered with tanned hide, which they fasten round their necks or arms, by a leather thong. They adopt this precaution for fear of being robbed on their journeys. Since the theft which had been committed on me, I had become suspicious, and I never went out without adopting some precaution for the security of what I left behind me. Still I went twice a day to the mosque, that I might appear extremely pious, for I saw the necessity of blinding the negroes, some of whom were not well disposed towards me, and declared that I was a white. The Mandingoes are certainly not fond of the whites, and they hold the name of a christian in abhorrence; and yet they do not despise Europeans. It is religious fanaticism alone that makes them view us unfavourably, and even if they had discovered who I was, it is possible that they would not have ill-treated me, though they would very probably have robbed me, and prevented me from continuing my journey. I found the inhabitants of Kankan as troublesome, and as much addicted to begging, as those of Cambaya, and not more generous. I received only a few colat-nuts from them; but the chief certainly made me a present of a bit of meat, at the solicitation of Mohammed, a Moor who was settled here. I had not asked Mohammed to make this request, but he, reckoned on getting his share of the feast; and accordingly he and I made a good supper of the chief's present.

The 5th of July was the festival of the Salam, which is always celebrated with great pomp by the Musulmans. Lamfia had on the preceding day asked me whether I intended to buy any meat to celebrate the festival. I told him, that as I had a long journey to perform, with but little to defray my expences, it behoved me to be economical, if I did not wish to be left on the road: he made no reply, but did not appear well pleased. I was present at the festival in company with my guide. It was held on an extensive plain east of the village, not far from the Milo. In passing through the streets, I observed several venerable old men, clothed in short scarlet mantles, the edges of which were trimmed with a yellow sprigged cotton, in imitation of gold lace. They walked separately, and were followed by a numerous train. As they proceeded along, they chanted *Allah-akbar, Allah-akbar, la illa il-Allah, Allah-akbar,* &c.; these words were repeated by their retinue, which increased in number every minute. In their right hands they held lances, and they wore red caps on their heads. On arriving at the plain, I saw a numerous concourse of people attired in a motley variety of costumes. The greater part wore the dress of the country, consisting of a coussabe, trowsers, a pointed cap, and sandals. Several of them were bedecked in old scarlet coats of the English soldiers, which they had procured at Sierra-Leone, or the Gambia: others were wrapped in old European cloaks, of various colours, and had European hats on their heads. In short, they had bedizened themselves in all the rags and tatters they could collect; and no doubt every one had put on his complete full-dress suit, in honour of the important occasion. All the men were armed with guns, lances, bows, and arrows, which, during prayer, they laid on the ground. The old men in the red cloaks arrived, followed by crowds of people. The chief soon appeared on horseback, escorted by two or three hundred Mandingoes, forming a file on each side of him; these Mandingoes were all armed with muskets. A flag of rose-coloured taffeta was borne before the chief. The almamy, or spiritual chief, followed Mamadi-Sanici, who may be called the chief magistrate: both were escorted by a guard, carrying white silk flags, which had in the centre a small piece of red, in the form of a heart. Mamadi-Sanici was dressed simply, but neatly. The almamy, however, was magnificently attired; he wore a fine scarlet mantle, trimmed with gold-lace and fringe, which had been presented to him by Major Peddie, during his stay at Kakondy, on the Rio Nuñez; for, when the Major was setting out to explore the interior of Africa, he sent presents to the different chiefs, in order to conciliate their favour.

The old men who wore the red mantles had evidently taken a pattern from the almamy's. The music of the festival consisted of two large drums, exactly resembling those used at Cambaya, which I have already described. The almamy repeated the prayer with an air of sincere devotion. It was a solemn spectacle to behold so numerous an assembly all kneeling in adoration of their God. The prayer being ended, the old men in the red cloaks formed a canopy with some white pagnes; beneath the canopy a seat was placed for the almamy, who, having taken his allotted station, read a long prayer in Arabic, of which, certainly, none of his auditory understood a word. After this prayer, the chief, Mamadi-Sanici, harangued the people, and a man standing by his side repeated in a loud voice what he said, that every one might hear. I was told that he exhorted his subjects to transfer their trade to the Wassoulo, Baléya, and the Fouta-Dhialon, adding that the road to Bouré was so extremely dangerous, that all dealings in that quarter must be suspended until further orders. After this short harangue, the crowd hastily retired. So rapid was their movement, that the gates were not large enough to allow the people to pass; men and horses mingled together in the rush. Women attended the festival, but they kept at a respectful distance from the men. They likewise joined in prayer. As soon as the ceremony was over, the paschal lamb was slaughtered, and the people regaled themselves during the rest of the day: feasting is indeed the greatest enjoyment of the negroes. Lamfia attended the festival arrayed in my woollen wrapper, and, being determined on making a grand display, he held my umbrella over his head the whole time, under the pretence of shading himself from the sun. Before we left his home, he had asked me to attire myself in this manner, but I declined it, and told him that he might have the use of the umbrella for the occasion. This was market day, and I did not perceive that it was more thinly attended on account of the festival. I went thither to get a little cassava for my guide, who began to be less attentive than heretofore; probably because I had no more fine presents to make him, he had given me no breakfast. By way of excuse for this neglect, he told me, that as it was a festival, and market-day, his women were busy; but we had two who had nothing else to do but to prepare the food of the family, and they were supplied with wood by the slaves, who pick it up in the fields.

The rest of the day passed off without any further rejoicing. At supper, which was later than usual, the women assembled to take their repast together, and they made themselves very merry; but, their games are far from being so lively as those of the idolatrous negroes of Baléya and Amana. They leaped and danced about the hut and the yard, holding a piece of meat in their hand, and biting at it in a disgusting manner. Music and dancing are forbidden among the Musulmans, and consequently their amusements are far from equalling in frolic and gaiety those which prevail among the pagans. After supper I was visited by an old marabout, who had come from Ségo; he looked at me with an expression of great curiosity, and could not help laughing at the length of my nose, assuring me that he had never seen any thing like it; he lavished benedictions upon me, as well as Lamfia, whose behaviour to me he praised highly. Lamfia greatly commended my religious zeal. This marabout confirmed the news which I had heard of a war between Ségo and Jenné, and he advised me to go by the way of Sambatikila. My host cut off two or three ells of the cloth of native manufacture, as a present for the marabout, who took care to give him a good dose of flattery. As soon as he had received the present, he went off, loading Lamfia with fresh benedictions, and praising his generosity.

On the 6th of July, being alone in my hut, I took the opportunity to examine my merchandise, which, unfortunately, was not under lock and key. I discovered, that some one had been meddling with my things, for the packets of glass-beads were not tied up in the manner in which I had left them; I immediately looked over carefully all my baggage, and, to my mortification, I found that I had been robbed, and that my most beautiful beads had disappeared. Fortunately I had on the eve of the festival hid my amber, my coral, and a little silver, in a small bag, containing cream of tartar and purgative salts. The thief had begun to open the bag of salts, but when he saw what it contained, he had thrown it aside, and fallen upon the glass beads: a razor, which I had lent on the preceding day to Lamfia, to cut his mustaches, and which he had often begged me to give to him, had also disappeared. This man believed me to be richer than I was. He thought that I possessed silver, gold, and a good stock of amber, and coral; he frequently asked me to sell him some, but I always took care to tell him I had none. On the day of the festival, I went out to the market, and also called upon a Mandingo, who wished to accompany me to Jenné and thence to travel to Mecca. He was about thirty-five or forty years old, and, notwithstanding his zeal for religion, he could not prevail on himself to disobey his father, who was very averse to his undertaking such a journey. Disobedience in such a case might well have been excusable, since it arose from a desire to please God.

I took care to let my host know that I was aware of his having been alone in my hut: I told him this in the presence of several persons, who came to see me. He appeared to be much vexed at the loss I had sustained. He made a great noise, assuring the Mandingoes who were present, that every person had gone out to prayer on the day of the festival, and that no one remained in the house but a little girl, ten or twelve years old. Not being able to throw the blame, as he before did, on the poor Foulah of the Fouta-Dhialon, he ordered the young slave to appear, and, addressing her in a severe tone, laid hold of both her hands in one of his, and threatened to beat her, if she did not name the person who had been in the hut during our absence. The girl declared that no one had entered, and that she had not quitted the hut. Lamfia then suspended his threats, lest the girl might say something to criminate himself. He loosed her hands, and said to the by-standers, that it was impossible I could have been robbed. I was pretty sure that this theft had not been committed by strangers; for I took the precaution, previously to going to prayer, to deposit my things in the millet jar, and no one besides Lamfia saw me do so. I did not at this moment mention to him the razor, which was also missing; but he continued to make a great disturbance, and to threaten the little slave, who, however, came off at last with the fright, as I did with the loss of my glass beads. When I reflected on the kind interest which this man had evinced for me, I could not fix my suspicions on him; and I secretly accused his wives, who had often appeared to wish for my glass ornaments. As for Lamfia, he constantly repeated that I could not have known how much merchandise I had, and that I certainly had not been robbed. This excited my indignation, and I looked angrily at him. He cast down his head, being unable to face me, and, from that moment, I deemed him guilty. I no longer accused any one but him, and determined to keep a vigilant look-out for the future. In the evening, he asked me very coolly if I intended to go the mosque: I replied, that I wished very much to go, but that I was apprehensive for the safety of the rest of my things, as the thief might not perhaps be so moderate as on the former occasion. At this he again hung down his head like a criminal. However, I endeavoured not to let my just suspicions be observed, or at least, not so as to make them be talked of abroad, which might have been attended with fatal consequences to myself: but, in spite of my caution, the affair became known. Being unable to stay continually at home to watch my property, I sent for a padlock to put on my bag. Lamfia, who still wished to appear extremely complaisant, took upon himself the trouble of making this purchase. I fixed the padlock on my bag, and, when I turned the key in his presence, he said to me, "Now, you will no longer run any risk of being robbed." — "Yes," I replied, "but that will not bring back my glass beads. It is now too late; I should have put a lock on my baggage sooner, if I had not thought that every thing was safe with you." He felt this reproach, and was visibly affected by it, but endeavoured to extricate himself from his embarrassment, by disputing the fact of the robbery, and observing, that a thief would not have been content with part of my goods, but have carried off the whole. This way of talking, however, served to confirm my suspicion; because, if the thief had been a stranger, he would probably have taken all, but he, fearing the consequences of detection, had pilfered only a part, in the hope that the loss would escape my notice.

The situation became painful; he feared that, if I continued much longer in the place, my complaints might be attended with more disagreeable effects to himself; he was therefore anxious to hasten our departure. In the evening I went with him to take leave of the mansa, and, though perfectly convinced that he had robbed me, I resolved to travel through the forest with him, rather than take the chance of being worse served by another guide. We did not find the chief at home, as he had gone to the ourondé to inspect his slaves. We therefore postponed our farewell interview until the following morning. On the same day the women and children assembled about me in the yard, and pretended to shew me glass beads similar to those I had lost. Lamfia affected not to notice these insults, fearing, perhaps, a new altercation with me. I stifled my displeasure, and waited patiently to see the end of this scene, without shewing any anger, which I was certain would only serve to prolong it. I had eaten nothing all day, and a little after sun-set, he gave me some rice very well prepared. Previously to this affair, he always took care to order his supper to be got ready early, that we might take that meal together a little before the sun went down, because, as he said, the Arabs do not like late suppers. Indeed, I could not but feel grateful for the attention he had hitherto paid me. When I fell asleep during the day in my hut, I was often surprised on awaking, to find pistachio-nuts roasted and properly prepared, laid down beside me. I was also indebted to him for always taking my part against any one who wished to injure me. I was nevertheless destined to be the dupe of his assiduities.

On the 7th of July we repaired again to the house of the mansa, to take leave of him, but he was still absent. On our way home I said to Lamfia, perhaps imprudently, that the thief had also taken the razor with which he had shaved himself on the day before the festival. He replied in a very confident manner, that he considered this impossible, and that it was certainly in my sack.

On our return to the hut, he begged me, in the presence of the Mandingo, to examine my baggage once more. After various useless searches, long discussions, and many goings and comings, the razor was at length found in the millet jar, where I am certain it had been that moment put, in the hope of persuading me that it had not been stolen but mislaid. Lamfia wished to restore it to me, but I would not take it, telling him that I wished to have at the same time, all the things I had lost. At this observation he appeared very much disconcerted. Two old men advised me to complain to the chief, if the thief did not immediately restore every thing he had taken. I seized the idea, and threatened to adopt it. He was alarmed, and requested me to wait a little. After a moment's reflexion he observed, that as I had been robbed under his roof, and as my person and property had been entrusted to his care by the chief of Cambaya, I was under his responsibility, and he therefore considered himself bound to make good whatever I had lost. On this condition I promised silence; but, finding that he was in no hurry to keep his word, and fearing to be plundered a third time, I followed the advice of several old men, who accompanied me to the chief of the district, to beg of him to give me a lodging, until an opportunity should occur for travelling across the forest of Wassoulo. Lamfia, who accompanied us, carried my sack. He had already several times proposed to go to the mansa, to submit to an ordeal, which consisted in passing a red-hot iron across the tongue. The person accused is acquitted if the iron do not burn him, but in that case the accuser is obliged to submit to the same ordeal. Judgment is pronounced against the party who refuses to undergo the operation. If it be the prosecutor, he must make reparation by giving the accused a present; if the latter, he must restore the value of what he is thus found guilty of stealing. This absurd custom, which ignorance has established, prevails throughout the whole of western Africa.

We found the chief in the midst of business. He was presiding over the council of elders, assembled at the women's mosque. We entered a hut, and soon afterwards the judges arrived. A native of Kankan, who knew something of Arabic, acted as my interpreter; I asked him to perform this office for me, as I did not understand the Mandingo sufficiently to make myself understood. He declared to the assembly, in terms which appeared to me very forcible, the manner in which I had been robbed; mentioning every particular, even the razor scene. Lamfia maintained, with great boldness, that I had not been robbed; he reverted once more to the loss of my paper, still accusing the absent Foulah. My interpreter answered, and stated in my name, that I could never sufficiently express the sense I entertained of the kind reception I had experienced from the inhabitants of Fouta-Dhialon, on my passage through their country; that so far from cheating me, they had behaved to me with the most generous hospitality; that there was no doubt that the person who had stolen my glass beads had also taken the paper. Lamfia, to justify himself, and defend his character, proposed to submit to the ordeal of red-hot iron, which often takes place among the people without any appeal to the judge. The mansa, however, ordered him to be silent. This chief, with whom I asked leave to lodge, advised me to remain with my present host, as he was to depart in two days, with a number of other merchants, to traverse the forests of Wassoulo.[51] I suspected that the mansa was afraid of being put to the expense of maintaining me, and I did not insist further on taking up my residence with him. I replied that I would rather return to Fouta-Dhialon than remain longer with this man, and I requested to be permitted to live with the worthy old Moor, who had continued to pay me amicable visits, and with whom I had always been on good terms. To this the assembly gave a unanimous consent. I left all my baggage under the care of the mansa, until a place should be procured for me in which I could lock it up safely. He urged me, with an air of kindness, to take my woollen wrapper to lay over me at night, observing that I should probably be cold.

I returned to my old quarters to get some medicines which I had left, because Mamadi-Sanici had desired me to prescribe for him. I took a negro with me, as I feared I should be insulted if I went alone; for, though most of the people took my part, and were indignant at Lamfia's conduct, I was apprehensive that his passion, excited by the scene which had just passed, would lead him to some excess. My precaution was not taken in vain, for he received me very ill, and made a good deal of difficulty in giving me what I demanded. He would have driven me from his hut, and even went so far as to attempt to strike me; but several persons who were present, interfered, and condemned his behaviour. In his fury he said, what he himself had a thousand times contradicted, that I was a christian, who was endeavouring to penetrate into the east, to take advantage of the Musulmans and to overreach them.

This scene, which I had foreseen, but which I could not avoid, vexed me exceedingly, for I was afraid it might lead to unpleasant consequences. However, no attention was paid to Lamfia's fury; he was looked upon as a rogue irritated at finding himself discovered; and I was told not to mind his accusations. I endeavoured to interest the natives in my behalf, pointing out to them my critical situation, alone and almost destitute in a strange country, and to crown my misfortunes, speaking the language but imperfectly. Many appeared to pity me, and these were the most zealous followers of the Prophet. I then went to the humble hut of my new host, who received me in the best manner he could. He even offered me the mat on which he was himself accustomed to lie; but this I objected to take, being reluctant to deprive the old man of it. He insisted however that I should have it, observing that it became me as a stranger to yield to him, and allow him, a native of the country, to do the honours of his little hut in his own way. I partook of his frugal supper, consisting of a small plate of tau, with some good gombo sauce, seasoned with salt. How happens it that, in every country, the poor man is always the most charitable? Because, being himself unfortunate, he measures another's wants by his own.

On the morning of the 8th of July, the chief sent for me, and I and the Moor Mohammed went to him. He was visiting the alkali, [52] a Foulah of the Wassoulo, settled at Kankan. He was one of the richest men in the town, and was also a member of the council. I found three or four Mandingoes of rank, who accompanied Mamadi-Sanici. An account was given to all present of the theft that had been committed upon me, and I took notice that Lamfia's good conduct to me, up to the time of the discovery of the robbery, was mentioned in terms of praise. It was decided that, as no proofs could be brought against him, he could not be punished; a decision which I thought very just. I was informed that the alkali was to be my host, because the sherif Mohammed was poor, and had no rice to give me; and, it was added, that the hut which I should occupy was protected by a lock and key; so that I need not fear any further depredation. The persons present then expressed a desire to examine my effects, alleging, as a reason for so doing, that in case of my being robbed again they might know what I possessed. I was not thankful to them for this precaution; nevertheless, though much against my inclination, I displayed my merchandise, taking good care to hide my notes, lest they might give rise to suspicion. Every thing was closely examined; the glass beads were counted and the cloth was measured. They did not however find my amber, for I had concealed it among some cream of tartar. I opened the packet which contained it, and shewed them the white powder, which they tasted, supposing it to be sugar. When undeceived, they were very anxious that I should give them some medicine: all declaring themselves to be unwell. After having examined every thing, they allowed me to pack up my goods, and none of them asked me for any thing except medicine. A hut was assigned to me, and I placed my property under lock and key, in a store-house, which was attached to my dwelling, a thing I had not before seen in the country. I was very well attended to, and supplied with every thing I could possibly want; but, as I did not wish to live at any one's expence, I proposed to buy rice, for myself at the market. This was opposed, however, and I was told that I should want for nothing.

This new host being very devout, I took care to be exceedingly attentive to prayers. But I impatiently looked for an opportunity to depart; and I was induced to hope that one would shortly occur. The rains had begun to be frequent; not a day passed over without a storm, and I was continually tormented by the thought that the country through which I should have to travel would be flooded. But even this was less distressing than the idea of staying in a place, where the quarrel which I had had with Lamfia promised me no security for the future. I was afraid that his ill-will towards me might give rise to something unpleasant. However, I was very comfortable with my new host, who was very rich, and much more generous than the generality of Mandingoes. He possessed numerous herds of oxen and cows, which supplied him with abundance of excellent milk. He often sent me some of it, together with a déguet, (a sort of couscous) an attention which no Mandingo had before paid me, with the exception of a sherif of the country, who gave me a little milk, because, as he said, we were relations. I was a neighbour to the Moor Mohammed, and every evening we took our supper together. He often came to bear me company, and he helped to while away my tedious hours, by introducing me to all his friends. This good old man, who was about sixty, was short, and had the features of an Arab; he was inconceivably active, and talked much, and with great rapidity. His wife, who was a negress, had borne him a son, who was at that time between twelve and fifteen years old. The lad was a poor looking creature, and his delicate health caused much anxiety to his old father. The mother was extremely industrious; she cooked all the victuals, and attended to the household concerns. Mohammed had a slave, whom he employed in cultivating a little garden, which surrounded his habitation. Three huts, built upon a piece of ground which the alkali had given him, served for the dwelling of himself and family. He had no field to cultivate, and his only resource was to go from place to place, asking the Mandingoes for rice, foigné, salt, meat, &c. for the maintainance of his family. In the middle of his garden he had a beautiful orange-tree, which bore very fine fruit. He told me he was sorry the oranges were not ripe enough for me to taste them. His poverty, together with the disinterested hospitality which he had extended to me, interested me exceedingly. I regretted that I could not meliorate his condition; but I forced him to accept a few small presents, for which he testified his gratitude in the warmest terms. Mamadi-Sanici sent to ask me for a remedy to give to one of his wives, who had sore eyes. I did not know what to give him, but as it was to my interest not to refuse him any thing, I put a little volatile alkali in water, and directed the eyes to be bathed with it, thinking that at all events it could do no harm. My presence, however, was required, and I went and bathed the patient's eyes myself. The mansa took the opportunity of asking me for an application for a bad foot, with which he had been afflicted for some years. I prescribed poultices of purslain, which grows spontaneously all over the country. The diseases which I observed to prevail among the people were ulcers on the legs, fevers, leprosy, elephantiasis, and goitre. I also noticed that several negroes had large white marks, of the colour of our skin, on their arms and legs, which I was told arose from ill health. I conjectured that they were marks of leprosy.

CHAPTER X

Further account of Kankan and its environs — Council of elders — State of trade, and civilization — Kissi — Bouré — Trade between Bouré and Bamako, Yamina, Ségo, Sansanding, and Jenné — Working of gold mines — Establishment of Bamako — Passage of the Milo, and several other tributary rivers of the Dhioliba.

The season was advancing. It was now the middle of July, and in August it becomes almost impossible to travel, the country being then entirely flooded: I was beginning to be very uneasy, when, fortunately, an opportunity occurred of starting for Sambatikila. I bargained with a Poulh[53] of the Fouta-Dhialon, who agreed to carry my luggage as far as the Wassoulo, for three heads of tobacco, worth about ten or twelve sous. My new guide, whose name was Arafanba, had a high reputation for piety; he appeared very obliging, and I was indebted to Mamadi-Sanici for recommending him. Our departure was fixed for the 16th of July; but before quitting Kankan I will give some further description of the place.

Kankan, the capital of a district of the same name, is a small town, situated at the distance of two gunshots from the left bank of the Milo, a fine river, flowing from the south, and fertilizing the country of Kissi, where it has its source. It runs to the N. E.: and discharges itself into the Dhioliba, two or three days' journey from Kankan. It is broad, deep, and fit for the navigation of canoes, drawing six or seven feet water. In the month of August it overflows, and fertilizes the neighbouring country. The following are the names of the villages which, as I was informed, are dependent on Kankan: Carfamoudeya, Diocana, Boucalan, Nafadi, Bacouco, Foussé, Sofino, Dio-Samana, and Kiémorou. The town is surrounded by fine thick quick-set hedges, which protect it much better than a mud or earth wall. It has two entrances, one on the west, and the other on the east. The population does not amount to more than six thousand; it is situated in a fertile plain of grey sand. None but very small hills are visible in the distance. In every direction there are small villages, or ourondés, for the slaves. These villages are ornaments to the country, for they are surrounded by fine plantations, where yams, maize, rice, foigné, onions, pistachio-nuts, and gombo are grown in abundance.

The inhabitants of Kankan are governed by a chief, called the *Dougou-tigui*, who never pronounces any decision without first convoking the council of elders, which usually meets in the mosque, and at which I was often present. The greatest silence prevails at these meetings; and, contrary to the usual practice of the negroes, each speaks in his turn, and those that do not conduct themselves properly are turned out. They are always very cautious in coming to a decision: they are afraid of committing an error, and therefore, deliberate leisurely. They are all Mahometans, and entertain a mortal hatred of pagans or infidels.

A market is held at Kankan three times a week, and, as I have before observed, all sorts of merchandise and necessaries of life are sold there. The Mandingoes are all traders, and travel a great deal. They go on foot to Sierra-Leone, Kakondy, Gambia, Senegal, and even to Jenné. Many of them spoke to me of M. Potin; a merchant at Senegal, and of M. Joffret, who belongs to the French factory at Albréda, on the Gambia. Their proximity to Bouré renders the people very rich, for they bring large quantities of gold from that country. In time of peace the women of Kankan go to Bouré to sell rice, millet, and various other articles of food, which they barter for gold. The men go to Kissi, where they procure handsome slaves, who are purchased each at the price of a cask of gunpowder, (containing twenty-five pounds), a bad musket (worth five gourdes) and four yards of pink silk. A Mandingo who possesses a dozen slaves may live at his ease without travelling, merely by taking the trouble to superintend them.

A brisk trade is carried on between the Kankan and the neighbouring countries, and it receives from the Wassoulo white cloth of native manufacture, which is highly valued in commerce; the inhabitants possess some hairy sheep, goats and abundance of horned cattle. These last are not so large as ours, and have a hump on the back, like those belonging to the Moors who inhabit the banks of the Senegal. The country also furnishes handsome horses, which, however, are far from attaining the excellence of the Arabians. I saw at the alkali's a mare which cost five slaves and two oxen; it was the finest animal I had met with throughout this part of Africa. The people rear a great quantity of poultry, and their cattle supply them with plenty of milk.

In their household affairs they are particularly neat and clean, and they are always dressed in very white cloth. They manufacture fine calico from the cotton which the women spin; they seldom sell it, but use it for their own garments. Each habitation is surrounded by a fence of straw or a thorn hedge. Within this enclosure are the huts, and on the outside of it is a small garden, in which the women and children cultivate maize and some tobacco.

The streets are broad and clean, and the town is shaded by numerous date-trees, papaws, bombaces, and baobabs.

At the distance of three days' journey south of Kankan is situated the first village of the Sangaran,. the name of which I have forgotten. Six days' journey further on, across the Sangaran lies the beautiful country of Kissi, which must not be confounded with Kissi-kissi, in the neighbourhood of Sierra-Leone. Lamfia, who made several journeys thither for the purpose of buying slaves, told me that the country is interspersed with mountains, and watered by numerous streams. The soil is very fertile, and the inhabitants cultivate a great quantity of rice, yams, foigné, and every necessary of life. They are all idolaters, and, like the Bambaras, they make incisions on their faces and other parts of their bodies. I saw several of them at Kankan, and I remarked that they all had very sharp and white teeth. Their hair, like that of the Mandingoes, is woolly, but they are lighter in colour; their noses are rather aquiline, their lips thin, and their faces nearly oval. The country is divided into several small states, which are governed by independent chiefs, who often wage war against one another for the sake of slaves, whom they sell at a high price. Some of these barbarians make it a business to lurk behind bushes, in order to surprise the unfortunate negro husbandmen in their fields, and mercilessly carry them off for immediate sale.

At the distance of a day and a half to the S. S. E. of Kankan is Toron, inhabited by idolatrous negroes, of whom I have before spoken. At two days' journey to the east, is the beautiful country of Wassoulo inhabited by Foulahs. At four days' (or perhaps five) to the N. ¼ N. E. of this city, descending the Milo, you perceive, the country, of Bouré three quarters of a day's journey distant, up the Tankisso, upon the right bank of which it is situated. I will give in a few words the information obtained from the negroes respecting this country. The city of Bouré is the chief town of the country bearing the same name. Tintigyan, Bougoreya, Fataya, Setiguia, and Docadila, are dependencies of it. These villages are not far distant from the Tankisso; for I was assured that the slaves carried thither upon their heads the goods brought by vessels, and make several trips in a day. The country of Bouré, the Mandingoes told me and they had visited it, is covered by hills, in which are many very abundant gold mines. The natives, who daily work them, are ignorant of the extent of these riches. Slaves are continually occupied in raising the earth; they employ for this purpose, baskets made of the branches of trees: the women wash this earth in calabashes; they use a great deal of water, and after shaking it well, they pour it off; thus, after several washings, the particles of gold are deposited at the bottom of the calabash, and are collected with great care: this gold is melted and, formed into rings or ingots. By this imperfect process, it may be supposed that a considerable quantity of gold remains in the washed earth; but they are not acquainted with the means of extracting it. Although the soil of Bouré is very fertile, no cultivation whatever is carried on: the inhabitants buy every thing of their neighbours; rice, millet, pistachio-nuts, pimento, every thing is bought with gold: they have horned cattle, and they breed some poultry. Before the war, Kankan furnished them largely with provisions, but, the communication being interrupted, no more are brought.

Bouré has a considerable commerce with Bamaka, which is six or eight days' journey distant, down the Dhioliba. The Moors carry to this country large quantities of salt and other merchandise which they exchange. The gold of Bouré circulates throughout the whole interior, and finds its way to the French and English settlements on the coasts; while Jenné, which was formerly considered as the country most plentifully supplied with this precious metal, has none excepting what is brought from this rich tract: Sansanding, Yamina, and Ségo, are similarly circumstanced. Opposite to Bamako, it is said, there is a cataract which the Mandigoes call Fada; but, according to the accounts I have received, it is not very high, as the canoes can descend and ascend, by a tow-line without even discharging their cargoes: this is the case during the swelling of the waters, when the cataract must be entirely covered.

The Mandingoes of Sansanding and Yamina and many saracolets carry to Bouré salt and European merchandise.

A well supplied market is held every day. This country is inhabited by Dhialonkés, who are partly idolaters; they have an absolute chief, who has the reputation of being a great warrior: he has many slaves employed in working the mines; and, besides the large quantity of gold that his labourers procure for him, each proprietor who digs for ore is obliged to give him half the produce of the day's work. This chief was at this time making war upon the large villages situated on the banks of the river. Sansando, a considerable place, and capital of several smaller ones, held him in check; this village is almost opposite to Bouré, upon the right bank of the Dhioliba; it is also inhabited by idolatrous Dhialonkés. This war, or rather this pillage, did much injury to commerce. The canoes, which arrived loaded with merchandise, were often plundered by the inhabitants of Sansando, who are extremely envious of the wealth of Bouré. Boucary is the name of the chief of this rich country: although not a zealous Musulman, he treats with respect all persons of that religion, particularly the marabouts or priests. He has the utmost confidence in *grigris*, and never travels without having his clothes covered with them. Naturally very suspicious, he has several dwellings, and never sleeps twice in succession at the same: he has a great number of wives. At the gate of his court yard there is a triple guard, and, before any one can reach his presence, he must pass through five or six more houses equally well guarded. At this moment he was also at war with the village of Damsa, inhabited by pagans and situated upon the Milo, between Kankan and Bouré, which intercepted the communication between the two districts. It is desirable that attempts should be made to establish a factory at Bamako; this post would command the commerce of the interior by attracting the produce of the gold mines, which is exported in part to Kakondy, the Gambia, and Sierra-Leone. Senegal, on account of its distance, cannot participate in this traffic, because the Mandingo merchants would be obliged to traverse Kankan, Baléya, Fouta-Dhialon, Bondou, Fouta-Toro, and part of Cayor or of the Wâlo country, to arrive there. It would, in the first instance, be requisite to ascertain the distance between Bamako and the point of the Senegal to which vessels can ascend—I mean above the rock of Felou. After having established a factory near this cataract, another should be formed where the river ceases to be navigable. It is to be presumed that from this second station at Bamako it would not be more than eight or ten days' journey; and from this important point the caravans of salt and of European commodities would proceed to Bamako. It is perhaps to be feared, that the natives would oppose this plan; but they might soon be brought to think more favourably, by shewing them the great advantages to be derived from the arrangement, and by paying them annual duties: the conduct of these people will always be governed by interest. The Moors, who carry on the greater part of this commerce which enriches them, would oppose to the utmost of their power this project of an establishment; but the duties that would be paid to the negro king would smooth away all difficulties; for the Moors pay no tribute whatever.

On the 16th of July, about nine in the morning, after having made a slight breakfast of rice, we prepared to set off; I presented to my host a little tin drinking mug, which he seemed to wish for, and with which he was very much delighted. After having escorted me to the end of the village, he left me with his benediction. I was accompanied by old Mohammed, who had shown me much kindness during my residence at Kankan; he had often told me that if he and his son were alone he would come with me to Jenné. We travelled about a mile to the east, across a plain, where we saw many little *ourondés*, surrounded by flourishing fields of maize. We arrived on the banks of the Milo, which I found very rapid, and as broad again as when I saw it before. We crossed it, with our baggage, in a canoe about fifty feet long and exceedingly narrow; it was formed of two trunks of trees, united lengthwise and fastened together with cords; it was about eleven o'clock when we reached the right bank. The good Moor testified great regret at parting and after having broken in two a colat-nut, which we ate together, he left me with good wishes for the success of my journey; when he was a little way from the bank, he turned his head towards me, bade me adieu once more, and wished me a speedy return to my country.

We left the banks of the river, and directed our course to the east for a couple of miles, through a well cultivated country. In some places I perceived, on a level with the ground, red and porous rocks, which appeared to be of the same nature as those at Sierra-Leone. We crossed a large rivulet on a very tottering bridge, which was rather dangerous to the merchants, who were all laden; one of them, having happily arrived at the further end of the bridge, could not keep his balance any longer, and fell into the water; but received no injury: this stream falls into the Milo. We halted at Sofino, a village dependent upon Kankan, and inhabited by Wassoulo Foulahs; the country is for the most part covered with nédés and cés; the land round the village is well cultivated, and more attention is paid to agriculture than at Kankan. We took up our abode in a hut, the inside walls of which appeared to have been whitewashed, whether with lime or not I could not tell, but it looked like it. We roasted some pistachio-nuts, which we ate while we were waiting till it should be time to set off; we were to travel by night through the woods, which are said to be infested by robbers. Our little caravan was composed of fourteen persons, Foulahs, Mandingoes, and saracolets. It might be about half past one when we set off, and the weather was cool, dark, and foggy. We proceeded eastward, walking at a great rate, and in perfect silence, lest we should be overheard by robbers, who would infallibly have stripped us.

We penetrated into the woods, and journeyed on through herbage of such height as to be above our heads. We came to the dwellings of a few Foulahs, whose appearance was not prepossessing, either as to countenance or dress; their clothes were hanging in rags, and, though they were almost a quarter of an inch thick in filth, we could still perceive that they had once been yellow. Their faces were adorned with a bushy beard, which was likewise very filthy, and their noses were disgustingly full of snuff. These are detached families, engaged in cultivating rice, yams, foigné, and pistachios: the soil is black and fertile; I never met with any at Kankan which was equally productive. We bought of these Foulahs a few yams for supper, for which we gave them tobacco and some glass ware. They looked at me with some curiosity, and when we left them they told us to beware of the *caffres* (infidels), who were very numerous in the woods. At night-fall we were overtaken by rain, which rendered our journey much more fatiguing and troublesome than it had been. To complete our discomfort, it became very dark, and we walked without knowing where we were setting our feet; towards eight o'clock we had lost our road, and were forced to stop. We sat down under the trees, with the rain pouring upon our backs, and not daring to cough or clear our throats for fear we should bring robbers upon us; we were silent and sad. A little before night we had seen three men without baggage and armed; they were sitting on the ground and held their guns on their knees; this attitude, and the expression of their countenances had rendered us a little suspicious of their intentions, but our number no doubt deterred them, and they were afraid that they should not be strong enough. At Kankan, I had been told that robbers continually attack the Mandingoes who traverse these woods, but never the caravans of saracolets, because they know that the latter carry guns, and that the Mandingoes are unarmed: the saracolets, when they cross the forest, always make it resound with numerous discharges of musquetry.

When the rain was over we contrived to light a fire, though not without some trouble; one of my companions tore off a bit of his pagne, laid powder upon it, and then putting it under the lock of his gun, contrived to set fire to it. We cut off a few branches of trees, to make a sort of hut to shelter us for the rest of the night; the rain had no sooner ceased, than we were beset by swarms of mosquitoes, which gave us no rest. Two of our companions, armed with poniards and lances, went in search of water, with a vessel which we had brought for that purpose; when our fire was lighted, we cooked upon the embers four yams and a few pistachios for supper, and, after this frugal repast, we stretched ourselves on wet leaves round the fire. As nearly as I can calculate, we had then travelled twelve miles from Sofino, in an easterly direction, over a good, but rather gravelly soil. The rain prevented me from using my sandals, and I was forced to walk barefoot over the gravel which gave me great pain. While I was lying by the fire, I could not help reflecting upon the suffering and fatigues I should have to endure, if I continued my journey during the season when the rain is perpetual; I thought also of the danger there would have been in venturing through these woods with no companion but Lamfia, who had proposed that I should do so, and would very likely have plundered me without mercy. I had time, in the silence of this vast wilderness, to indulge my melancholy reflexions, which were interrupted only by the notes of some night birds, and by the croaking of frogs. This was a dreadful night; I got no sleep, and I thought that it would never be morning.

On the 17th of July, day-light at last appeared, dissipating the vapours of the atmosphere, and reviving all nature. We ate some of the roasted yams, which we had over from the preceding night, and after this light meal, we set off towards the east, and crossed a large rivulet by a bridge that was nearly in ruins; every moment we were in danger of falling into the water, but we got over in safety; it was constructed on the same principle as that at Cambaya. The inundation of this stream, the banks of which are well-wooded, covered all the neighbouring country; the water was up to our knees, and we walked with great pain, on account of the gravel which cut our feet.

In the course of the day we crossed eight large streams, which are all tributaries to the Dhioliba. The soil is every where much the same, but the country was rather less wooded than what we had seen the evening before. We found plenty of nédés and cés, and I also remarked some ferruginous stones. We travelled at a very quick pace, and only halted when our porters were exhausted; we then ate a few raw pistachio-nuts to refresh us. I had great difficulty to keep up to this speed; fortunately, however, it did not rain that day. The road was still so covered with water from yesterday's rain, that I could not wear my sandals; I suffered sadly from the gravel, and my left heel was quite raw. At six in the evening we arrived thoroughly fatigued at Diécoura, the first village of Wassoulo, surrounded with a wall eight or ten feet high, and containing eight or nine hundred inhabitants.

We had travelled twenty-four miles, in an easterly direction, since morning; and, finding ourselves in the Wassoulo territory, we bore to the E. S. E. for six miles more, over a good soil, capable of producing excellent crops. When we arrived at Diécoura, I sat down upon an ox-hide, which had been spread under an orange-tree in front of our hut. The inhabitants assembled in crowds to see me; they looked at me with great curiosity, but did not teaze me with troublesome questions, as the Mandingoes had done. They seemed to agree with the description of them given by the inhabitants of Kankan, that is to say, to be exceedingly mild in their manners. They are pagans. The men use large pipes, with a tube as thick as a man's little finger, and three feet long; they are of earthen-ware, of a grey colour, and very well glazed; the bowl is as big as a coffee-cup, and the designs upon them were so well executed that I could scarcely believe that they had been made in the country; the evidence was so strong, however, that I was at last convinced. The inhabitants were very inquisitive, and wanted to know who I was, and whither I was going; but they did not teaze me. They are naturally lively, and amuse themselves under the great bombaces, where I saw all the young people assembled; they had a band of music, such as I had not before met with; twenty musicians were performing at once, upon separate instruments, several of which were made of wood, hollowed, and covered with sheep-skin. Mungo Park found a similar musical instrument amongst the Mandingoes to the north of the Dhioliba, which he describes as being made of an elephant's tusk; these, however, were of wood; they are twelve to fourteen inches long, and in the shape of a very straight horn; at the narrow end there is a hole on one side to blow into; and they produce very harmonious tones with this instrument. They have also a great drum and a tambourine, made of a small calabash, covered with sheep-skin, with iron rings round the rim, which make an agreeable jingling. Two little negroes, gaily dressed, with plumes on their heads, were jumping in cadence, and accompanied the music by striking two pieces of iron together; they were dressed almost like the little French tumblers.

The leaders of the band of musicians wore cloaks adorned with Guinea fowl's feathers, and they had ostrich plumes on their heads; many of them were shaking, in cadence, a round calabash, with a handle six inches long, and covered with net-work, containing some large beans, which, in spite of the rattle they made, accompanied the music very well. The musicians walked in a file, playing and moving in time; the women and children followed, dancing and clapping their hands. I was greatly amused with watching them, and their dance was free from all indecency. They passed part of the night in this diversion; and the two great drums produced a good effect. Since I had left the coast I had met with nothing that pleased me so much as this scene; I was never tired of their music, which seemed to me harmonious, although it had in it something wild: it is worthy of the traveller's attention. Our host gave us a supper of boiled foigné, which was accompanied with herbs, but rather unpalatable for want of salt and butter; we ate our portion however with a very good appetite, for we had taken nothing that day but a bit of yam and some pistachio-nuts. The saracolets bought milk, and cooked their rice, which they invited me to share with them.

Four days' journey to the east of Diécoura is Morila, a village surrounded with walls, where a market is held; and to the E. N. E. of Morila is the town of Kankary, situated on a river, which runs to the south and falls into the Dhioliba. This town belongs to the Bambaras of Ségo, and has a considerable market. I obtained the above information from the natives of the country.

My goods had gone forward with my guide, who went to Kimba to one of his acquaintance, but I was so fatigued that I preferred sleeping in the village to going any farther; we were to rejoin him the next day: the absence of my baggage preventing me from paying my host, one of the saracolets was so obliging as to discharge the debt with a few trinkets of glass, and he would never afterwards allow me to reimburse him.

On the 18th of July, we took leave of our hosts at six in the morning, and directed our course E. S. E. for about a mile. We crossed the Lin in a canoe, so ill-contrived, that we thought it would have upset; it was made of a crooked trunk of a tree, and was very narrow and leaky; every time we stirred, it inclined so much that the water came in over the gunwale. The Lin is a large stream from the south; its current is rapid, and it falls into the Dhioliba. We travelled another mile in the same direction, over a well-cultivated plain, and I saw many labourers all around, who were hoeing the ground, and seemed to break it up as thoroughly as our French vine-dressers; they were not like the negro slaves of the Mandingoes, who just scratch up the surface of the soil two or three inches deep, to clear it of weeds: these men laboured in good earnest for a rich and plentiful crop. They are well rewarded, for their rice, and every thing else they cultivate, grows quicker and produces more abundantly than in Kankan. I have seen them harvesting the foigné; it is cut with a sickle, and, in many parts, they leave it on the ground exposed to the rain; they commonly drive two rows of stakes into the ground, and arrange the crop very skilfully between them, so that it has the appearance of a palisade; straw is laid on the top to keep off the rain, and they fetch the foigné from this store as they want it: nobody ever thinks of plundering a magazine of this kind.

I have seen the negroes tilling the field from which a crop had just been gathered in, to sow it afresh with another grain. The women were occupied in clearing away the grass, and in weeding the beautiful fields of rice with which the country is covered. The people are industrious; they do not travel, but devote themselves to the labours of the field, and I was astonished to find agriculture in such a state of advancement in the interior of Africa: their land is as carefully cultivated as ours, whether under the plough or not, according as the position of the soil permits inundation. We arrived at the little hamlet where my guide had rested; he gave me a very kind reception, and said that he had been unhappy at my delay, and that he expected me sooner; he had given his friend notice of my coming and of the circumstances that occasioned my passage through their country. These good negroes came to see me every day; they sat by me and looked at me with curiosity; they were all very dirty and covered with rags, but there was great sweetness in their countenances. They were not annoying like the Mandingoes, but contented themselves with staring at me, and saying to one another: "He is a white! what a good, looking man he is!" One of them, the head of a family, made me a present of a sheep, and in the course of the day, of a large calabash of new milk, in which he had put some dégué, and which I thought delicious. I offered to share it with my companions, who would not taste it, till I had finished my meal; I did not expect so much delicacy from the Mandingoes, for my guide was one.

I walked about in the neighbourhood of our habitation, and was delighted with the good cultivation; the natives raise little mounds of earth, in which they plant their pistachios and yams; and these mounds are arranged with some taste, all of the same height and in rows. Rice and millet are sown in trenches; as soon as the rainy season commences they put in their seed around their habitations, and when the maize is in flower they plant cotton between the rows. The maize is ripe very early and they then pull it up to make room for the other crop. If they do not plant cotton, they turn up the ground after the maize is got in, and transplant the millet into it; a practice which I never remarked in Kankan. I was surprised to see these good people so laborious and careful; on every side, in the country, I saw men and women weeding the fields. They grow two crops a year on the same land; I have seen rice in ear, and other rice by its side scarcely above the ground. The country is for the most part very open; the only trees which are preserved by the husbandmen are the cé and the nédé; these are very common and very useful to the inhabitants. I never saw, as I have done in Fouta and Baléya, trees cut off four or five feet from the ground; the Foulahs of Wassoulo are careful to take up the roots, and leave nothing in their fields that can be injurious. In short, as I said before, they are as careful in their husbandry as our own farmers. I had many visiters all day long; the weather was stormy, and in the evening there was much lightning in the south, and a high wind from the S. W.; rain fell in torrents during part of the night, and the thunder was tremendously loud. In the evening my companions fell to work to kill the sheep which had been given to me, and we had a pretty good supper. Many of the Foulahs took leave of us to go to the market at Morila.

On the 19th of July, at nine in the morning, we left Kimba; our host's son served us as a guide. We travelled a mile to the south, and crossed a wide river, which was running from west to east, at the rate of two knots and a half an hour; in this place it was eight or nine feet deep; its banks which are rather high and barren, are composed of grey argillaceous earth, and in some parts of red earth mixed with small gravel. I inquired the name of this river, and nobody could inform me what it was; at last an old woman told me that it was the Sarano, and that is the same which passes by Kankary. We crossed in a very long and very narrow canoe, which leaked as if it had been a basket; I was not particularly well pleased to find myself in the middle of the river in this frail bark, from which we were continually baling out the water with a calabash: my guide Arafanba stood up in the boat and sang prayers out of the Koran with a loud voice; he was no doubt praying that God would grant us a safe passage. About eleven o'clock we reached the right bank, without any other damage than getting some of our things wet. We continued our route to the south, over a grey sand full of gravel. The surrounding country, which is very well cultivated, is inundated and covered with nédés and cés; we saw the rice in flag with its head just above the water. After proceeding for four miles in this direction, mid-leg in water, we halted at a neat village, where, for a few strings of beads, we bought milk and nédé flour which we mixed with it for our dinner; after which we proceeded two miles further to the south. We came again to the Sarano, which we had just crossed; at some little distance from its right bank is a range of hills of no great height, formed of earth and red porous rock. In this part the width of the river is considerable, and its course from south to north. We continued in the same direction for four miles. I perceived some fine fields of rice in ear, and a number of young herdsmen tending their cattle; they had flageolets of bamboo, with which they produced very harmonious sounds. Proceeding along the bank of the river, we reached Mauracé a little before sun-set; a hut was assigned to us, and the hospitable chief sent up a supper of foigné, with an unpleasant dish of herbs without salt.

On the 20th of July, at eight in the morning, we bade adieu to our host; we travelled eleven miles to the S. E. Throughout the whole country, which is very open, are small hamlets of ten or twelve houses, shaded by nédés and cés; the surrounding land is well cultivated, and I saw some fine fields of cotton; upon the whole, less attention is paid to the cultivation of that article in these parts, than to any other; they sow broad-cast, and the plants stand so close together, that they have not room to grow. About half past one, we halted under the shade of some nédés, near a hamlet, the inhabitants of which came to sell us milk and the fruit of the nédé, which we ate in haste, and then continued our route to the S. S. E. for three miles, over a gravelly soil, on which it was very painful walking, for my feet were extremely sore. We proceeded through a plain diversified by a few hillocks and rising grounds, which have no general influence upon the uniformity of the soil, and crossed a large rivulet, where I saw some bombaces and baobabs, intermingled with the nédé and the cé. The day was stormy; we halted at Kandiba, a neat little hamlet overshadowed by nédés. A hut was allotted to me and my guide, and another to the rest of my companions; in our's we had some foigné straw, which served us for a bed. All the inhabitants of the village and neighbourhood came to see me in the course of the evening, and lighted wisps of straw to have a better view of me; they formed a circle round me, were quite delighted to see me, and paid me many compliments, which my modesty will not permit me to repeat; they appeared very gentle and sprightly. The chief sent us a supper.

On the 21st of July, at nine in the morning, we continued our journey, towards the east, for twelve miles, over a gravelly soil, in some parts varied by a very productive red earth. We crossed a stream on the most incommodious bridge I had yet seen, for it was only a tree, the branches of which hung over the rivulet; my companions, who had loads on their heads, tottered every instant, but we had the good fortune to cross without any mishap. At two in the afternoon, we halted at Sigala, a little village where the prince of Wassoulo resides; my guide introduced me to his presence; a man went before to announce us, and we were permitted to enter his hut, where we found him lying by the side of his dog: the animal, which was of a long-eared species, with a sharp nose, and red hair, did not seem pleased with our visit, for he growled much when we approached him; his master pacified him, and we took our seat near the prince, on his ox-hide. My guide told him that I had been taken prisoner by the christians, and that I was returning to my native land; that I had been very well received in all Fouta, and that the prince of Kankan recommended me to his care.

Baramisa seemed very well disposed towards me; he appeared very lively, and addressed many questions to Arafanba, who said, in order to please him, that though I did not know him, I often asked about him on the way, and wanted to see him, with which he seemed flattered. I remarked in his hut a tin tea-pot, a copper dish, and many other vessels of the same metal. From the antique form of these vessels, I guessed that they might be Portuguese. The tea-pot was oval, and supported upon a circular rim at the foot; the handle, which projected a good deal, rose higher than the lid and the lid itself was crowned with a knob, which ended in a point at the top. The dishes were round, like those of pewter, used in Europe; a copper bowl, with a handle and a round pedestal, served to keep his colat-nuts cool. Baramisa had a large gold ear-ring in his right ear, and none in his left; he takes snuff, and smokes, like his subjects, and is not a whit more cleanly; his hut was hung round with bows, arrows, quivers, and lances, two horse saddles, and a great straw hat. I did not perceive any gun. Our visit was short; we returned to the hut allotted to us, and the prince soon afterwards sent a calabash of milk and *dégué*, which he begged me to accept: I dispatched it with my companions. Baramisa sent for me again, and I went with my guide; he received me in his stable, where he was sitting upon an ox-hide, near a beautiful horse; he made us sit down by his side, and gave me some colat-nuts, which he had put into a copper vessel, with a little water. In our presence he distributed among some of his women a quantity of yams, which had just been dug up. This prince of Wassoulo is reckoned to be very rich in gold and slaves; his subjects often present him with cattle: his wives are numerous, and they have their separate huts, which form together a little village. Before you reach the residence of the prince, you have to pass through several large courts, surrounded with mud walls, and kept very clean. His dwelling is as simple as that of any of his subjects; consisting only of a few round huts, with mud walls; on the outside of these walls, a few stakes are driven into the ground to support the timber work, which is like a pigeon house, and covered with straw; the ground-plot of these huts may be fifty or fifty-five feet in circumference, and they are twelve or fourteen feet high. The environs of this little village are well cultivated, and abounding in pistachios, rice, yams, maize, and a thousand other useful productions. I saw, for the first time since I left the coast, a few specimens of the *rhamnus lotus*, mentioned by Mungo Park. The prince sent us a pretty good supper of rice, cooked with sour milk, and added a little salt, by way of a luxury; we had rain all the evening, and the air was damp and cool.

Oh the 22nd of July, about nine in the morning, we took leave of Baramisa, making him a present of a little gunpowder, and a few glass trinkets for his women. We travelled to the S. E.; the soil, though full of small gravel, is well cultivated; cés and nédés we saw in abundance. After we had proceeded about thirteen miles, we crossed a large stream, upon a tottering bridge; the country is for the most part very open, and, from time to time, I saw a few small hills of porous red stone. We halted, at five in the afternoon, at Fila-Dougon, which is the last village of the Wassoulo territory, towards the east. The kind inhabitants gave us their own suppers, for we had eaten nothing that day. The Foulahs came in great numbers to see us; I showed them my umbrella, which they thought little less than miraculous, not understanding how it was possible that I could open and shut it at pleasure. Our fore-court was not clear all the evening, and many of them even came late at night, with wisps of lighted straw, which amused me extremely; they all exclaimed, with a smile when they saw me, "How white he is!" and then they repeated the compliments I had received over-night, adding, "We never yet saw so white a man." They inquired of my guide, whether the colour of my skin was natural; for these simple and quiet creatures, who never travel, have no idea of white men, beyond what they may happen to pick up from the Mandingo traders, who traverse their country. They are so frank, inoffensive, and hospitably generous to strangers, that, I think a christian might travel undisguised among them without encountering the slightest difficulty.

CHAPTER XI

Wassoulo — Manners and customs of the inhabitants — Flourishing state of agricultural industry — Hospitality — Kankary — Sambatikila — Reflections on the sale of slaves — Scarcity — Description of the residence of the almamy — Commerce — Smiths' work — Bambara villages — Arrival at Timé — Ranges of mountains.

Wassoulo is a country inhabited by idolatrous Foulahs, who are herdsmen and agriculturists; they rear a great number of horned cattle, and some sheep, and goats. I have seen among them horses of a small breed, and incapable of supporting much fatigue. They have also poultry, on which they set a high value, and which can only be bought for gunpowder, tobacco, salt, or glass-wares. They take especial care of their young fowls, collecting them every night in a sort of round basket, and carrying them into their huts to protect them from cold, and soon after sun-rise every morning, they are again set at liberty to run about round the house; they are seldom fed with grain of any kind, but live upon insects, herbs, and the grains of rice or millet, which fly out of the mortars while pounding. The men take care of the poultry, and bring out of the fields heaps of earth swarming with termites, which the fowls immediately devour. All the inhabitants have dogs to protect their houses; but I did not see dogs' flesh eaten in Wassoulo, as in some parts of Bambara.

The country is generally open, and diversified by a few hills; the soil very fertile, and partly composed of a rich black mould mixed with gravel: the country is watered by the Sarano, and by many large streams, which fertilise the soil; it brings forth in abundance every thing which is necessary for man in an unsophisticated state. The inhabitants are gentle, humane, and very hospitable, curious to excess, but much less teazing than the Mandingoes. Their food is very simple: they eat, like the people of Kankan, rice, tau, foigné, without pounding; to these they add a sauce made of leaves of different herbs; or of roasted pistachio-nuts. They seldom use salt, which is a great luxury, and eat meat only on feast-days; in their sauces they mix (besides gombo) the leaf of the baobab, dried and pounded; they also eat the fruit of this tree, which they steep in water or milk, and which, like nédé, is very sweet and nutritious.

The women manufacture earthen pots for their house-keeping; for this purpose they use a grey clay, which they find on the banks of the streams; they knead it, and clear it of all extraneous matter, and when of the proper consistence, it is easily worked: having brought it into the right form, they polish it by degrees with their hands, and the vessels, when finished, are placed in the shade to dry slowly, for the heat of the sun would crack them; when half dry; they are again polished with a piece of wood made for the purpose; in this way they become quite shining, and are again set to dry. Before they are completely hardened, they are exposed to a gentle sun, and eight or ten days afterwards they are piled one upon another, between two layers of millet-straw, which is set on fire to complete the baking. Vessels which are thus made come out quite glazed and of a greyish colour; they are usually round, with a little rim round the top, and no handle; they very much resemble what are made all through Fouta-Dhialon and Kankan. The amiable inhabitants of this happy country live as if they were all of one family. Each hamlet is composed of twelve or fourteen huts, or even fewer, surrounded by a clumsy and tasteless wooden palisade. In the centre of this little group of huts is a court, into which they all open; the cattle are shut up in this court at night; but the calves have a separate enclosure; it is the business of the women to milk the cows. There are usually two outer doors to this court, at each of which is a forked piece of wood, which you are sometimes oblige to stride over, as it is not always very easy to squeeze past it; and I have found it very troublesome, on various occasions, in my Arabian costume. These forks are thus placed to prevent the cattle from straying at night, and there is another entrance without this kind of barricade through which they are brought in and out.

The women, who are employed in cooking, perform their operations in the open air. The inhabitants are in general very dirty and ill-clothed; their costume resembles that of the natives of Toron; and, like them, they use tobacco and snuff. They plait their hair in tresses, wear ear-rings of small beads and necklaces, and iron bracelets on their legs and arms, like the women. They are Foulahs, but do not speak the Foulah language. Their complexion, which is lighter than that of the Mandingoes, is of a darker hue than the negroes of Fouta-Dhialon. I tried to discover whether they had any religion of their own; whether they worshipped fetishes, or the sun, moon or stars; but I could never perceive any religious ceremony amongst them, and I suspect that they are careless on the subject, and trouble themselves very little with theology: if they had any specific belief of their own, instead of encouraging Musulmans and grigris, they would Scorn them, and adhere to the superstition of their country. Small hamlets are to be seen at short distances from one another all over the country. The inhabitants grow a great quantity of cotton, of which they manufacture cloth, and sell it to dealers, who carry it to Kankan. The looms which they use for weaving cloth are like ours, but smaller; the breadths are not more than five inches wide; the slays are of reed, and they have a shuttle like ours with small bobbins, which they fasten to the shuttle with a thin bit of wire, or a small piece of reed; they do not weave fast. The women sit in their courts, and spin cotton; as they do not understand carding, their thread is coarse and uneven; they use the same kind of spindle which is employed by the negresses of the Senegal.

They have in the country smiths, who make poniards, iron bracelets, and agricultural implements; these last consist chiefly of a hoe eight or ten inches long, and five broad; I did not observe any other. With this instrument they make trenches, clear away the weeds, and cultivate the ground as well as we can in Europe. They have a small axe to cut down the trees which grow in their fields, and they take care to destroy the roots, which I had not seen practised since I left the coast. The inhabitants of Wassoulo carry on little traffic, and never travel; their idolatry indeed would expose them to the most dreadful slavery if they did. Gentle and humane, they give a friendly reception to all the strangers who come among them. They grow a great quantity of tobacco; when it has run to seed, they gather the leaves, dry them in the sun, and reduce part of them to snuff, of which they consume a great quantity; the rest is reserved for smoking. They have a pair of large tongs, like a smith's a foot long, to light their pipes with. The young men shave their heads, like the Mahometans. Most of them are very expert in the management of the bow and arrow, and I have seen them amuse themselves with shooting at a mark in a tree. The children, who are all naked, are early addicted to bodily exercises. These people have a habit of making incisions in their faces, and filing their teeth; they have several wives, like all other idolaters, who are most submissive to their husbands; a woman always drops on one knee when she hands any thing to her husband, and the same ceremony is observed to strangers of distinction. I never saw any kind of illness in the country; they are all robust and healthy. Though vegetable butter abounds amongst them they make little use of it; they prefer animal butter for culinary purposes, and reserve the vegetable for pains and wounds: they also grease their hair with it, and rub it over their bodies, which gives them a rank smell. They form a great contrast to the inhabitants of Kankan in the article of cleanliness; for they are altogether filthy and disgusting, and never wash their clothes, which are always of a black or yellow colour. They wear on their heads a cap eighteen inches in height, the top of which is very narrow, and hangs down on the back or shoulder; I could hardly guess the original colour, so completely was it always disfigured with dirt and butter; when it drops off in rags they provide themselves with a new one. The women have no other covering than a pagne, which they wrap round their loins; on their heads they wear a strip of the manufacture of the country, which serves as a head-dress. I never saw any of them smoke, but they take a great deal of snuff, and also rub it on the inside and out of their gums.

On the 23rd of July, at seven in the morning, we took leave of our hosts, who had given us a very good supper of rice the evening before. We directed our course E. S. E. and passed a little village, the name of which I have forgotten. At one of the cabins I asked for a little water to quench my thirst; a female slave brought me some in a calabash: she knelt down as she presented it to me. We heard distant thunder, but had no rain. We continued our progress to the S. E. for eight miles, and passed Banankodo, a large village of the Foulou, containing four or five hundred inhabitants; it is shaded by large bombaces and boabab trees. The country over which we travelled was under water, and the plain quite open: it was about noon, when, after having gone three miles more, we halted at Yonmouso, a little hamlet similar to those of the Wassoulos. Arafanba fired his piece in token of rejoicing on our arrival at this little village, where he had friends, with whom we went to seek a lodging, and they forthwith prepared a hut for us, in which we passed the night. I had met on the road a Poulh of Foulou, accompanied by his wife, who carried upon her head a breakfast of foigné and milk: as this man had questioned my guide respecting me, and was doubtless interested about me, I accepted with pleasure the breakfast which he offered to me. I wished to pay him in glass-wares, but he persisted in refusing all compensation. When I arrived at Yonmouso this man brought several of his companions to see me: he said nothing concerning his generous hospitality to me—a reserve that I admired greatly in a negro. He asked to see my umbrella; I hastened to gratify him, and it excited, as before, the admiration of all: to amuse them, I opened and shut it repeatedly. The hut was not cleared of people the whole evening; but their visits were very short, and their manners reserved: they also had recourse to wisps of lighted straw to see me the better, and liked the looks of me. Many gave me milk, and at the beginning of the night a pretty good supper of boiled yams pounded, with gombo sauce, which we seasoned with a little salt, and to which roasted pistachio-nuts were added.

The 24th of July we remained amongst these good people to rest from our fatigue. My guide gave five or six charges of powder for a kid: we ate part of it for our supper; and our host, to whom a small portion was given, presented us with some good sour milk and boiled rice for our breakfast the next morning. In the course of the day, we had a visit from a Poulh of the Fouta-Dhialon who was settled in this country. My guide presented him with a piece of kid, and I with a sheet of paper, for which he overwhelmed me with grateful acknowledgments. In the evening, many Foulahs from the neighbouring parts, attracted by the report that there was a white man in the place, paid me a visit; they lighted straw, and were very much amused at the length of my nose. They all said that I was a fine fellow, and went away very well pleased. Our host supplied us with a supper of yams, to which we added a piece of kid.

On the 25th of July, in the morning, the Foulah to whom we had given a piece of kid, sent us a plentiful breakfast of rice, besides a fowl and some milk; after making our meal we took leave of our host; my guide made him a present of a few strings of beads, and two little bits of scarlet cloth an inch and a half square. It was eight o'clock when we set off. We directed our course to the S. S. E. and travelled twelve miles in that direction without stopping; the country is generally open, but abounding in nédés and cés; the soil full of small gravel, and, in many places, of volcanic stones. We crossed several streams with well wooded banks, near which were neat cottages of the Bambaras, who were peacefully cultivating their little fields of yams; the country is not so well peopled as that of Wassoulo. We halted towards two o'clock, at Manegnan, a village inhabited by Bambaras; it contains about eight or nine hundred inhabitants; the natives call this part of the country Foulou, and like the Wassoulos they speak the Mandingo language; I did not perceive that they had any particular dialect. They are idolaters, or rather, they are without any religion; their food and clothes are like those of the inhabitants of Wassoulo; and they are equally dirty. At the entrance of the village I passed the *banankoro*, where all who are disengaged meet together to smoke their pipes and converse; I saw a number of old men there. The banankoro is a large hut, covered with straw, and open all round; the roof is supported upon stakes driven in a circle, and at equal distances. Round logs of wood are placed on the ground near one another, to serve as seats; these logs are so ancient, that they have become highly polished by use.

On reaching our lodging, I was visited by many of the old men, who had seen me pass when they were assembled; some of them gave me colats and a fowl for supper; these negroes seemed to me as gentle and humane as the Foulahs of Wassoulo, whom they resemble extremely in their countenances, their apparel, their customs and habits of life. They were never weary of looking at me, and said that they had never seen a white man; for the Moors of this country do not travel. Part of the evening was stormy, which at first prevented the inhabitants from seeing me; but they made themselves amends after the rain was over, crowding round me till eight o'clock in the evening with the same eagerness and curiosity; they also lighted straw, and paid me the same compliments as the people of Yonmouso.

On the 26th of July, at seven in the morning, we gave a present to our host and prepared to set off. I perceived that the village was surrounded by a wall, and that the inhabitants cultivated tobacco round their houses, for their own use. I was followed by a crowd for about half an hour; we crossed an inundated plain of indigo, which grows spontaneously, and afterwards passed over a very tottering bridge; here the villagers left us. I saw some cultivated land, but not in such good order as what I had left behind me. The husbandmen bring their fowls with them into the fields, to eat up the insects. We continued our course to the S. E.; and travelled eleven miles briskly enough; the country around us was level, and better wooded than what we had crossed for the last few days. We arrived at Nougouda a walled village, inhabited by Bambaras; and stayed there some time to change porters; we also bought a little milk and dégué to refresh ourselves. We then continued for five miles more to the south; at a considerable distance to the S. W. ¼ S. of our route, I saw three very high mountains with flattened peaks; we travelled two miles to the S. S. E. over a woody country, covered with ferruginous stones, and not cultivated. About four in the afternoon, we reached Tangouroman, a walled village which contains about three or four hundred Bambara inhabitants; we were nearly tired out, for we had travelled at a great rate, because my guide wished to reach his own home before night. The village is shaded by fine bombaces and baobabs. The poor inhabitants were unable to provide us with a fowl, or even with milk, and they found it difficult to give us a supper; they brought us a dish of foigné, with a sauce of herbs, which they had prepared for themselves, and supped on a bit of boiled yam; after which frugal repast, they fell to dancing merrily and kept it up all night. I remarked in our host's court, many little bundles of straw supported upon stakes or large stones, to keep it from the damp, which is excessive in this country; in these magazines they store their provision of rice, millet, pistachio-nuts, and yams, which are never plundered. I have not seen a single beggar between Kankan, or indeed Baléya, and this place. Arafanba went to sleep at Sambatikila; for my part, I was so fatigued with my day's journey, that I staid where I was, with the saracolets and a Foulah of Fouta-Dhialon. Our host made a present of a fine Barbary duck to my guide, who was considered in this country as a marabout of importance; we should have liked very well to eat it for supper, for we could find nothing to buy, but he kept it for his own private use.

On the 27th of July, at six in the morning we took leave of our host, after having paid him for our entertainment. We gave him four strings of beads, with which he appeared to be satisfied. In crossing the village I perceived that it was as dirty as its inhabitants; we were up to the ancles in mud. We directed our course to the S. S. E., and I saw nothing on my way but some poor fields of foigné, yams, and pistachios, in very bad order; I did not perceive any maize, which would be very useful to the inhabitants. The greater part of the land is a black mould intermingled with gravel; cultivation is almost entirely neglected. Twelve miles to the left of our road, we saw a chain of hills of inconsiderable height extending towards the N. E.

A little way from Sambatikila, we met my guide who was coming to meet us; our host, who the evening before had given him a duck, had sent his little daughter with us to Sambatikila, and Arafanba, recollecting I suppose that this Bambara was by no means rich, sent him back his duck; I was rather surprised at this conduct in a Mahometan towards an infidel. My guide told me that the almamy was anxious to see me, and sorry that I had remained behind the evening before; I told him jokingly, that the prince would soon have the pleasure of gratifying his curiosity.

It was nearly nine o'clock in the morning, when we made our appearance at Sambatikila, which is surrounded by a double wall, ten or eleven feet high, and ten inches thick. We proceeded immediately to the almamy's, and were ushered into an ante-room, where we waited till some one went to announce us. The chief admitted us immediately to his presence, and we found him reclining under a little shed in his court; he raised himself and extended his hand to me with the customary salutations, *salam alécoum; alécoum salam; enékindé; a kindé;* after having touched me, he rubbed his hand upon his face and chest, to communicate the salutary effect; for he is very religious, and has much faith in the sanctity of the Arabs. He was extremely polite, and told me that he was happy to receive a man whose country was so near Mecca. I told him that I meant to go thither; and he put many questions to Arafanba, who was eager to tell him all he had heard about me at Kankan. This old chief was dressed in the Arabian fashion; his clothes were exceedingly clean; he wore a turban of a red and white striped stuff manufactured in the country. Our visit was very short; he lodged me in one of his son's houses, together with the two saracolets and the Foulah; the son appeared to me very poor, but he gave us a neat habitation, and took great care that we should have warm water wherewith to perform our ablutions before prayer. I expected that the king would provide for our support, but he left us the whole day without food, presuming that my guide would take care of us; the guide sent us a breakfast of boiled yams, and sauce without salt. After this frugal repast, which we ate with considerable appetite, as it was then late in the day, I sent to my guide for the goods of mine which he had brought the night before; to reward him for the attention which he had paid me on the journey, I made him a small present of cloth, a pair of scissors, and some paper, with which he was delighted and thanked me heartily. He had been kind enough to pay all my expenses on the way, and never asked for any compensation. In the course of the day I was visited by many Mandingoes, who live at Sambatikila; one of them gave me some milk, which is not quite so plentiful here as in Wassoulo. It rained all the afternoon; I went, nevertheless, to the mosque to show the inhabitants that I was a zealous Musulman. At night-fall my guide sent us a small supper of rice, with which we contented ourselves, because we could get nothing else.

On the 28th of July, the almamy, recollecting, I suppose, that it was his duty to feed the strangers, sent us a dish of rice without salt, with a sauce of *zambala*,[54] and a supper of yams with a similar sauce.

On the 29th of July, we had nothing to eat the whole of the day; I bethought myself of calling upon the almamy, who seemed to have forgotten that he had strangers at his dwelling, or thought that they were accustomed to fasting. He did not hurry himself however, for it was six o'clock in the evening when he sent us some yams, boiled and pounded, with a little bad sauce; and we were unluckily obliged to share this light repast with a Mandingo, who happened at that moment to be prowling about our hut; he came and sat down by us, and needed no pressing, for he had probably tasted nothing since the evening before. I have often been obliged in the same way to share the little food I could get with these hungry and idle parasites, who would rather starve than work for themselves. As our host neglected us so completely, we went out to procure some rice and yams for ourselves; but we could find nothing in the village, for the devout almamy had forbidden the customary market twice a week, under pretence that it interfered with prayers. We sent to a neighbouring village, but were equally unsuccessful; so we were forced to be content with the small portion which our host allowed us. We were informed that provisions were scarce, that there was not enough to last till next harvest, and that the scarcity extended to the neighbouring country.

On the 30th of July, a caravan of saracolet merchants arrived at Sambatikila, on their way to Foulou to purchase slaves, whom they sell again in Foulou or Kankan. All the goods which are sold at the European settlements on the coast are destined for this infamous traffic: the slaves are not exported, it is true, but they are no better off than if they were. Slavery may perhaps be abolished in civilized Europe, but the wild and covetous African will long continue the barbarous custom of selling his fellow-creatures. It is so pleasant to live in idleness, and to enjoy the fruit of the labours of others, that every negro does all in his power to become a slave owner; their ambition is limited to the posession of twelve or fifteen slaves, whom they employ entirely in agricultural labour. These poor creatures are ill-clothed, and work very hard; but I never saw them ill-treated. They are commonly obliged to provide for their own support, and have a field to themselves, which they cultivate for this purpose; they grow maize and cassava round their huts, and find them a great resource. In the evening the almamy of Sambatikila sent us nothing, and we had made up our minds to fast, when we were agreeably surprised, about seven o'clock, by the sight of a dish of boiled rice without salt, which was sent by my guide, Arafanba, who knew that I was suffering from scanty diet. In truth, I could not be too grateful to this generous negro, who deprived himself for my sake of part of his supper; at a time when he found it very difficult to provide for his family. Provisions were so scarce and so dear in the village, that nobody thought of eating more than one meal a day, and the night was chosen for the purpose, because the negroes would rather go without food all day than retire to rest without supper.

On the 31st of July, at six in the morning, the almamy, recollecting probably that he had given us nothing the day before, sent us some rice for breakfast. A good saracolet, belonging to the caravan which had just arrived, and who had travelled often to Jenné, brought me some rice and milk, which he begged me to accept: I gave him some glass ware in return for his present. He was acquainted with many Moorish merchants at Jenné, and assured me I should be well received by them. This negro spoke a little Arabic; he told me, that on my road to Jenné I should find provisions very scarce, salt in particular. The son of the almamy came every now and then to see us, and to inquire whether we wanted warm water for our ablutions; he took care that we should never be short of *water*, but as to provisions, he did not inquire very particularly, and I suspect that the poor devil was little better off than ourselves; I noticed that he passed the whole day without food, as if it had been the Ramadan, and at night, after prayer, he ate a little tau with four other negroes. In spite of these compulsory fasts, they all seemed very merry, and never failed to go every morning to chant the Koran; the almamy himself also chanted from time to time. His son came sometimes to offer me his scanty supper, which I always refused, knowing that he had nothing else for himself.

On the 1st of August, I went with one of my companions to pay a visit to the almamy. We entered an apartment, which served the double purpose of stable and bedchamber, with the royal bed at the further end; this bed was a platform, six inches high, six or seven feet long, and five or six wide, upon which was spread an ox-hide, with a dirty musquito-curtain to keep off the insects. The room might be thirty or thirty-five feet long, and ten or twelve wide; it is constructed of earth, which they have not taken the trouble to make into bricks; the walls are seven, or seven feet and a half high, and a foot thick; the roof is supported upon wooden posts, planted within the side walls, and covered with straw; there are three entrances, the doors of which are also formed of straw. No furniture is visible in this royal apartment; but there were two saddles hanging up against the wall from the posts, a great straw hat, a drum, which is only used in time of war, some lances, a bow, quiver, and arrows; these were all its ornamements, excepting a lamp, formed of a piece of iron, supported upon another piece of the same metal, stuck into the ground: vegetable butter, which has not consistency enough to be made into candles, is burnt in this lamp. Two other apartments, of the same dimensions, serve as magazines for the produce of the fields and other valuables. The large inner enclosure contains several common huts, in which I saw some looms like those employed on the coast. The old prince was lying down on his bed, and he made us sit by him. He was saying his prayers, and held in his hand a rosary two feet and a half long, the beads of which were as large as bullets; he appeared very attentive. He addressed his conversation to me, and begged me to make his compliments to the elders of Mecca and Medina when I arrived there; after which he asked me to wait a moment. He went out into the court and returned immediately followed by a slave carrying on her head a calabash of rice, with some disagreeable herb sauce, which he gave me; he then dismissed me, promising that he would soon find me an opportunity for me to go to Jenné. The absence of salt rendered this rice unpleasant; but I had now ceased to be dainty, for hunger is sauce to all sorts of food, as I have often experienced in the course of my travels. Shortly after a Mandingo sent me an excellent dish of rice cooked with milk.

Since the 27th of July the rain had been incessant; the weather was still cold and damp. In the evening of the 1st of August, the almamy sent a man to tell me, that there was an opportunity for going to Jenné, and that if I liked to take advantage of it, he would furnish me with a guide to Timé, whence the caravan would start. I had a wound on my left foot which I was doctoring with lint, and could not heal; but I preferred suffering on the road, painful as my wound was, to remaining any longer in a place where there would soon be a horrible scarcity. I sent word to the chief that I wished to set off as early as possible.

On the 2d of August, at six in the morning, the almamy sent me some rice and a piece of a sheep which had been killed the day before, which I shared with my companions. About eight o'clock Arafanba came to me, and we went together to take leave of the chief. He called me to his store-house, and opened a little door, so low that a man must stoop double to enter; one of his women then drew out a bracelet wrapped in rag, of which he made me a present; it was silver and worth about three francs; I had brought him a pretty present of coloured muslin, paper, and strings of beads. Arafanba, my former guide, told him that I had very little merchandise with me and was sorry I could not offer him a more suitable present; he smiled and accepted it with pleasure.

The old man again desired me not to forget him when I should be among the venerable sheiks of Mecca; I promised that I would not and took my leave. A minute or two afterwards he came to the hut where I lodged to return my visit; he was on horseback, and had on his head a straw hat large enough to serve for an umbrella. He was going to his ourondé to look after his slaves; he told me he was sorry he had not thought in time of having a grigri made by the hand of an Arab; he wished me a good journey and left me. About ten o'clock, my new guide came to tell me it was time to set off; it had been raining all the morning and the rain was not yet over, but we did not stop for it. Before I proceed, however, I must give some account of the fine country which I am leaving.

Sambatikila is a large village surrounded by a double wall; it is independent and inhabited by Mandingo Musulmans. It is much larger than Kankan, but not so well peopled; there are many large vacant places in the interior of the village; the streets are narrow, crooked, and, at this season of the year, full of mud. The soil, composed in some places of black mould, and in others of grey sand mixed with earth, is very fertile, but very little cultivated; the country is covered with cés and nédés. The inhabitants are engaged entirely in commerce; they go a few days' journey to the south of their village to buy colat-nuts, and these they carry to Jenné and barter for salt; this traffic is not very lucrative, because the journeys are long and troublesome, and they have to purchase food on the road, and to pay for lodgings and transit-duty in all the villages.

A small quantity of very handsome cloth is manufactured in this neighbourhood, from cotton purchased from the Bambaras. The average price of a slave in these parts is thirty bricks of salt (a brick is ten inches long, three wide, and two or two and a half thick: there are larger and smaller bricks, and the value varies accordingly) a barrel of powder and eight parcels of beads of a bright chesnut colour; or, a gun and four yards of rose-coloured taffeta are also the price of a slave. The trade of Sambatikila is not brisk; and is far from equal to that of Kankan; the want of a market injures it greatly, and the inhabitants are poor. Their crops are not sufficient to last from one year to the next, and they are forced to buy rice from the Bambaras, paying for it with salt, which the others cannot procure in any other way. The Mandingoes would rather go without food part of the day than work in the fields; they pretend that labour would take off their attention from the Koran, which is a very specious excuse for their laziness.

Their flocks, which are not numerous, consist of sheep and goats; they also rear poultry; the few horses they have are of a very small breed. The son of the almamy with whom I lodged had performed several journeys to Jenné; he told me without any fear of compromising his dignity, that he had carried a load of colat-nuts on his head, as well as his companions. I questioned him as to the length of the journey; and he told me that it took two months and a half or three months to get thither, and that it was not possible to make more than two journeys in a year.

The title of almamy, or king, is hereditary; the eldest son of the sovereign always succeeds. He has usually four wives and a great number of children. He is the only chief at Sambatikila, and if disputes arise the elders assemble at the almamy's house, or at the mosque, to administer justice. Guns are not as common in this village as at Kankan, for I saw nothing but bows and arrows hanging up in the houses which I visited.

About ten in the morning, we commenced our journey; Arafanba, the two saracolets, and the Foulah, conducted me as far as the bank of a rivulet, which the natives call Oulaba, and which waters the neighbourhood of Sambatikila; we crossed in a wretched canoe, which was nearly upset more than once: it was made out of a single tree, but was now old, broken, and patched with pieces of rotten pagne, which would not keep out the water; fortunately the stream was not very wide, and we arrived at the right bank without accident. Arafanba accompanied me for a mile, and parted from me with great regret, after charging my guide to take care of me. Arafanba was the most amiable and agreeable Mandingo I had seen; and (what even now surprises me when I think of it) he never asked me for any thing, and appeared quite contented with the very moderate present which my means allowed me to make. We travelled E. S. E. for two miles, over a very fine black mould, intermingled with gravel; I saw only a few poor fields of foigné not yet in flower, though the harvest was over in Wassoulo; we crossed a tottering bridge, and arrived at Cagnanso, a little walled village which we did not enter. I noticed a shop belonging to some smiths, who were not better lodged than those which were on the coast; they make, however, agricultural implements, poniards, bracelets, and barbs for their arrows; the iron they use comes from Fouta-Dhialon. The environs of this village, which are inhabited by Bambaras, are uncultivated, but thickly studded with large trees, and covered with straw, which last impeded my progress greatly, causing me terrible pain, by fretting my wound and rubbing off the plaster; this, added to the water which covered the roads, and the rain which fell in torrents, fatigued me extremely. I longed to find a shelter where I might rest myself; we nevertheless continued our journey towards the S. S. E. After walking seven miles, we passed Coro, another walled Bambara village, which contains about four or five hundred inhabitants; the environs are no better cultivated than those of Cagnanso. We proceeded six miles further to the south; the country is woody and flat, and the road covered with gravel; which rendered walking very fatiguing. I saw no signs of cultivation, and we crossed several marshes. About three o'clock we halted, thoroughly fatigued, at Timicoro, a small Bambara village. The environs are woody, and covered with high straw; the fields are five or six miles from the huts, whether on account of the soil being better, or to save the grain from the ravages of goats and poultry, I know not. My guide took me to the house of one of his acquaintance, who supplied us with a small, damp, and dirty lodging. I had a good fire lighted immediately to dry my coussabe and my breeches; for the rain had been pelting at our backs all day; it continued through the night, and it was a small constant rain, which rendered the air cold. At this village I saw many goats and fowls, but the inhabitants have no horned cattle. At night-fall, the men came home from work; they were all neatly naked, having nothing but a tight cotton band which they pass between their thighs. I remarked that these men had necklaces on their necks, ear-rings of glass beads, and a great many amulets, such as goat's horns, sheep's tails, &c. All these things supply the place of grigris, in which they have great faith. They gave us a supper of tau, with herb-sauce, but no salt; I ate a little of this dish, but the sauce was so bad that I could not relish it.

In the evening a dispute arose between two men of the village, who began to fight, and would even have used their poniards, if the inhabitants had not collected round them to make peace. Nothing was heard but the shrieks of the women, who made great lamentations, and the crowd was immense; all spoke at once, and shouted to make themselves heard, so that there was a tremendous uproar. My guide informed me, that the chief of the village was blind, otherwise he would have come to the spot and restored order. I never could learn what was the cause of this scuffle, which took place precisely in the court where we lodged, and lasted a very long time, though the rain was pouring in torrents.

On the 3rd of August, in the morning, my guide cooked a small yam on the coals, and I roasted a few pistachio-nuts, which we ate together; after having presented our host with some small glass beads, we proceeded on our journey; it was then about nine o'clock. It still rained hard, and my umbrella was of little use, because the high grass, and the bushes which covered the road, wetted me as much as the rain. We travelled towards the south; at some distance from Timicoro, I saw a few poor fields of foigné and yams in a bad state of cultivation; the owners had not even taken the trouble to grub up the bushes. We passed the village of Yango-Firé, situated near a rivulet, where I saw plenty of poultry. We proceeded at first to the south, and then towards the east. We passed Brokhosso; to the S. E. of which I perceived a large hill, which appeared to be entirely destitute of vegetation. After crossing some fields of foigné, and others of french-beans, the first that I had seen since I left the coast, we arrived about half-past one in the afternoon, at the neat little village of Timé, inhabited by Mandingo Mahometans; it is shaded by a number of enormous bombaces, and by a few boababs; we had travelled about ten miles. Three or four miles to the east of Timé, we noticed a chain of mountains, which were probably eighteen hundred or two thousand feet high; this range stretches from north to east. That which faces the village is more elevated, and covered with fine vegetation, except on the summit, which is very bare.

CHAPTER XII

Abode at Timé — Weekly market — The traveller falls seriously ill of the scurvy — Is nursed by a negress — Rainy season — The author prevented from joining the caravan departing for Jenné — Fertility of the neighbourhood of Timé — Desperate condition of the traveller — His recovery after four months' illness — Description of a funeral.

My guide conducted me to the residence of his brother, who was from home; but a good old negress, who, judging from her wrinkled countenance, must have been sixty years of age, received me into her hut. She spread a bullock's hide upon the ground for me to sit on, and gave me some soup, consisting of herbs stewed in milk, and seasoned with salt; I could not eat much, for I was feverish and had shivering fits. I lay down on a mat near the fire (it was the old negress's bed) and fell asleep; but the master of the house arrived, and I was soon roused. He appeared very kind, and gave me some yams, to which he had taken care to add some salt. He then took my bag, saying he would conduct me to the chief of the village, a venerable old man of the tribe of the Bambaras, but professing the religion of Mahomet. The chief received me very well, and made me sit down on a bullock's hide, near a good fire, which kept his hut free from damp. The brother of my guide, who had conducted me to the chief, was his son. The old man informed me that I must remain with him until the departure of the caravan, which was shortly to set out for Jenné. I therefore returned to the humble dwelling of Baba's old mother. Alas! little did I think how long I was doomed to be her guest. I gave the good old negress a piece of raw meat, of which the chief had made me a present on my visit to him, and requested her to cook it for my supper. On tasting it I discovered it to be the flesh of the wild boar. I manifested some repugnance to eating it, and began to fear I should compromise myself; but my young guide from Sambatikila, who was less scrupulous, advised me to follow his example, assuring me that the meat was very good. The Mandingoes, notwithstanding their superstition, do not scruple to eat the flesh of the wild boar, though expressly forbidden in the Koran. My host sent me for supper some yams with a fowl, which he had just killed as a treat for us on our arrival.

On the 4th of August, the chief of the village came to see me, and brought me some colat-nuts and yams for my supper. The caravan was preparing to depart for Jenné, and my foot was not yet healed. The rains were incessant. I had to pass through a country intersected with rivers and large streams, which at this season overflow their banks, and marshes flooded with water. All this would of course render the journey dangerous and disagreeable. I reflected leisurely what plan I should adopt. I thought that with my wounded foot, which was getting worse and worse, I should incur the risk of being left on the road, or perishing in the marshes; for the Bambaras, who are an idolatrous people, would not willingly have allowed me to stay among them, and would probably have robbed me of all I possessed. I therefore determined to let the caravan depart without me, thinking it best to pass the month of August at Timé, and even to remain there until my recovery. I informed my host of my resolution, telling him that I would make him a present of a beautiful piece of coloured cloth and a pair of scissors, with which he appeared very well pleased. I was informed that there was a market once a week in the village, where I might purchase any provisions I wanted; The Bambaras of this part of Africa, which must be traversed in proceeding to Jenné, are poor and wretched. They do not trade beyond their own country. Not having joined the standard of the Prophet, they cannot travel but at the risk of being captured and made slaves. They are in general indolent. Their soil, unlike that of the Foulahs of the Wassoulo, is ill cultivated, and their tillages are disgustingly dirty. Their food is very bad; they eat all sorts of animals, dogs, cats, rats, mice, serpents and lizards; nothing escapes their voracity. They cultivate a little cotton, which they exchange with the Mandingoes for salt. I observed weaving in some of their villages; but they make little cloth, scarcely enough to clothe themselves, for they go almost naked. They may have as many wives as their means enable them to support. They have but few slaves, and are always armed with bows and arrows.

These people are governed by a multitude of petty independent chiefs, who often go to war with each other. In short, they are in a savage state, compared with the nations which follow the religion of the Prophet. They have no idea of the dignity of man. If I had been obliged to remain among them, my merchandise would have roused their cupidity, and being unrestrained by any sort of fear, they would probably have robbed me without scruple. Among the Musulmans, on the contrary, I was protected by the shield of Mahomet. In the little village of Timé I found every thing very abundant. The market, which is held once a week, enabled me to procure any thing. This market is supplied by the Bambaras of the neighbourhood, who come hither to dispose of the surplus of their provisions. Among other living things they bring fish, which they catch in the streams that water their plains.

On the 6th of August, the Mandingo merchants, who intended to set off for Jenné, put fresh leaves to their colats, to keep them damp, and counted them all over. They are also in the habit of damping them with water to preserve them.

On the 6th the caravan set off in a torrent of rain. The travellers about fifteen or twenty in number, both male and female, carried each of them on their heads a load of three thousand five hundred colats, a weight which I could scarcely lift. They bring back, on their return, salt in the form of loaves or flat cakes. The inhabitants assured me that the value in salt of three thousand five hundred colats, when brought back to Timé, was the price of two slaves; but the profit, as I subsequently ascertained, is not considerable; for great expenses are incurred on the road, not only for subsistence, but also for duties of transit. The price of the colats, a fruit which does not grow in this country, varies considerably. On returning from these journeys, the traders travel far into the south to procure colats, with salt and cloth, which they manufacture with cotton purchased from the Bambaras, and spun by their women.

On the 17th of August, Baba gave me a large hut to live in. Here I installed myself as well as I could. A mat spread on the damp ground, over which I laid my cotton wrapper, was the only furniture of the place. This hut also served as a warehouse and contained yams and rice.

On the 8th, I found myself very ill in consequence of the badness of the food, and I had an attack of fever. I took a few doses of sulphate of quinine, which had the effect of abating the fever for a few days. My host seemed much concerned at my indisposition. He searched through some old books which contained verses of the Koran, and brought me a scrap of paper well fumigated on which was written a charm in Arabic characters, assuring me that it was an excellent remedy for the disorder under which I was suffering. He directed me to copy it on a little piece of wood which he brought me; then, to wash off the writing with some water which I was to drink: he observed that this would to a certainty relieve me. To please him I copied the writing as he directed and when he was gone washed the bit of board; but instead of drinking the water I threw it away, which had quite as good an effect, for next day I found myself tolerably well. My host, of course, attributed my amendment to the efficacy of his remedy. I often received visits from the Mandingoes of the village. They were as troublesome as those of the Kankan, asking me continually for paper, powder, and various other things. The women tormented me for glass trinkets. They thought my skin very white, laughed at the length of my nose, and played me some childish tricks. In short, I agreed very well with the inhabitants of Timé, and was tolerably comfortable, with the exception of their food, which was detestable, chiefly on account of the want of salt. However, I purchased a little salt for my own use, and by degrees I became accustomed to the simple mode of living in this country.

On the 14th of August, the chief came to visit me. He begged me to write him an amulet, and in order to render the grigri or charm the more efficacious he made me a present of a kid. The amulet which he wished to have was to preserve him from diseases in general: I promised to exert all my skill to satisfy him. It would have been imprudent to refuse what he asked; for, in spite of the precaution I had taken of telling him that I had left my country extremely young, he imagined that I could speak and write Arabic very well. Five or six Mandingoes of the village immediately seized the kid and skinned it. They took care to reserve for themselves the stomach of the animal, which they put on the fire and broiled without taking the trouble to wash it. They shared this dainty morsel with some persons whom curiosity attracted round them. They were very expeditious and had soon cut up the kid; and without ever asking my leave on the subject, they made presents of small pieces to the neighbours and relations of my host; for in this country meat is a great luxury and is only eaten on festival days. The people eat the flesh of goats and sheep only, for they have no bullocks. The negroes gave the old chief a shoulder of the kid for his supper, and the remainder was reserved for me and Baba's family. Baba asked me what I intended to do with the skin of the animal. I consigned it to his disposal, and he immediately went and exchanged it for a lump of salt to season our meat, which was boiled in a large pot, and was destined to be kept for several days. The old negress, named Manman, a name very common throughout all the country, performed the office of Cook. This good creature was very kind and attentive to me. She brought me herself twice a-day a little rice and tau, the food which composed all my meals. I gave my host a pair of scissors, with which he appeared much pleased: it was an article of great rarity and high price at Timé.

On the 15th, I went to thank the chief for his present and gave him the amulet, which he received very gratefully. He immediately wrapped it up in a piece of cloth, which he rubbed over with wax and then enclosed it in another envelope, consisting of a piece of tanned sheep-skin. He tied this precious object with a little piece of string and hung it round his neck. He overwhelmed me with thanks and wished me a speedy return to my country.

The sore on my foot, instead of healing, grew worse. The month of August continued stormy: the rain poured down day and night: the sky was cloudy and the air heavy and cool. At intervals an east wind blew and was followed by a small, cold rain. The sun but rarely appeared. My hut was exceedingly damp. The water filtered through the wall which was made of earth and very thin. I was in a continual vapour bath and frequently ill, owing to the insalubrity of the air and the inconvenience of my new dwelling, in which I could not kindle a fire on account of the intolerable smoke. Throughout all the interior of Africa, the negroes never make chimneys. They kindle their fires in the middle of their huts, and leave the smoke to find its way through the roofs, which are in consequence thickly lined with soot.

During the rainy season, the Mandingoes scarcely ever go out of doors. They lie all day in their huts beside a great fire, and sometimes make coussabes to amuse themselves. When any circumstance obliges them to go out, they wear a kind of clogs with wooden soles two inches and a half thick, which keep their feet dry. The women pursue their occupations, going out to procure wood and water without any regard to the state of the weather. They never wear any covering on their feet whether the ground be wet or dry.

I intended to set out about the end of August; but at that time another sore much larger than the first broke out on the same foot. I suffered considerable pain, and my foot was so swelled that I could not walk. I begged the old negress to procure me some baobab leaves. She boiled them, and I made them into a poultice which I applied to my foot. This allayed the inflammation, and in the course of two days I found myself better. Having no rags for dressing the sore, I was obliged to use for that purpose pieces of the cotton which formed my turban. The old negress did not approve of this: she alleged that it would be better to dispense with the poultices than to destroy such a beautiful piece of cloth. The baobab leaves soon reduced the swelling of my foot; but the sore still continued as large as ever, being twice the size of a six-franc piece. I dressed it with lint which I had already used, and though I washed it, it was not very clean and did me no good. My host, who sympathised in my misfortune, sent one of his slaves to procure a root, which I recognized as having a caustic quality. He boiled it in water until it became tolerably soft, and then bruised a piece with a stone, and made a sort of salve of it. The first day he attended me himself: after washing the wound with the water of the decoction, he spread upon it some of the unctuous paste produced by the root, and then, instead of rag, he bound over it a leaf having a strong aromatic smell. On the following days, the old negress dressed my foot morning and evening, and she often consoled me with the hope of a speedy cure. In gratitude for her attention I made her a present of a piece of coloured cloth, which pleased her exceedingly. She had probably never before possessed any thing so beautiful; her son presently came to thank me, and very seriously asked me who had made the flowers on the cloth. I smiled at his simplicity, and told him that it had been made by the whites. He answered, still preserving his gravity, that he thought none but God could have made any thing so beautiful. I remained a month in my hut, constantly lying on the damp ground, for I was unable to walk, though I did not suffer very great pain. The month of September seemed to promise a return of fine weather; but appearances were delusive. The rains, to be sure, were not so incessant, but we regularly had rain every day, until October, when it became less frequent. The rain, which poured in torrents always set in with hurricanes, blowing from the east and south-east. In proportion as the rain diminished the heat increased, and the air became more salubrious. My foot got better, and I hoped to set off about the end of the month. It may well be imagined that I looked forward to the period of my departure with no little anxiety, and notwithstanding all the kindness that I experienced from my old nurse, I was impatient for the moment when I might have the pleasure of bidding her farewell. On market-days I gave her glass trinkets to purchase my weekly supply of rice and foigné, which she made her son's wives cook for me. She herself brought me twice a day a portion of tau and rice in a wooden platter, and in a little earthen vessel soup made of herbs or pistachio-nuts, to which I added a little salt and vegetable butter, without which these messes would have been scarcely eatable. For a few glass beads, I readily procured vegetable butter, called in the country *cé-toulou*, which, though collected in abundance, is not much eaten by the inhabitants, as they prefer selling it. This butter is tolerably good; but it is necessary to cook it with the food with which it is eaten, otherwise its flavour is not very agreeable. The natives use it for pains and sores. I have seen in the country a tree, which like the cé produces a butyraceous substance; it is called by the natives *taman*. The butter of this tree is of a yellow colour, like ours. It is firm, notwithstanding the heat of the climate, and does not contract any bad flavour. I liked it better than the butter of the cé, which is less firm, and of an ash colour. However, the natives assured me that the produce of the cé is more wholesome than that of the taman, and I saw many who would not eat the latter, alleging that it made them ill. For my part, I frequently ate it and never experienced any bad effect from it.

The Mandingoes of this part of Africa have more resources for food than the negroes who inhabit the neighbourhood of the Senegal, who have, in fact nothing but millet. Their food too is better cooked, and, excepting salt, which they have a great deal of trouble to obtain, they possess all that is necessary for supporting life; yams, maize, rice, honey, foigné, beans, giraumons, and pistachios, grow abundantly in this happy land: on the Senegal, on the other hand, all these things are wanting, though salt is easily procured. The expence of cultivation in this part of the country is low. The slaves merely break up the surface of earth, to destroy the weeds, and the seed is then sown. In planting yams, the ground is trenched up, for the root does not thrive well in a level soil. Every thing grows here very rapidly. The soil, which is composed of excellent black sandy mould, is fertilized alternately by the rains and the tropical heat, not less than by the numerous streams which wind through every part of the country; thus the land rewards with interest the labour of the husbandman. The foigné, which is sown during the month of May, is gathered in July. This grain is very useful, to the negroes, for it often happens that their supplies of provisions are not sufficient to last them till the following year. They might make two harvests in the course of the year, as is done in Wassoulo, if they were not too indolent. The foigné is abundant throughout the whole of the south. The women take great pains in separating it from extraneous matters. They expose the grain to the heat of the sun, after which they put it into a mortar and clear it from the chaff, which requires considerable time and trouble. The bran is afterwards extracted in the same way, as on the Senegal; the foigné is then pounded a second time, and when the grain is thoroughly cleared, it appears white and of about the coarseness of gunpowder. It is next washed and drained through a basket, in which it is allowed to remain until it swells a little. After this it is again consigned to the mortar, and a few strokes of the pestle suffice to reduce it to flour. If it were not wetted, the process of trituration would require longer time. The flour thus produced is made into a sort of pudding or paste called tau, which is the sangleh of the negroes of the Senegal. When this tau is baked it is put into a calabash, and seasoned with a sauce made of giraumon leaves, various herbs, and allspice; a little gombo is also added to render it glutinous, but neither salt nor butter is used in this sauce. The yams are cooked in a different manner. They are first boiled, and then pounded, and they are eaten with a sauce composed of dried fish reduced to powder, a little gombo, allspice, and zambala, or nédé seeds boiled, dried, and pulverized; which gives them a very agreeable flavour. Though the nédé seeds are very abundant in this country, yet the women use them but sparingly in their cookery, because, to preserve them all the year, they must be steeped in brine, and salt is scarce in this part of Africa. In general the sauces are strongly seasoned with allspice. At meal-times the guests assemble round the dish, and each in his turn takes a handful of yams, rolls it up in his hand, makes a hole in it with his thumb, and dips it into the sauce. When the rice is well cleaned and boiled in water, the cook adds to it a sauce made of pistachios and leaves of Guinea sorrel, but no salt. This article being expensive is used only at festivities, or on occasion of the visits of strangers of consequence. The people themselves are so accustomed to dispense with it, that they cannot feel the want of it as a great privation. Yet they invariably use a little salt whenever they eat meat, and I have heard them say that they would rather postpone their entertainments for a few days than go without salt. When they kill a kid or a sheep, they collect several of their neighbours, but they do not feast together. Each carries away his share to regale himself with his family at home.

The inhabitants of Timé are Mandingoes, and they all make journeys to Jenné. I inquired of them the distance from one city to the other, to ascertain whether they agree on this point with the people of Sambatikila. They all assured me that I required two months to go, and two months to return; but that they could only make two journeys in the course of the year, because they were obliged to travel to Teuté and Cani, a fortnight's journey to the south of Jenné, to purchase their colats. I also learned that the inhabitants of those villages themselves go very far to the south, to a place called Toman, to procure these colats. On their return they cover them with leaves, and then bury them under ground to preserve them. This fruit may be kept fresh for nine or ten months by taking the precaution to renew the leaves. The colat-tree flourishes in the south; it is very abundant in the Kissi, the Couranco, the Sangaran and the Kissi-kissi. It is a general article of trade in the interior; for the inhabitants, having no kind of fruits, highly esteem the colat, and, indeed, regard it as a sort of luxury. Old men who have lost their teeth reduce the colats to powder by means of a small grater, consisting merely of a bit of tin in which they make holes very close together. The Bambaras are very fond of the colats; but as they have not facility for going to the country where they grow, they purchase them with cotton and other produce of their agricultural industry.

The colat-tree resembles the plum-tree in size and form. The leaves are alternate, and about twice as broad as those of the plum; the flower, which is small and white, has a polypetalous corolla; the fruit is covered with a brownish yellow husk or rind, within which is a pulp, which is at first pink or white; but which, on attaining full maturity acquires a greenish hue. The same tree bears fruit of both colours. The colat-nut is of the size of the chesnut and of the same degree of hardness. At first it appears to have a bitter taste; but after it is swallowed it leaves a sweet flavour, which the negroes like very much. A glass of water taken immediately after one of these colat nuts, has the effect of having been sugared. The nut easily splits in two without changing its colour; but if one of the two halves be broken and exposed for a moment to the air, the pulp which was previously pink, or white, becomes of a rust colour.

I wished to ascertain the distance from Jenné to Timbuctoo; but nobody could give me any positive information on the subject. The inhabitants seemed to think it immense. Their journeys being merely commercial speculations, they pay little attention to geography, and very often they do not even know the names of the villages which they pass through. The negroes in this part of Africa are not so hospitable as those on the north of the Dhioliba, or even in the neighbourhood of the Senegal. They are generous only among themselves, and if they shew any kindness to strangers it is merely from motives of interest. This I attribute to the numerous caravans which are continually passing through their country, for, if they were to receive and entertain all the strangers who visit them, they would soon be ruined. The merchants purchase their provisions, and get them cooked by the women who follow the caravans. These negroes dress precisely in the same way as those who inhabit the regions further to the north. The dress of the women differs only in the mode of arranging their hair. They generally have their heads uncovered. Some plat their hair and fasten glass beads at the end of each tress; others have merely a tuft of hair at each side of the head; sometimes they take a piece of cotton of the manufacture of the country, about three yards long, and roll it round their heads, bringing it very forward upon the forehead.

About the end of October the rains ceased entirely, the days became exceedingly hot and the nights cool. I observed that the negroes are all extremely subject to take cold, which I attribute to their habit of lying near a great fire in their huts, and then going out thinly clad. My host Baba, who, during the first month of my abode at Timé, had paid me great attention, no doubt on account of the pretty presents which I had made him, began to neglect me. When I was long without giving him any thing, he was constantly begging of me and manifesting his ill-humour. On the other hand I was tormented by the women, who came in crowds to ask me for glass beads. I was at once an object of curiosity and aversion to them. They ridiculed my gestures and my words, and went about the village mimicking me and repeating what I said. Their gossip attracted fresh visiters to my hut; in short, from morning till night they were before my door, and when I went out I was followed by a troop of women who called after me in their own language—"The Arab is not good, he does not give us any thing"—(*Larab-magné atemo-oço*). Sometimes I got rid of them by giving them a few glass beads; but they soon renewed their attack. During the first month I was not molested in this way; but, when they became better acquainted with me, they grew intolerably troublesome. My sore foot was the object of their ridicule, and the difficulty I experienced in walking excited their immoderate laughter. Such are the beings among whom I was obliged to live. Their treatment of me arose not so much from any bad feeling as from stupidity and ignorance, for they are little better than savages. When I occasionally asked such of the women as most tormented me for water, they would hasten to fetch it for me. The men were not more hospitable than the women. If they did not amuse themselves at my expense they reproached me for giving them nothing. I told them that I had a long journey to perform before I could reach Mecca, and that the little stock of merchandise which I had would, perhaps, be insufficient to pay my expenses thither, in which case I should be unable to proceed. They did not appear to be moved by these representations, but, pointing to my woollen wrapper and my leather bag, they said—"Look there, you have a wrapper and a bag full of stuff and different merchandise. The Arab does not give us any thing; he is not good"—(*Mi casa fani abeyan nanfoulo abé. Larab featemo—oço amagné.*) They entertain extravagant ideas of the wealth of the whites, and even of the Arabs, whom they rank in the same class; and hence they conclude that a white man travelling through their country ought to make them liberal presents. I saw a Mandingo of the village, who had been several times at Gambia and at Albreda. He spoke of a Mr. Waterman, a merchant at Gambia, and of M. Jaffrot, of Albreda. He complained bitterly of the want of generosity shewn by the whites, who, he said, had large warehouses full of merchandise and yet gave away very little. This negro excited the curiosity of his countrymen, who assembled round him to hear him describe the wonders which he had seen on the coast. To convey to his hearers an idea of the large size of the houses of the whites, he compared them to ten or twelve mosques like that of Kankan, which, as I have already mentioned is a square unsightly building, capable of containing about three hundred persons. He described in glowing terms the way in which the Europeans dress and eat, which greatly astonished the simple negroes, who imagined that there were no other dresses than theirs in the world, and that the custom of eating with the fingers was universal. When I first arrived at Timé, I was frequently visited by a negro who asked me a thousand questions respecting the way in which I had been fed by the christians. He used to seat himself very close to me, and often upon my baggage, and on my manifesting displeasure at this, he withdrew somewhat out of humour, declaring that I was a christian. He, doubtless, hoped to make me purchase his silence on this subject; but as he was the only one who troubled me in this way, I was resolved that he should gain nothing by his insolence. I was a stranger, but under the protection of the almamy of Sambatikila, which, I suppose, inspired a sort of respect. The old negress continued very attentive to me, and I therefore promised to make her a handsome present at my departure, and in the mean time, I occasionally gave her a few glass ornaments.

By the 10th of November the sore in my foot was almost healed, and I hoped to profit by the first opportunity of setting out for Jenné. But, alas! at that very time, violent pains in my jaw informed me that I was attacked with scurvy, and I soon experienced all the horrors of that dreadful disease: the roof of my mouth became quite bare, a part of the bones exfoliated and fell away, and my teeth seemed ready to drop out of their sockets. I feared that my brain would be affected by the agonizing pains I felt in my head, and I was more than a fortnight without sleep. To crown my misery, the sore in my foot broke out afresh, and all hope of my departure vanished. The horror of my situation may be more easily imagined than described, — alone, in the interior of a wild country, stretched on the damp ground, with no pillow but the leather bag which contained my luggage, with no medicine and no attendant but Baba's old mother. This good creature brought me twice a-day a little rice-water, which she forced me to drink; for I could eat nothing. I was soon reduced to a skeleton, and my situation was so deplorable that at length I excited pity even in those who were least disposed to feel for me.

Suffering had deprived me of all energy. One thought alone absorbed my mind — that of death. I wished for it, and I prayed for it to God, in whom I reposed all my confidence, not in the hope of cure, for that I had relinquished; but in the hope of another and a happier state. This was the only consolation I experienced during my long sufferings, and for that I was indebted to the religious principles which I had imbibed during the numerous adversities of my wandering life: for, we are so constituted that it is often only in misfortune, and when bereft of friends, that we turn for consolation to that God who never withholds it.

At length, after six weeks of indescribable suffering, during which time I subsisted solely on boiled rice and water, I began to feel better and to reflect on what was passing around me. I scarcely ever saw Baba. I could easily perceive that I was a trouble to him and his family, and that they were tired of the burthen of a man who was continually ill. The presents which I had been obliged to make them every now and then were rapidly exhausting my means, and my baggage was becoming so scanty that I feared I should not have sufficient merchandise to complete my journey; for, ill as I was, I did not now renounce the idea of continuing it. I would rather have died on the road than have returned without making more important discoveries. I reflected on the best means of proceeding to the Niger, where I might hope to embark for Timbuctoo, the mysterious city which was the object of all my curiosity. I never for a moment reproached myself for the resolution which had brought me to these deserts, where I had suffered so much misery. I saw with regret the fine season advancing. The roads were passable and the marshes dried up, and every thing concurred to make me regret the time I was losing at Timé. Finding that I did not get better, Baba was moved with compassion and came to see me. He sat down by me, and, after inquiring how I was, he told me that he would bring me an old woman who understood my disorder. I thanked him for his kindness. The old woman came: she examined me attentively, and consoled me by saying that she would give me a medicine which would do me good, and that I should soon be quite well. She added that my disorder was common in the country, and that people who were attacked by it lost all their teeth if remedies were not promptly applied.

She commenced her treatment by forbidding me to eat meat or salt, or even to drink the rice-water with which the old negress had supplied me. In the evening, she brought in the corner of her pagne some pieces of red wood: this she boiled in water, with which she desired me to wash my mouth several times a day. I punctually obeyed her directions. The water was very acrid and had the effect of a strong astringent. However, I experienced but little relief. My cure promised to be very slow, and I felt no symptoms of convalescence until about the 13th of December. The sore on my foot, to which I had applied a diachylon plaster healed with my improving health. The weather was fine. The wind blew frequently from the N. E. and sometimes from the north. I went every day, supported on a stick, to take the air and amuse myself at the banancoro, a place, which, as I have already stated, is the rendezvous of idlers. Here it is shaded by large bombaces. The old men resort thither to spend a portion of the day, not to smoke like the Bambaras, for the inhabitants of Timé do not smoke, though they take a great deal of snuff. They amuse themselves by talking about trade and their former journeys. The young people also assemble there to dance all night.

I bought some fowls, as I wished to have food at once wholesome and succulent. The old negress cooked the fowls with a little rice. My appetite and strength gradually returned, and I was soon able to walk without a stick. I now anxiously looked forward for an opportunity to depart; but, as it might be some time before such an opportunity should occur, I thought it advisable to look out for a guide to conduct me to Tangrera, a large town which, the natives informed me, was ten days' journey from Timé, in the direction of E. N. E. From Tangrera caravans of Mandingo merchants frequently go to Jenné, Ségo, Sansanding, and Yamina. I had considerable difficulty in procuring a guide, though there were in the village numbers of idle Mandingoes, who spent the whole day in gossipping at the banancoro. At length, I found one who promised to accompany me, but only, within two days of Tangrera, which I thought I might easily reach by joining a party of merchants on the road. I promised my guide a little iron saucepan, to which he had taken a great fancy, and which I generally used for my ablutions. He was also to have a pair of scissors, a yard and a half of beautiful coloured cloth, and two sheets of paper. However, on the day appointed for our departure, he found some excuse for absenting himself. I saw that he was trifling with me, and I was obliged to put off my journey till another day. Baba continued to behave very ill and often spoke harshly to me. He seldom came to my hut, and when I bought any thing he contrived to make me pay more than its value, for the people who sold me provisions were his relations or friends. I have also one reproach to make against the old negress, who, in other respects, behaved very well to me. On market days I gave her some glass ornaments to purchase my weekly supply of grain; but she always discovered that there was too little. To satisfy them, I ought to have provided sufficient for their maintenance as well as mine.

One day Baba informed me that his brother, who had departed in the preceding August, had come home, and that he was gone to Teuté to procure colats, with the intention of returning immediately to Jenné. He told me I might go with him. I learned this news with considerable pleasure. This was about the end of December. Baba had received from his brother some salt, of which he made little presents to his neighbours and his wives. The latter came immediately to sell it to me for glass beads. Baba sent his youngest brother with some loaves of salt to Kany, to purchase colats and to barter them for goats or sheep.

I experienced fresh annoyances from Baba. He stole my salt to give it to his horse, which was not worth his keep. Nothing could persuade these people that I was not rich. In spite of the privations which I imposed upon myself, they still persisted in believing that I had plenty of gold and silver. To destroy this illusion, I determined to shew them the contents of my bag; but before I gave them this proof of confidence, I took the precaution of concealing any thing which might excite their cupidity. They are ignorant of the value of amber and coral, which their women never wear, and they saw mine with indifference.

On the 1st of January, 1828, I had the satisfaction to learn that Baba's brother had returned from Teuté, where he had been buying colats, which he was shortly to go and dispose of at Jenné. It was night when the old negress came to inform me of her son's arrival. I saw a dozen Mandingoes who accompanied him. They were covered with little bells; these, when they walked, made a noise that excited the curiosity of the people, who all ran out to see them.

On the 2nd of January, the travellers made little presents of colats to their friends and relations, who had come on the preceding evening to make inquiries about their journey. Baba's brother received from his friends, in return for the presents, two large calabashes full of tau and rice, together with some meat and salt. The neighbours were invited to partake of the entertainment. They were about fifteen or twenty in number, but that did not prevent them from sending a small portion of the feast to such of their relations as could not attend. The old negress regularly brought me my little portion, and as I was soon to leave the place, she paid me increased attention.

Our departure was fixed for the 9th of the month. The interval, during which Baba's young brother, Karamo-osla, stayed at Timé, was spent in rejoicings. Five or six meals were eaten in the course of the day; for, besides the food sent by friends and relations, the family took their dinner and supper as usual; indeed, I have frequently seen them rise in the night to eat. I visited the old chief, to acquaint him with my intended departure, of which, however, he had already been informed. He made me sit down beside him in his hut, and gave me some colat-nuts. He also begged me to accept some yams, which he ordered his slaves to carry home for me. He said, that since I was going away, and he should probably never see me again, he would request me, before I went, to write for him a charm against bad eyes. After satisfying him, I went with Baba to see a field of yams of his own cultivating. He had several free Bambaras at work for him. They throw up the earth into little ridges, as I have before mentioned, without taking the trouble to remove the young trees, which, when the yams take root, serve as sticks for them to climb up. We seated ourselves near a large heap of yams, which Baba had purchased with salt from the Bambaras, his neighbours, and which he intended to plant in his field. While a party of the labourers were engaged in selecting those which would be best for planting, some of the yams were cooked, and we ate them for dinner. When the proprietors visit their lands, they have no other food than yams, and the slaves always take care to steal a few and to conceal them under ground, that they may eat them secretly. The young lads carried on their heads baskets of yams, to give them to the men whose business it is to plant them. When they had done work, I observed that Baba paid his labourers in kind. On leaving me, each of the poor Bambaras gave me a yam.

A cold north wind had prevailed since the end of December. I could very well bear my woollen wrapper, and was glad, during the day, to seek the genial warmth of the sun. The negroes, who are naturally chilly, covered themselves with the woollen wrappers which they buy at Jenné; and in the month of December, they kindled larger fires than usual in their huts. I perceived that at this season the trees lose their leaves, and the negroes burn the dry herbs which surround their habitations. The eve of our departure was a grand festival. A young Mandingo negro was celebrating the funeral of his mother, who had been dead about a fortnight. On the very day of her death, I had been attracted to the neighbourhood by the sound of the music. I saw in the court-yard, two large drums, made like ours, and some persons were beating them, and clashing cymbals. These cymbals consist of two pieces of iron, about five inches long, and two and a half wide. The two negroes who were beating the drums, held these cymbals in their left hands. Each of the pieces of iron has a ring, one is passed over the thumb, and the other over the fore-finger, and by a movement of the hand they are struck together in regular time. The women of the neighbourhood brought little presents, by way of shewing respect to the deceased. A large circular basket was placed exactly in the centre of the yard to receive the offerings. The women, having deposited their presents, assumed a grave look, and, ranging themselves in a file, marched along, keeping time to the music, and making motions with their hands and heads, expressive of sorrow. Sometimes they beat time, by clapping their hands, while they sang a melancholy song. This scene continued the whole of the day. I inquired whether the presents which had been brought in honour of the deceased, were to be buried with her; for the Bambaras observe this superstitious custom. The Mandingoes told me that it did not prevail among them, and that the presents would be appropriated to the celebration of the *dégué-sousou*, at which I was present, and which I will describe as I saw it.

The son of the deceased bought a lean kid, for the entertainment of part of the guests, especially the musicians. Early on the morning of the day appointed for the festival, he called with Baba at my hut, where I was sitting by the fire, for the morning was cool. They both sat down by me, and the young man begged me to sell him some gunpowder to celebrate his mother's funeral. He told me he would pay me in cowries,[55] which were beginning to be current at Tangrera, and without which, I could not purchase food. I had about a flask of powder, which I had carefully preserved, thinking that it would be useful to me at Jenné. However, I gave him as much of it as was worth a thousand cowries; for I thought that by refusing I might render myself disliked. I had some difficulty in striking the bargain. They sent about every where in quest of horns for measuring the powder, and they could not get any large enough. To satisfy them, I must have given them all my stock. The 8th of January was the day fixed for the ceremony, which took place near the humble habitation of the deceased, beneath the shade of large bombaces, to all appearance coeval with the soil in which they grew. The band of music consisted of four large drums, as many pair of cymbals, and six hautboys, like those of Wassoulo, which I have described. The musicians were all Bambaras, for the Koran prohibits the Musulmans from applying themselves to music.

Four little boys, whose bodies were covered with leaves of trees, well arranged, and whose heads were adorned with plumes of ostrich-feathers, held in each hand a round basket; with a handle, in which were bits of iron and pebbles. They kept time with the music, jumping, and shaking their baskets, the contents of which, produced a strange jingling. There were two leaders of the band, who regulated the intervals when the performers were to play. They wore beautiful mantles of cotton net-work, very white, and fringed round. On their heads they had black caps, edged with scarlet, and adorned with cowries and ostrich-feathers. The musicians stood at the foot of a baobab. The assemblage was numerous, and all were well dressed. The men were tricked out in all their finery. I saw several with little coussabes, of a rusty colour, and almost covered with amulets, rolled up in little pieces of yellow cloth. Some were armed with muskets, and others with bows and arrows, as if prepared for combat. They also wore large round straw hats, of their own native manufacture. They walked all together round the assembled circle, leaping and dancing to the sound of the music, which I thought very agreeable. Sometimes they appeared furious, firing their muskets and running about with threatening looks. The men with bows and arrows, also appeared as if on the point of rushing on an enemy, and they pretended to shoot their arrows. The men were followed by a number of women, all neatly dressed, having about their shoulders white pagnes, which they tossed about from side to side, while they walked to the sound of the music, and observed profound silence. Those who were fatigued withdrew, and their places were immediately supplied by others. When they left the party, they ran away very fast, and were followed by some of the musicians, who accompanied them, playing, as far as their huts, where they received a present of some colats. About the middle of the festival, all the male relatives of the deceased made their appearance dressed in white. They walked in two files, each carrying in his hand a piece of flat iron, which they struck with another smaller piece. They walked round the assembly keeping time and singing a melancholy air. They were followed by women, who repeated the same song in chorus, and at intervals clapped their hands. Next came the son of the deceased, who was well dressed, and armed with a sabre. He did not appear much affected, and, after having walked round the assembly, he withdrew, and the warlike dance were renewed. The whole festival was arranged by two old men, relatives of the deceased. They addressed the assembled party, and delivered an eulogium on the good qualities of their departed kinswoman. The festival ended with a grand feast, during which, the goat which was killed in the morning, was eaten. I remarked, with pleasure, the good order which prevailed throughout the whole of the entertainment, which was kept up with great merriment. The young people danced almost the whole of the night. The son of the deceased withdrew from the supper which he had provided for his friends, and came to partake of ours.

The day, which I had so long and anxiously looked for, at length arrived. But, before I quit this beautiful country, I will endeavour to give a description of it, as well as of the character and manners of the people among whom I lived five months.

CHAPTER XIII

Description of Timé and its environs — Character, manners, and customs of the inhabitants — Period of circumcision for males, and excision for females — Manufactures, trade, and agriculture — Indigenous plants — Diseases.

The village of Timé is situated at the distance of two days' journey to the south of Sambatikila, fifteen to the north of Teuté and Cani, and ten to the north of Tangrera. The number of inhabitants is about five or six hundred, consisting partly of Mandingoes, and partly of Bambaras. A wall separates the two nations, but they live together on a friendly footing, notwithstanding the difference of religion; for the Mandingoes are Mahometans, and the Bambaras pagans. Such, however, as are the offspring of a Mandingo mother consider themselves superior to the unmixed Bambaras; they nevertheless, remain idolaters.

There is a chain of mountains to the east of the village. During the rainy season, the clouds collect in such masses around the summits of these mountains, that for five months and a half it rains almost without intermission. I did not experience any extraordinary heat during the rainy season. The air is always cool and damp, which renders it very unhealthy. In the months of December and January, a variable, but northerly, wind prevails, which still farther cools the atmosphere. The soil consists of good black mould and sand. In some parts it is irrigated by a number of small rivulets, the overflowing of which, fertilizes the land. The birds of the Senegal also inhabit the well-wooded banks of these streams. Green parrots are common, but I saw no paroquets.

The Mandingoes, who are naturally indolent, make their slaves work hard.[56] Those who have no slaves, are obliged to cultivate their own fields, but in that case they labour so inefficiently, that their harvest does not maintain them during the whole year. They, therefore, purchase from the Bambara negroes, who sell their surplus grain to procure salt.

The slaves, being regarded by the Mandingoes as their principal wealth, are not ill-treated; their food is the same as that of their masters, though sometimes it is not quite so abundant; they are dressed in a coarse pagne, which they wear to the last rag: they go naked until they are eighteen, or sometimes older. When they are not looked after, their natural indolence causes them to neglect their work: but towards that fault their masters are rather indulgent. They never punish them severely, except for theft or desertion. When it is suspected that a slave intends to run away, irons are put on his legs.

The Mandingoes measure time by years, months, weeks, and days, and I observed that they never miscalculated. They reckon the month by lunar revolutions, and twelve months make one year, which is called *sang*; their weeks consist of seven days. The market is held in the village once every week. They do not measure the day by hours, but divide it into four parts; the forenoon, until eleven o'clock, is called *soyoman*; from that hour to four o'clock, *télé*;[57] from four to seven o'clock, *oula*; and the night is called *soudo*.

The Mandingoes of this part of Africa are all traders; they travel much, even in the rainy season, but, being obliged to carry their merchandise on their heads, they take little with them, and journey at a slow pace. Their trade of course is not lucrative. They never travel without having about their garments abundance of amulets, or grigris, covered with scarlet. The inhabitants of this part of Soudan are not hospitable. The merchants are, therefore, obliged to purchase their provisions, and to pay for their lodgings, besides discharging the transit-duty, levied in each village. A considerable part of their profit is consequently expended in each journey. They carry bows and arrows, for fire-arms are not common in that country. They never travel without a small pot of vegetable butter, which they carry at their girdle, and every evening, after washing with warm water, they grease the head, face, and part of the body. They are so accustomed to anointing themselves in this manner, that the journey would be quite uncomfortable if they omitted to use the grease-pot. When they return from their journeys, they indulge in idleness and gormandizing, leaving agricultural labour to their slaves. They often go to the ourondé, where the slaves reside, to see if every thing be in good order, and to encourage them to work. They sometimes send them a good supper of foigné, which they make their wives prepare.

The Mandingoes have usually two meals a-day; they breakfast at eleven o'clock, take supper at seven in the evening; in the morning they sometimes eat a little rice porridge, which they call *baya*. The poor have but one repast a-day, but the greater part of them visit their neighbours to partake of their meals.

The negroes are extremely fond of social meetings. In the fine season, after evening prayer, they assemble with the whole neighbourhood, to take supper together. Each wife brings her husband's supper on her head.

Some have tau, others yams and rice; the sauce is usually separate, in a little plate called *birit*. These parties are always very merry. These worthy Musulmans vituperate those whom they call infidels, laugh heartily, and amuse themselves at the expense of absent friends. The women are not admitted to these meetings; they eat in their huts with their children, but never with their husbands. At the age of ten the male children take their meals with the father. When the repast is finished, the women come and collect their household utensils.

A custom which I observed to prevail generally among the negroes appeared to me very singular. At the end of every meal they thank each other reciprocally, and afterwards run through the village, repeating their thanks to every one they meet, which is equivalent to saying that they have dined or supped. It is easy to judge of the quality of the repast of which they have partaken, according to the expression of greater or less satisfaction with which the word signifying *thanks* is pronounced. Some of them came to the door of my hut also to ejaculate their thanks.

The Bambaras, who are all pagans, marry as many wives as they are able to maintain; but the Mandingoes have never more than four: they do not, however, marry them all at once, but at different periods, sometimes after intervals of three or four years. Every new wife occasions considerable expense, which they cannot defray, unless success in trade has enabled them to accumulate some profits. They must purchase slaves to present to the parents of their mistress; for otherwise no wife is to be had. This kind of dowry varies in amount, according to circumstances. If the female be of a good family, if she be handsome, or if her possession of superior qualities be generally acknowledged, the parents require three or four slaves, or the value of that number in merchandise. These unfortunate beings become henceforth the property of the mother. When the girl to be married is neither of a distinguished family nor handsome, then only two slaves are given. Throughout the whole of this country I met with no instance of a young woman living in a state of Celibacy; pretty, or plain, they all get married. These wives are, however, only so many servants, whom the men secure to themselves, and of whose running away they have no reason to be afraid. The bridegroom must deliver his slaves before he obtains possession of his bride, to whom he also makes some little presents, besides sending her every day large calabashes full of rice. The two months prior to the nuptials form a holiday time for the bride, and the mother invites the neighbours to take part in the merrimaking. These customs undergo some modification in each country: at Cambaya, for example, if the bridegroom gives three slaves, two are for the mother-in-law, and the third follows the bride to the house of her husband. At Timé, and at Sambatikila, the relations of the bride receive every thing. When the bridegroom has gone through every formality, and made all the requisite presents, if the betrothed, or any of her relations, should after all refuse to conclude the marriage, they are obliged to indemnify him for all the expenses he has incurred; on the contrary, if the objection be made by the man, whether from jealousy or any other cause, he loses all he has given. When, however, a discussion arises between the bridegroom and the family of the bride, and the match is in consequence broken off, every thing that the relations have received must be returned. Among a selfish and avaricious people, it is a necessary effect of these rigid regulations, that the first engagements are seldom dissolved. In the result the women are always the victims; for the men, looking upon the other sex as an inferior order of beings, are always absolute masters in the domestic circle. Quarrels are, however, frequent, for the husbands are extremely rigorous, and the wives are not very tractable. These unfortunate women may indeed be considered on a level with the slaves as to the severe labours imposed upon them. They go to distant places for wood and water; their husbands make them sow, weed the cultivated fields, and gather in the harvest. When they travel with a caravan, they carry burthens on their heads, while the husbands proceed at their ease on horseback. The poor women are often severely reproved for the slightest mistake they commit; they then cry, storm, and run about the village, complaining loudly of the injustice of their husbands; little attention is however paid to them, for the husbands, in their own opinion, are never in the wrong, and the dispute ends by the wife receiving a sound drubbing; she then weeps and screams, until the elders of the village come to her relief and restore peace for a time to the hut. I observed, that after a beating they become very gentle. It is certain that they are not vindictive; and indeed they would gain nothing by being so. On the third or fourth day after the quarrel they are as cheerful as ever. The wife dare not lift a hand against her husband, even in her own defence; and she never ventures to indulge in the least joke upon him. The husband always speaks in the tone of a master: in fact, his wives are merely servants.

I asked Baba why he did not sometimes make merry with his wives: he replied, that if he did he should not be able to manage them, for they would laugh at him when he ordered them to do any thing. Their marriages are celebrated by feasting and dancing, all the population of the village participating in the rejoicings; the consumption of eatables is great, and the husband pays all the expense: those who cannot attend have their suppers sent to them in calabashes; others who are absent have their share kept for them till they return home.

When the young bride repairs to her husband's village, a fresh entertainment is prepared for her reception. Gaiety always prevails on these occasions. No religious ceremony unites the husband and wife; nevertheless, the link by which they are bound cannot be broken; for the dowry which the husband has given is a solemn act, which cannot be undone. The wife is not the less unfortunate: let her husband beat her as much as he pleases, she cannot obtain a separation, except by restitution; but that is with her impossible, since she possesses nothing, and her parents, if they should be able, would not restore what they have received.

With respect to physical suffering the fortitude displayed by the women is remarkable. While pregnant they continue to perform the severest labours until the very last moment of their time. They give birth to children without uttering a complaint, and one would almost believe that they are delivered without pain, for on the following day they resume their usual occupations. I observed that the child is born white, with only a shade of yellow, and that it grows gradually darker until the tenth day, when it is quite black. The new-born infant is bathed in a calabash of tepid water, and not in the river as several travellers have asserted. Adults seldom bathe in cold water; still less do children. The mothers watch over their infants with great tenderness, seldom trusting them to the care of others. They always suckle them themselves, and they carry them every where on their backs, fastened up in their pagne, as is the custom in almost all the negro countries. In all the parts of Africa which I have visited, boys and girls go about naked until the age of puberty.

The male Mandingoes are circumcised between the age of fifteen and twenty. The excision which females should undergo, when they are marriageable is often delayed until they are promised in marriage. I even saw a married woman, who, after having a child, submitted to this operation. It is always performed by women, and on several patients at once, who are thereby rendered for some time unable to work. In this state they are taken care of by their mothers, who bathe the wound several times a day with an indigenous caustic; with the use of which they are acquainted. Their female neighbours go in quest of the wood and water of which they stand in need.

The day of circumcision is always a rejoicing day.

On the following day, the girls who have undergone the operation promenade the village accompanied by an old woman. They stop at every door to solicit donations, the old women speaking for them. The young women never go out without a reed which they carry in the left hand. They also wear on this occasion a man's cap of a large size, the front of which is supported by a piece of flexible wood put inside to make it stand up. With this head-dress these girls look like giantesses. Instead of a reed, I have seen some of them carrying an iron arrow, as an emblem of the circumcision.

The persons whose hospitality is appealed to on the part of the newly circumcised, hasten to prepare, each in his turn, victuals sufficient for a great dinner or supper, into which they put salt, and which is distributed among the patients. All their friends and neighbours follow this example if they please; but those who are betrothed must not fail, and they continue to send dinners to the circumcised until their recovery, which in general is not completed until six weeks after the operation. Their fathers, who never live in the same hut, also send them more provisions than usual. Large platefuls of rice or tau are distributed by the mothers among the neighbours and relations. On these occasions I was never forgotten. The good negress, my landlady, always took care that I should have my share.

The fathers and mothers are extremely fond of their children, and they, in their turn, have a great veneration for their parents. Indeed, respect and obedience to the old is a rule rigorously observed. In all these countries I never saw a mendicant. The aged who are unable to support themselves are always maintained and treated with respect by their children. In this part of the interior I saw a blind man, but he did not beg, as is the custom for such persons in other negro countries. Many travellers have asserted that the children retain a stronger attachment to their mother than to their father; but for my part, though I had an opportunity of studying their character for some time, I cannot say that I observed this difference in their affection. When they have any business to transact they follow in preference the advice of their father, and they would feel extreme reluctance to disobey him; for the father is always the supreme head of the family. I shall cite, by way of example, Arafan-Abdalahi, a Mandingo of Kankan, a man of forty or forty-five, who relinquished the pleasure, and even the religious duty, of performing a pilgrimage to Mecca, that he might not displease his aged father whose consent he could not obtain. I did not observe that the Mandingoes quarrel often. It is dangerous to insult them and still more to offend their parents. They are however vindictive, inquisitive, envious, liars, importunate, selfish, avaricious, ignorant and superstitious. They are not strictly speaking thieves since they do not steal from each other; but their probity with respect to others is very equivocal and in particular towards strangers, who would be very imprudent to shew them any thing that might tempt their cupidity, such as scissors, knives, glass trinkets, gunpowder, paper, &c. articles which are exceedingly rare and valuable in those countries. The Mandingoes do not trust any thing, even in the hands of their relations, without first counting or measuring it several times. In general they are distrustful and far from scrupulous about the means of obtaining what pleases them. During my stay at Timé, I heard that a Bambara belonging to a distant village had killed one of his comrades, which occasioned much consternation in the neighbourhood, but I was never able to learn whether the murderer suffered any punishment for the offence. I can, however, affirm that such crimes are rare among the Bambaras, and never committed by the Mandingoes. These latter despise the poor Bambaras, whom they look upon as infidels, but I had good reason to think that they are themselves avaricious and inhospitable, and I firmly believe, that I should have perished during my illness, if I had not possessed wherewithal to pay for my food; and for my personal security I was indebted to my disguise. They all manifested the most decided aversion to the name of christian; for they entertain the very worst idea of us. However, they are not altogether devoid of sensibility: they pay much attention to their countrymen in sickness, and even to those of their own religion. It must be remembered that I was to them an indifferent being, and yet, some of them evinced sincere compassion for me. I however, experienced more hospitality and less annoyance among the Foulahs than from the Mandingoes.

When a negro enters the house of a chief or a man of quality, he leaves his sandals at the door, and announces himself, by repeating three times *Salam alékoum*. This formality is not observed towards their equals until after the door is closed.

Earthen pots are not manufactured at Timé, but are procured from the Bambaras, who barter them for salt and colat-nuts: all these pots are of an oval shape, and I have seen some of them from eighteen to twenty inches deep: they are of a grey colour and not so well made as in the Kankan and the Wassoulo. The women employ their leisure moments in spinning cotton, from which is manufactured a kind of coloured cloth; this cloth is exchanged on the road to Jenné for cowries, the money with which they purchase salt. The Mandingoes of Timé do not live as well as those of Kankan and the Fouta. Like the Bambaras they eat all kinds of quadrupeds, except cats and dogs. My host Baba had three slaves, only one of whom, was able to work. The other two, and especially a little boy, were treated with harshness, because they were unable to make themselves useful. He was therefore obliged to employ day-labourers. The people of Timé are not so neat in their dress as the inhabitants of the Fouta and the Kankan, but they are better clothed than the Bambaras. Two days after the birth of a child, the event is celebrated by dancing and feasting.

They are accustomed, summer and winter, to bathe in warm water, every evening on returning from the fields where they work; the women take care to have the water ready. They have fires every night in their huts, for they are naturally chilly.

I have seen among the Mandingoes at Timé large nets made of cotton and the bark of trees twisted together; with these nets they go out to hunt the gazelle and wild-boar. Having discovered the traces of the animals in the woods, they spread their nets, and scour the surrounding country in order to drive the game into them. As soon as the animal is caught it is killed with the poniard. They generally assemble in great numbers for these hunting expeditions, which however, often prove unsuccessful. When they kill an animal they always turn its head to the east. The women never kill poultry; that business is always performed by the men. The inhabitants of Timé do not however kill much poultry, though they breed a great deal; they prefer selling it to travellers; they keep some goats and sheep, but neither oxen nor cows, although the soil produces excellent pasturage. There are some cows in the neighbouring villages but they are never milked.

Caravans of saracolets often pass through Timé on their way to the south to purchase slaves. The saracolets are not a nation but, as I have before mentioned, a class of merchants, who travel in every part of Africa. There are saracolets in all the negro countries, Mandingoes and Bambaras, Fouta-Dialonkés, in Kayaya, Bondou, &c. They are all Mahometans, and use in conversation among themselves a particular dialect, which the other negroes, even those of their own nation, do not understand. They scarcely ever remain in their native country, and have every where the reputation of being rich and very much inclined to theft.

When a stranger arrives at Timé, who happens to find any relations or friends there, if he does not immediately go to them, as soon as they hear of his arrival they prepare a great dinner for him. This repast, of which a fowl seasoned with salt forms part, they send by their wives to the new comer. They do not touch it themselves, but prepare a dinner for themselves as usual. Soon afterwards they call on their friend and receive his thanks; and, should they even find him at his meal, they would not partake of any portion of it. After his repast the stranger goes to pay his visit, which he would not have done, if the fowl had not been sent to him. This custom is very general throughout the country.

The huts of Timé are neither so large nor so neat as those of the Fouta and Kankan, though they are built in the same form, and surrounded by a similar wall of earth, six feet high and five inches thick; it is the women's business to cover this wall with cow-dung, which is purchased at the market for a few colats. The huts are roofed with straw, and contain no furniture except some mats spread upon the ground, which serve for seats in the day-time and beds at night, a few earthen pots for culinary purposes, wooden plates, calabashes, spatules for stirring the tau, and an earthen jar to hold water. The women keep their wood in a corner of their huts, lest their indolent neighbours might make free with it to save the trouble of procuring some for themselves. When they collect their wood, they make little presents of portions of it to the aged women in their vicinity. The inhabitants of this village do not use large earthen jars for holding grain, like the people of Fouta and Kankan, which shows that they neither grow so much, nor are so rich as the latter. Half a mile from the village there is a beautiful clear spring, where the inhabitants fetch water for their consumption. This spring is shaded by large trees, the name of which I do not know, but which would I believe, be very fit for building. The few productions of the soil cultivated by the people of Timé are left in the fields, with small pieces of written paper affixed to them, to keep off thieves; and no one ever touches them. During my stay at Timé, I only saw one man whose yams had been stolen out of the ground; but, said the negroes, they were not protected by grigris.

The butter-tree, or cé, is very abundant in the neighbourhood of Timé. It grows spontaneously, and in height and appearance resembles the pear-tree. The leaves grow in tufts, supported by a very short foot-stalk. They are round at top, and when the tree is young, they are six inches long. When the tree grows old the leaves become smaller, and resemble those of the Saint-Jean pear-tree. It blossoms at the extremity of its branches, and the flowers, which are small, grow in clusters, and are supported by a very strong pedicle. The petals are white, and the stamina are numerous and scarcely perceptible to the naked eye. The fruit, when mature, is as large as a Guinea-hen's egg, of oval shape, and equal at both ends. It is covered with a pale-green pellicle, beneath which is a green farinaceous pulp, three lines thick, of an extremely agreeable flavour. The negroes are very fond of it, and I liked it myself. Under this pulp there is a second pellicle, very thin, and resembling the white skin which lines the inside of an egg-shell. This covers the kernel, which is of a pale coffee colour. The fruit being disengaged from the two pellicles and the pulp, is enclosed in a shell as thin as that of an egg, and the kernel is of the size of a pigeon's egg. The fruit is exposed several days to the sun, in order to dry it, then pounded in a mortar, and reduced to flour which is of the colour of wheat bran. After being pounded, it is placed in a large calabash; luke-warm water is thrown over it, and it is kneaded with the hands until it attains the consistence of dough. To ascertain whether it is sufficiently manipulated, warm water is thrown over it, and if greasy particles are detached from the dough and float, the warm water is repeated several times, until the butter is completely separated, and rises to the surface. The butter is collected with a wooden spoon, and placed in a calabash. It is then boiled on a strong fire, being well skimmed to remove any pulp that might remain with it. When sufficiently boiled, it is poured into a calabash with a little water at the bottom to make it turn out easily.

Thus prepared it is wrapped in the leaves of the tree, and will keep two years without spoiling. The butter is of an ash-grey colour and as hard as tallow. It is an article of trade with the negroes, who use it both for food and for anointing their bodies. They also employ it to burn for light; and they told me that it was an excellent ointment for pains and sores. The fruit of the cé is much larger in Baléya and Amana than in Timé. The seed of this tree, which is so valuable to the people of these countries, could not be transported to Europe for sowing, unless packed in small earthen vessels, otherwise it loses its germinative power, which does not last long. I have already mentioned that there is at Timé a fruit called *taman*, which also produces an unctuous substance very good for eating and more firm than the cé. It might be advantageously employed in Europe for burning. The grease or fat, called by the natives *taman-toulou*, is extracted by the same process as that employed with the cé. The tree, which produces the *taman* grows on the banks of rivulets, and is very common in the south. These two trees are so abundant at Cani and Teuté, that the inhabitants of those places, I was told, though possessing plenty of cows, never eat any butter except that produced by the trees. Palm-oil is also met with here, though not in great quantity. The kernel of the taman is of the size of a horse-chesnut, somewhat elongated, of a beautiful pink colour, deepening a little towards the outside. It is exceedingly hard; and the women, after setting it on the fire in earthen pots, crush it between two flints, previously to pounding it in the mortar. The butter of the taman is of a light yellow colour. It is firmer than that of the cé, and has no smell. I preferred this to the other.

Indigo grows spontaneously in the environs of Timé. The women use it for dyeing their cotton thread; which the men weave into cloths. The process employed to extract the dye is very simple. They do not take the trouble to cut the plant, but gather the leaves, which they bruise; and then making them up into small cakes they lay them in the sun to dry.

This process has been followed for a very long period. When the dye is wanted, the cakes are bruised, and put into a large earthen pot, made for this purpose; cold water is then poured over them and time is allowed for the leaves to soak. After leaving them twenty hours to ferment, ley is made with the ashes of the straw of foigné, and cold water is added. This has the effect of dissolving the indigo. The dye being thus prepared, the articles to be dyed are put into the pot.

Cotton requires to be thus soaked for a whole night, or even longer; and when taken out, I have seen it of a beautiful blue colour. In proportion as the water diminishes, more is added, and the same leaves serve to dye for a whole week; but the first tint is always the finest.

I saw, in this country a climbing plant, with a very broad leaf, and containing a large quantity of blue dye. It is very common at Sierra-Leone.

The young women do not dye the cotton thread; that task is always consigned to the old women, who also cultivate little gardens round their huts, where they raise various kinds of herbs which they use for making their sauces, &c. In these gardens they also grow tobacco, which is sown in September and transplanted in October. Very little attention however is bestowed on its cultivation. That which I saw at Timé and in its neighbourhood is of a small species, and it is not gathered until it runs to seed. The leaves, after being dried in the sun, are reduced to powder. This is the only way in which the inhabitants use tobacco. I never saw any prepared in the European manner at Timé.

They have small hard beans of a grey colour which they boil. The giraumon also grows here. It is cooked with pistachio-nuts and pimento. This last plant, so common in hot countries, does not thrive well here; the inhabitants therefore purchase it in their journeys to the south, where they also procure a long kind of pepper which they are very fond of. They call it cani, the name of the place whence it is brought, and merchants carry this pepper to Jenné to exchange it for salt.

The most common distempers at Timé are ophthalmia, eruptive sores, swellings of the neck and throat, fevers and leprosy. Scurvy also makes its appearance sometimes. I never saw any deformed person in these parts. Colds are very common.

CHAPTER XIV

Departure from Timé, January 9th, 1829 — The name of Kong, applied by Mungo Park to a chain of mountains, is a generic term — Use of bells in caravans — Loubakho — Cacoron — Dancing and music of the Bambaras — Sananso — Dhio — The oil palm-tree — Talé — Customs of the inhabitants — Borandou — Grotesque mask — Tangrera.

On the 9th of January, after a slight repast of yams, which the old negress prepared for us, we got ready to leave Timé. I made my hostess a handsome present, which she received with pleasure, and I also gave Baba some merchandise, which I had promised him, as a compensation for the time I had stayed with him.

About nine o'clock in the morning we left the village, after taking leave of the good old chief, who wished us a prosperous journey.

My guide brought his wife to carry my baggage, which had now become very light, and his brother Baba was to accompany us a short distance on the road. We directed our course to the S. S. E. and gained the foot of the chain of mountains, which is composed of masses of granite. In crossing this chain, I observed several trees growing among the rocks, principally the cé. Numerous springs rise in the mountains and fertilize the country, the soil of which, composed of black mould mixed with grey sand, is exceedingly fertile. The country was stripped of all its charms: the grass was burned up, the trees had lost half their foliage, and the birds had flown from the woods to the margins of the streams. All was sad and desolate, and the dreary appearance of the hills of granite augmented the sombre effect of the scene. We entered a Bambara village named Dsagoé, where I saw several fine plantations of tobacco, of which the inhabitants consume a great quantity. We rested for a moment under the shade of a bombax, and refreshed ourselves with a calabashful of water, given to us by the inhabitants, who pressed eagerly round me, and kept their eyes fixed upon me. The morning's journey had fatigued me, for I was still weak, and could scarcely walk; which sufficiently proved that, if I had followed my inclination to set off sooner, I should not have been able to accomplish the journey. We took our leave of these inquisitive people, and proceeded towards the S. E.

over a country covered with large rocks of quartz. We saw some Bambaras preparing the ground for the purpose of planting yams.

After proceeding about ten miles, we arrived about two o'clock in the afternoon at Kimba, a small village where the caravan bound to Jenné was waiting. At the distance of about two miles from this village there is a chain of mountains extending from N. E. to S. W. and as high as those we crossed in the morning. I at first imagined that these might be the Kong mountains, mentioned by Mungo Park, though it is impossible to suppose that he saw them, as they are low, and at a considerable distance from Ségo. I may also observe that Kong is not the name, which the natives give to these mountains, for among the Mandingoes, Kong or Kongké signifies mountain. Park, no doubt, confounded the general with the particular name. The country is entirely covered with hills. In the village I saw some tobacco growing. As my breakfast had been but slight, I went up to a Bambara, whom I saw sitting in his hut with a calabash of yams, and asked him to sell me a few of them for some glass trinkets which I shewed him. The good negro immediately took out a handful of yams, which he put into a calabash with some sauce, and gave it to me. I presented him with some glass beads in payment, which he was at first reluctant to accept, but I forced him to take them as a present for his wife. At night-fall he paid me a visit at my hut, and made me a present of a very large yam.

With the exception of the good old chief at Timé, who was, indeed, of the Bambara nation, no inhabitants of that village ever paid me so much civility, during the time I stayed there.

In the village of Kimba I saw several men, assembled under a tree, playing at various games, which I had seen played by the negroes of the Senegal. Small holes made in the sand served for a chess-board, and bits of wood, five inches long, for the men. In this village I saw, for the first time since I left Fouta-Dhialon, the women sitting with the men, and mixing in their conversation, while employed in spinning cotton. The Mandingo women do not enjoy this privilege. Baba's brother prepared us an excellent supper of rice, and sauce made of pistachio-nuts, with some salt to render it more palatable.

On the 10th of January, about nine in the morning, the caravan prepared to depart. The women, with heavy loads of colats on their heads, took the lead, followed by the men, similarly laden. They all had a bell hung at their breasts; some had as many as a dozen attached to different parts of their dress. These appendages produce a deafening jingle, which highly pleases the negroes. They were all armed with bows and arrows, and marched in a file like a procession. The chiefs and the proprietors of merchandise leading the asses, closed the rear.

On leaving the village, Baba quitted us: he did not appear much affected at our separation; however, he recommended me to his brother, to whom I promised to make a handsome present on arriving at Jenné, and I placed my baggage on his ass. The negroes give several names to this city: they call it Dhienné, and often Dhiendé.

We advanced to the S. E., crossing several large rivulets, which delayed us some time, for the asses threw their loads off their backs, and the negroes were obliged to push them forward to make them advance. At length we entered the village of Zangouiriré, which contains from three to four hundred inhabitants, of the Bambara race, the only people met with on this road as far as Jenné. We continued our journey over a level country: the soil was fertile, and composed of grey sand, mixed with black earth. We had a chain of low hills both to the right and left of our road. Every minute the asses were throwing off their loads, which caused great trouble and delay. Among the female slaves who accompanied our caravan, I observed with pain, girls of twelve or fifteen years old carrying heavy loads of colats on their heads. The poor creatures were unable to endure the fatigue, and sometimes let their burthens fall. The heat was excessive, and an easterly wind annoyed us extremely; we had, however, the comfort every now and then of getting some water to quench our thirst. In about an hour and a half, we arrived at Dioumiégué, having travelled nine miles. The women belonging to the caravan had gone a little in advance, and prepared dinner for the men, who had no sooner came up, than they fell to eating, and then they lay down to rest themselves. The people came in crowds to look at me. They appeared very gentle and refrained from importuning me. Some of them made my guide presents of yams, which we ate for supper; others gave him colat-nuts. In the village I observed many small herds of oxen and cows. The latter are not milked.

We quitted Dioumiégué on the 11th of January, at six o'clock in the morning, after paying our passage-money to the chief. We kept to the east along a very fertile plain, where I perceived some husbandmen planting yams. Leaving the plain, we crossed a chain of hills, composed of large blocks of granite, intermixed with white quartz, veined with bright rose-colour. We crossed many small rivulets, which made a thousand windings in the passes of the mountains. We travelled two miles to the east, along very difficult roads, and then descended into a plain well cropped with yams, and thronged with people engaged in agricultural labour. After proceeding about ten miles in the same direction, we arrived about noon at Sinisso, where we halted. This village is surrounded by a wall, and contains about a hundred huts. My umbrella, which my guide displayed to the notice of the inhabitants, greatly excited their curiosity. The hut where we lodged was full of visiters the whole evening: for those who had obtained a sight of the wonder eagerly told their companions, who came running in their turn to behold it. They could not understand how the machine could be made to open and shut at pleasure. They called it a *libri*, a word in their language, signifying a hat; but notwithstanding their curiosity, they were far from being so troublesome as the Mandingoes.

At this season of the year, the women cook in the open air. For this purpose they kindle fires in their yards, round which the men sit and take their meals. They all invited me to partake of their supper of boiled yams.

On the 12th of January, at five in the morning, after paying for our lodging, we left this village, and directed our course to the N. E., over a soil consisting of a mixture of earth and gravel, but which is, nevertheless, very fertile. Having proceeded about four miles, we arrived at Salasso, through which we passed without stopping. Again continuing our course for four miles, we arrived about the middle of the day at Loubakho, where we halted. Loubakho is a large walled village, containing from six to seven hundred inhabitants. It is situated in a beautiful plain of very rich grey sand. About six or seven miles N. E. of the Village, there is a high pointed mountain, which extends N. W. and E. S. E. The inhabitants of Loubakho keep some horned cattle, and they brought us milk, which we purchased with glass beads. In the afternoon I received a visit from a saracolet, who had come from Sambatikila, and was proceeding to Jenné. As it is the custom in this country to make some presents to visiters, I directed my guide to give him in my name some colat-nuts; for which he overwhelmed him with acknowledgments. I also gave my guide a bit of coloured stuff to make him a cap. In the evening I purchased a large fowl for our supper. My guide gave it to his woman to cook; and after boiling it, she made a very good sauce of the liquor with pistachios, and a little salt for seasoning. I expressed a wish that we should partake of the fowl together. The Mandingoes, however, out of respect declined taking any. This was an instance of self-denial, which I was far from expecting; In the evening it lightened in the west. The day had been extremely hot, but during the night I could bear my woollen wrapper.

On the 13th, at four in the morning, we prepared to depart; but, before I proceed farther, I will endeavour to give a description of the whole economy of our caravan. It was composed of from forty to fifty Mandingoes, and thirty-five women, all carrying loads on their heads. There were eight chiefs leading their asses, about fifteen in number. With these chiefs were their slaves and women, whose business it was to carry the baggage and cook at every halt for the whole caravan. The women always proceeded first, and the men in the rear. The ringing of their bells gave notice of their approach. The Mandingoes are very fond of bells, the jingling of which diverts them on their journey. They make these bells themselves of iron and copper, which they purchase at Jenné, and in other markets on the banks of the Dhioliba, where they likewise procure bells ready made. On arriving at a village, the women of the caravan fetch water and bruise the millet for dinner. This meal being over, they prepare warm water for the men's baths: the water is heated in large vessels, which they borrow from the people of the village where they stop. This task being ended, they again set about bruising millet for supper. It is the business of the slaves to procure fire-wood for cooking. The free negroes are exempted from all this trouble; they lie down and rest themselves until their meals are ready: they then go through the village with their calabashes, containing colats, which they exchange with the inhabitants for cowries. With these they purchase grain for the supply of the caravan. The women employ their leisure moments in spinning cotton, which they purchase with the colats given to them by their husbands. I have seen them spin by the light of a lamp fed with vegetable butter; the produce of this labour is their own little perquisite. On their arrival at Jenné, they sell their spun cotton for cowries, with which they buy salt and glass trinkets. The women likewise wash the men's clothes. The men, as soon as they have rested themselves, inspect the loads of colats, especially those which during the journey have fallen from the asses' backs. They cover the fruit with fresh leaves, in order to keep it cool; they then go into the village to dispose of their cloth; they also settle the payment of the passage money; for all foreign merchants, however numerous they may be, are obliged in every place they halt to pay for the whole of the company, a small tax, the amount of which sometimes varies, but is generally about twenty colats for each load: these twenty colats are worth two hundred cowries, (about twenty sous, French money). When the caravan is numerous, which often happens, for it gains accessions on the road, some person who has but a small load goes forward, and arrives first in the village to procure lodgings for his companions; he then deposits his load and returns to meet his friends, whom he directs to their respective destinations. Those who do not adopt this prudent precaution have the trouble of seeking through the village for a place to put up at, and are often obliged to proceed farther. It is customary for the parties who first reach the village to return and help the others with their burdens, especially when the journey has been long.

On the 13th of January, we set out at four o'clock in the morning, in order to take advantage of the cool air. We proceeded to the N. E. for the distance of four miles, over a soil composed of very hard grey sand. The country was pretty flat, with the exception of some granite blocks, rising six or seven feet above the ground. The cé was very abundant, but the nédé much less common than in the parts through which we had previously journeyed. We passed near Couraniso, and then the road became rather stony. We went on for five miles more without seeing the least trace of cultivation, and at ten o'clock in the morning arrived at Cacoron, where we halted. This village contains from five to six hundred inhabitants, to whom I was an object of great curiosity. As I had not yet breakfasted, I went to a Bambara woman, who was pounding boiled yams; I bought some of her for a few glass beads, and she gave me separately, in a small pot, some gombo sauce. On dipping my yams into this sauce, I discovered, to my great mortification, some little paws, and immediately ascertained that the sauce was made of mice; however, I was hungry, and I continued my meal, though, I must confess, not without some feelings of disgust. The negroes, when they take their yams without sauce, never mash them: those which I bought from the negress were ready prepared. In the evening I saw many women chopping mice to make sauce for their suppers. I observed that they gut the animals, and, without taking the trouble of skinning them, merely draw them across the fire to singe off the hair: thus prepared, they lay them in a corner of the hut, and it is not unusual to keep them there for seven or eight days before they are cooked. The mice, which make their way into the jars of millet, are caught by the women and children without the aid of traps.

Though there is abundance of poultry at Cacoron, yet the negroes eat it only on holidays. I wanted to buy some, but could find nobody inclined to sell any. An old Bambara made me a present of some pistachios and a yam. I found the people here more hospitable than they had been represented to me. I am convinced that a European, travelling in a plain, unostentatious style, would experience no annoyance, that is, if he were not imprudent enough to display any valuable goods; in this case, he would run the risk of being robbed: but I am far from believing that these kind-hearted and simple people would be guilty of any cruelty towards a traveller.

The neighbourhood of Cacoron is covered with cés and nédés. The inhabitants make a great quantity of butter, which they sell to strangers. I scarcely ever saw so gay a people as the Bambaras. At sun-set they assemble under the great bombaces, at the entrance of the village, and dance all night to music which is not unpleasant. Attracted by this music, I stopped to observe their gambols, and was highly entertained. I was with a young Mandingo belonging to our caravan, who was particularly attentive to me. Men and women mingled together formed a large circle round a fire, jumping and keeping time to a band of music, consisting of three great drums and several hautboys. The musicians were dressed like those of Timé, having white cotton mantles, and ostrich-feathers on their heads. The dancers kept time with the music by a careless kind of motion of their arms and heads. The women had pieces of cotton cloth, which they held at both ends and waved in the air. The only figure of the dance consisted in going round the fire. The musicians kept themselves a little aloof, while the dancers, following each other in a file, went round the fire, leaping and shaking their legs about. I was much amused with this dance, in which there was nothing indecent, but I could not stay to look at it as long as I could have wished, for the capering of two or three hundred negroes raised an insufferable dust.

Throughout the whole of Bambara, and, according to the account of some negroes, even to a considerable distance south of Cacoron, the same music prevails. It is certainly one of the best and most agreeable I heard during my travels among the negroes. These people spend the greater part of the night in dancing; their dispositions are gentle and humane, and they are content with the present, without troubling themselves about the future. They have scarcely any clothing, generally wearing a sort of girdle, ornamented with cowries, which, after going round the waist and between the legs, is brought up in front to tie. To these girdles are attached fringes of cotton, which descend to the knee. The old men wear the usual pagne, and generally in the most filthy state. The women likewise wear pagnes, which are tied round their loins, and descend to their knees; they plat their hair in tresses, and rub their bodies all over with butter. The men shave their heads, like the Mahometans; but some tufts of hair are left, varying in size, according to the fancy of the wearer. Their skin is of the same colour as that of the Foulahs of the Wassoulo, and like them they have aquiline noses, thin lips, woolly hair, and sharp-pointed teeth; they make incisions on their faces and bodies.

In this country they make a sort of beer, or hydromel, of fermented millet and honey. They are very fond of this liquor which they drink till they intoxicate themselves.

On the 14th January, at five in the morning, we left the cheerful inhabitants of Cacaron, and proceeded three miles to the east over a level country, the soil of which was composed of very hard grey sand. We came to a mountain of black granite entirely barren. It extends north and south, and is about two hundred and fifty paces high. We advanced, five miles further in the same direction. On the way we passed some large blocks of black granite.

About nine in the morning we halted at Tisso-Soman, a pretty village, lying between two small hills of very pale granite. In the centre of this village I saw a number of wells seven or eight feet in depth. The ground in which they are dug consists of sand mixed with coarse grey gravel, and at the bottom of the wells is some grey clayey earth, with pieces of rock, the nature of which I was unable to determine. The clay is of a whitish grey, and very slippery. I was unable to judge of its quantity by what was thrown up and left round the edge of the wells. The water was very good; but rather white in colour.

The women of the caravan seated themselves round these wells to wash their millet.

After a light breakfast, consisting of tau and a bad sauce made of herbs, we left the village. About two o'clock we took an easterly direction, and proceeded about six miles, over a soil similar to that which I last described. Our progress was somewhat impeded by large blocks of granite, which we encountered at every step, and on either side of us were small hills of the same material. At sun-set we halted at Sananso, a large walled village, containing seven or eight hundred inhabitants. I seated myself near a hut, to rest after my fatigue; but the chief of the village invited me to sit by him, on some large clumps of wood, raised a little above the ground and placed near the door of his hut. Above these seats there was a sort of canopy, made of branches of trees. The chief had a little fire beside his seat, and the smoke was so disagreeable that I could not stay longer than a few minutes. He asked me some questions concerning the whites and their mode of living, and seemed satisfied with my answers.

The village is situated in a large, well cultivated, and fertile plain. At a little distance from it there is a mountain of granite entirely barren. In this village we met a caravan of Mandingoes, some of whom were going to Jenné and others to Sansanding. Some were laden with cloth, and some with colat-nuts. The chief of the village assigned to me a hut built of earth, the only one in the place, the others being all of straw. He had a fire kindled, and requested me to go in and lie down: but, on entering, I was nearly suffocated. The hut had a flat roof covered with earth, and the smoke, being unable to obtain a vent above, had no outlet but the door. Straw huts are not subject to this inconvenience. I speedily retired from this oven in which I could not breathe, and prepared to pass the night in the open air; but my guide, being informed of the reason which prevented me from remaining in the hut, explained the circumstance to the chief, who immediately selected another lodging for me, where I passed the night with a Mandingo belonging to our caravan. Some strangers sent us a little supper very well cooked.

On the 15th of January, at six in the morning, we proceeded northward about seven miles, among rocks of granite on a fertile soil composed of sand. I observed the cé and the nédé in great abundance and the land well cultivated. About eleven o'clock we arrived at Dhio, a large walled village containing about eight or nine hundred inhabitants. On entering the place, I observed a number of women assembled in a spot which seemed to be set aside for their recreation. Some were nursing their children who were quite naked, and others were asleep. The old men have also a place where they assemble to smoke their pipes, and where they spend a great part of the day. It is called the banancoro,. as among the Mandingoes. I also saw some tobacco plantations in the little gardens adjoining the huts. The village is disgustingly dirty.

At six in the morning of the 16th, we prepared to depart. On going out I saw some palm-trees of the species which produces oil. They are not by far so thriving here as on the coast. We proceeded E. N. E. over a very fertile soil, consisting of grey sand mixed with fine gravel. The country was woody; I observed some tamarind-trees and many cés. About nine in the morning, after travelling six miles and a half, we reached Niourot, a little village, where we could purchase nothing but with cowries, which are the current money among all the inhabitants of upper Bambara. They receive them from the European merchants who trade on the western coasts, and from the Moors on the shores of the Mediterranean. The cowries are just beginning to be current in this part of the country. The price of a fowl is eighty cowries. In the language of the country *kémé* signifies eighty, and to express a hundred the people say eighty and twenty, or *kémé nimouya* [58]

We were lodged in a very large hut where I saw, not without astonishment, two seats resembling sofas, each made out of the trunk of a tree. I regarded them as curiosities among a people who have no carpenter's tools. The legs, the arms, and the back, were all made out of one piece of wood, which was of a red colour and very hard. These sofas were really executed with some taste; they must have been a work of considerable time, but in those countries time is not so valuable as with us. The people have no other tools than small hatchets and poniards.

I observed that our host kept about a dozen little dogs, which, when sufficiently fattened, were destined for food. He had also a number of chickens; he fed them with termites, which his children brought from the fields. In general I did not see in this part of the country those great hills of the white ant (termites) which are found on the shores of the Senegal, where they are sometimes eight or nine feet high; those which I saw here are not more than eighteen inches or two feet high. In this village all the heads of families have huts or cabins built of earth, like that which the chief of Sananso allotted to me. The women's huts are of straw. We procured a little millet for our supper, for which we paid in colat-nuts. The wells are at a little distance from the village, and, if I may judge from the rope used for drawing up the water, they are not above twelve, or fifteen feet deep.

At half past six, on the morning of the 17th of January, we took leave of our host, whom we had taken care to pay on the preceding evening.

On leaving the village we met several Bambaras, who had about twenty dogs tied to a single cord; these animals were, I was informed, going to be fattened. As soon as they saw us they saluted us with such a loud barking that we could not hear ourselves speak. Our road lay to the N. N. E. and we passed a large village, the name of which I could not learn. We continued to travel over a soil composed of grey sand; the vegetation was the same as it had been for several preceding days. After travelling about eleven miles, we halted about eleven o'clock in the morning at Talé, a village containing three or four hundred inhabitants. They gave us several huts to lodge in. The huts in this village are not so large as in those which we had previously passed through; but they are of the same form. I walked through the streets, which are narrow and dirty. My appearance excited the curiosity of the Bambaras, but they did not annoy me. The women, who were exceedingly dirty, have all a bit of calabash, or a thin slip of wood, stuck into the under lip. I could scarcely persuade myself that this was a mere matter of taste, and questioned my guide upon the subject: he assured me that it was the fashion of the country. I was equally at a loss to conceive how this bit of wood, which was merely stuck through the lip, could keep its place. The women allowed me to see that this curious ornament was brought through to the inner part of the lip, and they laughed heartily at my astonishment. I asked one of them to remove the piece of wood from her lip; but she told me that if she did so the saliva would run through the hole. In short, I was quite amazed that coquetry could induce them to disfigure themselves in this manner; yet it is the general custom of this country. I saw young girls eight or ten years of age, who had in their lower lip little pieces of wood of the circumference of a pen, pointed at one end and stuck into the flesh. They renew it frequently, and every time use a larger bit of wood, which gradually widens the hole, until it becomes large enough to admit a piece of wood of the size of a half-crown piece. I observed that this singular and inconvenient ornament contributed to their uncleanliness.

The old men are provided with a bull's tail for the purpose of driving away the flies, which are very numerous and troublesome in this country. I did not see in this part of Africa any of those musquitoes which are so tormenting to travellers in the neighbourhood of the Senegal.

The inhabitants of this village are kind, affable, and hospitable: they invited me to partake of their little suppers of yams and mouse sauce.

Their huts are small and dirty. They cultivate rice and yams; their crops usually remain in the fields all the dry season, and when the rains commence they remove them to little straw store-houses, which are erected in the middle of the court-yards. The people are poor; they possess but few slaves, and scanty herds and flocks; but their soil, being fertile and well cultivated, yields them more than they want. I saw but few horses, and these were miserable-looking animals. I did not observe that the inhabitants of this village worship a deity. Like the people of Wassoulo, they have no religion; but they entertain a high respect for the disciples of Mahomet and the Koran, which they regard as a sort of magic. They always wear *saphies*,[59] suspended from their necks and different parts of their bodies. They hang them up at the entrance of their huts, as a protection against fire, thieves, and other accidents.

Throughout all this part of the country there are Mandingo villages, the inhabitants of which are Mahometans. They are independent of the Bambaras, as at Timé, Sambatikila, Tangrera, and other villages further southward. The Bambaras call them *Diaulas* or *Jaulas*, and though they might, owing to their superiority of numbers, molest them if they chose, yet they refrain from doing so, and go to their villages to sell them the superfluous produce of their harvest. The Bambaras, in general, speak the Mandingo language; but they have a particular dialect, which, owing to the rapidity with which I travelled among them, I had no opportunity of learning. This country is at the distance of a month's journey from Ségo; but it is independent of the latter. It is governed by a number of petty chiefs, who receive provisions by way of tribute; but they are moderate in their exactions, as they know the poverty of their subjects. The Mandingoes look upon the Bambaras as great thieves; yet the little store-houses which stand defenceless in their yards are always respected. But the Bambaras, like their accusers, whenever they see glass trinkets, scissors, knives, or locks and keys, things which to them are as valuable as gold, cannot resist the desire of possessing them; and, being too poor to buy, they endeavour to obtain what they want, not by force but by cunning. Throughout all the country I did not see a woman with ear-rings or a gold necklace. All their ornaments consist of the glass trinkets, which they procure from the merchants who come from Jenné. My guide, Karamo-osila, advised me not to shew them the contents of my bag; but I had no need of this advice. I should have taken good care not to open it in their presence, for, notwithstanding my good opinion of the people of these parts, I had no inclination to put their honesty to the test.

On the 18th of January, at six in the morning, we again set out, and travelled nine miles and a half northward. The soil still continued gravelly and the vegetation unvaried. About ten o'clock we arrived at Borandou, a village containing four or five hundred inhabitants. The huts are chiefly built of earth and have terraced roofs, which render them very inconvenient, because the smoke has no outlet but the door. The streets are dirty, narrow and crooked. There is a market twice a week for the strangers who happen to be in the neighbourhood, and whenever caravans pass another market is opened for the sale of provisions. I exchanged a few glass beads for some cowries, with which I purchased a little milk. This refreshed me, for it was long since I had tasted any. I saw some women in the streets carrying things to sell, which they cried, as in our European towns. I also observed that the Bambaras hang on the outside of their huts the heads of all the animals they eat; this is looked upon as a mark of grandeur. Every morning when they go to the fields they carry fire with them for roasting yams. They drink river water, and when they think they cannot obtain it, they bring water from the wells in calabashes. In the evening I was looking attentively at an old woman who had a piece of calabash in her lip, and I again reflected on the singularity of the custom; she and her companions laughed at my astonishment, and when I rose to go away she beckoned me to stop for a moment, and fetched me a yam of which she made me a present.

The inhabitants of this village make earthen pots. Their wells are ten or twelve feet deep, and the ground in which they are dug is gravelly. They contain good water, of a whitish colour.

At three o'clock in the afternoon we left the village of Borandou. We proceeded northward, to the distance of six miles, over a beautiful open country. In a plain at some distance from the village I saw many large ronniers, or rondiers. The cé was also very abundant. About sun-set we arrived at Syenso a large village, surrounded by walls, and containing a population of about six or seven hundred. On entering it I saw under a large baobab a man singularly dressed. The whole of his body was covered except his hands, and feet. His dress was entirely black, and his trowsers, his waistcoat, and the cap, which covered his face as well as his head, appeared to be all in one piece. The cap, which was of a square shape, was adorned with beautiful white ostrich-feathers and on the part which came over his face, like a mask, the eyes, nose and mouth were marked with scarlet. I was informed that this man was a sort of revenue officer and magistrate, and that he was the collector of the passage duties. He was armed with a whip and the inhabitants give him the name of *Naferi*. All the strangers of the neighbourhood, as well as the caravans which come to the village, pay the passage duties in cowries. The men and women stopped as they passed him, and if any refused to pay the required contribution he had recourse to his whip. Under a tree at a little distance from him I observed a great heap of cowries, which were guarded by a man not masked; they were, I suppose, the day's receipts. The tax is levied according to the quantity of merchandise, and varies from five to a hundred or two hundred cowries. As the market of Syenso is always well supplied, the duties paid by the traders render the chief of the village very rich.

These custom-house officers are also entrusted with the police of the village. They run, cracking their whips, after the children who make a noise in the streets; but they do not exercise their authority unless when they wear their uniforms. Our caravan was not stopped at the place where the passage money is usually received; but when we arrived, the officers came round to collect the duties. The masked officer looked at me with astonishment, and pointing at me with his finger, asked the other travellers, who the white man was. He continued pointing at me until I was at a considerable distance from him, as if he could not recover from his surprise.

About six o'clock on the morning of the 19th of January, we set off, taking a north-easterly direction. We travelled about seven miles over a soil composed of a mixture of sand and gravel; but very fertile. I remarked several fields which had been recently sown. The country is very open. On the road we found at least three hundred persons going to the market of Tangrera, where we arrived about nine in the morning. At at little distance from the village I saw a man dressed precisely like the officer of customs, whom I had seen the day before at Syenso. He pointed at me with his finger and seemed as much astonished as the other had been. The negroes threw cowries to him, which he counted very carefully, and when the payments were incorrect he seemed very much disposed to use his whip. Tangrera is resorted to by numbers of strangers and is a place of active trade, so that the duties levied by the chief on merchandise produce a considerable revenue. Every day a vast concourse of people repair to the market, which is also visited by caravans from the south, as well as from Ségo, Yamina, and Kayaye. They bring salt, which they exchange for colat-nuts and the cloth of the country.

Tangrera is a sort of entrepôt for these goods. The traders who come directly from the south, and do not wish to go as far as the banks of the Dhioliba, transact business in this town.

At Tangrera an unforseen disappointment occurred to me. My guide, on his arrival, took care to ascertain the value of merchandise. He learned that at Jenné colat-nuts were of very little value, and he consequently determined to proceed by way of Sansanding. I was much vexed when he informed me of this resolution, for I was very reluctant to venture either into that town or Ségo, in both which places I thought I was likely to meet with some unpleasant adventure. I knew that several Europeans had travelled in those parts, and, therefore, there was reason to fear that the inhabitants had become somewhat suspicious. Besides, that direction did not correspond with my plans, on account of the war between Jenné and Ségo, which intercepted all communication between the two countries.

I accordingly resolved to remain at Tangrera, until I should find an opportunity of going to Jenné. My guide accompanied me to the chief, to whom the old chief of Timé had recommended me. I was also accompanied by a saracolet of the country, who had travelled long among the Moors. He spoke the Moorish language very well, and he told me that he had been at El-Arawan, which they call Arawani.

Before I visited the chief, who is of the Bambara sect, I had had a conversation with the saracolet. He advised me to say that I was poor, and the lightness of my baggage, which was carried by my guide, sufficiently proved the truth of the assertion. By way of precaution, I took off my girdle, which contained some pieces of money for I was afraid that the chief would examine my property. The chief was a venerable-looking old man. We found him lying upon a bullock's hide, which was spread upon the ground, beneath a large bombax. He was superintending some labourers, who were employed in building huts. One of his brothers, a Mandingo converted to Mahometanism, accompanied us. My guide presented me to the chief, observing that the chief of Timé had requested him to receive me kindly. He then briefly related my adventures, the way in which I had been captured and brought up by the christians, and finally my abode of five months with his brother Baba at Timé. He described in feeling terms the illness and suffering I had undergone. The chief was so old that he could not speak to me; but he manifested his friendly feeling towards me by signs. When I was taking my leave of him he promised to forward me on the first opportunity; I was quartered with a saracolet, whom I supposed to be a Musulman. He had been so formerly, but since his return from his travels he had been in the habit of drinking the beer of the country. He lodged me in a neat little hut, and ordered one of his wives to prepare for me a dinner of rice, with pistachio sauce, and I gave the cook a little salt to season it. My host took me out to shew me the village; he conducted me to some Mahometan Mandingoes, whom I found assembled in large earth-built houses, which served as places of rendezvous for the men, and schools for the Musulman children. There are several of these places in the village. When I entered some were employed in making pagnes, and others in reading the Koran. They immediately laid aside their occupations, and I became the subject of conversation. They made me seat myself beside them on a bullock's hide, and they sent for a Moor who had come from Sansanding with a caravan of salt, which he wished to exchange for colats.

This Moor was of a very dark complexion. He said that he was a native of Waleth. He asked me many questions about my country and my parents.

He inquired their name which I immediately invented. I told him that my father was named Mohammed-Abdoulkerim, and my mother Mariam, and that my father was a merchant at Alexandria. He asked me whether they were still living. This question was most absurd, as I had just told him that I had left my country in my earliest childhood. I repeated this statement, and he replied— "Since you do not know whether your parents are living, why are you going back to your country? You might as well profess your religion in any other." I replied that I hoped to find a brother who would, doubtless, make over to me part of the property left by my parents. I added that the delay which I had experienced in prosecuting my journey was a great disappointment to me, and that I wished to avoid travelling during the ensuing rains. He asked me why I did not go to Sansanding. I observed that that would take me considerably out of my road, and might prevent me from reaching Jenné, whither I wished to go. He confirmed the report I had heard of the war between Ségo and Jenné; "but," added he, "you might by the road I have mentioned proceed to El-Arawan and thence to Mecca." He likewise told me that all the caravans destined for Jenné had set out, and that I was likely to remain at Tangrera a considerable time before I might find a favourable opportunity to depart. He then left me, and in a few moments returned, bringing a large piece of salt and eighty cowries, which he begged me to accept, observing that I should find salt very dear on the road. The Mandingoes, by signs, expressed their approbation of this generous conduct. This little present was very agreeable to me, for it served to assure me that, even if my resources were exhausted, I should find charitable persons inclined to assist me. My host took me to the market, where I saw a great concourse of people. The market was well supplied with all the necessaries of life, such as rice, yams, foigné, butter, animal and vegetable, salt, snuff, cloths, colats, dried fish, calabashes, butcher's meat, poultry, and also bullocks and sheep. I observed too, some European articles, glass-beads, gunpowder, flints, &c. I saw many women in the market, with flat earthen plates, in which they sold cakes, fried in vegetable butter. These cakes are called maumies, They are sold for cowries, the only current money of the country. Cowry is called kaulo in the language of the natives. I observed in the neighbourhood of the market-place several poor creatures, sitting at the corners of streets, asking charity. I had not seen such a thing as a regular beggar since my departure from the coast. We sat down for a few moments in the shop of a tobacco-dealer, where a great number of people were assembled. He had beside him a heap of cowries, amounting, perhaps, to thirty thousand. These were his day's receipts. He offered me a little snuff; I thanked him, but observed, that I did not take it.

This seemed to astonish him, for the practice of snuff-taking is universal in the village. Throughout almost all Africa, the Mandingoes are the only people who do not smoke. I never saw a woman use a pipe. The snuff which I saw in the tobacconist's shop smelt very well, and, unlike the usual snuff of the country, it was of a light chesnut colour; that which I saw in the other villages was green, and had but a faint smell.

Both the men and women who were at the market seemed better dressed and cleaner than those I had seen on the road from Timé. Very few of the women had their lips pierced.

On returning to my hut, I saw three men masked, like those I have already described. They were running after the children, who were endeavouring to escape from them.

In the evening, I went to see Karamo-osila, and asked him to pay me for the gunpowder which I had sold at Timé, for the celebration of the dégué-sousou. It was he who had undertaken to pay me. He informed me that he could not pay me in cowries, as had been agreed, because the colats did not sell very well; but that he would give me merchandise for the value. After a moment's reflection, he added, that I had sold my powder too dear, and that I ought to be satisfied with eighty colat-nuts, which were at that time equivalent to half a gourde. This did not astonish me, for it was what I expected. The Mandingoes are invariably dishonest in their dealings with strangers, especially when they know that they are not running any risk by so doing. I complained not of this injustice: I knew that my complaints would be useless. He directed his slaves to select eighty small colats, and he gave them to me in exchange for my powder, which might fairly have been estimated at double that value. He assured me, that he was sorry to leave me at Tangrera, where I knew nobody, and that he should feel pleasure in conducting me to Sansanding, if I would go with him. He said he no longer regarded me as a stranger, since I had lived five months with his brother, who had recommended me to him.

I went to the dwelling of my host, where I spent the remainder of the evening. He came and sat by me to bear me company. He praised the honesty of his wife, and requested me to give her the care of my baggage, as the door of my own hut had no fastening. I was frequently obliged to go out, and, consequently, might easily have been robbed in my absence, and I thought I was less liable to incur any loss if I entrusted it to the care of the woman. My bag closed with a padlock, and, consequently, it could not be opened without my knowledge. My host provided for me a good supper of rice, with a sauce of dried fish; and, in return for his attention, I gave the cook some salt to season the supper of the whole family. This present more than paid for my repast. My host, seeing that I had colats, very frequently asked me for some. I observed that he drank a good deal of beer, and saw him, with several Bambaras, seated in his hut round a large vessel of hydromel. They had a little calabash, which they filled, and passed round one to another. They were all very merry, and my host was so intoxicated that he could scarcely speak. This habit of drinking rendered my residence with him unpleasant. His hut was large, built of earth, with a terraced roof. It had two doors, and a window in the roof, to admit the air. The cooking was performed at one end, not in the middle, as is usual in other places in this part of Africa.

CHAPTER XV

Cultivation of tobacco — Tangrera — Fara — Bangaro — Itinerant musicians — Débéna — Tiara — Part of the caravan proceeds to Sansanding — Bee-hives — Siracana — The Bagoé, a navigable river — The Lous — Bandiarana — Bridge over the Koua.

On the morning of the 20th of January, Karamo-osila came to take leave of me. He made me a present of ten large colats, and again assured me of his sorrow at parting from me. I was also vexed at the separation, for I had every reason to be satisfied with his conduct. He always defrayed the expenses of my living, with the exception of some fowls which I purchased myself, and I had only given him, as a compensation for his attention, a cap of coloured cloth, and the silver bracelet which I received from the almamy of Sambatikila. He left me, after wishing me a speedy departure and a pleasant journey. In the morning my host, who was then somewhat recovered from the carousal of the preceding evening, accompanied me on a visit to the chief of the village. Unfortunately I did not find the chief at home, and my host and I called on one of the sherif's relations, whom we found sitting on a bullock's hide, in a large hut, superintending the manipulation of tobacco. Six stout slaves were employed in this hard labour. Each was provided with a huge pestle, and the tobacco was pounded in a large mortar. It had an excellent odour, and was much paler in colour than ours. The slaves were quite naked, and the perspiration was running down their bodies. This merchant carried on a thriving trade; his house was always full of customers, and he had lying beside him a large heap of cowries, the produce of the day's sale. The tobacco cultivated in the country is of a very small species, like that at Timé, and the leaves are short and narrow. The people pay little attention to its cultivation, and are not accustomed to cut off the head of the plant, as we do. At Tangrera, the leaves are dried in the shade, and afterwards made up into rolls: they thus acquire a pale chesnut colour.

It was about nine in the morning, when we returned home. My host told me in a very phlegmatic tone that he was tired, and asked me for colat-nuts. Soon afterwards I went back by myself to visit the chief, whom I found at home, lying on an ox-hide, in a miserable straw hut. After the usual salutations, he sent for two women, who had been to Jenné, to be my interpreters, for he supposed that I spoke the language of that country, and was exceedingly astonished when I told him that I did not understand it. I asked him in the Mandingo tongue, when the caravans for Jenné would start, and he told me that the merchants who made that journey were gone to Boyoko, to purchase colats; but that they would soon return, and then if I pleased I might travel with them. The *soon* of a negro, however, often means fifteen or twenty days. I learned that Boyoko is a village inhabited by Pagans, and that a market for the sale of colats is held there. It is twenty days journey S. S. E. of Tangrera.

Uncertain whether to wait a speedy opportunity for departing, and fearful of passing a second bad season in the interior, I finally resolved to rejoin the travellers who had set out in the morning. I hoped that by going to Sansanding and thence to Kayaye, I should meet with some opportunity to start for Jenné, and if not, I could leave Sansanding for El-Arawan, situated in the desert; and on reaching that town, I could form some definitive plan. I went immediately to seek the Moor Mohammed, to whom I communicated my project, of which he entirely approved. He accompanied me home, where I showed him several beautiful glass-trinkets. However he was not tempted by them, and he even declined accepting a few sheets of paper, telling me I should have occasion for them on the road. After some persuasion, he at length consented to take one. He talked for a moment with my host, and they both went together to the chief's house, to ask him to send a man to conduct me to the village, where the merchants going to Sansanding, were stopping. I was assured that the place was not very far distant.

Tangrera is a large walled village, shaded by great bombaces and baobabs. A well-stocked market is held there every day. The greater part of the huts are thatched with straw, but all those belonging to the heads of families are built of earth and have terraced roofs. The place is inhabited by Bambaras and Mandingoes, who live together in a very friendly footing; the Bambaras are the more numerous. They often meet in the course of the day under trees, to drink their beer, of which they are very fond. I saw in the village several wild fig-trees. The inhabitants are traders and cultivators. They manufacture a considerable quantity of cotton cloth, and hold frequent communications with the towns on the banks of the Dhioliba. They rear horned cattle, sheep, and some goats, and I also saw several fine horses; a rare sight in this part of the country. Cowries are the only current coin at Tangrera. This village is of the same size as Sambatikila, and contains nearly the same population. I went with my host to see the mosque; it is built of earth, and surmounted by several small massive towers. It is a shapeless edifice, the interior is dirty, and suffocatingly hot. The Musulmans, whose indolence is an antidote to their religious zeal, have not even taken the trouble to clear away the rubbish which was scattered on the floor during its construction. To be sure, they do not go very often to the mosque; for they repeat their prayers at home. Several Bambaras invited me jokingly to drink beer with them, but I affected a great aversion to that liquor.

In the course of the day, I sold some glass trinkets, to procure provisions for my journey. My host directed one of his women to attend to this business; and she took care to reserve a good profit for herself.

About three o'clock in the afternoon, the chief of Tangrera sent me the man who was to carry my luggage to Fara, where I was to rejoin my guide from Timé. My host escorted me out of the village, when, after wishing me a good journey, he took his leave. He had, in the course of the day, eaten half my colats, but I was pleased to find that his wife had taken only a few grains of salt which had not been put in my bag. My guide informed me that he was the son of the king of Tangrera. When we had advanced a little into the woods, he tried to frighten me. He threw down my bag, which was by no means heavy, saying that he was very much tired, and that either I must carry it in my turn, or give him some cowries for his trouble. I promised that on our arrival at Fara he should be rewarded to his satisfaction. He seemed to doubt the sincerity of my promise, and made many objections. However, finding me determined to resist, he took up the bag again, and proceeded on his way; but at such a quick pace that I could scarcely keep up with him. A little before we reached Fara, I had the same scene over again. He assured me that we were yet very far from the village, an assertion which I could the more easily believe, because Fara is so surrounded by large trees, that it is not seen until you are close upon it. Though my guide was much stronger than I still I persisted in refusing to pay him before our arrival, well knowing, that if I had the weakness to yield to him, the prince of Tangrera would have left me to finish the journey alone, while he indulged a hearty laugh at my folly.

We entered the village towards sun-set, after crossing a little stream, in which the water did not rise above our ancles. I met several women of our caravan there, who appeared astonished to see me. We had travelled five miles to the N. N. E. During three of these miles the country was but slightly shaded by trees, and the surface of the ground was covered with stones, which caused me considerable pain in walking. I observed several cés and nédés. On my arrival I paid my royal guide, who joyfully returned home. Karamo-osila was very happy to see me again. He immediately informed all the people of the caravan of my arrival; they congratulated me on having rejoined them, and Karamo-osila expressed his regret at having left me alone among infidels. I gave a description of my host, who drank beer, and with whom I did not consider myself very secure; they all joined in laughing and ridiculing him. A fowl was bought to celebrate my return, and I furnished the salt for seasoning it. These merchants, not having made much profit, were obliged to be very economical. They seldom indulge themselves with fowls or fish, or with salt for seasoning their victuals. Sometimes I heard them say to each other: "It is a long time since we had any thing good; let us have a little salt in our supper." Three or four of the same company often form a sort of partnership; they then mess together, each in turn defraying the expense.

At six in the morning of the 21st of January, we left the village of Fara, and proceeded to the N. W. travelling over a soil composed of gravel and ferruginous stones. I also observed a good deal of red sand. The road was very level, and occasionally shaded with trees. I did not see any trees of very large growth; indeed, none so high as our apple or pear tree. Bombaces and baobabs, the giants of the vegetable kingdom in this part of the world, grow only in the vicinity of villages; I never saw any of them in the woods. Our caravan had prodigiously increased since leaving Tangrera; and our number was now between five and six hundred persons, all laden, and all going to Sansanding and Yamina, besides nearly eighty asses. At ten in the morning we halted at Bangoro, a small walled town, containing about three or four thousand inhabitants. On entering the town, four officers of the customs met us, and, stopping the caravan, they took from each Mandingo a hat, or some other article, by way of security for the duties they had to collect. They were armed with sabres, which they held naked in their hands, but made no use of them. Several negroes of the village came to their assistance, for they had plenty to do with such a numerous caravan. A discussion arose between the officers and the merchants, the latter not liking to be deprived of their hats; but at length the matter was arranged, and we entered the town. As soon as we were installed in our abodes, the officers came to receive their dues which were paid in colats. A little market was immediately opened under an enormous bombax. As I was going about, offering glass beads for sale, I was met by a saracolet from Tangrera, who, addressing me in the Mandingo language, requested me to follow him. He led the way to a hut, in front of which several of his comrades were sitting, some of whom spoke a little Arabic. He informed me that the Moor Mahomet, whom I had seen at Tangrera, sent his compliments to me, together with a hundred cowries, of which he begged my acceptance, wishing me a prosperous journey. The saracolet then presented his hand to me, saying *Bismilahi*; I understood by this, that he wished me to say a prayer, and I moved my lips for a moment, then with a serious air I blew upon his hand, which he drew across his face. He immediately counted me down a hundred cowries, adding to them twenty of his own, which were equivalent to a hundred of our country. After expressing my gratitude for this generous conduct, I took leave of the Moor, and hastened to communicate the good news to my guide, who loaded my benefactors with blessings. I immediately spent a few of the cowries in purchasing a fowl for my supper, of which I invited my guide and his companions to partake. They however out of compliment declined doing so, but I made them accept some portion of the fowl. We did not eat together, for I still bore marks of the scurvy: indeed that dreadful malady had entirely disfigured me. Karamo-osila had ordered his women to serve up my victuals apart from the rest and my guide, who was very attentive to me, often examined my allowance, and if he did not think it enough added some of his own to it.

I observed round the village some very high ronniers and several palm-trees. In the evening about a hundred women assembled in the market-place. Their dress consisted merely of a pagne fastened round the waist; and on their heads they had small straw hats, which fell a little over the ears. Several of them had in their hands tambourines, made of a calabash covered with tanned sheep-skin, and ornamented with iron rings, which produced an agreeable sound. They sung wild airs, and danced together keeping time to their singing and nourishing their tambourines. In this manner, they danced several times round the place, and then went off singing. I walked along the streets, which are narrow and dirty; I saw several men parading about, beating large drums, and women with tambourines, suspended from their necks; to these tambourines were affixed small boards covered with bells and little bits of iron, which being shaken struck against the instrument, and produced a very pleasing sound. I concluded that all these musicians were what are called at the Senegal *griotes*, or wandering minstrels, who make it their business to sing songs in praise of any who will pay them; those whom I saw at Bangoro were very modest, and did not, like their fraternity at the Senegal, teaze passengers for presents.

These people are always gay; and their cheerfulness forms a striking contrast with the dull, gloomy look of the fanatic Musulman.

The women of this place wear on their lower lip a piece of pewter fastened internally by a plate of the same metal; one end pointed, about two inches long and as thick as a quill, projecting on the outside of the lip. This curious ornament is a little varied according to the fancy of the wearers. The custom of piercing the lip is general among the female sex in this part of the country. It is an indispensable ornament to beauty, in the lips of these African coquettes and their admirers. I could not help laughing when I thought of the singular effect such an ornament would produce on the red and white lips of my own fair countrywomen.

On the 22nd January, at six o'clock in the morning, we bade adieu to the merry inhabitants of Bangoro. Our course lay to the N. W. We travelled five miles over a sandy soil covered with stones, and crossed two small dried up marshes. My guide told me that, when he last passed this place, he had experienced much difficulty, the country being at the time inundated, and that, if I had travelled with him in the preceding August, I should probably have been left on the road. The country is in general very naked. About nine o'clock we halted at Débéna, a town containing four or five thousand Bambara inhabitants. The place is surrounded by a wall and a market is held in it. In this market the people of the caravan went to display their salt and colats, which they exchanged with the Bambaras, who, for the value of ten cowries, can purchase seasoning for a whole family's dinner. However, they seldom indulge in this luxury, and when they buy salt, they reserve it for festivities and rejoicings. The town of Débéna is composed of several small hamlets, very near each other, and the market was held under a large bombax.

In all the inhabited places, situated on our route, we found markets well stocked with the productions of the country, as well as with fish, which is caught in the neighbouring streams, but which is never offered for sale, until it is dried. On my arrival at any village, I always went to the market, to purchase my breakfast. In all the villages between Tangrera and Jenné, there are in the markets women who sell small fried takes, which are very acceptable to travellers. They cost one or two cowries a piece, and as soon as the merchants arrive at a halting station, they send one of their women to the market to buy some of these cakes, which they eat, while dinner is preparing.

On the 23d of January, at six in the morning, we set off and proceeded nine miles, first to the N. N. E. and then to the E. N. E. The soil over which we travelled was composed of hard grey sand and some ferruginous stones. No vegetation was visible except cés and nédés. In this part, the country is very level.

We stopped about nine o'clock at Tiara, a village surrounded by a wall. A little before we reached it, we crossed a small river, which supplies the inhabitants with water. The village is shaded by bombaces and baobabs, and the inhabitants cultivate tobacco in the gardens surrounding their huts. The market is not well stocked, and we had a good deal of difficulty to procure millet for our supper. In the evening a man belonging to our caravan came to me joyfully and told me that we were going to Jenné. At first, I thought he was jesting with me, but my guide Karamo-osila came soon afterwards to inform me that it was determined we should take that direction, because there were already too many merchants going to Sansanding. Our caravan was indeed, exceedingly numerous. I cannot express the gratification I felt at this happy news, for it was not without great reluctance that I had resolved to take the road to Sansanding, a course which thwarted all my plans, and deprived me of all chance of visiting Timbuctoo. I made my guide a present as a token of the pleasure I felt at his resolution, and purchased a fowl that we might have a good supper. As my companions had before declined accepting any part of the poultry I bought for myself, for fear of depriving me of it, I insisted on their taking this whole of the fowl; but yet, at supper time, my guide himself brought me my portion of it.

I saw in this village a very large tree, the branches of which were fringed with small roots. At Tangrera I had observed a similar one. It also grows in the island of Saint-Louis in the Senegal. This tree, which is a species of *ficus indica*, is milky and viscous; the natives hold their banancoro in its shade.

On the 24th of January, at six in the morning, the chief part of our company took a N. W. direction, on their way to Sansanding. We took the road to Jenné, proceeding four miles to the N. E. over a very smooth soil, composed of hard grey sand, covered with ferruginous stones. We crossed several small streams, the water of which reached to our knees. The vegetation did not vary much; but I observed a tree which is common in the neighbourhood of the Senegal; it bears a round and rather flat fruit, and of the size of a golden rennet. It has a grey pellicle, and the pulp, of which the negroes are very fond, is of a greenish colour. The kernel is fibrous, and the leaves of the tree are pinnate, and as large as those of the ash. The negroes use the bark in distempers, employing it as a caustic. About nine in the morning, we arrived at Douasso, where we stopped. It is a small village without walls, containing about two hundred, or two hundred and fifty inhabitants.

I experienced great pain in my palate, for the sores occasioned by the scurvy, were not yet healed. During the halt, I kept myself apart from my companions, being unwilling that they should witness my sufferings, or the painful operations which I was myself obliged to perform, having no one capable of rendering me those disagreeable services. I drew from my palate a bone, which was connected with the skull. I asked my guide to procure some of the astringent, which the natives employ in such disorders. He immediately ordered one of his women to prepare me some and I used it with success.

Throughout all this part of Africa, even on this side of Baléya, the negroes place hives in the trees, for bees to settle in. They collect a great quantity of honey, of which they are very fond. These hives are made of the bark of trees, and covered with straw. I saw several green trees, entirely stripped of the bark for this purpose. In the environs of the village, millet and maize are cultivated. Markets are not held daily,. but some women came and sold us millet and pistachio-nuts for supper.

On the 25th of January, at six in the morning, we proceeded northward, at first over a sandy and well cultivated tract, and afterwards over a soil composed of red earth covered with gravel, and having ferruginous stones on the surface. This country is full of cés and nédés. We met a caravan of Mandingo merchants coming from Kayaye, where they had been buying salt. They had with them many asses, and the animals were adorned with fine scarlet bridles, which are sold in the markets on the banks of the Dhioliba. These bridles were studded with cowries, and bells; each ass had about fifty bells attached to his collar, so that their approach was audible from some distance. The salt appeared to me to be rather dark in colour, and very coarse in the grain. It was made up in cakes of two feet and a half long, one foot broad and two inches thick. An ass generally carries four of these cakes, and a negro two and a half; the women carry only two, but their burthen is augmented by calabashes and cooking utensils.

About nine in the morning, we reached Siracana, a large walled village, containing from six to eight hundred inhabitants. It is situated in an open plain. The soil, composed of grey earth, mixed with a good deal of sand, is in the proper season well cultivated; On my arrival, the Bambara at whose hut we went to put up would not let me in, because I was white and therefore, he said, I might bring him ill luck. I sat down on a stone near the hut; and here I waited exposed to the heat of a burning sun, until my guide and three other Mandingoes succeeded in bringing the simple and superstitious Bambara to reason. They gave him a glowing account of my adventures, and the manner in which I had been carried off by the christians. They told him that I was now on my return to my own country, near Mecca; that it would be a meritorious action to receive me, and that those who treated me well would go straight to paradise. The negro, convinced by these powerful arguments, admitted me into his hut, where I, as well as my companions, enjoyed the benefit of the shade. The negro was doubtless delighted by the assurance he had received of going to paradise, for in the evening he and some of his friends came to see me, and sitting down by me, they gazed at me attentively. He begged me to excuse the reception I had met with in the morning, which he said was entirely owing to a mistake, for he at first supposed I was a christian. He afterwards requested me to accept a fowl for my supper.

I saw in this village a female trader and manufacturer, a native of Ségo. She bought cotton and employed her slaves in spinning it. I visited the market, which appeared very dull; it was scantily supplied, and we had some difficulty in procuring millet for our supper. I saw in the market, cotton, earthen utensils, tobacco, and the fried cakes called maumies: the latter were sold by women, whose dirty appearance was by no means calculated to tempt customers. There were not altogether more than thirty women in the market, which was held under a great bombax.

Though there were some cattle in the village, yet we could procure no milk. There were in some of the huts beds formed of three or four trunks of trees, raised a little above the ground; we had one of these beds in our hut. Between the trunks of the trees, a small intervening space is left, into which I crept with the intention of taking a nap; but I found myself so uncomfortable, that I was glad to stretch myself on the floor, covered with my wrapper.

On the 26th of January, at six in the morning, we set out in the direction of E. N. E. We passed a small marsh, which, being dried up, afforded pasture for a few sheep. We also forded a river, which runs into the Dhioliba; the water was more than knee-deep at the part where we crossed. We pursued our course over a sandy gravelly soil, the country presenting one uniform aspect for the space of four or five miles. About eight in the morning we arrived at Sounibara, a small village, containing a population of about two or three hundred. Not being able to procure provisions here, we made no halt. After leaving the village, we passed some wells, fifteen or sixteen feet deep. The ground in which they were dug was composed of a reddish kind of sand, mixed with much gravel. I also observed veins of grey argillaceous earth mixed with gravel, about two feet and a half thick: the earth nearest to the water was argillaceous, and contained some flints. These wells afford abundance of good water, but it has a whitish tint from the clay. We saw a number of women employed in washing their pagnes. They draw the water from the wells in small calabashes, attached to ropes made of the bark of trees; and other calabashes of larger size served them to wash in. I saw that they used a kind of soap, called in the country *saboune* or *safnan*. These names are known throughout the interior, from the Senegal to Bondou, Caarta, and Cason. The Brakna Moors call their soap *sabon*. All these words bear a strong resemblance to the French *savon*.[60] The Bambara washerwomen, whom I have just mentioned, were stark naked, yet they manifested no shame at being seen in this state by the men composing our caravan.

We advanced three miles to the south, over a soil composed of grey sand and gravel. We halted at Fara about one in the afternoon. The country over which we had travelled was one immense forest of cés. In this part the cé surpasses every other tree in abundance, and the natives carry on a considerable trade in the butter which they obtain from it. They take it to Jenné, where they sell it to the caravans which stop at that town. In all the inhabited places through which I passed, I saw women carrying calabashes filled with this butter, some of which I often purchased. The price of a pound was forty cowries (about four French sous). The negro, whose business it was to provide millet for the whole caravan, on his return from the market informed us that it was much dearer than it had been for several preceding days. The expenses of each meal for our party, consisting of fifteen or sixteen persons, had usually been about eighty cowries: in the village of Fara, it amounted to thirty more. I was informed that the further we advanced towards Jenné, the dearer we should find provisions. Their high price is occasioned by the number of merchants travelling this way.

At six o'clock in the morning of the 27th of January, we left Fara, and took the direction of N. N. E. over a road covered with grey sand. We next reached the banks of the Bagoé, the White River of the negroes. Its course is from E. S. E. to W. S. W., its banks, which are thickly wooded, rise to the height of thirty or forty feet, and are composed of a yellow kind of sand, mixed with clay, together with some veins of grey argillaceous earth, about eighteen inches or two feet thick. The Bagoé swells in the rainy season, and inundates the neighbouring country, rendering it very marshy. Indeed, to some distance over land, the flood is so great that canoes pass through it. The river is nearly as wide as the Milo at Kankan. It is deep, and navigable for large canoes. It has many windings, and after flowing for the space of five or six miles W. S. W. it turns northward and falls into the Dhioliba. According to the information I collected from the natives and Mandingo travellers, the Bagoé comes from the south, passes Teuté (whither they go to buy colat-nuts), and then falls into the Dhioliba a little below Ségo. We were a long time crossing it, great delay being occasioned by the quantity of our baggage, as well as by the discussion about the fare, which we had to pay in cowries. The negroes, who are naturally chilly, kindled a fire, and seated themselves round it, to settle the price to be paid for the passage. The Bambara who owned the canoe gave to each individual a piece of wood, which was returned to him as they stepped ashore; thus he secured himself against any mistake which might have arisen from the confusion and the number of persons. The canoe in which we crossed was tolerably large. It was near noon when we reached the right bank. The current was slow, flowing, perhaps, at the rate of a knot and a half an hour.

We continued our course to the N. E., and, about two o'clock, arrived at a neat village, called Courounina, where we halted to dine. After eating a little boiled rice, with some bad herb sauce, and paying the chief the passage-duty, we again started, taking a N. E. direction. After crossing a little stream, we arrived, shortly before night-fall, at Missabougou. The country through which I passed during the day resembled all that I had seen for several days preceding, and was well cropped with millet, pistachios, &c. The inhabitants thronged to see me; they looked at me with earnest curiosity, saying, that they had never seen a Moor so white as I was.

A little after sun-set, as I was standing by the fire, boiling some pieces of bark to wash my mouth, which was still very painful, a young negro of our caravan, who had shewn me marks of attention during the whole of the journey, informed me that I must not stay out too late, because, if the Lous should see me, they would beat me unmercifully. I did not know what he meant, and asked him to explain himself. He told me that throughout the whole of Bambara, there are men who live all day in the woods, in huts made of the branches of trees. They have with them boys, to whom they teach the mysteries of their ceremonies; Every night they issue from the woods, accompanied by the boys, running about the village, uttering frightful cries, and making a thousand hideous contortions. On their approach, the terrified inhabitants shut themselves up in their huts; but there are some men, added the negro, who are not afraid of the Lous. I immediately conjectured, that these Lous must be an association similar to that of the Simos, which I have already described as existing among the people who inhabit the banks of the Rio Nuñez, and also among the Timannees. I was confirmed in this supposition, when the young negro informed me that, on rejoicing days, they give notice of their intention to shew themselves openly. They come and join in the festivities of the day, and then return to their habitations, laden with presents of every kind, which all, and particularly the women, are eager to bestow upon them. The young negro, from whom I learned these particulars, had made several journeys through this country, and had acquired an acquaintance with the manners of the people, which a stranger can obtain but slowly and imperfectly. He, moreover, informed me that the Lous drink the beer of the country, with which they frequently become intoxicated.

In the evening, I heard some strange howlings in the vicinity of the village. I made no doubt that the Lous had commented their nightly incursions, and felt great curiosity to see them. I cautiously crept out of my hut, and took my station behind a little palisade, whence I could see without being seen. I soon saw a man advance. His head was covered with a piece of rag, and from various parts of his body were suspended bells and little bits of iron, which made a horrid jingling noise. Before he entered the village, he announced his approach by running round it, uttering frightful howlings, and rattling his noisy appendages. He was followed by a number of boys, dressed like himself. I heard some old men, who were sitting conversing together at their doors, call out to the Lou, not to go that way, as there were people there; and he and his retinue immediately turned another way. During a great part of the night I could get no sleep, on account of the howling of these savages.

At six next morning, we left Missabougou, and travelled six miles N. E. Our road was covered with ferruginous stones. About nine in the morning, we halted at Badiarana, a village containing about eight or nine hundred inhabitants. The market was abundantly supplied with all the necessaries of life. The inhabitants maintain a considerable trade; merchants from Ségo and Yamina bring salt to Badiarana, which they exchange for cloth of native manufacture, and cowries. Mandingoes coming from the market of Jenné also traffic at Badiarana, to procure a supply of cowries for the remainder of their journey. I inquired of several merchants the distance of this place from Ségo. They all concurred in telling me that Kayaye, a large commercial town, was nine days' journey north of Badiarana, and that Ségo was nine days' journey from Kayaye in the same direction.

As we approached the village, the chief stopped the caravan in a field to count the loads. To guard against any mistake in the payment of the passage-duties, he gave to each merchant as many pieces of wood as he had loads. Each load was charged at the rate of twenty colat-nuts, the price of the latter being from fifteen to eighteen cowries a-piece in the village. The chief lodged us in some large huts. On our arrival, I immediately visited the market, where I bought some maumies and sour milk. The market is kept in very good order. The dealers, who were ranged in two rows, were neatly dressed, and behaved with great civility to those who bought their commodities, which consisted of the produce of the country. Their shops were filled with cotton, raw and manufactured, salt, millet, allspice, long pepper, pistachios, zambalas, the fruit of the baobab, and the dried leaves of that tree, which are used in cookery. I also exhibited my ware, and sold some glass ornaments and pieces of coloured calico, which strongly excited the admiration of the negroes. I afterwards went, accompanied by my guide, to visit the chief. I found him seated in a large hut, surrounded by some Mandingo merchants, who were engaged in discussing their affairs. The wife of the chief had seen my glass trinkets, and she begged her husband to buy some for her. I sold him about twenty beads, at thirty cowries each. Several women purchased from me little bits of coloured stuff, measuring about eighteen or twenty inches long, and four broad, for each of which they paid me three hundred cowries, worth twenty four French sous. One of the confidants of the chief, who received the colats in payment of the passage-duties, presented me with ten very fine ones, which he begged me to accept. This man's hands and feet were covered with leprosy. My companions found a sale for some of their colats. At supper time, as I was taking the air in the court, I saw the chief of the village stretched upon a mat, with his head supported on a log of wood, and beside him stood a young negress, who was attending upon him. Shortly afterwards, six or seven of his wives brought him by turns a calabash of tau for his supper. He tasted a little of the contents of each calabash, distributed a portion to some Bambaras, who were lying beside him, and the cooks successively carried away the remainder. It is the custom of this country for the wives of a rich man, each to prepare her own supper separately, and then to carry it to the head of the family before she touches it herself. The wives of the poorer class cook the supper of the whole family, and perform this office by turns. I was pretty near the chief, and was much astonished that he did not invite me to partake of the repast, a custom which is so generally prevalent in these countries. The wells at Badiarana are dug seven or eight feet deep, in a soil consisting of mixed sand and gravel. There is grey argillaceous earth at the bottom of these wells, and the water, though rather white, is pleasant to drink.

On the 29th of January, at six o'clock in the morning, we set off, proceeding northward, over a road covered with ferruginous stones and red gravel. After crossing a large stream, we reached Timbala, where we passed the remainder of the day, being all greatly fatigued.

On the 30th of January, at six o'clock in the morning, we left Timbala. After travelling some distance N. N. W. I was shewn the road leading to Ségo and Yamina. We turned N. N. E., taking the road to Jenné, and, after proceeding eight miles in that direction, we halted. At a short distance from Timbala, we saw several women cooking maumies, which they sold to the people of the caravan. They had some difficulty in supplying us, for we all wanted some, under the expectation that we should have to travel a considerable distance without halting. However, this plan was changed, and about ten o'clock we stopped at Touriat, a little unwalled village. Our road, during the morning, was over very hard grey sand, and shaded by bombaces, baobabs, and cés; the latter were very abundant. A man belonging to our caravan being ill, his companions subscribed together for the purchase of a kid, for, since our departure, they had scarcely eaten any thing but tau, and herb sauce without salt. My guide gave me a bit of the kid, about the size of an egg; for it was divided among so many, that even my allowance was more than fell to the lot of some of the rest.

The country round the village is very open, and the soil level. The cé and the nédé are more numerous than any other trees. Touriat contains between three and four hundred inhabitants.

On the 31st of January, at six in the morning, after proceeding some distance N. N. E., over a soil composed of hard sand, and covered with ferruginous stones and gravel, we arrived at Magna-Gnounan, where we stopped to dine. In the neighbourhood of the village there are some pretty little gardens, planted with onions and beans, which the inhabitants cultivate carefully: they use the leaves for making their sauces. I also saw some fields of tobacco, which, in this place, is cultivated no better than at Timé; but it is of a finer kind: the leaves are broad and very long, and, if it were well attended to, it would thrive as well as that cultivated in Europe. The village of Magna Gnounan is walled, and contains about two hundred and fifty inhabitants; the environs are well wooded with mimosas and large baobabs. I saw some cotton plantations; but they appeared to be neglected. I sat down beyond the boundaries of the village, in the shade of a baobab, and roasted some pistachios for my dinner, which I shared with some of my companions.

At the distance of a mile South-east I observed two hills, about a hundred, or a hundred and twenty fathoms in height: they appeared to be clothed with fine vegetation. Under the baobabs, on the outside of the village, a little market is held; but it is ill supplied, and nothing is sold in it but pistachios and millet. About half-past two o'clock we left Magna-Gnounan, and proceeded six miles northward, over a road covered with ferruginous stones and gravel. The butter-tree still continued to be abundant. We crossed four streams, all tributary to the Dhioliba. A little before sun-set we halted at Khoukhola, where we passed the night. This neat little village is shaded by numerous baobabs, with the fruit and leaves of which the inhabitants trade. I saw some huts built of bricks baked in the sun.

At six in the morning, we resumed our journey in the direction of N. N. E. The soil over which we passed was composed of hard grey sand, mixed with white and pink calcareous stones. After travelling four miles, we came to a large stream, and next arrived at Kiébala, a small village, where we settled the passage duties, without being detained more than an hour. I saw in this village several wells; pieces of wood were fixed round them to prevent the earth from falling in. I also observed some tobacco-plantations. The caravan stopped in a field without the village; not far from this spot I saw a tree, to the branches of which were tied pieces of string, leather, cloth, &c. Under the tree were some empty earthen vessels, ranged in regular order. I was informed that this was a burial place. It is the custom of the Bambaras to deposit in the graves of the dead, provisions, cloth, and various other things, keeping a portion of these articles, which they hang upon a tree near the burial place, and putting the eatables into earthen vessels. If, during the night, dogs, or any wild animal, should devour the latter, it is believed that the guardian spirit of the deceased has been banqueting at his grave. These superstitions prevail only in some parts of the country.

Continuing our course N. E., on a soil similar to that which we had passed over in the morning, about ten or eleven o'clock, we arrived at Sérasso, where we passed the rest of the day. This village, which contains a population of about three hundred, is situated in a well cultivated plain, covered with cés, nédés, bombaces, baobabs, and mimosas. Since we left the village of Fara, yams and rice had become very rare. They are but little cultivated, owing, no doubt, to the dryness of the ground; for rains are not so common in this direction as further to the south. Millet of both kinds and maize are, however, cultivated here; the former in great abundance.

On the 2nd of February, at six o'clock, we left Sérasso, and proceeded eastward, in order to cross a bridge at a short distance from the village. This bridge is built, like that of Cambaya, across the Tankisso, except that it is covered with straw, and then with a layer of earth. It had steps on each side, a precaution which I had not hitherto seen among the negroes. This bridge is more convenient than any other I saw in the interior. At its entrance were stationed two negroes, who were sitting beside a little fire, though the weather was any thing but cold. The heat here is nearly the same as at the Senegal; but it varies a little. The two negroes received the passage-duties: they demanded twenty cowries for each load of colats. The Mandingoes would have preferred paying double the amount in kind; for they had not much money. The men and women passed gratis. We were delayed for a considerable time by the stubbornness of the assess; the negroes had infinite trouble in getting them across; two were carried as far as the middle of the bridge, and then they darted off at full gallop. The natives of the country are not required to pay passage-duty; this contribution is only demanded from foreigners. I asked several persons the name of the stream we had just crossed. They told me it was called Koua, a name which I know is common to all streams. We advanced four miles E. N. E., across a level plain, covered with large trees; the soil was composed of hard grey sand, and here and there I perceived some blocks of black granite.

About nine in the morning we halted at Mouriosso. The houses in this place are surmounted by terraces built of bricks baked in the sun. Shortly before we entered the village, we crossed a stream, on the banks of which I saw gardens containing fine beds of onions. These gardens are cultivated by the women, many of whom were employed in weeding. They water the ground frequently. Near the gardens are wells, two feet deep, whence the water is taken in calabashes to which no ropes are attached. The soil of these gardens is black, rich, and very productive. They are surrounded, by fences of dry briars and thorns, to keep out the poultry. Several of the women whom we saw in these gardens had no other clothing than wretched pagnes fastened round their waists. They came to sell us tops of onions to put into our sauce. We paid them in cowries with which they bought glass beads to adorn themselves. They sometimes wear necklaces of chesnut-coloured beads, which are preferred in the country to all others, because they are the cheapest.

On our arrival a market was immediately opened under a large tree, the branches of which were covered with roots, like one I saw on a former occasion and which I have already mentioned. The market was supplied with millet, a little rice, pistachios, onions, and zambalas. There were also some women selling maumies, some of which we bought, as our dinner was not ready.

The village is composed of numerous little enclosures, each of which is occupied by one family. The place contains a population of about two hundred. The people cultivate round their little habitations water-melons, giraumons, and calabashes, the stems of which they train up to the roofs of their huts. The fields surrounding the village are sown with small millet: I saw some persons employed in weaving; but smiths, if there be any, are not common, for I did not see one.

CHAPTER XVI

Oulasso — Facibrisso — Toumané — Implements of husbandry — Couara — Koraba — Douasso — Kong — Baunan — Garo — Forges — Nibakhasso.

About two o'clock in the afternoon, we left the village of Mouriosso, and proceeded in the direction of E. N. E. over a hard soil, composed of grey earth mixed with sand, and studded with ferruginous stones and gravel. It was barren in the extreme. About six in the evening we halted at Oulasso, a village, the huts of which are enclosed and built like those of Mouriosso, and containing three or four hundred inhabitants. In this village we found a caravan of Mandingo traders coming from the south, where they had been buying colat-nuts, which they intended to sell at Jenné. A large hut was assigned to us; but we could not stay in it on account of the heat and smoke. The fire was lighted at the further end of the hut, which might be about twenty feet long by eight broad, and the smoke had no outlet but the door. The fire consequently produced the same effect as a furnace. I passed the night under a mimosa, which grew before our hut, having covered myself with my wrapper, for the air was cool.

As the village was too small to afford lodging for two caravans several of the merchants slept, like myself, in the open air; however, they took the precaution of lighting fires. These fires, glimmering through the village, had a very curious effect. They served for the women to cook by; at our last halting station we had procured millet enough for the supper of the whole party; it was well we had taken this precaution, for we could get nothing at Oulasso. The soil in the vicinity of the village consists of very productive sand, in part cultivated. The Bambara inhabitants did not understand the Mandingo language; but we had the good fortune to meet with a woman who acted as our interpreter.

On the 3rd of February, at six in the morning, we proceeded in the direction of N. E. Our caravan was now very strong, being augmented by that which we had joined the preceding evening. We pursued our course over a soil composed of sand and very hard earth, covered with stones and gravel, which rendered the road very fatiguing. The country was, however, well wooded with cés and nédés. We crossed three large streams, by which we were detained a long time on account of our asses. The banks of these streams were thickly wooded, and in the shady parts grew many palm-trees. The natives are not aware that this tree furnishes an intoxicating liquor; they extract the oil, which they are very fond of, and with which they anoint their bodies. The palm-tree does not grow so abundantly here as on the coast. About ten o'clock in the morning we arrived at Facibrisso, where there is a great market for colat-nuts, allspice, long pepper, which is brought from the south, cloth manufactured in the country, and salt brought from the banks of the Dhioliba, besides a considerable quantity of millet, cotton, pistachios, and other native produce. The huts, which have flat roofs and only a ground-floor, are built of bricks baked in the sun. They are extremely inconvenient and so slight that they frequently fall down. All the villages, as far as Jenné, are built in the same way, and in general shaded by numerous bombaces and baobabs. The inhabitants gather the fruit of the baobab and sell it to the caravans. They even carry it to Jenné, where it is scarce, and from Jenné it is exported to Timbuctoo. The cé and the nédé are astonishingly abundant in all this part of the country. Proceeding towards the north, the baobabs become less common and the bombaces surpass them in size. The ronnier is abundant in some places.

On the 4th of February, at six in the morning, we set off in the direction of E. S. E. over a very good fertile soil. We crossed a river, after which we proceeded along a road covered with gravel. After travelling four miles we reached Toumané, where we found a numerous caravan on its way from Jenné. These traders brought us the unwelcome information that colats were very plentiful and very cheap at Jenné. This news was very disheartening to the poor merchants from Timé.

I went to see the market, which I found better than those of the villages through which I had previously passed. It was held under a sort of penthouse, which kept off the rain in bad weather. It was very well supplied with all the productions of the country. I even saw butcher's meat and European commodities, such as cloth, muskets, powder and glass trinkets. The female traders managed their business cleverly. I bought some maumies, which were better made and superior to those in other villages. I saw some wild Guinea fowl, which are very common in this country: they are sold at the same price as common fowls. There were in this village many strangers from Ségo, Yamina, and other places. The inhabitants paid no particular attention to me, all taking me for a Moor. I found them mild and civil towards strangers; they were very neatly dressed, in comparison with the inhabitants of the villages which I had visited. My guide, Karamo-osila, discouraged by the news brought by the merchants from Jenné, resolved a second time to proceed by the way of Kayaye and Sansanding. This decision would have annoyed me extremely if the rest of the party had concurred in it; but he and his associates were the only persons who approved the plan. I made a bargain with an old man from Timé who was going to Jenné, and promised that on reaching this town I would give him a beautiful piece of cloth if he would allow his ass to carry my luggage. This arrangement seemed to please him. On the evening of our separation, I wished to make a third present to my guide, consisting of a piece of coloured cloth; but he declined accepting it, telling me, that in serving me he had not been influenced by motives of interest, but by the wish to perform an action which would be agreeable to God and the prophet. He added that I had a long journey before I should reach Mecca, and that, as my resources were not great, they would if I made frequent presents soon be exhausted. I was not to be duped by this; I perceived that he wanted something else: in fact he asked me to sell him a pair of scissors and some paper. Being convinced that I should be thought greedy if I sold him these articles, I promised to give him them at our parting, which was to be the next day. During the journey I had lent seven hundred cowries; partly to my guide and partly to other persons of the caravan. They all faithfully repaid me.

On the morning of the 5th of February, I went, accompanied by Karamo-osila, to call on the man from Timé, with whom I was henceforth to travel. At parting from my old guide, I presented him with the pair of scissors and the paper which I had promised him. He asked me for some cowries to enable him to pursue his journey, under the pretence that his colat-nuts would not sell, and that he should be unable to purchase provisions: I paid little attention to his request. Although I had every reason to praise his conduct, yet I parted from him without regret, for I was continually annoyed by his people, and principally by his wives, who took pleasure in tormenting me. I was their butt, and a constant subject of amusement to them. Indeed, during the halts, from the annoyance which I experienced, I might have fancied myself still at Timé; the men never took the trouble to make them hold their tongues.

At seven o'clock on the morning of the 5th of February, we separated, Karamo-osila going to the N. N. E. and we to the east. At a little, distance from the village we crossed a stream by a very substantial bridge. There were between six and seven hundred persons and thirty or forty asses to pass. Many travellers with their women forded the stream, being up to their waists in water. It was a terrible scene of uproar and confusion. Every one was loudly disputing about the amount of the passage-duty, which was paid in cowries. Our caravan had been augmented by a number of merchants who traded in cloth, allspice, and long pepper. Having reached the opposite bank of the stream, we proceeded towards the N. E. along a fine level road. The country was open and interspersed with cés and nédés. The soil, composed of grey sand, was broken here and there by little hills. We crossed a dry marsh, covered with rich pasture, into which the natives turn their cattle. The inhabitants of the neighbouring villages are so industrious as to make dikes. They are raised to the height of three and a half, or four feet, so as to confine the waters of the marsh, which would otherwise inundate the country in the months of August and September.

About nine o'clock in the morning we halted at Oulasso, a village composed of three or four small enclosures of equal size, and containing about three hundred inhabitants.

At six in the morning of the 6th of February, we again set out and proceeded six miles N. E. over the same kind of soil as on the preceding day. The country was covered with bombaces and baobabs. We halted about nine in the morning at Chesso. This village is formed like Oulasso, of several little enclosures, very near to each other. The surrounding country is very bare. There is a marsh, on the borders of which the natives cultivate onions, beans, giraumons, &c. There are also within the village many bombaces and baobabs. On arriving at the hut allotted to us, I saw at the door a very dirty woman baking cakes in an earthen frying-pan made in the country. I bought some of them, not being able to procure any others; as there was no market in this village. Our hut, which was very narrow and low, scarcely afforded room for us and our luggage. However, I was obliged to pass the night in it.

My new companions clubbed to buy a goat. I gave seventy cowries for my share, and unfortunately I could not eat it, the meat being hard and badly cooked. An hour or two after supper, the negroes fell to eating the head half roasted on the ashes; and after they had gnawed the bones they gave them to the slaves.

The want of a market renders this place extremely dull. Its long, crooked streets are very dirty, and contain pools of filthy water, through which we were obliged to wade mid-leg deep in mud. Around these pools the inhabitants grow herbs for their sauces. My supper, consisting of the liquor in which the goat was boiled, helped to recruit my strength, exhausted by travelling every day without intermission.

At seven o'clock in the morning of the 7th of February, we left Chesso, taking a N. E. direction. The soil was level and covered with ferruginous stones and gravel. The vegetation was similar to that which I observed on the preceding days, but I also saw some specimens of the *rhamnus lotus*. We continued our journey over a grey sandy soil, producing millet and various other things. A fresh breeze blew from the north, and I should have been glad to warm myself, my clothing being but slight and falling in tatters about me.

We arrived about nine in the morning at Pala, where we halted for the rest of the day. This little village has a well stocked market. I perceived in the neighbourhood many furnaces for smelting iron, which is found on the surface of the soil. I saw also the implement employed in the cultivation of the soil, the only one, I believe, with which these people are acquainted, for I saw no other. It is a hoe, a foot long and eight inches broad. The handle, which is about sixteen inches in length, slants very much. In reaping they make use of a sickle without teeth, as at Wassoulo.

At eight o'clock, on the morning of the 8th of February, we left Pala, and proceeded to the N. E. over a soil composed of white hard sand. The country is very open, but here and there are to be seen many mimosas and cés. The cé, which as I have before stated, furnishes abundance of butter, grows spontaneously throughout the interior of Africa. It would thrive admirably in our American colonies, where its introduction would be a great service to humanity. To the inhabitants of those regions the gift of this useful plant would be more valuable than a mine of gold. It was nine o'clock in the morning when we arrived at Maconeau, a pretty village, containing from three to four hundred inhabitants, and situated in a well cultivated plain. Near the village there is a low hill, extending from N. W. to S. E.

On the 9th of February, at six in the morning, we directed our course N. E. and proceeded about a mile ascending the hill where I saw many white calcareous stones. We descended by a very difficult road into a fine, firm sandy plain; along which we proceeded five miles. Although our daily journeys had not been very long, I was nevertheless greatly fatigued. If, at times, I sat down while hot under a tree to rest awhile, I was instantly chilled by a cool wind. These sudden transitions caused those frequent colds which I may rank among the greatest miseries I suffered during my travels. In sleeping in the huts I experienced a similar inconvenience. The large fires which the negroes are accustomed to make occasioned a suffocating heat, and the wind penetrating through a badly closed door, chilled me with cold; I sometimes coughed so much that I could not sleep, and sat up part of the night; I occasionally adopted the plan of sleeping out of doors, in order to enjoy a more equal temperature, but from this I found little relief. I was exceedingly ill, and so hoarse that it was necessary to come very close to me to hear me speak.

We met a caravan of traders coming from Jenné, where they had purchased salt; they had with them some horses, which they had also bought at that place. About nine o'clock in the morning we halted at Couara, a pretty village, where we found an abundance of all the necessaries of life. The inhabitants grow a great deal of cotton and millet, and are supplied with water from a stream which runs E. N. E., half a mile from the village.

At eight o'clock in the morning of the 10th of February we quitted Couara, and crossed the river called Koraba which delayed us at least three hours. This river is narrow and deep, and its banks, which are very high and well wooded, are composed of a red argillaceous earth, mixed with sand, gravel, and fragments of rock. The current is very rapid. The Koraba makes great ravages during its inundations, sweeping away masses of earth, and enlarging its bed; in return for these encroachments, however, it fertilises the country. This river comes from the south and flows rapidly from N. E. to east; on its right bank there is a chain of hills extending from south to E. N. E. The natives and the Mandingo merchants assured me that this river passes Kayaye, a considerable town, where a well frequented market is held, five days' journey N. N. W. of Couara, and that it falls into the Dhioliba in the neighbourood of Ségo. The Koraba is navigable for vessels of from sixty to eighty tons; in the part which we crossed it was ten feet deep, and from fifty to sixty fathoms wide. It is called by some the Couaraba; several women from the village had stationed themselves on the bank of the river, to sell maumies. I bought some for my breakfast. We had two canoes to cross the river; the boatmen were very hard in their demands upon us; they made us pay in advance, and counted their cowries two or three times over, to be assured that we had not deceived them. I was impatient at this delay. The asses also gave us infinite trouble; it was necessary to make them swim over, for the canoes were too small to receive them; when they got into the middle of the river, these animals turned and would have gone back to the bank which they had just left. At length, one of the negroes, whose patience was worn out, put cords round the necks of the asses, and fastening the other end round his own waist, swam across, whilst the other Mandingoes, who were behind, beat the animals and thus forced them on. We reached the right bank without experiencing any other difficulty. I asked a Mandingo negress to give me some water in a calabash, and she was good enough to add a little millet-flour to it. It was near noon when we left the bank of the river and proceeded towards the N. E. over a clayey soil. The country in general was very open. I perceived some *nauclea Africana.* The soil is covered with ferruginous stones, and in every direction are to be seen hills of no great height, most of which extend from N. W. to east and are covered with cés, at least those which I saw. About half past two in the afternoon, having proceeded four miles and a half, we halted at Douasso a village shaded by numerous baobabs and bombaces. The wells, which were between twelve and fourteen feet deep, afforded clean and pleasant water.

The surrounding country is very level and covered with nédés. Part of our caravan remained at Couara, not being able to cross the river that day. We were to wait for them at this village. I visited the market, which I found supplied with fish, fresh and dried, a great deal of millet, some rice, pistachios, maumies, and plenty of cotton. The women of our caravan obtained some colat-nuts from their husbands, to purchase this last article. They spin it, and, as I said before, whatever profit it produces, is their own. I saw some persons weaving under trees. In the evening our host presented us with a fowl, some pistachios, and a fresh fish of the carp kind, which is very common in the marshes: to catch it, the natives use a basket made of the branches of a tree. My old guide, whose name was Kai-mou, returned thanks for the present by a long prayer, and after assuring our host that he would go to Mahomet's paradise, he gave him eight colat-nuts, valued in that country at forty-eight cowries.

After supper I took my seat on a sheep-skin in the court, to enjoy the cool air. Here we saw a Mandingo merchant, a native of Kong, who was returning from Jenné to trade in salt. He was alone, and carried his merchandise on his head. I entered into conversation with him, and obtained all the information I could respecting his country. He told me that Kong, his native place, was a large town, the capital of a district, inhabited by Mahometan Mandingoes. From Douasso, where we were, he said it would take him a month and a half to travel to Kong, with his load on his head. I asked him in what direction his country lay, and he several times pointed to the S. S. E. and S. ¼ S. E. I had a pocket compass, which I was afraid to make use of, except when alone. Had it been seen, it would probably have brought me into trouble. In order to ascertain as correctly as I could the situation of Kong, as described by the Mandingo, I remarked attentively the place where he sat, and fixed upon an object near the point of the horizon, which he had indicated. Next morning, without being seen by any person, I satisfied myself of its situation. The merchant told me that, on his return, he should leave Tangrera on his left, and pass through a great trading village, inhabited as he said, by Mandingoes, and a month's journey from Douasso; he called it Dierisso. From that place he said it would take fifteen days to reach Kong. He likewise told me that the soil of his country was level and sandy; but very productive in millet, rice, yams, cassava, giraumons, cés, nédés, baobabs, and other useful trees and plants, and that his countrymen were rich in oxen, sheep, goats, and poultry. They have also horses, which must be a small breed, for he compared them with those of the country in which we were.

I learned from my informant, that a market is held every day in the town of Kong. The country is watered by numerous small streams, but it contains no rivers. The people grow a great quantity of cotton, of which they manufacture beautiful cloth, highly esteemed in trade. There are no gold-mines in Kong. Gold is brought thither from Baunan, which is fifteen days' journey further south.

Baunan produces colat-nuts and a great quantity of gold, which the inhabitants exchange for salt and cloth. The soil of Baunan, although fertile and hilly, is uncultivated. The inhabitants, who employ themselves in working the mines, obtain provisions from their neighbours. The Kong trader told me that he had been many times at Baunan, and that beyond Kong there were no Bambara negroes; the people had, indeed, curly hair, but they spoke a different language. They are all idolaters, and do not travel, having markets of their own. The Mandingo merchants trade in Baunan, and go in caravans to Jenné, taking with them gold, colat-nuts, allspice, and long pepper. The negro, from whom I learned these particulars, told me that there were at that time many traders of his country at Jenné, and that I might, perhaps, see them. From Kong, caravans of pilgrims sometimes go to Mecca. The Baunan country, to which this negro alluded, is most probably the Tauman, which I heard mentioned by the good old woman at Timé.

On the 11th of February, as we were still sojourning at Douasso, awaiting the arrival of a party of our companions, who remained behind, I thought I would make an observation, at least approximatively, of the meridian altitude of the sun, by measuring a shadow at noon. For this purpose, I stationed myself near a large baobab, at a little distance from the village, in order to escape notice; but, notwithstanding this precaution, I had nearly involved myself in a serious scrape. Owing to the peculiarity of my colour, I was immediately missed from among my companions; I was sought for and discovered under the tree: as I was rising to look at the road, I perceived at a little distance some women, who walked round me to watch me; on seeing me writing they ran to inform the men, who thought themselves all lost, imagining that I was a sorcerer, and had bewitched their village; they assembled in great numbers, and made a great disturbance, desiring my guide to prohibit me from writing any more. I confess that I was not quite at ease as to the consequences of this affair. Some persons came to me and declared, in an authoritative tone, that I must relinquish my magical operations; they even shook me by the shoulders, and used threats to me. I had foreseen that, if observed, I should excite suspicion, and accordingly took the precaution of writing on the ground where I was making my observation the sacred words, *Bism' Allah erralmân errahym* (in the name of the merciful and forgiving God); but the ignorant Bambaras could not read writing. Fortunately, I had finished my observation when this unpleasant scene occurred. The people gathered round me, and asked me what I had been doing: I told them I had been making an amulet, which was a safeguard against all sorts of illness, and my guide heartily seconded this evasion. At length they appeared satisfied; some begged me to write similar grigris for them; and, had I complied with the requests of all, I might have continued at work all day. I gave to two Bambaras a little bit of paper, on which I had written some Arabic characters: they appeared much pleased with the present, and wrapped it up very carefully in a bit of dirty rag. On returning to my hut, it was some time before I entirely recovered from the agitation into which I had been thrown. Old Kai-mou, my guide, asked me why I had remained so long under the tree: he told me that I had exposed myself to danger, for the Bambaras were not well disposed people; that I must be on my guard with them, and, in future, if I wished to write, I must remain in my hut; as for himself, he was fully persuaded that I had been writing grigris. In the evening our company arrived.

On the 12th of February, at six o'clock in the morning, we left the superstitious inhabitants of Douasso, and proceeded northward over a tolerably level soil, covered in some places with ferruginous stones and gravel.

We proceeded four miles and a half in this same direction. As we advanced the soil became sandy and well cultivated. The country was generally open, yet there were some cés and nédés, *rhamnus lotus*, and *nauclea*. We met a numerous caravan from Jenné, laden with salt. This caravan was composed of about two hundred men, sixty women, and twenty-five asses. About nine o'clock in the morning we halted at Sanasso. From Toumaré to Jenné wood is so scarce, that the greater part of the inhabitants burn millet-stubble. Sanasso is shaded by bombaces and baobabs. Like all Bambara villages in this region, it is built of bricks baked in the sun. The houses have only a ground-floor: they are very dirty, and surrounded with walls.

On the 13th of February, at six o'clock in the morning, we proceeded on our journey, in a direction N. N. E. After advancing six miles, we crossed an extensive dry marsh. The country was even more open than that through which we had passed on the preceding day. The soil, which was level, consisted of grey and very hard sand. About nine o'clock in the morning, we stopped at Garo, a large village, containing from eight to nine hundred inhabitants. It is situated in a beautiful plain, fertile in cotton and millet. Round the huts tobacco is cultivated. A great market is held at this place.

At six o'clock in the morning of the 14th of February, we proceeded northward, and journeyed four miles over the same kind of soil as on the preceding day. About eight o'clock we halted at the village of Béré, the environs of which are covered with cés and nédés. I observed a great deal of ferruginous stone on the surface of the soil. Here are several furnaces for smelting iron. We lodged with a smelter, who explained to me the process which he employed in his business. The stones containing particles of iron are first broken with a large hammer. They are then put into a furnace, having a fire both above and below. These furnaces are constructed like those in Fouta-Dhialon, which I have already described. The iron, when melted, is run into a convenient form, and carried to Jenné to be exchanged for salt. The forges are constructed like those of Senegal; but the Smiths of Béré have not so many tools. Their bellows are made of two sheep or kid skins; they have a very small anvil and two large hammers. They use charcoal, although it is very scarce. The forges are in a long and narrow building, rudely constructed, having seven doors opening to the west. At Béré I disposed of some glass trinkets. The poor Bambaras seemed quite enchanted with the beauty of the things which I exhibited; I took care, however, to shew them very little.

At six o'clock in the morning of the 15th of February, we set out in the direction of N. N. E. and proceeded five miles over a soil similar to that observed on the preceding day. About nine o'clock we halted at Nibakhasso, a village containing, from six to seven hundred inhabitants, and having a well stocked market. The people were celebrating a festival, and amusing themselves by singing and dancing. The old men were assembled round great calabashes filled with beer, drinking, singing, and smoking. Some musicians helped to enliven the scene. A very fat dog was killed for the occasion, and broiled with the skin on. Although it was almost raw, the owner speedily disposed of it: each person bought a small piece for five or ten cowries, devoured it greedily, and washed it down with a draught of beer. The flesh was of a reddish colour, but looked very well; and I dare say it was much better than that of the camel which I was afterwards obliged to eat in the desert. Our Mandingoes exhibited their stock of nuts, and sold some of them to the merry Bambaras. I also disposed of those which I brought from Tangrera, and which they bought in preference. There are people in this country who make beer and sell it retail. I had a great wish to taste it, but my character of Musulman rendered that impossible. On holidays, these dealers in beer station themselves at the scene of festivity, and are soon surrounded by the lovers of this liquor, which they sell in small calabashes. I observed that they looked very sharply after their payment, and refused to serve those who had no money. In the evening, the inhabitants of the place were almost all intoxicated. They brought out about twelve or fifteen horses, and made them prance about to the sound of drums. The young people danced all night. Old Kai-mou, my guide, was so extravagant as to buy a large fowl for supper, and I gave him salt to season the sauce. We made an excellent meal.

At six o'clock in the morning of the 16th of February, we again set forth, and proceeded four miles in a N. N. E. direction. The soil was composed of sand and gravel, and the vegetation consisted of numerous cés and nédés, some mimosas, wild figs, *rhamnus lotus*, and bombaces. At eleven o'clock in the morning we arrived at Wattouro. We met a caravan of traders returning from Jenné. They informed us that the war between Ségo and that town interrupted all communication, and that the Moorish traders were afraid to go to Sansanding on account of this war. They also told us that colat-nuts fetched no price at Jenné. The market at Wattouro, which was in the shade of some bombaces, was well supplied with dried fish, millet, a little rice, and butcher's meat.

CHAPTER XVII

Dwarf cotton — Coloni — The Iolas, a Foulah tribe — Bancousso — Carabara — Marshes — Ropes made of the hibiscus — Brick-making — Construction of houses — Kerina — Foudouca — Medina — Lotus bread — Touma-dioman — Marianan — Arrival at Galia on the banks of the Dhioliba, opposite to Jenné.

On the 17th of February, at six o'clock in, the morning, we proceeded northward. The caravan, intimidated by the reports of the war with Ségo, and being in the neighbourhood of that town, put itself on the defensive. At a little distance from the village we halted, to put ourselves in order. The men carrying loads, who were all armed with bows and arrows, were divided into two bodies, and between them the women were placed; while the old merchants, and the chiefs of the caravan, driving their asses, brought up the rear. I seated myself to see them pass, which occupied at least a quarter of an hour. The order of our march was well observed, and had an imposing effect. When we wished to rest, the advanced guard halted with the women. The rear went forward to a certain distance, and then rested in its turn, till those who had stopped first should come up. The old men with the asses being now in the van halted till the whole caravan had passed, and resumed their usual place in the rear. We proceeded four miles N. N. E. on a soil similar to that which we passed over on the previous day. About eleven o'clock we stopped at Saraclé, a little walled village, having a very well supplied market. At the entrance of the village I observed a well: the soil in which it was dug, consisted of greyish earth, mixed with sand and gravel.

The well was from fifteen to eighteen feet in depth, and the water it contained clear and pleasant to the taste. It had no enclosure, and near it was a great hole, forming a pond, into which the negresses throw the water in which they wash their clothes. Although this water was very dirty, both men and women washed their faces in it every morning; and many persons belonging to our company followed their example. In the neighbourhood of Saraclé there are some mimosas, and a great quantity of cés and nédés. Many traders from Ségo, and other adjacent places, attended the market. From some of these people I learned that the capital of Bambara was four days' journey N. N. W. of Saraclé. I sold in the market some glass wares, and some pieces of coloured calico, between eighteen and twenty inches long and four broad, for three hundred cowries each, (equal to one franc and fifty centimes). The women rolled these pieces of cloth round their heads, drawing them rather forward upon the brow. They wear no other kind of head-dress.

On the 18th of February, as we were preparing to depart, one of old Kai-mou's men laid hold of my baggage with a disdainful air, and threw it on one side, telling me in a very uncivil tone that henceforth I must carry it myself. I paid no attention to this impertinence, and turned my head another way, having nothing to do with the man, though I could plainly perceive that his intention was to insult me. During all the time I was among the Mandingoes I never saw a man so insolent as this: he was full of self-sufficiency, and often insulted the Bambaras whilst selling his merchandise to them. He despised them, and considered himself their superior. He met with one, however, who, instead of giving way to him, shook his fist in his face, and threatened to punish him for his insolence. Our braggadocio who, like all cowards, was brave only when he believed himself the stronger, was silent immediately, and even appeared somewhat frightened. The dispute drew together a numerous crowd of Bambaras, and might perhaps have led to serious consequences. At the moment of our departure Kai-mou gave orders for arranging the loads, and the man who used to carry my bag placed it amongst his baggage; I knew very well that all this was occasioned by a little misunderstanding which had occurred at Wattouro between me and my old guide, and which arose out of the following circumstance. Being in the market I bought some rice for twenty cowries; I asked my guide, who had likewise purchased a similar quantity, to put our shares together. He declined this, assigning some reason which I could not comprehend. I perceived that he spoke in an authoritative tone, and I answered him in the same manner. He was several days without speaking to me, and even cherished a sort of animosity against me.

At six o'clock in the morning, we proceeded N. E. over a very level sandy soil. The country was very open, but I saw here and there some cés, nédés, mimosas, and *rhamnus lotus*. The caravan advanced in the same order as on the preceding day. The heat, which was greater than usual, became overpowering. After proceeding four miles we halted at the village of Bamba, which is shaded by baobabs. At the market I observed that the women wore glass rings in the nose; and some had these ornaments made of gold or copper. This village contains from three to four hundred inhabitants. I was assured that, after travelling N. W. three days longer, we should see the Dhioliba, and that the fourth day would bring us to Ségo.

In the evening we were harassed by parties of female singers, who, by dint of importunity, extort money from travellers. Old Kai-mou gave them two colats to get rid of them. Afterwards, perceiving me in a corner, they came to me; but, as I had nothing to give them, I left the room, at which they did not seem well pleased. These itinerant singers are followed by a number of well dressed girls, each of whom carries a little calabash to receive what may be given, whilst the concert is going on. Shortly afterwards we were attacked by another set of beggars, who sing prayers from the Koran in a loud voice. These singers stood at the doors, and the people gave them some colat nuts.

At six o'clock in the morning of the 19th of February, we proceeded in a N. E. direction. We travelled three miles through a very open country, the soil being similar to that which I had observed for several preceding days. I saw many fields of cotton of a very small species. On the road, a poor woman carrying a heavy load was taken in labour and delivered in a cotton field. We went forward, leaving the poor creature in the care of two females. Next morning I was much surprised to see her following the caravan, with an empty calabash on her head. Her countenance had undergone a change.

We halted at Sanso, where we passed the remainder of the day. In the environs of this village were many plantations of cotton, of a kind which I had not before seen, either on the banks of the Senegal or in the neighbourhood of Sierra-Leone. It does not grow higher than five or six inches above the ground. It has very few branches, and the plant has the same appearance as the large cotton. The wool which it produces is of inferior quality, very short, and not of a good white. I likewise saw here a cotton plant which grows to the height of four or five feet. Dwarf cotton is cultivated at some distance from the village. It is very abundant, and is sown at random among the millet as in Wassoulo. This cotton is annual. A great deal of it is sold to the women belonging to the caravans which are continually passing through the country. The inhabitants also make with it a narrow cloth, which is manufactured throughout all the interior; for, in proportion as I advanced towards the banks of the Dhioliba, I perceived a great change in the industry of the natives. Here they are much better clothed; they apply themselves to trade, their markets are better supplied and their agricultural operations are more carefully performed. All sorts of provisions are dear here: indeed it is frequently difficult to procure them at all, owing to the great number of strangers passing this way. In this part of Bambara the only kind of grain is large and small millet. Rice grows in very small quantities. Yams which are so useful in the south, are here small and so inferior in quality that they are very little cultivated. In the market I sometimes saw a dozen at most. They were extremely dear. Travellers buy them and roast them in the ashes to eat at their departure in the morning on the road, when they rest. The environs of Sanso are wooded with cés and nédés. The butter extracted from the cé, is sold at Jenné to the caravans which pass through the village. The greater part of the inhabitants have nothing to burn but millet stubble, for wood is so scarce that those who have it prefer selling it in the market.

At six o'clock in the morning of the 20th of February we set out proceeding in a N. E. direction for six miles, through a level, open country, the soil consisting of hard grey sand. I saw a few *naucleas* and nédés. The heat, already very powerful, was increased by a burning wind from the east. About eleven we halted at Saga, a very pretty village, shaded by bombaces. I now found myself less an object of curiosity than hitherto. Every one took me for a Moor. My beautiful coloured cloth and my glass wares wholly occupied the attention of my companions. Throughout all this country the costume is nearly the same as in the south, except that it is neater. The women likewise wear their hair platted; they may be compared with the Mandingo women of Timé and Tangrera, but not with the Bambara females who wear scarcely any clothing. They have also rings at the nose such as I have before described.

On the 21st of February, at six o'clock in the morning, we took a N. E. direction, and proceeded five miles and a half, the caravan still observing the same order as before. The soil was similar to that we had passed over for several preceding days, except that it was a little more gravelly. The surrounding country is well cropped with millet, and I observed some *rhamnus lotus*. At ten in the morning we arrived at Coloni, a little village situated in a beautiful, fertile and well cultivated plain, surrounded by a great number of large bombaces. On my arrival, I seated myself on the ground in the shade of a tree under which there were some female traders, from whom I bought some boiled pistachios for my breakfast, to which I added some cakes. While I was taking my frugal repast, I was accosted by a Foulah of Massina, whom I had seen at Sanasso. He seated himself beside me on the ground, and several of his comrades soon followed his example. This negro already knew all about me, and he related my history to the rest. He told them that I was a sherif, and that I had come from amongst christians, for whom they testified the greatest aversion. After annoying me by their teazing questions, they advised me, when I arrived at Jenné, to visit Ségo Ahmadou, who would certainly give me some handsome presents and a guide to conduct me to my native country. All these Foulahs were settled at Coloni, and were natives of Massina, a country situated a little to the north of Jenné. The village of Coloni is the first of those of which Ségo Ahmadou is chief, and it forms part of the little kingdom of Jenné. This country was conquered from the Bambaras by the Foulahs. Ségo Ahmadou has erected mosques here. The Bambaras, who do pot profess the Mahometan religion, pay a small tribute to the chief: there are many Mandingoes settled in this country, where they are usually called *Iaulas, Diaulas,* or *Iolas*; they are the principal traders. The Foulahs who inhabit this country follow no occupation but the duties of religion; they have numerous slaves, who cultivate the land, and provide for the wants of their masters. These Foulahs wear the same dress as those of the Fouta-Dhialon; they are also as clean as the latter, and resemble them in hair, complexion, and features; they are tall and well made men, and have rather a dignified deportment; they speak both the language of Fouta and that of the Mandingoes: they are all armed with three or four lances, which they hold in one hand; these lances are fixed on slender shafts about five feet long. The village of Coloni, which is surrounded by two mud walls, contains a population of about four hundred, consisting of Foulahs, Bambaras, and Mandingoes: it is shaded by large mimosas and some bombaces. We were lodged in a hut belonging to my acquaintance, the Foulah, who came to see me very often; he was almost always accompanied by some of his friends, who gave me colat-nuts, of which these people appear to be exceedingly fond. As to my host, during his frequent visits, he overwhelmed me with questions, but made me no present: he asked me whether I had any gold to sell; for he supposed that as I had come from Bouré, where it was very abundant, I must have some. Though I assured him that I was poor and had no money, yet he constantly repeated the same inquiry. In the evening, a man of our caravan bought a kid, by way of speculation. He divided it into small portions, which he sold among his comrades for eighty cowries each. I bought one of the pieces, having fared very badly for several days past. I had it cooked for supper, sharing it with my guide and some of his people. The room in which we were to pass the night was so dreadfully smoky that I determined to sleep in the court. I had caught such a cold that I could not sleep; my continued cough affected my lungs and brought on a spitting of blood.

On the 22nd of February, as we were preparing to depart, I had to encounter a repetition of the scene which had taken place at Saraclé. The same negro had the insolence to throw my leather bag down at the door, telling me that I must take it on my own head, for the man who had hitherto carried it was ill. I took no notice of him and went away, though, owing to his insolence on several former occasions, I had been obliged to exercise great self-command to refrain from replying to him. I stopped for a moment to buy some maumies for my breakfast, for I understood that we should have a long journey before we made a halt. I saw all the people of the caravan ranging themselves in order, with their loads on their heads, and my luggage still continued lying on the ground. As my guide had not reproved the insolence of the negro, I thought he did not wish to take charge of my things, and, taking a mat and some trifles which I had given to a negress to carry, I determined to stay in the village, and change my guide. The old man, with the ass, who had not yet set out, told me that I was wrong to take the things from the woman, who was already somewhat in advance, and, that I should have taken no notice of what the negro said. He observed that he was the only master there, and that as the man who had hitherto carried my luggage, had really some ailment in his neck, he would put my bag on the back of his own ass. He added, that if he had intended me to carry it, he would have told me so himself. However, I am fully persuaded that had he seen me inclined to carry it he would willingly have allowed me to do so, for his ass was already sufficiently loaded. I declared that if I again experienced such treatment, I would change my guide; for, paying as I did, I might find one any where. I had made him a present of a piece of coloured calico and some paper, and I was to pay him for his services on arriving at Jenné. I complained that he had not repressed the insolence of his slave. He appeared much out of humour, and having with a very ill grace put my luggage on the back of the ass, we continued our journey. I followed him, carrying the mat on which I slept, an earthen vessel, and my umbrella; when we rejoined our party, some of the women relieved me from this little burden. Several Foulahs of Coloni escorted me to a little distance from the village, and, at parting, they begged me to give them my blessing. One of them put his hand in mine, and the others in succession did the same. I muttered a few verses of the Koran, and to make an end of the ceremony, I blew upon their bands, which they rubbed over their faces, devoutly exclaiming, *Alam-doul-illahi*, and went away satisfied.

We had now come up to the caravan, which had stopped for a short time to range itself in the order which had been observed on several preceding days. We proceeded five miles eastward over a good road. The country was better wooded than that through which we had passed the day before, and was in many places covered with stubble. The soil consisted of firm sand. We crossed a stream, which delayed us a considerable time. Both men and women threw off their clothes and forded it, the water being up to their waists. Those who had no loads to carry crossed it by a tottering bridge, consisting of a row of perpendicular poles planted in the bed of the stream, to which other poles were negligently tied in a tranverse direction. The negroes stepped upon these transverse poles, and held by the upright ones: they every moment ran the risk of falling into the water; however, we all got across without accident. The banks of this stream are well wooded. We continued our course five miles to the S. E. over a sandy soil, the surface of which was covered with gravel. The excessive heat rendered our journey very fatiguing. About eleven in the morning we arrived at Bancousso, a large village containing a population of five or six hundred, and situated in a well cultivated plain, shaded by baobabs. This village has a large market, well supplied with the productions of the country; I saw in it a great quantity of cloth, and earthen pots, which are made here.

At six o'clock in the morning of the 23rd of February, we advanced six miles to the N. E. We crossed a stream which was nearly dry, and then continued seven miles further in the same direction. The soil, which is level, is composed of grey sand, and in some places of red earth mixed with gravel. The country was open, and I saw but very few nédés and cés. We were greatly oppressed by the heat, and unfortunately found very little water on the road. About two in the afternoon we arrived at Gniapé, excessively thirsty and fatigued. The environs of this village are tolerably well cultivated. Old Kai-mou, my guide, had a serious quarrel with one of his wives: he threatened to strike her; she imprudently dared him to do so; and the old man, in a fit of rage, beat her unmercifully. The poor creature took up a stick to defend herself, but fortunately some Mandingoes of the caravan, hearing the noise, came and interfered. The woman, being prevented from taking her revenge, had recourse to tears, and, in the violence of her passion, struck her own bosom. This was the only time I ever saw among these people a wife presume to resist her husband. The animosity was long kept up between the parties, and they did not even speak to each other; at length, after the lapse of three or four days, a Mandingo negro endeavoured to effect a reconciliation; what he said, certainly had some influence, for he succeeded in restoring peace between the husband and wife. The woman was obliged to confess that she was in the wrong, for the husband would never have yielded. To ratify the peace, Kai-mou broke a colat-nut, half of which he gave to his wife, and he ate the other half himself. From that moment they were friends. The women of these countries easily forget this kind of treatment, to which they are accustomed.

At six o'clock in the morning of the 24th of February, we directed our course to E. N. E., and proceeded three miles across a country similar, to that through which we passed the day before. We met a caravan of Mandingo traders coming from Jenné, and halted, at eight in the evening, at Couriban-Sanso.

On the 25th of February, we started at sun-rise, travelling eight miles E. N. E. The soil continued unvaried, and the country very open. At ten o'clock in the morning we reached a small neat village, called Kimpana, where we passed the remainder of the day and the succeeding night.

On the 26th of February, at six in the morning, we again resumed our journey, proceeding six miles N. E., over a fine gravelly soil. I observed several specimens of the *rhamnus lotus,* and various other trees, of which I did not know the names. At ten o'clock we halted at Carabara, a village containing five or six hundred inhabitants. A great market is held here. The wells, which are without the boundaries of the village, are twelve or fourteen feet deep, and contain very good water.

On the 27th of February, we advanced six miles to N. N. W. The ground was covered with fine gravel; cés and nédés were becoming less frequent, but I observed some bombaces and mimosas. It was near eleven o'clock when we halted at the village of Nenesso, the environs of which are well cropped with millet and cotton, and I saw also some baobabs.

At ten in the morning of the 28th February, we resumed our course N.N.W., and advanced four miles over a sandy and well cultivated soil, in which grow many large baobabs. We halted at Nomou, a village situated in a beautiful open plain, where I saw some fine plantations of cotton and tobacco; the latter had long pointed leaves, and, if properly prepared, it would, no doubt, be as good as ours. The people take great pains in cultivating it. They first sow the seed in beds, and when the plant has attained a certain growth, they transplant it; for this purpose they prepare the ground by two diggings, and dividing it into little squares, the plants of tobacco are there placed at the distance of eighteen inches asunder; they are watered twice a day, there being wells for that purpose near the plantations.

The leaves of the tobacco are not gathered until the plant is in seed, as the practice of topping is not understood here. There is a great consumption of tobacco; for the people take snuff and smoke very much: smoking is indeed the only recreation of the old men; their pipes are of the same size and form as those used in the Wassoulo. They take snuff with a small brush or hair pencil. The dress, customs, and manners of the people in this part of the country vary but little.

At six o'clock on the morning of the 29th of February we directed our course to N. E. and advanced three miles through an open country, similar to that which we had seen the day before. We halted at Tamero. While I was in the market purchasing some cakes, a woman, tolerably well dressed, accosted me, and taking me for an Arab, requested me to go and see a Moor who was ill in the village. I followed her, and found the sick man, sitting under the shade of a bombax, employed in killing the vermin with which he was tormented. He seemed very poor, being no better clothed than myself, and he had a sore on his foot which prevented him from walking. He invited me to sit down by him, and then asked me whence I came. He was astonished when I told him that Alexandria was my country: he said he had heard of it, but that it was a great way off. He told me that he was a native of Tafilet, whither he wished to return, but that he was prevented from so doing by his inability to walk. He lived with a good Mahometan negro, who supplied him with food out of mere charity. The miserable condition of this poor creature excited my pity, and I gave him a few glass beads. On returning home I told my guide that I had seen a Moor who knew my country; Kai-mou seemed much pleased at this and appeared more cheerful than usual.

At the market I saw some good dried fish, which I bought for supper, and my travelling companions partook of it. The village of Tamero is, like all the others, composed of several walled inclosures. It is shaded by baobabs, and contains a population of about three or four hundred. The fruit and leaves of the baobab are carefully gathered and the inhabitants carry on a great trade in them.

On the 1st of March, we set out at six in the morning, and travelled five miles N. N. E. Shortly after leaving the village we crossed a large inundated marsh, being up to our waists in water. This marsh is frequented by numbers of aquatic birds, as the pelican, the egret, the trumpet-bird, the marabou, the puffin, the Barbary duck, the teal, and various other species, which I could not distinguish. The natives do not shoot these birds, gunpowder being with them a very scarce article. Having crossed the marsh, we passed over a tract, the soil of which was composed of a kind of loose sand. Here I observed tamarind-trees and samps in abundance, as well as the *rhamnus lotus*, the cé, the nédé, and the baobab.

About nine in the morning we halted at Syenso, where some of the inhabitants were engaged in storing the fruit of the baobab. For this purpose they break the shell with a large piece of wood, and then take out the pulp, which, after being thoroughly dried in the sun, they slightly pound to extract the fecula, which is much esteemed in this country. The people put it into their sauces and use it as a substitute for honey in preparing their dokhnou. At Syenso ropes are made of the *hibiscus cannibinus*, or hemp, discovered at Gambia by a Frenchman named Baudery, and which is also used on the Senegal. No machinery is employed in making these ropes; they are merely twisted by hand, consequently they are not very strong, especially as the hemp, which is not wetted before it is used, is gathered when very dry. I bought two of these ropes, which were about six yards long and an inch thick: I paid for each fifteen cowries, (equivalent to a sou and a half.) I met with a man from Jenné, who was very kind and civil to me. On my complaining of fatigue, he advised me to be patient, as we had not far to go before we should reach Jenné.

At six in the morning of the 2nd of March, we left Syenso, and advanced between north and east the distance of seven miles. A little beyond the village we crossed a marsh, in which the water was knee-deep. The surrounding country is covered with rich pasturage. About eleven we stopped at Somou, a village situated in an open and well cultivated plain. I was astonished at the great quantity of fish, which I saw in the market; I bought some for supper and found it very good. I also purchased some lotus bread, which had a very pleasant taste: it was rather acid and in colour resembled gingerbread. It was made of the fruit of the *rhamnus lotus*, mentioned by Mungo Park. There were in the market some women selling millet stubble, which is used for fuel on account of the scarcity of wood. I also saw a small quantity of sulphur in sticks; it is brought from the markets of Jenné, Ségo, Sansanding, and Yamina, but I know not what use is made of it here. All the villages on this road, from Oulasso to Jenné, are built of bricks baked in the sun. These bricks, which are a foot long, eight inches broad and a foot thick, are made without the aid of a mould. The earth, being mixed to a proper consistence, is spread upon the ground, and when half dry it is shaped into the form of bricks, which are laid in the sun, and turned from side to side until sufficiently baked. The houses, or rather huts, are eight or nine feet high, twelve or fourteen long, and eight wide. The walls are eighteen inches thick and rudely built, the bricks being not even cemented together. They have all flat roofs, which are supported by thick posts, placed within at suitable distances from each other, and similar posts are erected for the same purpose in the middle of the room. The whole is so badly constructed that the wall cannot for any length of time support the roof, which is very heavy, and consists of untrimmed branches of trees covered with earth. The huts have in general but one door and no chimney, and when fires are kindled in them, which is the case every evening, the smoke is unbearable. For my part I always preferred sleeping in the open air. These huts are entered by door-ways about five feet high and of the usual width, and they are closed by very weak and ill joined straw doors. Each inhabitant has several of these houses, and in his court-yard a little round store-house, made of earth and thatched with straw, in which provisions are kept. The villages in this part of the country are very dull and far from being so cheerful as those further southward. I was no longer amused by witnessing the dancing and merrimaking of the people.

On the 3rd of March, at sun-rise, we set out and proceeded five miles north-east. When we had advanced a mile and a half from Somou, we crossed a great marsh, where the water was knee-deep. In this marsh there are many fish and aquatic birds. In the direction of N. W. it forms a great lake and in the S. E. it is filled with high grass and weeds. We went seven miles further N. N. E. The soil, consisting of hard sand, was level and open. About noon, we arrived, much fatigued, at Kinana, a village containing about two hundred inhabitants, and surrounded by an infinite multitude of ronniers.

On the 4th of March, at ten in the morning, after proceeding two miles N. N. E. we turned to E. N. E., then again to N. N. E. having travelled altogether about ten miles. The aspect of the country was barren, being covered with volcanic stones and red gravel. About eleven o'clock we reached Kirina, a village surrounded by bombaces and baobabs, containing a population of about five or six hundred. The inhabitants are, for the most part, rope-makers. They sell their ropes to the caravans which pass through the country, and also take them to Jenné. They are used in making the canoes employed in the passage to Timbuctoo. Some of these ropes are made of hemp; but most of them of the bark of trees and of the leaves of the ronnier. Some claspknives were offered us for sale. They were tolerably well made, and it was the first time that I had seen any such articles in the interior. They were not of European manufacture; I presume therefore that they had been brought from Tafilet.

There were in the village some wells, twelve or thirteen feet deep: the soil in which they were dug was full of gravel and small pebbles. They contained good clear water.

On the fifth of March, at six in the morning, we left the village of Kirina, and advanced four miles N. E. over the same sort of soil as on the preceding day. We halted at Foudouca, another village, shaded by nédés and baobabs. Here we found provisions very dear. Foudouca contains about five or six hundred inhabitants, which is the average amount of the population of all the villages as far as Jenné. They are, as I have already mentioned, walled, though sometimes only partially; a village being occasionally composed of four or five little enclosures, in each of which reside several families. The wells are usually seven or eight feet deep.

At sun-rise on the 6th of March, we again set out and advanced six miles, first to N. E; and then to N. W. The soil still continued the same; but the country was more open than it had previously been. I saw many millet fields, which had been cultivated in the rainy season. Some of the stubble yet remained on the ground. About eleven in the forenoon we halted at Medina, the environs of which are well cultivated. The market is small, but well supplied. I saw in it some very fine fish both fresh and dry. The fresh fish, I was told, had been caught in the Dhioliba. It was about two feet and a half long and one in circumference. It had no scales, and the head was rather long. This fish had only one large bone and no small ones. I bought a piece for my supper and found it excellent. There is no better fish in Europe. I also saw in the market a great deal of lotus bread. It had a somewhat saccharine and acid taste, owing, to the fruit being gathered before it is ripe. It is very common in this part of the Soudan. The inhabitants sell it at Jenné, whence it is conveyed to Timbuctoo.

At six in the morning of the 7th of March, we pursued a N. E. direction. The soil continued the same as it had been, for several preceding days; I saw however some naucleas. At ten in the morning we halted at Courignan, a village situated in a plain covered with gravel, which nevertheless, is cultivated in the rainy season. As far as the eye can reach, nothing is to be seen but bushes at considerable distances from each other. Near the village there are some ronniers and bombaces. In the market, which is well supplied with necessaries, I saw some butchers. They skewer together bits of beef and suet, which, after being broiled or merely smoke-dried, they sell to their customers.

On the 8th of March, about seven in the morning, we prepared for departure. At the entrance of the village we were met by the butchers, who on the preceding evening had boiled the heads and feet of the animals which they had killed, and now offered them for sale to the people of the caravan. This detained us a little while, as we all bought something to eat before dinner, which we should not have till late. After advancing eight miles to the N. E. over a soil composed of hard, red sand, strewed with gravel, we crossed a marsh, choosing a narrow part which was dry, though it was flooded elsewhere. Rice is cultivated on the higher parts of this marsh, on which the negroes have constructed dikes to check the inundation. After crossing the marsh, we came to a large village, called Touma-dioman. We did not stop here, but proceeded five miles to the N. N. E. over a soil composed of hard sand, but less gravelly than it had been on the preceding days, and covered with mimosas, cés, nedés, and the *rhamnus lotus*. The road was thronged with people, travelling from village to village with various commodities, such as millet, cotton, dried fish, &c., and caravans of dealers in salt.

At the village of Touma-dioman there are two large ponds of muddy water, to which both men and beasts went to slake their thirst.

About one in the afternoon, we stopped at Manianan, a large village, with a well furnished market, in which the dealers are sheltered from the heat of the sun by small straw huts. The ronnier grows abundantly in the neighbourhood of this village, there many Iolas are settled: they are an artful, but industrious people, and devote themselves to trade and the manufacture of cotton cloth. Manianan is situated on an eminence, which is nearly surrounded by large ditches formed by nature, which serve as fortifications to the village. These ditches contain a great deal of water, which, though impure, is nevertheless drunk by the inhabitants. I saw several children in small canoes made of pieces of plank joined together, amusing themselves by paddling about in these ditches, on the edges of which the women of the village throw dirt and all sorts of filth. One of my fellow travellers bought an ass here, for which he paid eleven thousand cowries.

We started from Manianan at eight in the morning of the 9th of March. On leaving the village on the north side, I saw several huts built like those of the Foulah shepherds, and in the surrounding fields there were cattle, goats, sheep, and some asses. After proceeding three miles over a soil composed of loose sand, in which in many places the vegetation is similar to that which I had observed on the preceding day, we came in sight of Tomga, a village which, like Manianan, is surrounded by deep moats and numerous ronniers.

On the 10th of March, at six in the morning, we set out, proceeding two miles north and then three miles N. N. W. We crossed an inundated marsh, being up to our waists in water. Here I observed the blue and white nymphæa, the seed and root of which the natives use as food. In the marshes are to be seen a few small shrubs at great distances from each other. In many inundated places it was found necessary to unload the asses to get them through the water. The men took the loads on their heads, and it was only by supporting themselves with sticks that they could maintain their equilibrium.

About eleven in the morning, we arrived much fatigued at Galia (or Cougalia), situated on a slight elevation, on the bank of the Dhioliba. Galia is a hamlet consisting of five or six earth huts, and an equal number of straw cabins, of the same shape as those of the Foulahs. The neighbourhood, to some distance, is not inundated at this season. I saw many ronniers, and, on the bank of the river two large tamarind-trees, which serve to vary the uniformity of the landscape. In this little village are settled some Foulahs, whose business is to convey in canoes the numerous caravans going to Jenné. I found them very civil. I purchased from them a little milk, and some pistachios, for we could not procure either millet or rice for supper. In the evening, I saw several large canoes, descending the river on their way to Timbuctoo. The Dhioliba, which, in this party seems to come from W. ¼ N. W. flows slowly to N. E., its current running about a knot and a half an hour. The water was tolerably clear, but it had a whitish tint. The banks of the river are, for the most part, open and low, except before Cougalia, where they are somewhat high, and composed of grey argillaceous sand. Here and there, small veins of red clay are observable. At a little distance, in the direction of N. E. I perceived a small island, which, though dry at this season, is under water during the inundations of the river, which are periodical. The market of Cougalia, is held on the bank of the river, in the shade of two tamarind-trees. It was scantily supplied; but, fortunately, we had provisions with us. We bought some dried fish. Our caravan was so numerous, that we could not all find lodgings within the village. The greater part of my companions took up their quarters in tents, which were erected in the fields, and consisted of poles driven into the earth, and covered with pagnes.

CHAPTER XVIII

Crossing the Dhioliba — Abode at Jenné — Description of the town — Manners and customs of the inhabitants — Trade — English and French goods — Buildings — Population — Schools — Religion — Food and clothing — Geographical details — Course of the river — The Massina — Residence of the sherif of Jenné — A dinner — Use of tea, sugar and porcelain — Preparations for my departure for Timbuctoo.

On the morning of the 11th of March we prepared to leave Cougalia. We crossed the river in frail canoes, about thirty feet long and very narrow, made of a single trunk of the bombax. They were very inconvenient and every moment threatened to upset. However, we succeeded in getting the asses on board; for the river was too wide for them to swim across. I should imagine that its breadth in this part is five hundred feet, or two hundred and fifty ordinary paces. I thought it narrow in comparison with its width at Couroussa, in the country of Amana, which is much nearer to its source. At first, I supposed that what I saw at Cougalia was only an arm of the river, forming the island of Jenné. It is very deep, for in the middle our people were obliged to use oars, their poles not being long enough to reach the bottom. It was noon when we landed on the right bank, and several musket-shots were fired in token of rejoicing. The heat was intense. I walked a short distance along the bank of the river, where I saw many mimosas, of the same kind as that which grows in the water on the banks of the Senegal, and which is also very abundant in the interior. On inundated ground, however, it does not exceed the height of five feet. It is thorny, the branches are slender and the pod is hairy; it contracts its leaves on being touched.

On leaving the banks of the Dhioliba, we proceeded six miles W.N.W. We crossed a dry marsh, on which there was not a single tree to shade us. On this marsh rice is grown during the inundations. The ground consists of grey argillaceous earth, mixed with a good deal of sand and numerous veins of red clay, like that which I had seen on the banks of the Dhioliba. I observed several slaves who were engaged in agricultural labour. They used large hoes like those employed in the Wassoulo.

A little before we reached the island of Jenné, the soil changed to a hard sand, over which the inundation does not appear to extend. Some shrubs were growing upon it.

About half past two we arrived on the bank of a secondary branch of the Dhioliba, which comes from the north in this part, and forms the island on which is situated the town of Jenné. In fording it the water was up to our waists. Its current is very rapid, and its bed is wide and sandy. We saw a great number of traders crossing the water. They were coming from Jenné and returning to their respective countries with merchandise.

Having crossed this branch of the river, I thought myself on the island of Jenné, but, before we could reach the town, I found that we had to cross a second branch as deep as the other. After crossing the first branch we found ourselves at the extremity of a large island, separated by this marigot, and formed by an arm of the river, which branches off at Ségo and rejoins it at Isaca, a village situated at the distance of a day and a half's journey from Cougalia. Within this large island is situated the island of Jenné, which is surrounded by a secondary arm of the river. I saw in the port, many large canoes: some afloat waiting for their cargoes and others ashore, to undergo repair. I was astonished at the size of these canoes, of which I shall say more hereafter.

When we landed, there were several negroes assembled at the water-side. My guide addressed himself to one of them, a good-looking Mandingo, and asked him whether he could give us a lodging. He conducted us to his habitation, the outside of which was well enough, but the inside did not correspond with its external appearance. From consideration to me in my assumed character of an Arab, I was lodged in an upper room, where I should not be so much exposed to damp as in the lower part of the house. The room was exceedingly wretched and dirty. It might be about twelve feet long, five wide, and of a proportionate height. The floor, which consisted of planks of rough wood, was better made than any I have seen among the Bambaras. It was, however, very uneven, and covered with rubbish, a heap of which lay in one corner of the room, as the floor was undergoing repair. The only furniture the apartment contained was a mat spread upon the floor. The steps, which led from this room to the yard were of earth, and so narrow and steep as to be very dangerous to descend. My old guide and his people were lodged in the store-room on the ground-floor.

When we were fairly settled in our new abode, Kai-mou called together the master of the house and two or three old men who lived in the neighbourhood, to whom he related the circumstances which had occasioned my journey to Jenné. They listened to his story with great attention, and seemed to be much interested about me. On my expressing a wish to become acquainted with the Arabs who were settled in the town, and to place myself under their protection, they agreed to conduct me in the evening to sherif Sidy-Oulad-Marmou, a Moor of Tafilet, who was reputed to be very rich. This interview being ended, my old guide asked me to go up to my chamber; he ascended before me and seated himself on the mat. He began by congratulating me, and then addressed me in a long speech, in which he assured me that I ought to consider myself very fortunate, in having reached Jenné without experiencing any serious disaster or being ill-treated by the infidels. He said it was very astonishing that, considering my white colour, which was so strange to the people, I should have travelled over so large a tract of country without being robbed. He added that I was in a great measure indebted to him for my safety, and that he trusted I would reward him for his important services. He then paused and looked me stedfastly in the face, as much as to ask me what I thought of his speech. I saw that he wished to be paid without further delay, and I immediately gave him a pair of scissors, two yards of coloured calico, three sheets of paper, and a string of thirty red glass beads for his wives. In France these trifles might have been worth about five francs, but at Jenné their value was at least three times as great.

The old man had partly supplied me with provisions on my journey, for which I made him some little compensation by presents, consisting of bits of cloth. At all events, it would have been difficult to travel cheaper in Africa. Poor Kai-mou was however perfectly satisfied; indeed, my generosity seemed to have exceeded his expectations, and he joyfully overwhelmed me with blessings. I wished to go immediately to the Arab sherif; but he insisted on my staying to dine with him, observing that, next day we should have time enough to go and see the Moor, to whom he promised to speak in my behalf. He ordered one of his women to buy some fresh fish and rice, to make amends for our bad living the few preceding days. Our host, who was already prepossessed in my favour, came to accompany me to the mosque, to attend the six o'clock prayer. I saw there several Moors, all of whom were very well dressed. They took no notice of me.

On my return home my guide sent for me, and we sat down together with his people in the middle of the yard, to partake of a supper which we found exceedingly savoury, for it was seasoned with salt. I did not pass a very tranquil night, owing to my anxiety respecting the reception I might experience from my new countrymen.

On the 12th of March, about eight o'clock in the morning, my guide and I went to visit the Moors. Our host, by whom we were accompanied, went first to call on one of his friends. He entered the house and left us at the door, where we remained at least an hour. I was, at first, rather uneasy at this strange conduct, but was afterwards informed that the people of the house were at their breakfast. When the repast was ended, they came to invite us in, and gave to each of us half a colat-nut. After this they presented to us a calabash of couscous, which they had had the politeness to set aside for us. The want of lalo (the bruised leaf of the baobab which is put into the couscous) rendered it very unpalatable. They put on the top of the couscous some bones which they had themselves been gnawing. We afterwards went all together to the sherif. As I was passing through the market, which appeared to be abundantly supplied with all kinds of merchandise, I was accosted by a well-dressed negro. The man knew by my countenance and by my tattered dress that I was a stranger. He asked me whence I had come and who I was. He told me that he himself was a native of Adrar. As my companions were going on first, we had not time for further conversation, and I saw no more of the man. On reaching the sherif's house, which was near the market-place, I saw four Moors sitting in the street upon a mat and some little round cushions, made of badly tanned sheep-skin with the wool still remaining on it. One of them, a man of about forty, was much whiter than myself.

My companions, without any ceremony, told them who I was and whence I had come, adding that my resources were exhausted and that I appealed to them for hospitality. Their astonishment was extreme. They gazed at me with curiosity and said one to another: *Aich kount hadé?* (what means this?) I saluted them: they returned my salutation and gave me their hands. They then again asked me who I was. I told them as well as I could, for I spoke their language very imperfectly, that I was an Arab and a native of Alexandria. I added that my father, a zealous Musulman and a very rich merchant, had ships like those of the christians; that I had been made prisoner when very young by the French; but that I had escaped from them, with the determination of returning to my country and embracing the religion of my fathers; that I was almost destitute, and had come to claim their protection to enable me to reach Timbuctoo, whence I should proceed to Alexandria, my native city. They paid great attention to all that I said; but they did not appear to be quite convinced of the truth of my story. They observed that Alexandria lay to the east, and that I had come from the west, and they asked me how I had effected my escape from among the christians. Fortunately, I was prepared with an answer: I related a long story in which I said that the christians, having captured me at Alexandria, conveyed me to their country, which is in the north; that they had educated me, and that when I grew up, the christian to whom I belonged took me with him on board a ship, which, after two months' voyage, brought us to the coast of the negro country. "The whites," continued I, "possess little villages on the coast, where they have commercial establishments, in one of which I remained a considerable time. I had the care of a store-house and my master who regarded me as his son, reposed entire confidence in me. Profiting by my continual intercourse with the Foulahs, I endeavoured to learn their language, and, after communicating to some of them the secret of my birth, I was induced by their reiterated entreaties to leave the christians and to retire to their country; but before I attempted to execute this plan I wished to earn money sufficient to defray the expenses of my long journey. This object I at length attained, and one night I made my escape with some Foulahs, who conducted me to the Fouta-Dhialon, where I was presented to the king of that country."

I closed my narrative by a pompous eulogium on the sovereign of the Fouta, mentioning in high terms of praise his generosity and his zeal for the religion of Mahomet. My story appeared plausible enough, and its veracity was no longer doubted. Having left my country so young, there appeared nothing extraordinary in my being imperfectly acquainted with its language. I also mentioned that what little Arabic I knew had been picked up on my journey. The Moors asked me numerous questions about the christians and the way in which they had treated me. They all inquired whether I had been beaten and treated like a slave; whether I had been prevented from praying; and whether I had eaten pork and drunk brandy. I answered that the christians were a humane people; that they treated their prisoners kindly, but that they did not tolerate among them the exercise of the Mahometan religion,[61] in which," said I, "they place no more faith, than we do in christianity." On hearing this they all exclaimed: *Allah akbar!* (great God!) "What! did you not pray among the christians?" continued they. "No; I left my country so young that I had not learned our prayers, and the christians of course did not teach me them." — "But did you not pray when you were in the Soudan with the Mahometan Foulahs!" "Yes, but I took care not to be observed." "Did you sometimes pray to the prophet?" — "I did so internally."

When I confessed that I had eaten pork and drunk brandy they were all horror-struck and exclaimed in Arabic: "Ah! great God, why did you do that!" — "Because," replied I, "my master obliged me." I observed that, had I been willing to continue such a life, I should have remained among the christians; but that it was to avoid the commission of such heinous sins, that I had undertaken my long and perilous journey. "He is right; he speaks truly," they then repeated, looking at each others. Among other questions, I was asked whether it was true that the christians eat their slaves. This absurd question was not asked by the Moors of Tafilet, who appeared tolerably well informed, but, by some roving Moors, who happened to be passing by and stopped, out of curiosity, to hear our conversation. The Moors of Tafilet looked at them with an air of contempt and superiority, and told them that the whites were not cannibals. Those who had asked the question laughed too, and I suppose they had been merely joking. I informed them that the Europeans had no slaves now. They asked me why? "Because," replied I, "they say that men are all equal in the eye of God, and that there ought to be no slavery." They admitted that this was very true, and that it was very fine for the christians to think so. "But why," continued they "were you detained as a slave?" I replied that I was not detained, and that if I had remained in France until the end of the war, I might, like others of my countrymen, have returned home, but, being in the Soudan with the christian, my master, the latter, who had no child, regarded me as his son and would not part with me. "His fortune," added I, "could not tempt me. I despised it when I thought of a future life and the paradise of Mahomet." They congratulated me on these praiseworthy feelings. They questioned me about the food of the christians, in what direction they turn the heads of the bullocks and sheep which they slaughter, whether they knock the animal down or cut its throat, whether the christians eat with their fingers, and sit on the ground. I should fill whole pages were I to repeat all the questions that were put to me.

When the examination was ended, the sherif desired the negro, my host, to conduct me to the chief of Jenné. Thither we went, still accompanied by my guide. We entered the little corridor of a mean-looking house, and were desired to wait in the first room we entered, where many other persons were likewise waiting for an audience. A bullock's hide was brought for us to sit upon. At the extremity of the corridor, there was a door, which opened upon an inner staircase, leading to the first story. On my being announced, the chief came down stairs and seated himself at the foot of the staircase, the door still remaining closed. The chief did not speak Arabic, and he desired that I should be asked whether I understood the Mandingo language.

The man who stood guard at the door repeated the answer in a loud voice, to enable the chief (who I suppose was somewhat deaf) to hear. He then requested to know whether I spoke the Bambara language. One of the Moors, whom I had seen with the sherif, now joined me. On his being announced, the door of the staircase was immediately opened, and all present had the gratification of seeing this mysterious chief. He was advanced in years, very fat, almost blind, and very simply dressed. The Moor eagerly advanced, and giving him his hand by way of salutation, told me to do the same; I immediately did so. It was a distinction of which I was not a little proud, for it is not granted to every one. The Moor again informed the chief what my intentions were; he added that, being very poor I threw myself on his hospitality. The chief, after listening attentively, said that until an opportunity should occur for my going to Timbuctoo, on my way to my native country, I should remain with the sherif who, as a rich man and a descendant of the Prophet, would take care that I should be well treated. Before I left him, this negro chief requested that I would myself repeat the story I had related in the morning, which I briefly did, the Moor who had joined acting as interpreter. Of all the Moors whom I had seen during the morning, the sherif had given me the coolest reception. The chief sent one of his people to conduct me to the residence of my new host, and I returned among my new countrymen, whose presence had at first somewhat alarmed me. I fancied that they could all read in my countenance the deception which I was practising upon them; but fortunately this was not the case. The man who accompanied me communicated the commands of the chief to the sherif, who replied that he was very ready to obey them. He made me sit down on the ground beside him, and he and the Moors who were, with him repeated all the questions which they had put to me before. The sherif appeared to be a man of greater consequence than the rest. He spoke but little, and retired into his house apparently not very well pleased at being burthened with me. He said nothing to me, but put a few questions to the Moors, who repeated them to me.

A numerous concourse collected around us; but it gradually dispersed, and at length I was left alone with the two Moors, who were very sociable. One of them, who was named Al-Haggi-Mohammed, called one of his slaves, gave her some cowries, and sent her to purchase four small loaves or cakes of rice, together with some butter and honey. She mixed the butter and honey well together, and then brought it to us in a neat pewter dish of European manufacture. The Haggi-Mohammed ordered her to carry it into a corridor on the first floor, and then requested me to go up to breakfast. I ate but little, and, when I went down to thank him for his attention, he begged that I would lie down and rest, saying that I must be much fatigued after my long journey. He conducted me into a house, which served the two-fold purpose of a lodging for his slaves and a magazine for his merchandise. He cleared out a little corridor, and, having ordered a mat to be spread upon the floor, told me that this was to be my chamber. He had a better house, in which he himself resided with his children. My umbrella attracted his attention; he asked me to let him see it: he opened and shut it several times and showed it to those about him. He called the sherif and shewed it to him. The sherif appeared to be a connoisseur in curiosities of this kind, and he admired it exceedingly; many negroes stopped to look at it, and seemed utterly lost in amazement. I told the Moor that I had brought with me some other luggage. He desired me to go and fetch it, and sent a person to conduct me. I went to the residence of my old guide to get my baggage, which I had left in my chamber; as there was no door to it, I might have had reason to repent this imprudence; but, fortunately, I found every thing as I had left it. Kai-mou asked me if I was pleased with my new hosts, for I had two. I replied in the affirmative. On my return to my lodging, the Haggi-Mohammed asked me what there was in my bag; he advised me if I had merchandise to sell it before my departure, as I should not dispose of it so advantageously at Timbuctoo, all the goods that are sold at Jenné being brought from that city.

I took my bag to my new lodging and opened it in order to prepare for the visit which I expected to receive from the Moors; I laid aside the money which I had in my girdle, and mixed my notes in pencil with some leaves of the Koran, so that, in case my portfolio should be opened the papers might be taken for a book of prayers. In the event of the notes being discovered, I had determined to say that they contained a narrative of the events which had occurred to me during my abode among the christians, which I wished to communicate to my family. But, in spite of all these precautions, I was not without anxiety. I took a view of the house in which I was to reside for some days. The first story consisted of several galleries, similar to those in which I was lodged, two small closets containing earthen vessels filled with water, a dirty water-closet, and a little court level with this floor, which received light only on this side. The ground-floor, which was distributed in the same way, consisted of store-rooms for rice and millet, and a stable for a horse. These store-rooms received light partly from a second court behind the house, and partly from a grated opening in the court of the first story. The gallery which I occupied was the most convenient and the cleanest apartment of the whole. Two staircases led up to it. They were made of earth, but were much better and more solid than that of the chamber which I occupied on my first arrival at Jenné. One of these staircases led to the entrance door, and the other to the lower court. Some of the Haggi-Mohamed's store-rooms which were filled with sacks of merchandise, were fastened with padlocks of European manufacture.

The court on the first story was partly roofed at the four corners. Pieces of wood, resting on the walls at little intervals from each other and covered with earth, formed a sort of terrace with a parapet running round it. On this terrace, to which there was an ascent of about ten steps, the Moors and even the negroes were accustomed to take their supper.

About noon a female slave brought me a large dish of very good rice, seasoned with meat and small onions.

The latter thrive well every where in the neighbourhood of Jenné. The Haggi-Mohammed came to inquire after my health. As I had eaten only a small portion of what he sent to me, he supposed that I was ill. He desired me to make myself easy; for now that I was among the Moors I should want nothing, and with the grace of God I should soon return to my country. Then sitting down beside me, he asked me what I should do when I went home, as I did not know my parents. I told him that at first I should be somewhat at a loss. "But," said I, "if you had a son among strangers, should you forget him?"—"Certainly not," replied he.—"Neither will my father forget me. When I get to Alexandria I shall find him out; and, even if both my parents are dead, I have a brother who will surely know me again." As I was very ill with severe cold, he procured, at my request, some dry gombo and had it boiled with honey. This, I found to relieve me very much. The cold affected my chest and I was quite hoarse, which was very inconvenient to me, having to answer so many questions.

I mentioned to the Haggi-Mohammed my wish to repay the cowries which he had expended on my account. He refused to accept payment, and desired me to purchase nothing, observing that I had only to ask for whatever I might want, and he would supply it. He sent for a barber to shave my head. This man was an expert operator; he did not hurt me in the least, though I certainly expected to suffer under his hands. The handle of his razor was made according to the fashion of the country, but the blade which was of European manufacture, was good. The barbers carry their razors in a small copper sheath. They do not use soap; a forbearance for which I was grateful, for the smell of all the soap that I met with in the country was extremely offensive: they merely wash the head with cold water. After resuming my turban, I paid a visit to the market; I was surprised at the number of the people I saw there. It is well supplied with all the necessaries of life, and is constantly crowded by a multitude of strangers and the inhabitants of the neighbouring villages, who attend it to sell their produce, and to purchase salt and other commodities. There are several rows of dealers both male and female.

Some erect little palisades of straw, to protect themselves from the excessive heat of the sun; over these they throw a pagne and thus form a small hut. Their goods are laid out in little baskets, placed on large round panniers.

In going round the market, I observed some shops pretty well stocked with European commodities, which sell at a very high price. There was a great variety of cotton goods, printed muslins, calicoes, scarlet cloth, hardware, flints, &c. Nearly the whole of these articles appeared to be of English manufacture. I saw however some French muskets, which are much esteemed. Among the other articles on sale, were glass trinkets, false amber, false coral, sulphur in sticks, and gunpowder which, I was informed, is manufactured in the country. I am not acquainted with the materials of which their powder is made, but it appears that they are pounded together in a mortar moistened with water. They form this powder into lumps of the size of a man's fist, which they dry in the sun. The purchasers allow it to remain in the same state until they are going to use it, when they crush it and put it in a powder-horn. When they load their muskets with home-made powder, they use a much greater quantity than they would think necessary of the European kind, which they value far more highly. Their powder produces but a weak explosion; it sometimes issues from the musket like a fusee, without any report.

While descending the Dhioliba to Tercy, I saw at a village a large calabash full of saltpetre which appeared very fine, but I cannot tell how the people procured it. I questioned a Moor, who merely replied: "It is powder," and I could learn nothing more about it. The dealers in colat-nuts occupy one end of the market. They are ranged in two rows, with each a small pannier of colats before him, which they sell retail at the rate of eight or ten cowries a-piece. The low price proves the great abundance of this fruit in the country; but the usual price is from fifteen to twenty cowries.

There are also butchers in the market, who lay out their meat much in the same way as their brethren in Europe. They also thrust skewers through little pieces of meat, which they smoke-dry and sell retail. Great quantities of fish, fresh as well as dried, are brought to this market, in which are also to be had earthen pots, calabashes, mats, and salt; but the salt in the market is only sold retail; that which is sold wholesale is kept in the warehouses.

There are great numbers of hawkers in the streets, who cry the goods which they carry about with them, as in Europe. They sell stuffs made in the country, cured provisions, colat-nuts, honey, vegetable and animal butter, milk and fire-wood. The last article, which is scarce, is brought by women from the distance of twelve or fifteen miles round. Millet straw is sold in the market and during my residence in this town, I saw, every evening, negresses purchasing each a certain quantity for ten cowries to cook their suppers: the ordinary faggots cost one hundred and twenty cowries, which are equal to twelve sous. Fortunately, this is not a cold country.

The Moors of Jenné do not keep shops. They employ confidential agents, or even slaves, to sell goods on their account. It is their custom to sit on mats before their doors, with some cakes of salt placed beside them, and in this way they wait for customers to buy their goods, or others who may wish to sell. Thus they accumulate, without giving themselves much trouble, great quantities of ivory, gold, rice, millet, honey, raw wax, cured provisions, and heaps of small onions. These articles they deposit in their store-houses, whence they forward them to Timbuctoo, where they have correspondents, who send them in exchange salt, tobacco, and European merchandise.

There are also marabouts among the negroes of Jenné, but the trade they carry on is not so considerable. The article they deal in are seldom of great value, but consist chiefly of the zambalas, tamarinds, pimento, long pepper, leaves and fruit of the baobab, gombos, leaves and fruit of Guinea sorrel, pistachios, beans, and a number of small articles which are brought at Jenné by the people of the caravans. They also send to Timbuctoo calabashes and earthen pots for culinary purposes. The wax purchased at Jenné is used for candles, which are made without moulds and generally consumed through the country. Quantities are sent to Timbuctoo, where there is a great demand for them.

The Moorish merchants resident in Jenné, about thirty or forty in number, occupy the best houses, which have besides the advantage of being situated near the market. The principal trade of the place is in their hands. They form companies of several partners, and are owners of large barges, which carry cargoes of native produce to Timbuctoo.

Jenné was called by the early travellers *the Land of Gold*. However, that metal is not produced in the environs, but it is frequently brought to Jenné by the Mandingoes of the Kong country and the merchants of Bouré. It forms a principal branch of commerce for these rich traders. They also deal in slaves, whom they send to Tafilet, and to other quarters, as Mogador, Tunis, and Tripoli. I have seen men leading these unfortunate beings about the streets, and crying them for sale at the rate of twenty-five, thirty, or forty thousand cowries, according to their age. I was grieved to see such an insult offered to human nature. Such of these poor creatures as I observed at Jenné in the families of Moors, who all keep a considerable number of them, are not the most to be pitied; they are well fed, well clothed, and not hard worked. Their lot would be preferable to that of the peasantry of some countries of Europe, if any thing could compensate for the loss of liberty. In general they become confidential servants, who take care of the house in the absence of the master, or pack the merchandise and ship it. I remarked that these masters often gave them cowries to purchase what they liked. It was pleasing to witness conduct so well calculated to promote fidelity adopted towards them. They are indeed entrusted with whole sacks of cowries to count, without any apprehension of their stealing them.

The town of Jenné is about two miles and half in circumference; it is surrounded by a very ill constructed earth wall, about ten feet high, and fourteen inches thick. There are several gates, but they are small. The houses are built of bricks dried in the sun. The sand of the isle of Jenné is mixed with a little clay, and it is employed to make bricks of a round form which are sufficiently solid. The houses are as large as those of European villages. The greater part have only one story, like Haggi-Mohammed's, which I have already described. They are all terraced, have no windows externally, and the apartments receive no air except from an inner court. The only entrance, which is of ordinary size, is closed by a door made of wooden planks, pretty thick, and apparently sawed. The door is fastened on the inside by a double iron chain, and on the outside by a wooden lock made in the country. Some however have iron locks. The apartments are all long and narrow. The walls, especially the outer, are well plastered with sand, for they have no lime. In each house there is a staircase leading to the terrace; but there are no chimneys, and consequently the slaves cook in the open air. The streets are not straight, but they are broad enough for a country in which no carriages are used; eight or nine persons may walk in them abreast; they are kept in good order, being swept almost daily. The environs of Jenné are marshy and entirely destitute of trees. Some clumps of ronniers are however seen on slight elevations at very remote distances. Before the rains set in, the plains receive some tillage, and are all sown with rice, which grows with the increase of the water of the river; the slaves are the cultivators of this grain. There was also on the banks of the river some gombo, tobacco, and giraumons. I was told that in the rainy season they grow cabbage, carrots, and European turnips, the seed of which is brought from Tafilet. In the marshes is found a kind of forage, which is cut and dried for the cattle. In places not exposed to the inundation they cultivate only millet and maize. The town of Jenné is full of bustle and animation; every day numerous caravans of merchants are arriving and departing with all kinds of useful productions. In Jenné there is a mosque built of earth, surmounted by two massive but not high towers; it is rudely constructed, though very large. It is abandoned to thousands of swallows, which build their nests in it. This occasions a very disagreeable smell, to avoid which, the custom of saying prayers in a small outer court has become common. In the environs of the mosque, to which I often went, I always observed a number of beggars, reduced to mendicity by old age, blindness, or other infirmities.

The town is shaded by some boababs, mimosas, date-trees, and ronniers. I remarked another kind of tree, the name of which, I do not know.

The population of Jenné included a number of resident strangers, as Mandingoes, Foulahs, Bambaras, and Moors. They speak the languages peculiar to their respective countries, besides a general dialect called *Kissour*, which is the language currently adopted as far as Timbuctoo. The number of the inhabitants may be computed at eight or ten thousand. This town was formerly independent, but it now belongs to a small kingdom, of which Ségo-Ahmadou is the sovereign. He is a Foulah, and a fanatical Musulman, but a great conqueror. With a very small number of followers, he has subdued several districts in the south of Bambara, where he has introduced his religion and enforces obedience. Jenné was his capital; but this zealous disciple of the prophet, finding that the great trade of that town interfered with his religious duties, and drew aside the true believers from their devotions, founded another town on the right bank of the river. He named it *el-Lamdou-Lillahi* (to the praise of God), the first words of a prayer in the Koran. At this place there are public schools in which children are taught gratuitously. There are also schools for adults, according to the degrees of their information. This devout chief is brother to the king of Massina, a country situated on the left bank of the Dhioliba.

Ségo-Ahmadou does not levy contributions on the merchants who resort to Jenné for the purpose of trade. Foreign merchants settled in the country are not subject to taxes any more than natives; but they send presents to the king, as well as to his brother, the chief of Jenné. I had often heard Ségo-Ahmadou extolled for his generosity; but the Moors told me that he was generous only to his own subjects. The inhabitants of Jenné are exceedingly active and industrious, and very much like the savage negroes I had seen in the south. In short, they are intelligent men, who speculate on the labour of their slaves; while, among the free-men, the rich devote themselves to commerce, and the poor to various trades and professions. At Jenné, there are tailors who make clothes which are sent to Timbuctoo; smiths, founders, masons, shoemakers, porters, packers and fishermen: every one renders himself useful in some way or other. Mats, made of the leaves of the ronnier, are used for packing up goods; they are manufactured by the inhabitants of the neighbouring villages, who sell them in the market. This matting is covered with a second envelope, consisting of a bullock's hide; that is to say, if the goods are worth it. The smiths are no better provided with tools than those I saw on the road: they execute the same work with the same scanty means. It is the business of the packers to sack the grain, and, in order to force as much as possible into the bag, they press it down with a piece of wood. When their bag is full, they put a handful of straw above the millet, and sew the bag. This is much more secure than simple packing.

All the inhabitants of Jenné are Mahometans. They do not permit infidels to enter their town, and when the Bambara people come to Jenné, they are obliged to repeat the Mahometan prayers, otherwise they would be unmercifully beaten by the Foulahs, who form the majority of the population. I found the inhabitants very civil to strangers, at least to those of their own religion; and they put traders in the way of disposing of their goods.

They have several wives, whom, however they do not ill-treat, like the negroes further to the south. The women never go out unveiled, and are not allowed to eat their meals with their husbands, or even with their male children. The girls, when they attain a suitable age, assist their mothers in cooking, washing and other household business. They occupy their leisure moments in spinning cotton, which they buy in the market, for in the marshy environs of the city it is not cultivated; however, on the west side, I saw a little field of cotton surrounded by a thorn hedge. It appeared to be of very inferior quality, and does not thrive well.

The people of Jenné know no other writing than that of the Arabs: almost all can read, though few understand it. There are schools for youth, like those which I have already described. After the children have learned every thing that is taught in these schools, they are sent to El-Lamdou-Lilahi; and when they know the Koran by heart, they are looked upon as learned men: they then return to their native places, and enter into trade.

The inhabitants of Jenné live very well: they eat rice boiled with fresh meat, which is to be procured every day in the market. With the fine millet they make couscous; this is eaten with fresh or dried fish, of which they have great abundance. Their dishes are highly seasoned; they use a good deal of allspice, and salt is common enough to enable every one to get it. The expense of maintenance for a single individual is about twenty-five or thirty cowries per day. Meat is not dear in this place; a piece which costs forty cowries (twenty centimes), is enough to furnish a dinner for four persons. They generally make two meals a day; all sitting round one dish, and each taking out a portion with his hand, like all the inhabitants of the interior.

Their houses are not furnished. They have leather bags in which they put their things; these bags are sometimes hung to a line put up across the apartment. The people always sleep on bullocks' hides, or mats, spread upon the ground. Hence they are very subject to rheumatic complaints, owing to the extreme dampness of the soil; for they cannot keep fires during the night on account of the scarcity of wood. The children, as well as grown persons, are very neatly dressed. They wear a coussabe made of cloth of the Soudan, generally white, which is the favourite colour; their trowsers reach to the ancle, and are not so full as those worn by the Mandingoes in the south; they have a hem at the waist in which is run a cotton string that ties above the hips. The Mandingo traders buy these trowsers and carry them to their country: I saw them at Sambatikila, Timé, and Tangrera. The people of Jenné never go barefoot, not even the children of the slaves. Their shoes, which are very neatly made, ressemble our European slippers; they have them of various colours. Their shoemakers use no lasts they get thin leather from Timbuctoo, whither it is brought by the Moors from Morocco. I saw no tanners in Jenné.

The most elegant head-dress worn in this place is a red cap, round which a large piece of muslin is rolled in the form of a turban. Men of inferior rank, like the saracolets, wear caps made in the country. The dress of the women consists of a coussabe with a pagne under it, I saw several females with sandals. They plat their hair and wear necklaces of glass, amber, coral, and gold ear-rings. Some also wear about the neck plates of that metal which are made in the country. I saw some with nose-rings; they all have their noses pierced, and those who are not rich enough to buy a ring have a piece of pink silk in its stead. They wear silver bracelets of a round form, and their ancles are encircled by flat rings of plated iron, four inches broad, which cover them completely.

The price of an ordinary coussabe of cloth of native manufacture is two thousand cowries; a pair of trowsers costs one thousand, and a pair of slippers three hundred. They are to be had either cheaper or dearer, according to the variety of form or colour. The Moors have magazines well supplied with European merchandise; such as white Guinea cloth, (for they have but little blue) calico, scarlet cloth, paper, muskets, powder, hardware, needles, silk, and sulphur. They sell all these things wholesale. They have also white sugar and tea; but it is only the very rich who can afford such luxuries. I was pleased to find at Jenné that one might use a pocket-handkerchief without being ridiculed; for the inhabitants themselves use it, whereas, in the countries through which I had previously passed, it would have been dangerous to suffer such a thing to be seen. A cake of salt, of the dimensions which I have described in a former part of this volume, costs ten, fifteen, or even twenty thousand cowries, according to the scarcity or abundance of the article; there are smaller cakes, which cost seven or eight thousand cowries.

The Moorish merchants derive considerable profit from their trade in salt. They have great influence over the negroes who give them credit for being richer than they really are. The poor Mandingo traders, after travelling for two months with loads of colat-nuts on their heads, are obliged to go through the streets of Jenné to sell them; for, being merely articles of luxury, they are not easily disposed of. It is true that a great many are consumed in the neighbourhood of Jenné and on the banks of the river as far as Timbuctoo; but the quantity which is brought from the south is immense, and they are consequently sold at eight or ten cowries each. Certainly at that price the poor Mandingoes can gain nothing; for the expenses incurred on their journey and during the time they stay at Jenné, the fares across the rivers, the passage-duties in the villages, and the requisite presents, absorb all their profits. The cowries obtained by the sale of their colats are appropriated to the purchase of salt, which cannot be bought with their merchandise.

As there are no inns in this country, the strangers are obliged to lodge in the houses of private persons, whom they pay in merchandise. They buy wood in the market for their cooking, and as provisions are dear in the town, they send their slaves to the neighbouring villages, where it is procured somewhat cheaper. The fishermen catch many small carp in the surrounding villages. They dry them by laying them on straw and then setting fire to it. This fish is bought by the poor people.

Ségo-Ahmadou, the chief of Jenné, maintains an active war against the Bambaras of Ségo, whom he wishes to subject to the standard of the prophet; but the Bambaras who are a warlike race, resist him. This war is very injurious to the trade of Jenné, because it interrupts all communications with Yamina, Sansanding, Bamako, and Bouré, whence the gold is brought which is circulated in the interior. The town of Jenné can no longer be considered as the central point of commerce. Yamina, Sansanding, and Bamako are, in reality, the entrepôts: those places are visited by trading Moors from all parts of the desert, and by the negroes of the Soudan, from Kong to Galam, Bondou, and the Fouta-Dhialon. Jenné cannot enjoy the same advantage on account of its distance from Bouré. Previously to the war, small canoes used to go from Jenné to Bouré, and return laden with gold. The merchants of Jenné suffer considerably by this war; but they are afraid to complain openly: indeed, they would not better themselves if they did. Several negroes informed me that since the war the Moors are forsaking this town, and taking up their abode at Sansanding.

I often went up to the terrace of the house in which I lodged. As far as the eye could reach, the country was open and marshy; there were to be seen a few clumps of ronniers at a great distance and some tamarind-trees on the most elevated parts of the banks of the river. To the west I could distinctly see a branch of the Dhioliba, which appeared tolerably large. I was told that it came from the neighbourhood of Ségo, and that that town was five days' journey west, or rather S. S. W. of Jenné. This branch, as I have already said, rejoins the river at Isaca. The island on which the town of Jenné is situated is formed by an arm of this branch, which comes from W. N. W. The island is about twelve or fifteen miles in circumference. I did not go round it, but that appeared to be its extent from my point of view. This secondary arm, or branch, is wide but rather shallow. On the north, of the town it cannot be crossed but in canoes; in other places it may be forded; when the water is low it is navigable for small canoes only, for its bed is full of sand-banks and the inhabitants are obliged to push their large empty canoes down nearly to the river, where the branch is navigable at all times. Thither the merchandise is conveyed in small canoes: this is a long and toilsome process, but the traders are not obliged to hire hands, having their own slaves to do the work. During inundations the branch is easily navigable for large canoes. Round the town I saw a great many canoes undergoing repair.

Jenné is situated in the eastern part of the island, on an elevation of seven or eight feet, which preserves it from the periodical inundations of the river. Its soil is composed of red argillaceous earth, mixed with a great deal of grey sand, among which I saw not a single stone.

Old Kai-mou, my guide, came to pay me a visit; he had been purchasing a fine cotton wrapper of the manufacture of the country. It consisted of narrow breadths sewed together like the pagnes. These wrappers are much esteemed by the negroes, who are very chilly; the Moors do not wear them: they have better which come from Morocco. My guide told me that he had not yet found purchasers for his colats. I asked him to go with me to Timbuctoo, where he could dispose of them more advantageously. He laughed at this, and said he should spend all he possessed before he got thither: I gave him some glass beads and he left me in good humour.

I conversed every day with the Moors, who, as I perceived, regarded the negroes as a race very inferior to themselves. They often used to say to me: "The negroes are ignorant brutes; when they see a Moor they think he is entirely covered with gold, however poor he may be. They imagine that we have gold between our skin and flesh."

At the distance of three days' journey N. W. of Jenné is situated the kingdom of Massina, inhabited by Mahometan Foulahs; almost all of them wear their hair in small tresses.

They often come to Jenné for the purposes of trade, and sell oxen and sheep for the daily consumption of the town. Their sheep are the finest that I have seen in the interior; they are large and have wool like those of Europe. The fleece is used for making wrappers, which sell at very good prices. These Foulahs also bring milk and butter to Jenné. Massina is very productive in rice, millet, pistachios, water-melons, giraumons, and onions. The inhabitants rear a good deal of poultry, and have a fine breed of horses. Every Moor on the island has his own horse. Massina is governed by a king, who is the brother and ally of Ségo-Ahmadou.

The dress of the people is the same as that worn by the inhabitants of Jenné, with the exception of the piece of muslin in the form of a turban. The men of Massina whom I saw had round straw hats with broad brims, and were armed with bows and arrows, and three or four javelins which they always carry in their hands. They sometimes go out without their bows and arrows; but never without their lances.

As I was one day sitting before my door with some Moors, several Foulahs stopped to look at me. They seemed very gentle, and were apparently much interested about me. One of them, perceiving a friend at a little distance, called him, and told him he would give him ten cowries. I was much astonished to see a man call to his comrade in the street, for the purpose of offering him so trifling a present. The man to whom the money was offered did not seem to be in want of it, yet he received it very gratefully. Ten cowries are of about the value of a French sou.

As I had been informed that I should depart for Timbuctoo, by the first opportunity, I selected some articles of merchandise, which I wished, to dispose of at Jenné. Not knowing their value, I gave them to the sherif and the Haggi-Mohammed to sell for me. They carefully counted the glass beads, and measured the cloth in my presence, and the sherif noted down the quantities of each on a hit of paper. They executed this commission very well: they were to be sure the principal gainers by it, for they bought the greatest part of the things themselves. Before the bargain was concluded, they did indeed ask me whether I was satisfied with the price they had offered. I was aware that it was too low; but I readily gave my consent to all they proposed, feeling that I was in a situation in which I might need their services. They certainly took advantage of me, but they were merchants who bought merely upon speculation. The Haggi-Mohammed, thinking that I had some other things in reserve, came to my lodging, and tried to prevail on me to shew him the contents of my bag. He asked me whether I had any gold or silver, observing that he should be very glad to hear that I had some, as it would enable me to support myself on my journey home. I assured him that I had none left, and emptied my bag in his presence, having previously taken the precaution of hiding my papers and money, for I expected that I should have to undergo this scrutiny. He saw some glass beads, amber, and coral, which I had reserved, and he again told me that as all those things were brought to Jenné from Timbuctoo, it would be advisable for me to dispose of them before I set out. I at first scrupled to do this, but at length yielded to his urgent solicitations. He particularly admired the amber, all of which he bought at two hundred cowries per bead, (twenty-two French sous), one-fourth of its value at Sierra-Leone, where I had purchased it. He bought part of the coral at a still lower rate; but the glass ornaments and cloth, though they fetched a low price, I sold more advantageously. For sixty coral beads, (No. 4,) he offered me two hundred cowries. On my declining to sell them at that price, he took them up, and putting them into the pocket of his coussabe, said, "I will give you a thousand cowries, (one gourde.).

In this manner he extorted my consent, though I am certain that had I insisted on it he would have returned them. The traders of Jenné obtain mock amber and coral from Timbuctoo, which they sell at very low prices. Haggi-Mohammed, who was very well satisfied with his bargain, gave me half a dozen dates, and shortly afterwards presented me with a very neat white coussabe, made of cloth of native manufacture.

In truth I stood greatly in need of it, for my own was absolutely in tatters. He also gave me about two yards of the cloth of the country to roll round my head in the form of a turban.

During my stay at Jenné I was very kindly treated by the Moors. I paid nothing for my maintenance, and was provided with every thing I could wish for. The sale of my merchandise was the only thing of which I had reason to complain. I often sat in company with the Moors, upon a mat which was laid down in the shade before the door, and saw them make their purchases. I also observed many negroes, who, as they passed the sherif, saluted him by kissing their hands. The latter gave them cowries from a little bag, which he kept beside him for that purpose. A young Moor, named Hassan, who was very attentive to me, advised me, when I should get to Timbuctoo, to take the road to Tafilet or Fez, whence I could go to Algiers and afterwards to Alexandria. He informed me that there had been at Timbuctoo a christian, who had been attacked and beaten on the road; that he remained a long time at Timbuctoo to recover, but that he afterwards died, he could not tell how. I asked him what could have induced a christian to go to Timbuctoo: he answered that it was only to *write the country*, (*Jektoub torab*.) I concluded that this christian was Major Laing, who I was aware had left Tripoli to proceed to the capital of the Soudan, by crossing the great desert. I deplored the unhappy death of the intrepid traveller, and reflected that in case of my disguise being discovered I should in all probability share the same fate.

At four o'clock on the 16th, I was requested to wait on the sherif Oulad-Marmou, to whose good graces the sale of my merchandise had somewhat recommended me. I was shewn into a large lofty room on the ground-floor, which was lighted from an opening in the ceiling. To one part of the ceiling was attached a cord, supporting a lamp, in which vegetable butter was burned by way of oil. A mattress was laid upon the floor above a mat; a brass candlestick of European manufacture, in which was a sort of candle or taper, and a small cupboard, formed in the wall, and fastened by a lock and key similar to ours, together with some sacks of grain, standing in a corner, were all that the room contained. I ascended by a good staircase to the terrace, where I saw several little closets, all empty, except one, which appeared to be the sherif's wardrobe, for some of his clothes were hanging to a cord, fastened, to the wall. I was requested to sit on a round leather cushion, near which a mat was spread: and I found myself in company with seven Moors and a negro, all merchants of Jenné.

A neat little round table was brought and placed before us; it had legs three inches high. I thought at first that it was a table for playing some game, for it was inlaid with pieces of ivory and brass, ranged in regular order; but on the entrance of a large pewter dish, containing an enormous piece of a sheep, which had been killed in the morning, and stewed with a great quantity of onions, I discovered that I had been invited to dinner.

The sherif had beside him a covered basket, containing several small round loaves, weighing about half a pound each, and made of wheat-flour and yeast. He broke some of them in pieces, several of which he placed before each of us. Although our dinner was somewhat in the European style, yet we had neither knives nor forks, but all ate with our fingers. I found that the bread was very good, and certainly I never expected to make such a meal that day. We all helped ourselves from the dish with our hands, but with a certain degree of politeness. The conversation, which was exceedingly lively, was all at the expense of the poor christians. I was again asked whether I had eaten pork and drunk spirits. I made them the same reply as before, at which they burst into laughter, and began to ridicule the Europeans.

Our repast being ended, tea was introduced. The sherif, on this occasion, seemed to make his very best display. He was evidently anxious to let his negro guest see his superiority. We were attended by a young and handsome female slave. A box was brought in containing a porcelain tea service, which the sherif himself arranged on a plate of copper, which served the purpose of a tea-board. The cups, which were very small, were placed within others of a larger size, which had feet like egg-cups. We each took four of these cups of tea, with white sugar; and, after dinner, of which the sherif did the honours admirably well, we took a walk on the banks of the river. We sat down for a few minutes to see the canoes pass by, and, afterwards, we all said the evening prayer together, it being too late to go to the mosque. We then each returned to our homes. I found a great difference between the Moors of Jenné and the Brakna Moors, among whom I had lived eight months.

On the 18th of March, the new moon was saluted with several discharges of musketry, and, on the 19th, commenced the feast of the Ramadan. The

Haggi-Mohammed asked me whether I meant to fast during the Ramadan. My interest was so much concerned in submitting to it, that I dared not venture to refuse; and, indeed, the fast was by no means so great a hardship to me now, as it had been in 1824. Then I had no shelter but a tent, whilst now, I was protected from the heat of the sun, in a cool well-aired house; so that I did not suffer much from thirst. At sun-set, a beverage, made of tamarinds, was brought to me, and, afterwards another, made of honey and sour milk, strained and dried in the sun, forming a kind of very hard cheese, which the Moors, who are fond of it, bring to Jenné. They reduce it to powder, and mix it with their drink. On the following days, a sort of pudding was brought to me, made of very white flour, mixed with a few tamarinds; so that I could patiently wait until supper was ready.

About eight in the evening, an enormous mess of rice, boiled with mutton was brought to me. In the course of the day, I had expressed a wish to buy some milk, for the purpose of mixing it with water, to drink in the night; but I could not get any at the market. However, about ten at night, the Haggi-Mohammed, sent me a good quantity of milk and also, a candle to light me at my repast. About one in the morning, I was supplied with a breakfast as abundant as the supper of the previous evening.

I soon found an advantage in this change of habits; for I was much better served in the night time than I had hitherto been in the day. Nothing could be easier than this kind of abstinence, which merely consisted in sitting up a little later than usual for the purpose of making a hearty meal, and sleeping away the hours devoted to abstinence. The slaves are obliged to observe the fast, but they, as well as their masters make ample amends in the night for their privations during the day.

On the 20th, I determined to make a present of my umbrella to the sherif. I thought it but right to do so, as he was to procure me a conveyance by water to Timbuctoo. He appeared highly pleased with the present. I thought that the Haggi-Mohammed was already sufficiently rewarded by the purchase of my amber and coral at a price much below their value; however, as I wished to continue on good terms with him, I made him a further present of a yard of calico, which I had reserved for myself.

At sun-set Oulad-Marmou gave me handful of dates, and a very fine water-melon. He repeated this present every evening until my departure: the umbrella had completely established me in his favour. The produce of the sale of my merchandise was valued at thirty thousand cowries, and the sherif bought cloth of the country for me to that amount, assuring me that it would sell well at Timbuctoo. The cloth was packed up in two pagnes, for which I was indebted to his liberality. He also gave me four yellow wax-candles, made in the country, which I burned on board the canoe, during my passage.

On the 22nd of March, I was informed that I could start next day for Timbuctoo. The sherif sent me in the evening, a new loaf and a very good mutton stew for my supper.

On the morning of the 23rd he sent for me to his house. I took with me my bag, which he ordered one of his people to carry to the canoe, as well as my package of merchandise. He mixed together in my presence a good deal of millet flour and honey. This preparation was intended to be put into water for my drink; and I found it very useful on my passage, during which I was extremely ill-used, as will be seen in the sequel. The young Moor, whom I have already mentioned and to whom I made a present of a pair of scissors, gave me a large supply of wheaten bread, which had been dried in an oven, and told me how it was to be eaten; they first soak it in water and then mix it with a good deal of butter and honey. The sherif informed me that he had paid the master of the caravan three hundred cowries for my maintenance during the whole passage. He, as well as the young Moor, and the Haggi-Mohammed, attended me on board the canoe, which might be of twelve or fifteen tons burden. This canoe was not going to Timbuctoo, but merely to convey us to another vessel of larger size, which was waiting in the river; for at this season the branch was not navigable by large boats. The cargo of our canoe consisted of various kinds of provisions, twenty slaves, women, and children, the stoutest of whom were in chains. On the shore there was a crowd of people waiting to see us start.

FOOTNOTES:

[1] A title given to several African sovereigns.

[2] *Grigri* a kind of writing which these people consider as a talisman.

[3] Negociations, traffic.

[4] A piece of cotton cloth of the country, six feet long and two and a half wide.

[5] Blue India calico. The pieces are about sixteen yards long.

[6] Couscous, a kind of pottage made with millet.

[7] The Tabasky is the last day of the Ramadan: it may be likened to our Easter Sunday.

[8] The Peulhs inhabit Fouta-Toro; they are also called Foulahs.

[9] Or Niegueh.

[10] The carrier-bullock is a particular species. It has a bunch on the back. After it has been castrated, it is accustomed while very young to carry burdens; and to make it the more tractable, a cord is run through its nostrils.

[11] The name given at the Senegal to an arm of the river.

[12] Piastres: at the Senegal five and six franc pieces are called gourdes.

[13] A sort of gruel made of the flour of millet or other grain.

[14] The negroes who inhabit the countries of Cayor, Wâlo, and Ghiolof, are called Wolofs. They all speak the same language, with some modifications in the different countries. This language is understood by the Foulahs of Fouta Toro and their neighbours, the Serreres, as also by the Moors who travel in those parts.

[15] This is the same thing as the *bakat* of the negroes of Wâlo; it is a *holcus*, the grain of which nearly resembles our millet—perhaps the *holcus sorghum*.

[16] A small basket of straw, resembling those of our shop-keepers: it is used for winnowing the flour for the purpose of separating the bran. The negresses are very expert at this operation, turning out the bran and the imperfectly pounded grain; the flour is left on the *layot*.

[17] To say prayers.

[18] I had chosen the name of Abd-Allahi as the most satisfactory to Musulman piety; it signifies *slave of God*.

[19] A sort of round frock without sleeves.

[20] Or *hassanyéh*. The Moors call those who bear arms *hassanes*; they are also called *harabis*.

[21] The marabouts are the priests; they are not armed and do not go to war.

[22] Instead of wool the sheep of this part of Africa are covered with hair: the coat of some of them is so short that it is impossible to shear them.

[23] The Laratines are the offspring of Moors and female slaves; they are slaves themselves, but are never sold, and proud of their origin; they sometimes refuse to obey their master. They are an intermediate race between the Moors and the slaves.

[24] Among the Moors, and also the negroes, it is always a marabout who kills the animals intended for food; they would not eat meat which had been killed by a slave, or even by a man who was not a marabout.

[25] A wandering tribe, spread all over the western parts of Africa. The Laobés are carpenters and pedlars; they are the Jews of this country.

[26] Or Douichs, see the Map of the Course of the Senegal below Moussala.

[27] Perhaps the Teja-Kants, or Takants, reputed to dwell further eastward.

[28] Or Ouled-Douleeme.

[29] Perhaps the Abou-Sebahs.

[30] A *coussabe* is a piece of cloth two yards long and three quarters wide, doubled and sewed together, with holes left for the arms at the top. Another opening is left for the head; so that it is a sort of shirt without sleeves.

[31] A sort of light, blue calico very coarse and thin in its texture, and used by the Moors for mosquito-curtains, and sometimes for coussabes for their slaves. It is sold at the Senegal at from eight to twelve shillings the piece of fourteen yards.

[32] A Moorish nation inhabiting the lower part of the river, westward of the country of the Braknas.

[33] Nobody is admitted to traffic without paying customs or dues; which are proportioned to the tonnage of the vessel and the value of the goods traded for. Government pays duty annually to all the princes on the banks of the river, with whom the inhabitants of St. Louis have dealings, to secure protection for their commerce.

[34] Worth about £ 166 sterling.

[35] Negro sailors are so called.

[36] This tribe has a market near the mouth of the river, known by the name of the post of the Darmancours or Darmankous.

[37] The name given to the Mulattoes.

[38] This establishment is so called from Richard, the gardener, who founded it, and *Tol*, which signifies a garden in the Wolof language.

[39] A French factory on the Gambia.

[40] The seracolets, or sarakolas, are a corporation of itinerant merchants who travel over Africa; it is an error to suppose that the sarakolas are a nation.

[41] Almamy is the name given to the kings of many of these countries.

[42] This is the name given by Europeans to this fruit in the African colonies; the Mandingoes call it *ourou*.

[43] Some inhabitants of Kakondy, acquainted with the manners of the Bagos, informed me that they make gods of any thing that comes into their hands, such as a ram's horn, a cow's tail, a reptile, etc., and sacrifice to them.

[44] The nédé is a species of mimosa, the fruit of which contains a feculent substance, which is eaten by the negroes of this part of Africa.

[45] A place which the masters of slaves allot to their agricultural negroes; they have each a hut and a piece of ground, the produce of which supports them.

[46] The *Cé* or *Shea* of Mungo Park.

[47] The sherifs are the descendants of the Prophet; they are the Arabian nobility.

[48] Arabs or Musulmans in general.

[49] The word Kaffre, or Kafir, means infidel, idolater.

[50] The boatmen who navigate this river are called sognios.

[51] The caravans assemble to travel in a body through these woods, which are infested with robbers.

[52] The title of a chief.

[53] Poulh and Foulah are the same.

[54] Zambala is the seed of the nédé, boiled and dried; it is pounded for sauce.

[55] A small univalve shell, which passes for money.

[56] A Mandingo who has eight or ten slaves is reckoned rich.

[57] Télé, day, sun.

[58] See the Mandingo vocabulary.

[59] Charms, like the grigris.

[60] The Arabic word for soap is *saboun*.

[61] I trust I shall be pardoned for this misrepresentation, for, had I admitted the liberty of worship, there were some among my interrogators who would have been acute enough to ask me why I had undertaken so toilsome a journey, since I could freely exercise my religion among a people, who, according to my own account had treated me very kindly.